BRITISH BANKING

British Banking

Continuity and Change from 1694 to the Present

RANALD C. MICHIE

OXFORD
UNIVERSITY PRESS

Great Clarendon Street, Oxford, OX2 6DP,
United Kingdom

Oxford University Press is a department of the University of Oxford.
It furthers the University's objective of excellence in research, scholarship,
and education by publishing worldwide. Oxford is a registered trade mark of
Oxford University Press in the UK and in certain other countries

© Ranald C. Michie 2016

The moral rights of the author have been asserted

First Edition published in 2016

Impression: 1

All rights reserved. No part of this publication may be reproduced, stored in
a retrieval system, or transmitted, in any form or by any means, without the
prior permission in writing of Oxford University Press, or as expressly permitted
by law, by licence or under terms agreed with the appropriate reprographics
rights organization. Enquiries concerning reproduction outside the scope of the
above should be sent to the Rights Department, Oxford University Press, at the
address above

You must not circulate this work in any other form
and you must impose this same condition on any acquirer

Published in the United States of America by Oxford University Press
198 Madison Avenue, New York, NY 10016, United States of America

British Library Cataloguing in Publication Data
Data available

Library of Congress Control Number: 2016935484

ISBN 978-0-19-872736-1

Printed in Great Britain by
Clays Ltd, St Ives plc

Links to third party websites are provided by Oxford in good faith and
for information only. Oxford disclaims any responsibility for the materials
contained in any third party website referenced in this work.

*I dedicate this book to my brother, Uisdean Macleod Michie
Born on the Island of Lewis, 11th October 1945
Died in Nottingham, England, 20th June 2015
An inspirational geologist*

Preface

This book is the product of my contribution to the Leverhulme Trust-funded Tipping Points Project that ran from 2010 to 2015 and was located at the Institute for Hazard, Risk, and Resilience (IHRR) at Durham University. I am enormously grateful to the staff at IHRR for the support they have provided over those years and all those, with one exception, who participated in the Tipping Points Project. I benefited enormously from interaction with an interdisciplinary team as it forced me out of my comfort zone to think about problems in new ways and so reach different conclusions. After an academic lifetime as a practicing financial historian the process was, at times, painful but rewarding. My only regret is that it had not happened to me earlier in my career.

I also benefited greatly from the advice of a number of others who were connected to the Tipping Points Project either formally or informally. One was Professor Phillip Cottrell to whom I owe a number of insights into British banking history. Sadly he is no longer with us. He could have produced a better book than this one. Another involved was Ian Bond who had a career at the Bank of England before retiring: he provided me with some rare glimpses into the official mind of British banking but bears no responsibility for the outcome. I would also like to thank Chris Lendrum, who spent his career at Barclays before retiring. From him I gained some understanding of what it meant to be a banker but he, also, bears no responsibility for the outcome.

I would also like to thank my wife, Dinah, and my children, Alexander and Jonathan, for listening to me when I went through my voyage of discovery regarding the history of British banking. I am sure they do not want to hear another word over dinner about the Lend and Hold Model versus the Originate and Distribute Model. I would also like to thank my friend, Francis Pritchard, for reading the book and helping to make it fit for publication. His contribution was, as always, invaluable. Finally, I would also like to thank David Musson for sticking by me when I switched from writing a book about the global securities market since 1975 to one on British banking since 1694. I still hope to deliver that book!

Contents

Figures and Tables	xi
Introduction	1
1. Context and Chronology, 1694–2015	16
2. Crises and Crescendo, 1694–1825	46
3. Consolidation and Competence, 1825–1914	70
4. Choice and Connections, 1825–1914	90
5. Complications and Co-operation, 1914–1945	125
6. Control and Compartmentalization, 1945–1970	162
7. Convergence and Conversions, 1970–1997	184
8. Competition and Complacency, 1997–2007	202
9. Catastrophe and Convalescence, 2007–2015	237
10. Comments and Conclusion	264
Appendices	271
Bibliography	291
Index	323

Figures and Tables

Figure 1.1. Trend in numbers of UK Banks 1700–2008	31
Figure 1.2. Trend in numbers of US Banks 1782–2009	33
Table 4.1. Joint-Stock Banks: Assets and Liabilities, 1911/14	95
Table 4.2. Number of Banks	97
Table 4.3. Number of Bank Offices	98
Table 4.4. Ratio of Bank Offices to Population	98
Table 5.1. Number of Banks	134
Table 5.2. Joint-Stock Banks: Assets and Liabilities, 1911/14 and 1921/4	135
Table 5.3. Joint-Stock Banks: Assets and Liabilities, 1921/4 and 1938	136
Table 5.4. Number of Bank Offices	142
Table 5.5. Ratio of Bank Offices to Population	142

Introduction

A central problem faced by any study of banking that attempts to cover three centuries is to find a definition of a bank that can be used throughout. As Wilkins observed recently, 'The word "bank" has different meanings in different countries and periods.'[1] The Bank for International Settlement defines a bank as a deposit-taking corporation though it makes an exception for central banks. This is a very narrow interpretation that fails to capture both the diversity of banking experience and change over time.[2] Recent scholarship in financial history has suggested that banks need to be studied within the context of wider developments in finance if they are to be fully understood.[3] Conversely, the study of banks cannot be regarded as simply another branch of business history. Banks play a key role in the monetary system, maintain a close relationship to government and are exposed to sudden crises. As businesses, banks are also the product of a complex mixture of national forces including the level of economic development, the legal environment, the pattern of corporate governance and the nature and degree of government intervention. The banks that emerged adapted to the domestic and international environment within which they operated, developing their response through a process of trial and error. As a result, the boundaries between different types of bank were in constant flux making any study focused on a particular subset flawed. All banks possessed both unique and common features and the balance between the two shifted over time.[4]

---

[1] M. Wilkins, 'Disjunctive Sets? Business and Banking History', in E. Green, M. Pohle-Fraser and I.L. Fraser (eds), *The Human Factor in Banking History: Entrepreneurship, Organization, Management and Personnel* (Athens: Alpha Bank, 2008), p.153.

[2] Bank for International Settlement, *Guidelines to the International Locational Banking Statistics* (B.I.S., September 2011), pp.6–11.

[3] O. Feiertag and I.P. Minoglou, 'European Banking Historiography at a Turning Point', in O. Feiertag and I.P. Minoglou (eds), *European Banking Historiography: Past and Present* (Athens: Alpha Bank, 2009), p.19.

[4] S. Battilossi, '"Ephors" from Growth to Governance: How Modern Theories Are Re-shaping Historians' View of the Economic Functions of Bankers', in Green, Pohle-Fraser and Fraser (eds), *Human Factor*, pp.89–94.

This makes both international comparisons between banks, and the development of a long-term perspective, especially hazardous unless the differences between countries and over time are fully understood. Capie and Woods, for example, have warned that comparing banking in the UK and the USA is inappropriate because of the difference between the two countries.[5] Grossman has successfully conducted such an exercise but only by confining himself to commercial or retail banking. What he emphasizes is the need to study Britain's banking history both because of its early development and the fact that it provided the model that was copied and adapted in many other parts of the world.[6] The intention in this book is to provide a study of British banking that is sufficiently broad to cope with its diversity over time, and is conducted at sufficient depth to produce meaningful results. Only when that is done can the past history of British banking be used as a reliable guide for those framing policies that will help determine its future structure.

For that purpose it is necessary to adopt some working definition of a bank that can be applied throughout the years from the late seventeenth century until the present. That definition can be neither too narrow so as to exclude much that was important in shaping the general development of banking nor so broad that the unique features of a bank are lost. In a very perceptive speech a previous Governor of the Bank of England, Eddie George, addressed the question of what was a bank. He posed the question, 'Are Banks Still Special?' at an IMF Central Banking Seminar in Washington DC on the 29th of January 1997. According to Eddie George the distinguishing features of a bank was that it took unsecured deposits, played a central role in the payments system, and provided a source of funding by intermediating between lenders and borrowers. Though he recognized that alternatives to all these roles were available he held to the opinion that banks remained special because of the liquid nature of their liabilities. It was this 'mismatch between their assets and liabilities which makes banks peculiarly vulnerable to systemic risk'.[7] Eddie George was making a claim for the special nature of banking at a time when it was under threat from the emergence of multi-functional global banks. Nevertheless, his conclusions can be applied throughout the history of British banking. In the light of the events that unfolded in 2007/8 his views might have deserved greater consideration at the time.

At no stage did a bank ever confine itself to a single strand of business. Whether banking was the pursuit of an individual or a transnational corporation, a bank had to continuously adapt its business model to take advantage

---

[5] F. Capie and G. Woods, *Money over Two Centuries: Selected Topics in British Monetary History* (Oxford: O.U.P., 2012), p.1.

[6] R.S. Grossman, *Unsettled Account: The Evolution of Banking in the Industrialized World Since 1800* (Princeton: Princeton UP, 2010), p.168.

[7] E. George, 'Are Banks Special?', *Bank of England Quarterly Bulletin* (February 1997), pp.113–18.

of new opportunities and respond to new challenges. If the definition of a bank is interpreted very narrowly it only captures those financial institutions that take in deposits from and make loans to, the public. Even then it omits a group of other institutions whose operations are very similar including various forms of saving and loan associations such as savings banks and building societies. All these borrowed short from the public and lent long and so incurred a maturity mismatch in the same way as banks, with whom they competed for the business of savers and borrowers. Conversely, there are those financial institutions that depended little on retail deposits but still faced a maturity mismatch as they relied on funds obtained through the money market. The likes of merchant banks, investment banks, discount houses, investment trusts, and finance companies all used short-term funds to finance long term investment. These other financial institutions are usually considered separately from commercial or retail banks even though there was a high degree of mutual interdependence and competition, leading to the combination of all financial activity in a single business such as was the case with a universal bank. Without considering the depth and diversity of all that banks undertook it is not possible to understand what was happening over time in and to banking.

In the context of the UK the task is made even more complicated when it is recognized that the British economy was a relatively open one. This exposed banking to global influences, especially as Britain was home to one of the most important international financial centres throughout the last 300 years. However, if the net is cast too widely then the entire financial sector is included, which fails to capture the unique features of banks, as emphasized by Eddie George in 1997 but ignored until the 2007/8 financial crisis made everyone aware of the accuracy of his analysis. The approach adopted here is to expand the focus to all financial institutions whose main business involved borrowing short and lending long, as that exposed them to issues of liquidity. At the same time the study recognizes that banks are different from those financial intermediaries that did not face significant liquidity issues, as was the case with most insurance companies and asset managers, and so these are not included.

Based on this approach there are three central elements that need to be considered in any study of British banking. The first is that banking provides a service to the rest of the economy. This service takes a number of different forms each of which is essential to the operation of a modern economy. A core function of a bank is to act as an intermediary between those needing to make or receive payments. The larger and more complex the economy became the greater was the need for a payments system beyond that provided by metal coins or paper notes. With billions of transactions between millions of people taking place on a daily basis, the facilities provided by banks became the core architecture of the payments system without which the economy could not function. Only when a problem occurred in this payments system was its value apparent. The existence of an efficient and reliable low-cost payments system provided by banks became accepted as a matter of routine. The result was to reduce the reliance placed on tangible forms of money to almost zero for all legitimate transactions, which meant a huge reduction in the costs involved. Achieving that position took a long time and required the banking system to devise ways of working that met the needs of an economy in which the provision of virtually all goods and services either took place through the market or involved a transfer paid to and received from the government ranging from the payment of taxes to the receipt of benefits.

This process involved a great deal of trial and error, and constant innovation, before a system was put in place that was trusted by everyone. Such a system required the participation of all banks for, without that, no bank-based payments system could operate effectively. Initially this meant that banks had to be willing to accept as a method of payment the notes issued by their peers. That progressed to the use of cheques drawn on each others' banks before reaching a stage in which customers' accounts were directly debited and credited through a centralized clearing system. What this meant was that banks were mutually dependent as they became integrated into a system through which all bank customers could make and receive payments through their own bank. The result was a major boost to economic integration both within Britain and internationally, as banks established links to each other that facilitated not only domestic payments but also the transfer of funds across different currency zones. However, this integration also exposed banks to counterparty risk as they carried uncovered exposures. Banks made payments to their customers when presented with the notes, cheques, or debits of other banks, trusting that they would receive the equivalent in return. That did not always happen and so the banking system had to devise ways of minimizing the risks involved in an inter-bank payments system while preserving the benefits it brought to themselves and their customers.

Vital as the payments system provided by banks was, the services they provided extended much further than that. Banks also acted as the intermediary between those with a surplus of money and those with a deficit, bridging their need through time and space. In providing this service a bank is different from an individual capitalist or a money-lender, as it functions by using funds supplied by others. A bank is also different from an institutional investor in terms of the nature of these funds. Though the direct participation of private individuals, or the issue of stocks and bonds to the public, institutional investors raise a permanent capital that can be invested for the long term. In contrast, apart from the capital provided by the owners of the bank, the funds upon which it operated could usually be withdrawn immediately or at short notice. As a result those managing a bank had to balance the possibility of these funds being withdrawn against the returns to be made by lending them to others.

Introduction 5

At the heart of this calculation was the knowledge that holding the funds as cash produced no returns while incurring expenses relating to staff, materials, and buildings. In contrast those needing to borrow funds would pay for the money obtained, offering the bank a higher rate of return if the loan was for a longer than a shorter period. If a bank retained as cash a large proportion of the money it raised through deposits and borrowings, while investing the remainder in short-term loans and assets that could be easily and quickly sold, not only would the owners of the bank and those lending it money receive a poor rate of return but the economy would be deprived of the credit and capital required to both operate and generate economic growth. Conversely, such banks would be resilient in the face of crises as they had the resources to meet withdrawals by running down their cash, selling assets, and not re-lending the money received as short-term loans were repaid. The reverse position prevailed if a bank retained a low proportion of deposits and borrowings as cash and used the remainder to make long-term loans and invested in illiquid but high-yielding assets. Under these circumstances the owners of the bank and the providers of the funds would receive a high rate of return and the economy would be well supplied with both credit and capital, generating a high rate of economic growth as a result. However, such banks would not be resilient when crises occur as they lacked both sufficient cash to meet immediate withdrawals while long-term loans remained outstanding and illiquid assets were difficult to sell.

Given these extreme positions all banks developed strategies to cope with the simultaneous need to generate returns while minimizing risks. Those banks with a large permanent capital could afford to take more risks, such as purchasing illiquid assets or lending long term, because they were less exposed to sudden withdrawals. Nevertheless, to the extent that they were dependent upon either retail deposits or short-term borrowing to finance their activities they had to ensure that they were always in a position to meet withdrawals or the need to repay a loan. Conversely, for those banks that relied heavily on retail deposits supplemented by short-term loans there was a constant need to be always in a position to meet withdrawals and redemptions. For each bank the result was a requirement to maximize cash and liquid assets over illiquid assets and long-term investment even though such a state would only be required in a crisis. What this meant was that the banking system as a whole was over-provided with liquidity in normal circumstances, representing a huge waste of financial resources. The solution devised, but only slowly, was to create a money market within which banks with surplus funds could lend to those facing a shortage but on a temporary basis and, ideally, receiving some form of collateral in return. As each bank had customers with different needs that constantly varied, some found themselves with funds in excess of demand while others could not provide the finance their customers required. What the inter-bank money market did was match these surpluses and deficits on a continuous basis, so releasing the untapped liquidity of the entire banking system for productive use. However, as with the payments system, such a step forward created risks. It could encourage individual banks to finance long-term lending and the purchase of illiquid assets using the short-term funds available from the inter-bank market because of the profits to be made. Illiquid assets and long-term loans generated a higher yield than the interest paid on short-term inter-bank borrowing. Problems then arose in a crisis when such a bank could not repay its short-term borrowing and so left other banks unable to access the funds they now required and had only lent out temporarily. Hence the need for collateral that could be sold if the borrowing bank defaulted as well as constant monitoring to ensure that banks only borrowed from the inter-bank market to finance temporary shortages and were always in a position to repay.

Nevertheless, there still existed the possibility that the entire banking system would find itself short of liquidity as was the case in a major crisis when the public rushed to withdraw funds and short-term loans were called in rather than being renewed. What was then required was a lender of last resort. This was a single individual or institution that was in a position to supply unlimited quantities of money on a temporary basis, until the crisis died down and trust in banks was re-established. Again, the emergence of a lender of last resort was a gradual process and one that required procedures to be put in place so as to prevent such intervention being relied upon by all banks, so removing constraints on bank behaviour. Hence the requirement that only those banks providing suitable collateral would receive temporary assistance as that was designed to prevent individual banks pursuing a policy of reckless but highly profitable lending, using short-term borrowing from the inter-bank market, secure in the knowledge that in a crisis they would be assisted directly or indirectly.

The secret of a successful banking system, measured by the contribution it made to the growth of the economy, was one that simultaneously delivered to both savers and borrowers and was resilient in the face of crises. Historical evidence remains divided on whether British banking ever achieved that balance. Over the last 150 years before 2007, British banking did become increasingly stable and financial crises were either avoided or of limited magnitude. Many claim, however, that this stability was achieved at the expense of economic growth. The verdict was that an overly conservative banking system delivered to neither savers nor borrowers and contributed to Britain's prolonged economic decline by denying industry the capital it required to invest in new technology and develop new products. In particular, this banking system was believed to exhibit a preference for short-term lending and the most liquid of assets so depriving the economy of sources of long-term capital. This complaint lies at the heart of the 'Macmillan Gap', first identified by the Committee into Finance in Industry that reported in 1931, and included Keynes among its membership. Implicit in this criticism was the belief that British banks had become so stable by then that they could afford to take greater risks. The one positive claim that could be made for British banks was that their focus on cash and liquid assets made them resilient in the face of financial crises. British banks were able to weather the financial storms produced by both world wars, and the global crisis following the Wall Street Crash of 1929, unlike the banks of most other countries. However, even that positive claim evaporated in the wake of the financial crisis of 2007/8 when the UK government was forced to intervene so as to prevent the failure of a number of major banks and so forestall a wider collapse. In the wake of that crisis it emerged that a number of British banks had embarked on a highly risky lending strategy that left them dangerously short of liquidity and so vulnerable when a financial crisis did take place. The outcome was a prolonged recession in which the economy took years to recover the position it had achieved by the eve of the crisis. Combined with the traditional verdict that has criticized British banks for being overly conservative, and so fostering an extended period of low economic growth, is the new one that accuses them of excessive risk-taking that resulted in a long and deep recession. The question that arises is whether either verdict is accurate. Should the conservative behaviour of British banks be linked to the long period of slow economic growth or to the benefits that came from stability? Conversely, should the debacle of the financial crisis of 2007/8 be related to the behaviour of the banks or the preceding period of rapid economic growth? Overall, what is the historical verdict on the degree to which British banks were able to balance successfully the demands placed upon them in delivering the service that a modern economy requires?

The second element to British banking is that it does not exist solely to serve the rest of the economy but is an industry in its own right. That position grew with globalization as British banks came to serve not only UK customers but also those of other countries, as they expanded their activities abroad. These activities were not simply an extension of existing British banks, as they opened offices, set up branches, and created subsidiaries abroad. Banks were also founded with British head offices, employing British staff, and owned by British investors but operating in countries around the world. Whether operating at home or abroad British banks provided employment and generated profits. In turn those working for banks spent, saved, and paid taxes, as did the owners of banks and even banks themselves when organized as companies. In this respect banks were no different from any other business contributing to economic growth directly through the services that they sold and the income they generated. This banking system was also an increasingly diverse one. Banking gradually emerged from being a subsidiary activity for those engaged in other pursuits such as the law, trade, or dealing in precious metals, to become a distinct business. However, no single type of bank dominated because there was a constant flux between those banks offering a general service to their customers and those that chose a highly specialized role. On the one hand there emerged the large commercial or retail banks that collected savings directly from the public and made loans to UK customers through a branch network managed from a head office. On the other hand there were small banks, conducting a highly specialized business of a largely wholesale nature from a single office. Across the spectrum, the business of one merged into that of another while at each end the business that banks were engaged in shaded into those provided by other components of the economy, whether that involved insurance companies, stockbrokers, or fund managers. The more sophisticated the economy the more it required specialized financial services while rising levels of income and wealth increased the demand for all kinds of banking activity. Banks had to meet the needs of all types of customers at all times whether that involved managing savings or providing loans to individuals, putting together complex arrangements for business finance or arranging trade credit on an international basis. At all times this was done against the background of domestic and global competition, which forced banks to innovate if they were to retain customers and generate profits.

The historical verdict on the performance of British banking as businesses is also mixed. Before the First World War British banks were seen as the model to be followed wherever they were in the spectrum of financial services. In terms of retail banking the combination created in Britain of an extensive branch network managed from a head office and involving highly trained and closely supervised staff, was not only rolled out within Britain but also copied by many countries around the world. British merchant banks also occupied a central role in international finance liaising between borrowers and lenders whether it was arranging the credit required for world trade or the funds needed by governments and business. Since then, criticism has grown that, as an industry, British banks were slow to develop new forms, as with the universal banking model, or adopt the latest technological advances providing major productivity advances as with computerization. For many British observers, retail banking had become a cartel by the beginning of the twentieth century, dominated by a few large banks that were immune to competitive pressures. It has been suggested that this encouraged a conservative culture, which was detrimental to innovation. At the wholesale level, British merchant banks were also slow to make the transition to the investment bank model, losing out to foreign competitors as a result. One outcome was the growth of shadow banks that were more responsive to customers and quicker to embrace new forms and new technology. The growth of the building society movement in the nineteenth century was one example of this while the decline of UK-owned investment banks in the late twentieth was another. There were also failed attempts by individual British banks to reach the scale of their international rivals from the 1970s onwards as was the case with the Midland,

Warburgs, and Royal Bank of Scotland, leaving them vulnerable to acquisition or forced to retrench after a crisis. As in the role played by British banking as a service, there is also considerable doubt about its performance as a business, especially in the light of the financial crisis of 2007/8. In the dash for growth in the decade that preceded that crisis British banks appeared to have abandoned the standards of behaviour that had made them such admired models around the world, without discovering the combination of dynamism and stability that delivered success to banks from other countries.

The final element that needs to be considered when examining British banking is the position of the City of London as an international financial centre. Over the last 200 years the City of London has become a magnet for banks from throughout the world and it remains so today. In a global economy banks need to interact with each other. This involves making and receiving payments on behalf of customers or matching debits and credits over different currencies and time periods. It also involves smoothing out imbalances in the funds they have available. Through the inter-bank market, banks borrow from and lend to each other on a continuous basis ensuring that they can meet the needs of all their customers all of the time, whether they are depositors or borrowers. The result of that is that the banking industry in Britain meets the needs of the world economy through the facilities it provides not just in other countries but also in London. British banks did not have to go abroad to participate in the global financial system for that came to them through the position occupied by the City of London in international finance. The City of London was neither an offshore financial centre in which the domestic component was non-existent, nor a domestic financial centre in which the international dimension was marginal. Instead, the two components long co-existed and were each of sufficient magnitude to rank of equal importance. This position had arisen because of Britain's extensive engagement in international trade and finance over the centuries and then the attractions London provided as a financial centre spanning different time zones and possessing an unrivalled depth and breadth of connections, expertise, and facilities.

The historical verdict on the City of London is very polarized. There are many historians who stress the City/Industry divide in which the interests of those in the City became not only detached from the rest of the UK economy but also antagonistic towards it, through diverting finance and talent away from other domestic activities. Others point to the influence of the City of London on the British government, leading to policies that favoured the financial rather than the industrial sector. Conversely, there are others who point to the fact that the presence of foreign banks in London generates considerable employment and income for the UK economy, and constitutes a major export industry. There are also those who see the success of the City as part of a process of international specialization in which Britain's long-term advantages lie in financial services, especially those related to banking. Finally, some suggest that the policies pursued by successive UK governments are actually detrimental to the City of London. Whatever the position taken, no study of British banking can ignore the international dimension derived from the UK hosting one of the world's leading financial centres since the beginning of the eighteenth century, whether that involves the presence of so many foreign banks or the engagement of British banks in the international financial markets located in their midst.

The approach taken in this book departs from the way that Britain's banking history has been written in the past. It makes the diversity of the banking experience central, along with the interaction between the principal components, whether that involved competition, co-operation or interdependence as in the operation of the payments system, the inter-bank money market and the relationship between the Bank of England and the rest of the banking system. Any analysis that moves beyond uncritical description examines the evidence from a particular viewpoint and that has the effect of distorting the conclusions reached. This study will be no different, so it is essential that the approach taken is made explicit, as much that might be considered either relevant and or even essential by others will be omitted or relegated to a minor role. However, the approach adopted by those others is equally flawed as their analysis is also driven by a particular view that contributes to the conclusions they have reached. This can be seen in the various approaches to British banking history that others have adopted.

One approach is to treat banks as part of the monetary system because of their ability to create money through the issue of bank notes and the provision of credit. This approach gives priority to the relationship between the banking system and the government as intermediated by the Bank of England. As Sir John Clapham noted in the first volume of *The Bank of England: A History*, published in 1944 and written during the Second World War, 'A banking system is closely associated with public borrowing and with what is almost the oldest and most closely guarded function of the state, the issue of money, that governments can seldom afford to leave it entirely unlicensed and uncontrolled.'[8] This emphasis on the connection between politics and finance has long underpinned much of the study of British banking, with its structure attributed to the influence of legislation passed in the nineteenth century. Shepherd held this view in his 1971 book, *The Growth and Role of UK Financial Institutions, 1880–1962*.[9] Going even further back in time, the beginnings of modern banking in Britain have been credited to the arrival in 1688 of a new king from the Netherlands, which possessed the most advanced

---

[8] Sir John Clapham, *The Bank of England: A History*, 2 vols. (Cambridge: CUP, 1944), p.2.
[9] D.K. Shepherd, *The Growth and Role of UK Financial Institutions, 1880–1962* (London: Methuen, 1971).

financial system at the time. The result is the view that the structure of British banking was the creation of state intervention. As Calomiris and Haber state, in *Fragile by Design*, 'the notions that banking systems can arise spontaneously, or that they could function efficiently without active government involvement, are utopian fantasies.' For that reason the conclusion they reached was that 'the extent to which banking systems are able to achieve the two key measures of success—abundant credit and the absence of banking crises—depends critically on the political environment.'[10] Though heavily influenced by the pattern of banking they have observed in the USA, Calomiris and Haber apply that conclusion to Britain's banking experience. A similar emphasis on the role played by the state in shaping British banking is also one taken up by Turner in his recent book, *Banking in Crisis*.[11] Like Calomiris and Haber, the underlying assumption in Turner's book is that banking was intrinsically unstable and without some kind of government intervention the result would be crisis after crisis. 'The final lesson from the history of British banking is that politics is the ultimate determinant of banking stability.'[12] The problem of such an approach is that it prioritizes the perspective of the Bank of England when studying the history of British banking rather than the business of banking in its own right. Such a perspective is increasingly at variance with the rest of banking as the Bank of England came under the control of the government over the course of the twentieth century, becoming government-owned in 1946. As Singleton observed in his history of central banking, 'The modern central banker must think like a banker, a public servant, and an economist, though this has not always been the case.'[13] The result is to relegate the study of British banking to the position of junior partner with priority given to the needs and actions of the Bank of England and the shifting priorities of the UK government. This is much more the history of political power than the history of banking.

Related to that approach is a perspective on the development of British banking derived from the position occupied by the Bank of England as lender of last resort, and its evolving supervisory role, long before that was formally recognized in the years after the Second World War. The research relating to that approach to British banking history has been gathered together in two collections involving Charles Goodhart. As Goodhart himself concluded, in 'Myths about the Lender of Last Resort', 'it is unthinkable that any government or central bank would now stand idly by and watch the closure of any of its major banks, the realization of large-scale losses on the bank deposits of its

---

[10] C.W. Calomiris and S.H. Haber, *Fragile by Design: The Political Origins of Banking Crises and Scarce Credit* (Princeton: Princeton UP, 2014), p.491.
[11] J.D. Turner, *Banking in Crisis: The Rise and Fall of British Banking Stability, 1800 to the Present* (Cambridge: CUP, 2014), pp.5–6.
[12] Turner, *Banking in Crisis*, pp.6, 11, 219.
[13] J. Singleton, *Central Banking in the Twentieth Century* (Cambridge: CUP, 2011), p.18.

citizens, if the authorities could avoid such events'.[14] This attitude towards the development of the banking system can be seen in the study conducted by the staff of the Bank of England into the Evolution of the UK Banking System. This focused on the emergence of very large banks with multi-functional and multinational operations. To regulators the emergence of such banks posed problems as to how to supervise them and what to do in a crisis if they had become too big to be allowed to fail.[15] Again, this approach is much more a history of British banking regulation and the role played by the central bank as lender of last resort, than a history of British banking.

Another approach is to focus on the role played by banks within the economy, with priority given to the contribution they made to the finance of manufacturing industry. In many ways the culmination of this approach to Britain's banking history was Carnevali's 2005 book, *Europe's Advantage: Banks and Small Firms in Britain, France, Germany, and Italy since 1918*. In keeping with many earlier studies throughout the twentieth century, this reached the conclusion that the core problem in British manufacturing could be traced to the inadequate finance provided by British banks. Again, however, the focus is exclusively on the commercial banks and ignores the variety of funding mechanisms available to British business unlike the position in many other countries.[16] Its conclusions are also contradicted by much of the research undertaken by those who have examined the details of British bank lending from the mid nineteenth century onwards, as reported in Capie and Woods, *Money over Two Centuries: Selected Topics in British Monetary History*.[17] This approach to banking history is much more from the perspective of the borrower than the lender. Little consideration is given to the constraints under which a bank operated because of the maturity mismatch between the loans it made and the funds it employed. When making a loan, a banker had to carefully balance the risks taken with the expected return within the context that depositors could withdraw their funds at short notice. That alone can explain many of the lending decisions made and the complaints from frustrated borrowers.

Related to the approach that prioritizes the perspective of the borrower was the absence of one that credited banks with the long period of stability

[14] C. Goodhart, P. Hartmann, D. Llewellyn, L. Rojas-Suarez, and S. Weisbrod, *Financial Regulation: Why, How and Where Now?* (London: Routledge, 1998); C. Goodhart and G. Illing (eds), *Financial Crises, Contagion, and the Lender of Last Resort: A Reader* (Oxford: OUP, 2002); C. Goodhart, 'Myths about the Lender of Last Resort', in Goodhart and Illing (eds), *Financial Crises*, p.241.

[15] R. Davies, P. Richardson, V. Katinaite, and M. Manning, 'Evolution of the UK Banking System', *Bank of England Quarterly Bulletin*, 50 (2010), pp.320–30.

[16] F. Carnevali, *Europe's Advantage: Banks and Small Firms in Britain, France, Germany, and Italy since 1918* (Oxford: OUP, 2005).

[17] Capie and Woods, *Money over Two Centuries*.

Introduction   13

experienced in Britain before the crisis of 2007/8. Unlike the histories of banking in other countries, especially the USA, but also Continental Europe between the wars, there were few significant banking crises in Britain in the twentieth century. Turner goes so far as to claim there were none between 1825 and 2007.[18] However, most others suggest that they continued to take place, pointing to those of 1866, 1878, 1890, 1914, and 1974 as worthy of serious consideration.[19] Whether there were repeated crises or not, the general belief in the stability of British banking rendered it meaningless to approach the subject from that perspective as the absence of activity produces little material for such a study. In contrast, the banking crisis of 2007/8 has generated considerable interest not only in what took place then but also in the context of British banking history. For Attack, what happened in 2007/8 was fundamentally different from anything that had happened in the past.[20] In contrast to Reinhart and Rogoff in *This Time is Different*, the conclusion to be drawn was that it had all happened many times before.[21] The result for the UK was to open up the question of the historical relationship between banks and financial crises as in the 2014 edited volume by Dimsdale and Hotson, *British Financial Crises since 1825*. This identifies a golden era of stability between 1870 and 1970, and puts forward various suggestions from different authors as to why that was the case.[22] What it does not do is explore in any detail the actual business of banking, focusing entirely on the crises and not the part played by banks in contributing to either instability or stability.

The actual business of banking and the way it was organized in each bank is the approach adopted in those books that prioritize banks as businesses, whether organized as small partnerships or large corporations managing diverse global operations. This approach gives the individual bank a distinct identity and makes it central to the narrative, emphasizing its achievements in the face of adversity. In *A Hundred Years of Joint Stock Banking*, by Crick and Wadsworth, which was published in 1936, the achievements of the successive generations that had built up the Midland Bank over the previous century are praised. 'In many ways the strong, unified banking system in England was the product of pertinacity and ingenious adaptation to restrictive laws, rather than of design or even unimpeded evolution.' The perspective of those writing from

---

[18] Turner, *Banking in Crisis*, pp.7, 53–4.
[19] C.M. Reinhart and K.S. Rogoff, *This Time is Different: Eight Centuries of Financial Folly* (Princeton: Princeton UP, 2009); Y. Cassis, *Crises and Opportunities: The Shaping of Modern Finance* (Oxford: OUP, 2011); C.P. Kindleberger and R.Z. Aliber, *Manias, Panics, and Crashes: A History of Financial Crises* (Basingstoke: Palgrave Macmillan, 2005).
[20] J. Atack, 'Financial Innovations and Crises: The View Backwards', in J. Atack and L. Neal (eds), *The Origin and Development of Financial Markets and Institutions: From the Seventeenth Century to the Present* (Cambridge: CUP, 2009), p.2.
[21] Reinhart and Rogoff, *This Time is Different*.
[22] N. Dimsdale and A. Hotson (eds), *British Financial Crises* (Oxford: OUP, 2014).

inside the banks was that they had achieved perfection not because of government intervention, natural evolution, or original design but through a process of continuous adaptation and response. Such a perspective was understandable from those who had experienced the shock of the First World War and the worst economic, monetary, and financial crisis the world had ever experienced, and had seen the large British commercial banks prove resilient. 'It is safe to say that, but for the process of structural consolidation, English banking could never have survived unmutilated the stress of the post-war period.'[23] A similar pride in the achievements of both individual British banks and the system as a whole emerged in the histories produced after the Second World War, as in *Lloyds Bank in the History of English Banking*, by Sayers, which appeared in 1957. The scale and diversity that Lloyds Bank had achieved by the First World War allowed it not only to emerge unscathed from that event but also contributed to the avoidance of any subsequent crises despite the problems posed by the Wall Street Crash of 1929, the collapse of the Gold Standard in 1931, the world depression of the 1930s, the long years of the Second World War, and Britain's subsequent economic difficulties. As Sayers observed in 1957, 'fiction writers of our generation portray our banking offices as the dens of sleepy unadventurous fellows whose only task is to follow the even tenor of their way. Things were not always like this; the nineteenth-century novelists could always give the story a fresh turn by bringing the local bank crashing down.' From the 1950s onwards British banks had become one of the symbols of British resilience and stability.[24] In contrast, by the end of the twentieth century a more sceptical view of British banking had emerged, highlighting its failures as well as successes in the light of Britain's own relatively poor post-war economic performance and the success of foreign-owned banks in capturing so much of the business conducted in the City of London. This can be seen in the history *Barclays: The Business of Banking, 1690–1996* by Ackrill and Hannah, published in 2001.[25] The weakness of these otherwise excellent business histories is that they emphasize what was unique about each bank, not what was shared and common. The achievements of each bank are attributed to the actions of the staff, not the environment within which they operated and the opportunities that existed.

Lastly, there is the approach that places banks within the financial system by emphasizing the role they played and their interaction with each other and how that changed over time. This approach tends to blur the distinctions

---

[23] W.F. Crick and J.E. Wadsworth, *A Hundred Years of Joint Stock Banking* (London: Hodder & Stoughton, 1936), pp.42, 345.
[24] R.S. Sayers, *Lloyds Bank in the History of English Banking* (Oxford: OUP, 1957), pp.108, 204–18.
[25] M. Ackrill and L. Hannah, *Barclays: The Business of Banking, 1690–1996* (Cambridge: CUP, 2001).

between different types of banks and emphasize, instead, the importance of both the payments system and the money market. It is this approach that is attempted here. As a consequence, the question of money and monetary policy is not addressed directly though it is touched upon where it is relevant to the performance and behaviour of those within the banking system. What is also neglected are the details relevant to individual banks including their development, organization, management, and staffing unless, again, that is relevant to the operation of the banking system. This focus should be kept in mind when following the account of British banking over the last three centuries presented here. It is an account neither of money and credit nor individual enterprise, interesting and valid as these are, but of a system and the way that individual components performed and interacted over time. In this sense the approach mirrors that adopted in Grossman's 2010 book, *Unsettled Account: The Evolution of Banking in the Industrialized World since 1800*, but applies it to a single country, the UK, while expanding it to include all those financial institutions that fit into the wider definition of banking as identified by Eddie George.[26]

---

[26] Grossman, *Unsettled Account*.

1

Context and Chronology, 1694–2015

INTRODUCTION

By the late nineteenth century there was an implicit belief that the British banking system that had emerged by then was as close to perfection as it was possible to achieve. While credit was given to the legislative changes made in the first half of the century, what had been achieved was seen to be the ultimate product of a process of natural evolution, combining the virtue of stability with the ability to meet the needs of both savers and borrowers. Nevertheless, even by the beginning of the twentieth century, there were some reservations being expressed about British banking, though the focus was not directed at the entire banking sector but at those large-deposit banks that had come to dominate it. This criticism of British banks centred on the complaint that they were too conservative in their lending, being only willing to provide short-term credit rather than long-term finance. The centralized nature of the British banking system exposed them to the attack that they were London-orientated, as that was where their head offices were, and so they neglected the needs of the provinces. This attack also extended to the merchant banks, as they were seen to be interested only in international investment and not the needs of the domestic economy. Over time this attack was used to develop a thesis that British banks contributed to Britain's economic decline through their failure to provide the long-term finance required by northern manufacturing industry. This was contrasted with the more interventionist behaviour of German universal banks or the more intimate connections with local business in the US unitary banking system. A product of this analysis was growing pressure on government to take a more interventionist stance with regard to British banking. This pressure emerged between the wars in the face of the difficult economic conditions experienced by British manufacturing industry and the mass unemployment that resulted. It emerged again after the Second World War in the face of growing international competition and Britain's relatively poor economic performance. No longer was it accepted that the British banking system was perfect and should be left untouched by government.[1]

All that British banks could offer in compensation was their contribution to economic stability, as had been exhibited during two world wars and the global economic, financial, and monetary difficulties experienced between them. Almost alone in the world British banks surmounted these problems without either a crisis or the necessity to call upon the government for assistance. That stability then continued after the Second World War. In their survey of banking crises Reinhart and Rogoff observed that there were none of significance in Britain between 1878 and 1991, despite the extreme pressures its banking system was placed under during these years, which destabilized other banking systems around the world.[2] Other surveys of banking crises produce slightly longer or shorter periods over which British banks exhibited their stability but all emphasize this key element in contrast to what took place elsewhere. Cassis suggests that the last significant crisis in British banking, prior to that of 2007/8, was 1890.[3] Kindleberger is also of this view,[4] while Grossman notes 'the remarkable banking stability that reigned in England following the Baring Crisis of 1890.'[5] Many place the beginning of stability somewhat earlier with the last significant crisis being that of 1866. Turner argues for an even earlier start date, claiming that the last crisis prior to 2007/8 was in 1825.[6] He is at variance with most other experts, such as Capie, who point to the importance of the crises that took place in 1836/7, 1847, and 1857.[7] Though some suggest that this stability ended in the crisis of 1973/4 or that of 1991/2 all are agreed that the crisis of 2007/8 brought it to a definite end. The only query about that date is the preference, especially at the Bank of England, for the year 2008 rather than 2007. That would place responsibility for the end of British banking stability not with the crisis that engulfed the domestic bank, Northern Rock, in 2007 but the collapse of the US investment bank, Lehman Brothers.[8]

---

[1] See R.C. Michie, 'The City of London and British Banking, 1900–1939', in C. Wrigley (ed.), *A Companion to Early Twentieth-Century Britain* (Oxford: OUP, 2003), pp.249–69; R.C. Michie, 'The City of London and the British Government: The Changing Relationship', in R.C. Michie and P.A. Williamson (eds), *The British Government and the City of London in the Twentieth Century* (Cambridge: CUP, 2004), pp.31–55.
[2] Reinhart and Rogoff, *This Time is Different*, p.87.
[3] Cassis, *Crises and Opportunities*, p.4.
[4] Kindleberger and Aliber, *Manias, Panics, and Crashes*, pp.184–8, 302–11.
[5] Grossman, *Unsettled Account*, p.190.
[6] Turner, *Banking in Crisis*, pp.7, 53–4.
[7] F. Capie, 'British Financial Crises in the Nineteenth and Twentieth Centuries', in Dimsdale and Hotson (eds), *British Financial Crises*, p.11.
[8] For a recent use of the 2008 date by the staff at the Bank of England see Z. Liu, S. Quiet, and B. Roth, 'Banking Sector Interconnectedness: What It Is, How Can We Measure It and Why Does It Matter?', *Bank of England Quarterly Bulletin* (2015), pp.2–8.

This long period without crises meant that the contribution made by British banks to stability was increasingly taken for granted. In the report of the Committee on Finance and Industry, commonly known as the Macmillan Committee, which appeared in 1931, it was noted that, 'It may be that we are too far removed in this country from the days of great banking failures and panics, and the ruin following from the destruction of confidence, to esteem at its proper worth the enormous value of an impregnable banking system.'[9] With the stability that followed, despite the world depression of the 1930s, the Second World War, and the problems of economic recovery after 1945, it can be easily understood why subsequent generations paid little attention to that element of banking.[10] This neglect of stability as an important element within British banking has been recognized as a fundamental flaw in the light of the 2007/8 financial crisis. It led to the implicit assumption by those regulating the banking system that the stability of banks could be relied upon, irrespective of what happened elsewhere in the economy or the monetary system.[11] Contributing to that attitude was the belief that stability was only partly the product of what the banks had done, and then to a lesser degree. Many have expressed the view that it was the legislative changes introduced between 1826 and 1844 that created the conditions for stability. As Rondo Cameron, one of the early pioneers of comparative banking history, observed 'one of the most important determinants of banking structure is legislation.'[12] This remains a commonly held view when combined with the role played by the Bank of England. Long before the Bank was taken into state ownership in 1946 it was regarded as the government's bank, expected to act in the national interest. Intervention by the Bank of England was seen as instrumental in the avoidance of banking crises in 1890, when Barings Bank was in difficulty; between 1929 and 1932, when the problems of Williams Deacon's Bank emerged; and the Secondary Banking Crisis of 1973–4.

More generally the stability is credited to the Bank of England having learnt how to play the role of lender of last resort, which meant that liquidity crises were avoided.[13] Liquidity crises were the main cause of bank failure leading to a

[9] Committee on Finance and Industry, *Report: Cmd* 3897 (London, H.M.S.O., 1931).
[10] Capie and Woods, *Money over Two Centuries*, p.333; N. Dimsdale and A. Hotson, 'Financial Crises and Economic Activity in the UK since 1825', in Dimsdale and Hotson (eds), *British Financial Crises*, p.53.
[11] Z. Jakab and M. Kumhof, 'Banks Are not Intermediaries of Loanable Funds: And Why It Matters', *Bank of England Working Paper*, 529 (2015), pp.1–57.
[12] R. Cameron, 'Banking and Industrialisation in Britain in the Nineteenth Century', in A. Slaven and D.H. Aldcroft (eds), *Business, Banking and Urban History* (Edinburgh: John Donald, 1982), p.107.
[13] F. Allen and D. Gale, *Understanding Financial Crises* (Oxford: OUP, 2007), p.2; M. Billings and F. Capie, 'Financial Crisis, Contagion and the British Banking System between the World Wars', *Business History*, 53 (2011), p.197; Capie and Woods, *Money over Two Centuries*, pp.3, 49–50, 329–34; Turner, *Banking in Crisis*, pp.8–10.

general panic, arising out of the maturity mismatch that was the characteristic of all banks. In a liquidity crisis, even solvent banks failed as they were not in a position to meet the demands of those customers wishing to withdraw their deposits or demanding an alternative to the bank notes they held. If liquidity crises could be prevented through the supply of additional money when a sudden shortage arose, then a subsequent panic and a run could be avoided. The secret was to provide the increased liquidity in such a way that banks would not come to expect that it would always be available, and so take increased risks thereby endangering the stability of the entire banking system. It was this that the Bank of England appeared to have perfected after 1866 and so the stability experienced until the crisis of 2007/8 has been credited to the Bank, rather than to the banking system as a whole.[14]

After the Second World War, with stability seemingly assured by the Bank of England, especially as it was now under government control, the pressure for government intervention in the banking system became irresistible. It was generally accepted that banks, especially those run from the City of London, were mainly responsible for the relatively poor performance of the British economy.[15] The solution for some was seen to lie in the state ownership of banks, but this only extended as far as the Bank of England in 1946. For others what was required was the creation of alternatives to banks and this did happen after the end of the war, with the formation of the Industrial and Commercial Finance Corporation, later to become 3i, as one of the initiatives. For many the key lay in increasing the degree of competition between the banks by removing the barriers that had existed between the various segments of the financial system. Increased competition would challenge the conservative attitudes towards risk-taking that were seen to be endemic within British banking, and force all participants to become more responsive to both savers and borrowers. The first move in this direction came from the Bank of England in 1970 with the removal of the controls that had restrained domestic competition in the 1950s and 1960s. The sudden ending of these controls did contribute to the banking crisis of 1973/4, but this was successfully dealt with by Bank of England intervention, so enhancing its reputation for ensuring stability.[16] Further changes came in the 1980s with the reforms associated with Big Bang, which covered not only the restrictive practices of the London Stock Exchange but also those of banks and building societies.[17] That was then followed in the 1990s with the radical re-structuring of banking regulation that

---

[14] For an in-depth discussion of these issues see Goodhart, Hartmann, Llewellyn, Rojas-Suarez, and Weisbrod, *Financial Regulation*. The extensive literature on the subject of 'Lender of Last Resort' has been brought together in Goodhart and Illing (eds), *Financial Crises*.
[15] See Michie, 'A Financial Phoenix, pp.15–41.
[16] F. Hirsch, 'The Bagehot Problem', in Goodhart and Illing (eds), *Financial Crises*, p.189.
[17] For Big Bang see C. Bellringer and R.C. Michie, 'Big Bang in the City', pp.1–27.

led to the formation of the Financial Services Authority in 1997/8.[18] In all of these the question of banking stability was either ignored or relegated to a minor concern in comparison with the desire to create a more competitive banking environment in Britain. Not until the crisis of 2007/8 did banking stability become a priority once again.

Given the way a bank operated and the activities that it was engaged in, governments inevitably became involved in supervising what they did. A bank posed a risk to monetary stability by issuing notes that passed from hand to hand as money but had no intrinsic value. A bank also posed a risk to financial stability by acting as repositories for the savings made by the public as these could be destroyed if it became insolvent. Collectively, banks threatened economic stability if one or more should collapse and so deprive the public of a payments system and a source of credit. The question for the relationship between banking and government was not whether there should be one but its nature and extent.[19] For Britain, as in other countries, that relationship became increasingly close over the course of the twentieth century, extending beyond the need to prevent or limit the risks inherent in banking to a desire to influence and control the entire system in the interests of government policy. This took place both at the national level and internationally, with the establishment of the Bank for International Settlement in 1930 and the International Monetary Fund in 1944.[20]

In the light of what happened in Britain, and globally, in 2007/8, a question exists whether this greatly increased government intervention in the banking system achieved even its first basic aim, which was to ensure stability, let alone all the secondary objectives that were set over the years. As David Peretz of the IMF admitted in 2010, when assessing his own organization's performance in the run-up to the financial crisis in the UK in 2007, 'To summarize, IMF staff did not foresee the risk of a crisis of the scale, nature or severity of the one that occurred in the UK.'[21] In Kindleberger's classic account of financial crises, as updated by Aliber after the events of 2007–9, it was acknowledged how difficult it was for governments to strike a balance between intervening too much or too little in the banking system. Too great a level of government intervention prevented those banks that were subject to control from operating efficiently and competitively, and so drove financial activity into areas that were completely unregulated. Conversely, too little by way of government

---

[18] For evidence that bank stability was not a consideration in the changes introduced in 1997/8 see E. Balls and G. O'Donnell (eds), *Reforming Britain's Economic and Financial Policy: Towards Greater Economic Stability* (London: Palgrave, 2002).
[19] Grossman, *Unsettled Account*, pp.101, 130–5, 146.
[20] Singleton, *Central Banking in the Twentieth Century*, pp.60–90, 113, 127–32, 167; Cassis, *Crises and Opportunities*, p.118.
[21] David Peretz, Speech: 'IMF Performance in the Run-up to the Financial and Economic Crisis: Bilateral Surveillance of the United Kingdom', 9 December 2010, pp.1–23.

regulation left the users of banking services open to abuse while leading to the build-up of risks. In between there was the issue of moral hazard, which arose when banks were so confident that governments would intervene in a crisis that they took excessive risks as the losses would be borne by the state while they would reap the profits.[22]

One way of answering the question of the degree and nature of government control is to examine what happened in British banking over the last three centuries. Over that period British banking discovered and then lost the balance between too much and too little government intervention in banking while avoiding the problem of moral hazard. Even the reservation that such a balance was only achieved at the expense of the British economy, through overly conservative behaviour, is no longer considered a valid one. As Battilossi concluded from a comparative survey of banking history, 'New research...has vindicated British banks from traditional allegations such as failure to engage in industrial lending, excess risk aversion and conservatism, or strong preference for liquidity of asset portfolio... it turns out that British bankers flexibly adapted their formal and informal screening and monitoring mechanisms to changes in the economic and business environment, parallel to the transition from the dominance of small local private bankers to a consolidated system of joint-stock banks.'[23] In the light of this conclusion possibly the British banking system did find the holy grail of financial stability without sacrificing the contribution it made to savers, borrowers, and the economy as whole. Whether that was the case or not, the history of British banking is a subject that demands detailed study, both in terms of long-term trends and the events and decisions that determined its composition and structure.

THE NUMBER OF UK BANKS

Certain features of the British banking system are well known.[24] Sometime in the nineteenth century it moved from a position of instability to stability but the precise moment is unknown and there is debate over the reasons why. Various explanations have been provided to explain this stability ranging from the role played by the Bank of England as lender of last resort, through the structure of banking itself with its ability to spread risk through an extensive

---

[22] Kindleberger and Aliber, *Manias, Panics, and Crashes*, pp.16, 25, 83, 194, 213, 227–46, 300.
[23] Battilossi, '"Ephors" from Growth to Governance', p.89.
[24] The data on the number of UK banks and building societies was assembled as one of the outputs from the Leverhulme Trust-funded 'Tipping Points Project' at the Institute of Hazard, Risk and Resilience, University of Durham, from 2010 to 2015. I would like to thank those involved for their assistance, especially Matthew Hollow.

branch network, to the professionalism of staff trained to assess risk.[25] However, the debate continues to rage on why the British banking system moved from a position of instability to one of stability during the 19th century, maintained that position during the 20th century, and then lost it at the beginning of the 21st century. This can be seen from the range of views put forward in the volume edited by Dimsdale and Hotson in 2014.[26] Related to this transition was the transformation of the British banking system from one of numerous banks that were small and vulnerable to one containing a small number of banks that were large and resilient. All this was achieved without any active involvement of the UK government, apart from permissive legislation that removed the monopoly of the Bank of England over joint-stock banking in England and extended limited liability to banking companies.[27]

Making it difficult to resolve the various explanations for the rise and fall of British banking stability is the absence of long-run data covering even such basics as the number of banks. Neither the government nor the Bank of England systematically collected this information. As Sheppard noted in his pioneering attempt to remedy this deficit, 'Unfortunately, before the mid-1950s, the coverage of the UK's financial statistics as published by the Bank of England or by the Government agencies was far from comprehensive.' In failing to do so they were typical of most countries, with the USA being the main exception. 'The published series of UK financial statistics for the pre-1954 years are not comprehensive enough for study of the UK financial system to be nearly as detailed as analysis of the US financial system has been.'[28] In the *New Dictionary of Statistics*, which was published in 1911, the compiler, Augustus D. Webb, was able to draw upon the Statistical Abstract of the United States for annual information on the number of US banks but lacked an equivalent source for other countries. For the UK he relied on the *Bankers' Magazine* for information about banks.[29] Despite this failure to collect such basic data, knowing the trend in the number of banks was considered important not only in the USA. In the UK, from its beginning in 1879, members of the Institute of Bankers attempted to estimate trends in the number of banks

---

[25] Capie and Woods, *Money over Two Centuries*, pp.64, 105, 329–32.

[26] N. Dimsdale and A. Hotson, 'Introduction' in Dimsdale and Hotson (eds), *British Financial Crises*, p.7; Capie, 'British Financial Crises', in Dimsdale and Hotson (eds), *British Financial Crises*, p.16; J.D. Turner, 'Holding Shareholders to Account: British Banking Stability and Contingent Capital', in Dimsdale and Hotson (eds), *British Financial Crises*, pp.139–40, 145, 153, 155; A. Offer, 'Narrow Banking, Real Estate, and Financial Stability in the UK, c. 1870–2010', in Dimsdale and Hotson (eds), *British Financial Crises*, p.158.

[27] Grossman, *Unsettled Account*, pp.3, 63, 72–6.

[28] Shepherd, *The Growth and Role of UK Financial Institutions*, pp.xi–xii, 111.

[29] See A.D. Webb, *The New Dictionary of Statistics* (London: Routledge, 1911), pp.52–62. This publication followed on from Mulhall's *Dictionary of Statistics* which did not reference the sources used in the compilation of data.

because of the implications that had for the current state of British banking.[30] In the 1960s Sheppard did try to remedy this historical deficit by estimating the number of UK banks for each year from 1880 until 1966, but this count was limited to those banks whose balance sheets were available. This meant that in 1962, for example, only 25 banks were included. Though they covered the largest banks operating in England, Scotland, and Northern Ireland they only included one private bank and three merchant banks along with a bank from the Isle of Man, the Yorkshire Penny Bank, and the Co-operative Wholesale Society. Despite the growing importance of other financial intermediaries they were all excluded because the publicly available information was considered insufficient. This series also lacks consistency over time as there are two major breaks in 1891 and 1920, and so it cannot be used to trace long-term trends in bank numbers.[31] Nevertheless, the need to know trends in the number of banks remains relevant today as it informs the debate about whether the causes of the financial crisis of 2007–9 were the product of a shrinking banking sector, dominated by a few banks that had become too big to fail, or due to increasing competition leading to risk-taking caused by an expanding bank population.[32] Though it is desirable to know the importance of individual banks in terms of their relative share of loans or deposits and the nature of their business, the number of banks does provide a basic starting point for any examination of a banking system.

For that reason attempts have been made by British historians to provide this information but, apart from Sheppard, it has been confined to either specific types of banks or for particular periods.[33] What is lacking is a comprehensive annual series that allows tipping points to be identified and then matched with possible causes, such as changes in legislation, or potential effects, as in the question of whether British banking was to become more concentrated or more competitive. Contributing to the difficulty in establishing the trend in the number of banks is the lack of a precise definition of a 'bank'. Many different types of financial institution undertook functions that might lead them to be classified as banks, such as collecting savings and/or making loans, but not all were classified as 'banks'. One such example were

---

[30] See R.W. Barnett, 'The History of the Progress and Development of Banking in the United Kingdom from the Year 1800 to the Present Time, *Journal of the Institute of Bankers*, 1 (1880); R.W. Barnett, 'The Effect of the Development of Banking Facilities upon the Circulation of the Country', *Journal of the Institute of Bankers*, 2 (1881); J. Dick, 'Banking Statistics of the United Kingdom in 1896, Compared with Former Times', *Journal of the Institute of Bankers*, 18 (1897); Sir D. Drummond Fraser, 'British Home Banking'.

[31] Shepherd, *The Growth and Role of UK Financial Institutions*, pp.113–14, 141, Appendix 1 and 2.

[32] See Davies, Richardson, Katinaite, and Manning, 'Evolution of the UK Banking System'.

[33] See L. Pressnell, *Country Banking in the Industrial Revolution* (Oxford: OUP, 1956); F. Capie and A. Webber, *A Monetary History of the United Kingdom, 1870–1982* (London: Allen & Unwin, 1985).

building societies as they were long engaged in accepting deposits and lending to finance house purchase and a number did become recognized as banks after 1986. No definition of a bank was incorporated into English law, and a number of different ones were used by different authorities at different times and for different purposes.[34]

In the Appendix at the end of this book, readers can find a detailed chronological account of the number of British banks between 1700 and 2008, British building societies between 1876 and 2010, and British trustee savings banks 1829 to 1967, and another for US banks from 1782 to 2013. They will also find two timelines, the first listing principal events in British banking between 1694 and 2012, the second, principal events in US banking between 1781 and 2010.

In the absence of an annual count of the number of British banks the more readily available information from the USA (See Table at Appendix 4) has been used as representative of trends in banking. US authorities began to count the number of banks during the nineteenth century, taking a very liberal view on what to include. With the introduction of deposit insurance, and the establishment of the Federal Deposit Insurance Corporation (FDIC) in 1933/4, a new annual count of the number of US banks became available. Given the assurance provided to savers by the FDIC scheme most institutions that collected deposits joined. However, even in the USA, the large savings and loan sector was not included in the FDIC scheme until its own provider of deposit insurance, the Federal savings and loan Insurance Corporation (founded in 1934), collapsed in 1989 and its successor organization, the Resolution Trust Corporation, merged with the FDIC in 1995.[35] What the US data show is a fairly continuous growth in the number of US banks during the course of the nineteenth and into the twentieth century before beginning a steep decline. The number of US banks reached 30,456 in 1921 and then halved to 14,146 by 1934. After this period of rapid decline, what the FDIC data show, with savings and loan institutions excluded, is that the 14,146 banks in the USA in 1934 fell only slowly to 12,715 in 1989. It was only in the 1990s and early twenty-first century that a rapid decline again took place, with the number falling to 7,284 in 2007 and then 5,876 in 2013.[36]

---

[34] See *Journal of the Institute of Bankers*, 'Memorandum by the Committee of London Clearing Bankers to the Company Law Amendment Committee', *JIB*, 65 (1944); Sir George Blunden, 'The Supervision of the UK Banking System', *Bank of England Quarterly Bulletin*, 15 (1975). For an authoritative discussion of what defines a bank and an attempt to count the number of UK banks see the chapter by Ian Bond in M. Hollow, F. Akinbami, and R. Michie (eds), *Complexity and Crisis in the Financial System: Critical Perspectives on the Evolution of American and British Banking* (Cheltenham: Edward Elgar, 2016).

[35] M.D. Bordo (ed.), *Financial Market and Institutions in Historical Statistics of the United States: Earliest Times to the Present*, Millenial Ed. (New York: CUP, 2006).

[36] Federal Deposit Insurance Corporation, *Historic Banking Database*.

This pattern in the number of US banks has led Grossman to suggest, in his authoritative comparative history of banking in developed economies, that there is a banking-population life cycle. An expansion in bank numbers is followed by a rapid decline involving a financial crisis and then a prolonged period of stability.[37] It was in 1929 that the Wall Street Crash took place, followed by a catastrophic banking collapse in the early 1930s. Similarly, there was a massive financial crisis in the USA in 2008 involving the failure or near failure of a number of major US banks. The causal link between consolidation and crisis was believed to run through the behaviour of bankers. With consolidation, there emerged banks managed by paid employees who could pursue highly risky strategies, secure in the knowledge that if their actions resulted in catastrophic losses they would not be held financially responsible while any gains would be well rewarded. This behaviour forced the US government to intervene so as to prevent a systemic collapse as the public's confidence in the entire banking system was undermined by successive failures. In 1934 the measure taken was the introduction of deposit insurance whereas in 2008 it extended to the direct assistance provided to a number of the largest banks. In the aftermath of each crisis the result of the consolidation was lack of competition among banks, which allowed bankers to become ultra cautious. The result was a shortage of finance, which deepened and prolonged the economic depression. This US experience has been extended to banking globally as an explanation for the global financial crisis of 2007/8, including that of the UK. According to Haldane and May, writing in 2011, 'There has been a spectacular rise in the size and concentration of the financial system over the last two decades, with the rapid emergence of "super-spreader institutions" too big, connected, or important to fail.'[38] However, the absence of long-term data on the number of banks in countries other than the USA means that the link between rapid consolidation and financial crisis is dependent upon the experience of one country, though it is generally applied. This is unfortunate because, as Calomiris and Haber have concluded, the result of legislative intervention in the USA was to create a 'uniquely unstable system'.[39] It is often a mistake to generalize about patterns in one financial system based on those observed in another because of the differences that exist, especially in banking, owing to national legislation.[40]

An annual count of the number of UK banks provides a first step in establishing the degree to which this US experience does apply generally.

---

[37] Grossman, *Unsettled Account*, p.17.
[38] A.G. Haldane and R.M. May, 'Systemic Risk in Banking Ecosystems', *Nature*, 20 January 2011, pp.353-4.
[39] Calomiris and Haber, *Fragile by Design*, pp.161-203.
[40] R.C. Michie, 'Financial Capitalism', in L. Neal and J.G. Williamson (eds), *The Cambridge History of Capitalism, The Spread of Capitalism: From 1848 to the Present*, v.2 (Cambridge: CUP, 2014), pp.230-63.

Only when that has been done can further research reveal whether the assumptions made about banking behaviour, and its causes and consequences, are correct. With such data for both the USA and the UK it becomes possible to compare and contrast the experience of each country and draw conclusions about the timing of events and the causality involved. To create such a series, recording the annual number of British banks for the UK, the *Bankers' Almanac Register of Bank Name Changes and Liquidations*[41] provides a potential source. This volume lists by name all British banks that were known to have existed, according to the records of the *Bankers' Almanac*. This information was then supplemented by a similar listing for the post-1992 period in the Bankers' Almanac 2009.[42] From these two sources it was possible to identify British banks dating as far back as the sixteenth century and up to 2008. Normally included in this source was the year in which the bank was formed and when it ceased to operate. Where the dates were incomplete this information was obtained from other sources. That did require some intelligent guesswork involving, for example, the first and last reference found for the bank. An element of duplication also exists in the information provided by the *Bankers' Almanac* as some banks operated under a number of different names. When operating as a partnership a bank could be known either by the names of the partners or through the location of its office or both. Thus, the same bank could generate multiple entries especially if it operated in more than one town or through linked partnerships. Such duplication declined as joint-stock companies replaced partnerships. Later, though, a number of banking companies chose to operate separate subsidiaries for particular parts of their business if it was necessary to distinguish these from their main operations.[43]

It is important to acknowledge these weaknesses in the information culled from the *Bankers' Almanac* so that the data series is not regarded as precise.[44] Nevertheless, the information obtained has made it possible to identify the number of British banks started and ended each year. That information is used

[41] East Grinstead: Reed Information Services, 1992.
[42] London: Reed Business Information, 2009.
[43] These were the most useful: Capie and Webber, *A Monetary History*; M. Davies, *The Origins and Development of Cartelisation in British Banking* (Bangor: Institute of European Finance, 1993); M. Dawes and C.N. Ward-Perkins, *Country Banks of England and Wales: Private Provincial Banks and Bankers, 1688–1953* (Canterbury: Chartered Institute of Bankers, 2001); F.G. Hilton Price, *A Handbook of London Bankers* (London: [n.p.], 1876 and 1890/1); J. Orbell and A. Turton, *British Banking: A Guide to Historical Records* (Aldershot: Ashgate, 2001); Pressnell, *Country Banking*; J. Sykes, *The Amalgamation Movement in English Banking, 1825–1924* (London: King, 1926); S.E. Thomas, *The Rise and Growth of Joint-Stock Banking* (London: Pitman, 1934); *The Times* Digital Archive, 1785–2008.
[44] Ian Bond, who acted as an advisor on the Tipping Points Project, provided a detailed critique of the banking database and remains sceptical of the reliance placed on the *Bankers' Almanac* as the single source.

to obtain the annual total by adding the number of banks started in any one year to the number already in existence from the previous year and subtracting the number ended in any one year from the total for the following year. (See Table at Appendix 1) The merit of relying on this single source in identifying the number of British banks is that it provides a degree of consistency over time in terms of those categories of financial institutions that were included. The *Bankers' Almanac* was established in London in 1845 as a specialist provider of reference data on and for the banking industry, and continues to do so today. After 2009 it ceased to produce an annual printed volume and, instead, switched to a digital subscription service.[45] Sheppard relied for much of his information on the *Bankers' Almanac*, noting the comprehensive nature of its coverage, but excluded in his count those banks that did not provide the balance sheet information he required.[46]

The *Bankers' Almanac* listed all UK-based financial institutions, including those located in Ireland, they regarded as performing the functions of a bank. Also included were those banks operating overseas if they had a British head office and foreign banks with a UK subsidiary. Selective subsidiaries of British banks, where they were separately constituted and had an independent existence, were also included. Excluded were foreign banks with only a branch or an office in the UK and those financial institutions not regarded as banks such as building societies and other mutual organizations. The defect of relying on this single source is that financial institutions may be included that otherwise might not be classed as a bank because of the specific nature of their activities, or excluded even, though they operated in many ways like a bank. An alternative approach would be to define a bank precisely and then only count those financial institutions that matched that definition. Such an approach does work for relatively short periods and for particular types of financial institutions. It has been used, for example, to count the number of country banks and the number of joint-stock banks.[47] However, when the objective is to create a long-run time series that is as comprehensive as that available for the USA, then a different approach needs to be taken in the absence of officially collected information.

Though the *Bankers' Almanac* did take an inclusive view on what constituted a bank, two important categories of financial institutions were excluded, namely building societies and savings banks. For the sake of completeness it was decided to count the number of each of these. Prior to the passing of a new Building Societies Act in 1874 it was not possible to construct a comprehensive annual series of the number of building societies. Even with that Act the dataset constructed is not a record of all the building societies in existence

---

[45] The *Bankers' Almanac* is currently owned by the Reed Group.
[46] Shepherd, *The Growth and Role of UK Financial Institutions*, pp.117–18.
[47] See Dawes and Ward-Perkins, *Country Banks of England and Wales*; Thomas, *The Rise and Growth*.

between 1875 and 2010. Prior to 1894 there was no legal obligation for building societies to be officially registered with the Chief Registrar of Friendly Societies. The majority of the larger, permanent societies did take up this option but many of the smaller, terminating variety did not.[48] The data itself was collected directly from the Annual Reports of the Chief Registrar of Friendly Societies. The problem with these Annual Reports prior to 1894, however, is that they only record the number of building societies registered/dissolved each year (not the total number of registered societies in existence at that time). Thus, it is necessary to work backwards from the 1894 Special Report produced by the Select Committee on Building Societies, commissioned in the aftermath of the 1892 Liberator Crash, where it is stated that there were at that time 2,158 registered societies still in existence.[49] From this starting point it is then possible to work out the number of registered societies by subtracting the number of societies registered/dissolved in the previous year. Finally, there is a gap between 1940 and 1950 owing to the fact that in 1940 a Miscellaneous Provisions Societies Bill was passed that suspended the need for societies to provide the Registrar with annual registrations during the 'emergency period'. However, Sheppard obtained data for those years and that has been used.[50] (See Table at Appendix 2). In contrast to building societies there is a series on the number of savings banks from 1829 to 1944. This was compiled by Oliver Horne for his history of British savings banks, which was published in 1947, and continued by David Sheppard up to 1967.[51] That is what is presented here. (See Table at Appendix 3).

KEY OBSERVATIONS

What the data reveal about the British banking system[52] is the degree to which it changed over the course of centuries. In terms of absolute numbers there

---

[48] See S. James Price, *Building Societies, Their Origin and History*, 2nd ed. (London: Franey, 1959); E.J. Cleary, *The Building Society Movement* (London: Elek Books, 1965); H. Ashworth, *The Building Society Story* (London: Franey, 1980).

[49] 'Special Report and Reports from the Select Committee on Building Societies (No. 2) Bill; Together with the Proceedings of the Committee, Minutes of Evidence, Appendix and Index' (London: HMSO, 1894), 58. There is a series in Shepherd, *The Growth and Role of UK Financial Institutions*, Table A 2.4. This differs at times from the series presented here in that it includes unregistered building societies where such information was known.

[50] 'Societies (Miscellaneous Provisions). A Bill to Amend the Law Relating to Trade Unions, Friendly Societies, Building Societies and Certain Other Societies for Purposes Connected with the Present Emergency, and to Make Further Provision with Respect to the Amalgamation and Transfer of Engagements of Trade Unions and Building Societies' (London: HMSO, 1940).

[51] H.O. Horne, *A History of Savings Banks* (London: OUP, 1947), pp.386–91; Shepherd, *The Growth and Role of UK Financial Institutions*, Table A 2.3.

[52] These are general observations focusing on broad trends. More detailed analysis, including support evidence and referencing, will be found in the subsequent chapters.

was a gradual rise in the number of banks until the middle of the eighteenth century, with the overall numbers remaining low. That was the followed by a rapid expansion that took overall numbers up to an all-time peak in 1810, when the total exceeded 1,000 individual banks. That peak was never again exceeded for a gradual decline then took place, punctuated with occasional rises and falls over the course of the nineteenth century. By the 1920s the number of UK banks had settled down to a figure of under 200, and slowly fell to half that over the next 100 years, though there was a brief flurry in the 1960s/70s. This stability in the number of UK banks, especially during the twentieth century, has led many to see British banking as a static system in which the existing banks were immune from the competition that came from new entrants.

This perception of British banking as a closed system is an incorrect one, as revealed by the data on the changing number of British banks. What is apparent is that, at no stage, were there no new entrants into British banking. The number of new entrants reached an all-time high in the late eighteenth and early nineteenth centuries but there were subsequent peaks such as during the 1830s and 1860s as well as in the 1980s and 1990s. Judged by numbers alone, British banking was a system in which established banks were always exposed to challenger banks, though the degree to which this took place varied over time. A similar verdict can be reached on the number of exits from British banking. Again, this contradicts the popular perception that British banks were long-lived institutions that were immune to failure. Especially in the era before 1826, when British banking was dominated by small partnerships, there was a process of continuous exits and entries as the personnel involved changed with each departure and new arrival. Though fathers were succeeded by sons these were the exception rather than the rule for it was not possible to rely on the maintenance of either inclination or competence over many generations, considering the limited degree of choice, especially as daughters were excluded from consideration. It was only with the coming of joint-stock companies that a semi-permanence in banking was possible. Even then mergers, takeovers, and bankruptcies took place on a regular basis, continually winnowing the number of banks. The result was a banking system that experienced numerous losses from among its numbers over time, not only in the eighteenth and nineteenth centuries but also throughout the twentieth. At no stage was British banking composed of a small number of banks whose survival was guaranteed whether through immunity from being acquired by a rival or the possibility of failure. Particularly when banks became answerable to shareholders their management was always conscious that a poor performance could result in their dismissal or an unsolicited takeover bid.

When entrants into, and exits from, British banking are combined, the impression generated is of a highly dynamic system never at rest. Again, this contradicts the impression of a system comprising a small number of long-established banks that neither faced competition from challenger banks nor the possibility that they would fail or be taken over. If that were the case complaints that it was a system characterized by being too big to fail, and so able to operate at the extremes of risk-taking or risk aversion, would have some support. As it is the absolute number of banks, and the constant activity in terms of entrants and exits, suggests that the British banking system was a constantly evolving one. This can be seen if the net position is examined through subtracting exits from entries. What this reveals is a system prior to 1810 in which entries outnumber exits with a high degree of volatility. No sooner had one bank ceased business, for whatever reason, but others took its place, so building up the number of banks. In contrast, after 1810 the process was reversed with exits outnumbering entrants with the result that the number of banks fell over time. That position was particularly noticeable in the early and late nineteenth century but was temporarily reversed in the middle years. During the twentieth century the level of activity was much lower but there continued to be both entries into and exits from banking that, briefly, increased numbers in the 1960s/70s and then led to a reduction from the 1990s.

If those businesses that competed with banks for savings and loans, but are not covered by the banking data drawn from the *Bankers' Almanac*, are included in the population of financial institutions a somewhat different picture emerges. As the number of banks declines in the first half of the nineteenth century the number of savings banks expanded. The number of savings banks then steadily declined from the mid nineteenth century onwards. This suggests that the forces driving consolidation among banks were also evident among savings banks even though they operated a much simpler form of banking.[53] In the second half of the nineteenth century the number of building societies also grew very rapidly, replicating what had happened to banks almost a century earlier. Again, though, after peaking in the 1890s the number of building societies then falls steadily throughout the entire twentieth century, supporting the conclusion that the forces leading to consolidation among banks of all kinds were strong once the period of initial expansion was over.[54] What the data reveal are the long-term trends evident across the entire range of financial institutions that accepted deposits and made loans, and so could be regarded as banks. These trends indicate that after a period of rapid expansion in numbers a process of consolidation took place though the precise timing varied according to the type of bank. It came first among retail and

---

[53] Horne, *A History of Savings Banks*, pp.386-91; Shepherd, *The Growth and Role of UK Financial Institutions*, Table A 2.3.

[54] Special Report and Reports from the Select Committee on Building Societies (No. 2) Bill, p.58. There is a series in Shepherd, *The Growth and Role of UK Financial Institutions*, Table A 2.4. This differs at times from the series presented here in that it includes unregistered building societies where such information was known.

commercial banks and took place later among savings banks and then building societies.[55]

TRENDS IN BRITISH BANKING

What the numbers suggest was that there were underlying economies of scale in banking that encouraged concentration over the course of the nineteenth and twentieth centuries. As the overall volume of banking business grew, driven by rising per capita income, the increasing complexity of a modern economy, and the need for finance, after 1810 it was delivered by fewer and fewer banks as shown in Figure 1.1.

However, the existence of economies of scale in banking is disputed, especially at the Bank of England. In the wake of the financial crisis of 2007/8 Andrew Haldane delivered a speech in September 2009 in which he claimed that 'There is not a scrap of evidence of economies of scale or scope in banking—of bigger or broader being better—beyond a low size threshold.'[56] This view was then given substance a year later when staff at the Bank of England produced a narrative on the evolution of the British banking system that disputed the conclusion reached by many others that economies of scale had driven the growth of ever larger banks, and even put forward the counter-suggestion that diseconomies of scale existed for the very largest banks. However, they did accept that the need for banks to meet regulatory requirements was an impulse towards greater scale as that allowed the costs of compliance to be spread. Possibly the reluctance by the Bank of England to accept that economies of scale drove concentration was an understandable product of the problems faced by

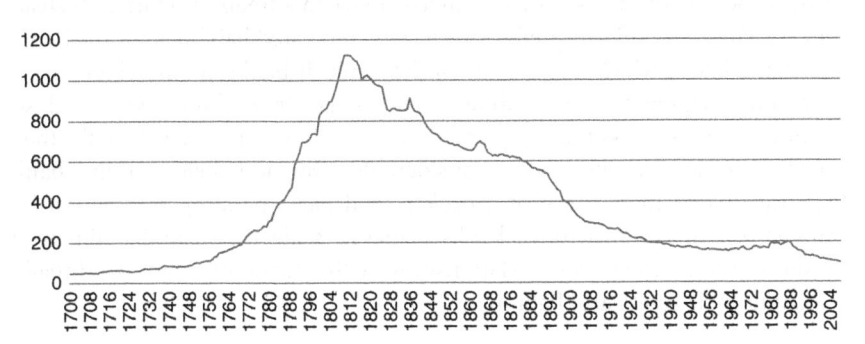

Figure 1.1. Trend in numbers of UK Banks 1700–2008 (annual data)
Appendix 1

---

[55] Grossman, *Unsettled Account*, pp.3, 63, 72–6.
[56] A. Haldane, 'Credit Is Trust', *Bank of England Quarterly Bulletin*, 49 (2009), pp.1–21.

regulators when banks became so big that they could not be allowed to fail. 'A financial institution becomes too important to fail when the potential losses to the financial system and wider economy associated with its failure or distress would be so large or uncertain that a government is unable to commit credibly not to intervene in support.'[57] However, this is not a new problem in the UK as such banks were emerging a century earlier, and the Bank of England not only coped with such a situation in the past but also turned it to its advantage when arranging the rescue of Barings in 1890, Williams Deacons in 1930, and the secondary banks in 1974. In a paper at the Institute of Bankers in 1900, Macdonald voiced his concern that, though the possibility was remote, if one of these large banks should fail the results would be catastrophic. The failure of such a bank would be 'nothing less than national, nay, an international calamity' and would result in 'widespread ruin and disaster.'[58] However, until the 1920s, when the Bank of England persuaded banks to refrain from future mergers unless it approved, the trend towards concentration begun after 1810 continued apace.

The reasons for such a trend have been explored by banking historians not only in the UK but also in other countries leading to the conclusion that it was a direct response to the changing environment within which banks operated over the course of the nineteenth and twentieth centuries, most notably the increased size of their business customers and their borrowing requirements, and the economic integration generated by the transformation of transport and communications beginning with the railway and the telegraph. The US position was the exception, Figure 1.2., and that was a product of legislation that prevented the emergence of large banks.

In other countries where no such legislative impediment existed, concentration within banking was the normal pattern. Banks did not simply connect lenders and borrowers as with any intermediary in a financial market. Instead they issued notes and accepted deposits, which created liabilities for the bank, and made loans, which were assets of the bank. If banks could achieve scale they could aggregate these liabilities and assets in different ways and so maximize the business that they could do, as well as minimize the risks they ran. This meant that there was a considerable value-added element in a bank that was absent in the case of a broker or dealer operating transaction by transaction. In contrast, once banks achieved scale they could build up a business maintaining close relationships with customers and continually matching their assets and liabilities.[59]

---

[57] Davies, Richardson, Katinaite, and Manning, 'Evolution of the UK Banking System', pp.320–30.
[58] J.C. Macdonald, 'The Economic Effects, National and International of the Concentration of Capital in Few Controlling Hands', *Journal of the Institute of Bankers*, 21 (1900), pp.370–9.
[59] Attack, 'Financial Innovations and Crises', p.3.

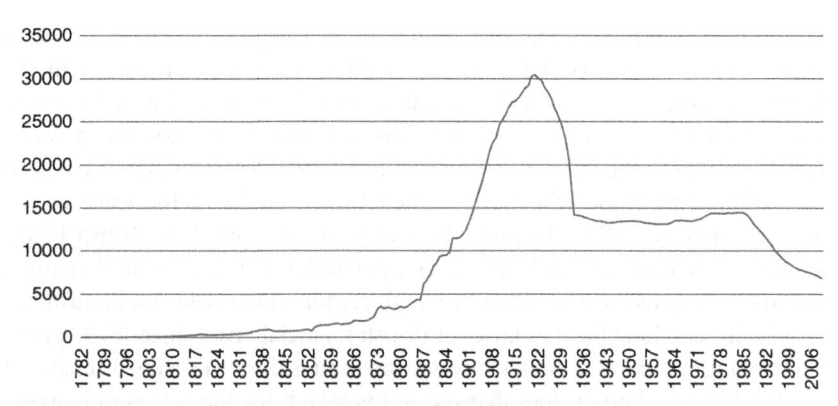

Figure 1.2. Trend in numbers of US Banks 1782–2009 (annual data)
Appendix 4

Scale allowed banks to balance their assets and liabilities across diverse locations and activities so releasing funds, that otherwise would have had to be kept in reserve, for productive employment with consequences for their profitability, while remaining resilient in a crisis.[60] In any crisis it was not the large banks that failed but the smaller ones resulting in a more concentrated system unless replacement banks appeared. The reason that there were increasingly fewer new banks in the nineteenth century was the ability of existing banks to capture more and more of the available business. A major explanation for this was the replacement of the small partnerships of the past with the joint-stock company. The joint-stock form provided banks with the management structure and legal status required to cope with the principal–agent problems inherent in any large organization. In a joint-stock bank staff could be recruited, trained, supervised, and directed in ways that were not possible in a partnership reliant upon family and friends.[61] Such were the advantages possessed by the joint-stock banks that they increasingly challenged for business in the field of international finance where bonds of family and religion had long been essential requirements. Increasingly, it was the joint-stock banks that became the trusted counterparties in the ceaseless flow of credits, debits, and payments that linked all banks together and underpinned international trade and finance. London-managed joint-stock banks not only provided banking services nationwide but also in such distant countries as Argentina, Australia, Brazil, New Zealand, and West and South Africa.[62]

---

[60] Grossman, *Unsettled Account*, pp.147–61.
[61] Cassis, *Crises and Opportunities*, pp.57–71; Capie and Woods, *Money over Two Centuries*, p.64.
[62] G. Jones, *Multinationals and Global Capitalism from the Nineteenth to the Twenty-First Century* (Oxford: OUP, 2005), p.266; G. Kurgan-Van Hentenryk, 'The Social Origins of Bank Managers', in Green, Pohle-Fraser, and Fraser (eds), *Human Factor*, p.177; L. Hannah, 'The

Important as numbers are, they, alone, do not capture all that took place within British banking over the course of three centuries. Particularly in the nineteenth century the economies of scale achieved by banks changed the very nature of the way they conducted their business and the relationship between them, including to the Bank of England. These fundamental changes have been little explored by those who have studied British banks in the wake of the financial crisis of 2007/8. Instead, there is an assumption that British banks had always conducted their business in a particular way until radical changes were made towards the end of the twentieth century. Dimsdale and Hotson, for example, in searching for the causes of British financial crises since 1825, ignore the changing nature of a bank's business assuming that it remained unaltered until the 1990s.[63] Turner does likewise in his search for the causes of banking stability.[64] From the perspective of those focused on explaining the causes of the financial crisis of 2007/8, banking practice in the UK changed little until after 1979, with the ending of exchange controls, or 1986 with the reforms introduced at the time of Big Bang, or 1997/8 with the new regulatory regime associated with the creation of the Financial Services Authority. The tried and tested model of Lend and Hold was increasingly replaced by the Originate and Distribute Model imported from investment banking practices developed in the USA.

In the Lend and Hold Model a bank maintained a close relationship with its customers using the deposits made by one group to lend to another on a continuous basis. In contrast, in the Originate and Distribute Model when a bank lent to a customer it re-packaged the loan as a security, which it then sold to investors, so releasing additional funds to be lent and re-packaged in the same way. In the wake of the financial crisis of 2007/8 this new way of conducting a banking business was seen to lie at the heart of what had gone wrong. Banks had come to rely upon funding through the wholesale market and when this suddenly froze, as it did in 2007/8, the most dependent banks faced an immediate liquidity crisis. This soon became a solvency one as it became impossible to price the value of the assets they held, in the form of re-packaged loans, against their liabilities to those who had lent them money, whether they were retail customers or other banks via the inter-bank money market. As these inter-connections between banks became known, and the risks they posed understood, the result was contagion spreading from those banks most exposed to wholesale funding to other banks that had either lent them money or bought the re-packaged loans.[65] This reversed the traditional

---

Twentieth Century Transformation of Banking and its Effect on Management Training for Bankers', in Green, Pohle-Fraser, and Fraser (eds), *Human Factor*, pp.190–6.

[63] N. Dimsdale and A. Hotson, 'Introduction', in Dimsdale and Hotson (eds), *British Financial Crises*.

[64] Turner, *Banking in Crisis*.

[65] Liu, Quiet, and Roth, 'Banking Sector Interconnectedness', pp.1–10.

view of the inter-bank market. Until the crisis of 2007/8 the inter-bank money market had been widely praised as a way of providing a bank with liquidity during a crisis as long as it was sufficiently deep and broad. There also needed to be a lender of last resort ready to intervene if the inter-bank market froze and so prevented those banks that had relied on it for liquidity obtaining what they required.[66] What is ignored in the current literature, but was familiar to an older generation of banking historians, was how and why the Lend and Hold Model of banking came to dominate over the course of the nineteenth and twentieth centuries. Only by understanding that, is it possible to explain why British banking became stable and then lost that stability prior to the 2007/8 financial crisis.

At the beginning of the eighteenth century the normal practice among banks was to make loans by issuing their own bank notes which then circulated as a means of payment, before being exchanged for coins minted by the state. An alternative was to issue Bank of England notes, leaving the responsibility for maintaining a reserve of coins, especially of gold, with that institution. In London, banks, other than the Bank of England, stopped issuing their own notes in the eighteenth century, using those of the Bank instead. Outside London the practice of banks issuing their own notes continued well into the nineteenth century, though they were exchangeable for those of the Bank of England as well as coin. Those receiving the bank notes, whether issued by the Bank or other banks, signed a bill of exchange promising to repay at a future date, often ninety days or three months later. The bank generated its profit by the difference between the value of the notes given to the borrower and the amount that was repaid, because a discount existed between what the bank paid the borrower and what it received when the loan was repaid. These bills were then either held by the bank until maturity or re-sold to those with temporarily spare funds, including other banks. The discount to face value at which bills were purchased gradually fell as the date of repayment came closer, creating innumerable buying and selling opportunities over the life of a bill of exchange.[67]

The Bank of England, from its establishment in 1694, was a ready purchaser of bills. It had lent its entire capital to the government, receiving in return a regular interest payment. In addition it received commission from the government for the business it conducted on its behalf as well as generating profits through accepting deposits and making loans to other customers. The Bank of England generated most of its profits through the issue of bank notes

---

[66] Allen and Gale, *Understanding Financial Crises*, pp.94–9, 154–5, 269, 282–3.
[67] My understanding of bills of exchange owes much to a number of discussions with Professor Shizuya Nishimura who was the author of the seminal work, *The Decline of Inland Bills of Exchange in the London Money Market 1855–1913* (Cambridge: CUP, 1971). His expertise in the subject of bills of exchange was unrivalled.

and their circulation. Its charter allowed it to issue bank notes, up to a stated amount, without the necessity of holding the equivalent in gold. The more of these it could distribute by way of loans, the more profit it could make and this was an important imperative for the Bank of England until at least 1914. The Bank was owned by investors who held its shares because of the dividends that were paid related to the risks involved, not through any sense of national interest or other altruistic motives.[68] It is important to recognize the pressure the Bank of England was under to pay these dividends as it dictated the way it operated as a bank until the First World War. It was during the First World War that the Bank acquired a quasi-statutory role and continued with that during the 1920s and 1930s, and into the Second World War before being taken into state ownership in 1946. According to Clapham, writing his history of the Bank of England from the perspective of 1944, 'the bank of the thirties, and even the twenties, of the current century was in many ways so unlike that of 1914.' It had become 'a non-competitive public institution with world-wide connections and influence, not eager for profit.' Before that, it operated like any other bank, though one possessed of a special position within the financial system.[69]

What a bank with the resources of the Bank of England was able to do in the eighteenth century was to operate a Lend and Hold Model on a grand scale. By establishing contact with numerous merchants, manufacturers, and retailers in London, the Bank of England was able to make them loans by issuing its notes, which then circulated among their suppliers and customers. When these bills matured, the Bank of England profited from the discount between the value of the notes it issued in return for the bills and the payment it received. It was the Bank of England's success in this business that led the other London bankers to stop issuing their own notes and, instead, use those of the Bank of England. Once in that position these other banks ceased to be competitors of the Bank of England and became its customers. These banks sold bills to the Bank of England, receiving in return Bank of England notes, which were then used to make further loans, so repeating the process. Initially these bills were the product of trade and industry being used to cover the period that goods were in transit or the delay between production and consumption. However, as banks became more involved, bills could also be used to provide short-term credit for all manner of activities, being either repaid on maturity or renewed so as to extend the time period of the finance provided. The links between London bankers and those that were emerging elsewhere in the UK during the second half of the eighteenth century also brought in bills from throughout Britain. As Bank of England notes did not circulate much outside London these country banks prospered by issuing their own notes, which were made payable in coin

---

[68] For the early history of the Bank of England see Clapham, *The Bank of England*.
[69] Clapham, *The Bank of England*, v.2, pp.417, 427.

or Bank of England notes either at their own office or in London through the bank that acted as their correspondent there. The development of an increasingly efficient and extensive mail service centred on London, allowed for the easy transmission of bills, notes, and instructions.

As the Bank of England was the only bank in England and Wales allowed to operate as a joint-stock company, with even partnerships restricted to a maximum of six partners, in the eighteenth century all other banks remained small outside Scotland, and later Ireland. Deprived of scale, one of the few ways a bank could grow its business outside London, where direct competition from the Bank of England did not exist, was to issue more notes and send the resulting bills to London. In London these bills could be re-discounted at the Bank of England, generating new funds that could also be lent. However, the Bank of England became wary of expanding its purchase of bills that carried a risk of default. What the Bank of England wanted were short-dated bills backed by collateral rather than long-dated bills involving no more than a guarantee of repayment. Thus, it both attempted to limit its purchases of bills and restrict the type it bought. In response, a new class of intermediary appeared in London in the eighteenth century—the bill broker. These bill brokers would buy and sell bills between banks in London, by-passing the Bank of England. Both on their own account, and in acting for their country correspondents, London banks were in the position of being either in receipt of funds they had no immediate use for or possessed of bills which they wished to sell so as to raise funds. Given the small number of customers each bank had, and the similarity among those for whom it catered, being defined by class, business, or locality, at any one time a single bank was highly likely to be either short of funds or possessed of an excess. What the bill brokers were able to do, by walking from bank to bank in London, was buy bills from a bank that needed to raise money and sell that bill to another bank that had spare funds, and do so throughout the day. Initially the Bank of England regarded these bill brokers as rivals, as they competed with it for bills. Gradually a relationship built up, with the bill brokers selling bills to the Bank of England and also borrowing from it to finance their holdings of bills, as they were willing to accept a wide range of bills both in terms of the time period they had to run and the purpose for which they had been issued. The result was that over the course of the eighteenth century an active Originate and Distribute Model of banking was established in the UK, especially in England, with the Bank of England and the London-based bill brokers at its centre. This contributed enormously to the expansion of banking as each bank was no longer dependent on matching assets and liabilities on its own but was now part of an increasingly integrated national money market.[70]

---

[70] The eighteenth-century origins of British banking are explored in chapter 2.

What restrained the issue of notes by all banks, including the Bank of England, was the need to redeem holders in coin if requested. Thus, a bank had to ensure that it held sufficient coin to meet redemptions. The calculation made was that only a proportion of the notes would be redeemed at any one time so allowing a bank to issue many more than it could redeem in coin. These notes were a liability of the bank as holders could request instant repayment. Conversely a bill was an asset to a bank as it represented a loan, which it expected to be repaid. Thus a bank matched its liabilities in the form of the notes it issued with its assets in the form of the bills it held. Apart from the solvency risk that the bank ran in the event of a borrower defaulting on payment when the bill became due, there was the liquidity risk. This arose because those holding notes could all demand instant repayment while bills were only repaid on maturity, though the ability to re-sell meant that funds could be raised when or if required. The problem arose when the ability to re-sell bills evaporated as it did regularly in a financial crisis. In particular, the Bank of England's priority was to safeguard its own liquidity and so when that was threatened it ceased to buy bills or, at least, cut back on purchases. This action ensured its survival but not those of other banks facing a liquidity crisis, as they could no longer access the money required to meet note redemptions. To cover that liquidity risk a bank needed to keep a store of coins to meet repayment but these generated no return and posed a security risk, being attractive to thieves. An alternative was to keep Bank of England notes but these could also be stolen and represented an interest-free loan to that bank. Another alternative was to attract deposits from those with spare funds as these could be used to supplement the capital invested in the bank by the partners, though that was limited by the cap on their number and the inability to operate on a joint-stock basis until 1826 in England and Wales. A bank accepted deposits in return for an agreement to pay interest on the amount received. These deposits were a liability of the bank as it was committed to repaying the amount placed with it when requested to do so. However, they represented a more stable source of funding than the issue of bank notes as deposits paid interest and were regarded more in the manner of an investment than a means of payment.

What happened was that as banks became larger and more diversified in the nineteenth century, they had less need to use the Originate and Distribute Model and, instead, increasingly relied on the Lend and Hold Model. Instead of operating on the basis of notes banks switched to using the growing volume of deposits as the basis of their lending.[71] This change in banking practice was made possible by the economies of scale possessed by the joint-stock banks that slowly emerged after 1826, becoming the dominant force by the late

---

[71] The nineteenth-century origins of British banking are explored in chapter 3.

nineteenth century. One example is Lloyds Bank. In 1865 it operated from seven offices and handled the business of 2,041 current accounts. In 1914 it operated from 879 offices and handled 333,090. A similar change took place with Barclays Bank, which began as an amalgamation of small private banks facing extinction because of the growth of the joint-stock banks. The scale of these banks gained them the trust of the public who were willing to place their savings on deposit with them without the assurance of any form of government guarantee. These joint-stock banks recruited from the widest employment pool available, rather than restricting themselves to relatives and co-religionists, and then trained, directed, and supervised their staff to a high level of professionalism. In turn those employees could expect to reach the level of top management if they prospered under the training they received, absorbing the culture of the bank where they worked. That also meant that those running these banks did not have to possess wealth in order to be in control, as in a partnership, but were the product of a meritocracy. Without independent means of their own, those running the joint-stock banks were fully aware that their future rested on having in place a system that forced staff to behave in such a way as to maintain the trust of their customers. At the same time those running joint-stock banks were aware too that they were also answerable to shareholders. Poor performance could not only lead to their dismissal, it could also encourage a hostile takeover bid, which, if successful, might well result in their removal. Thus banks had to balance the trust of those who used them with the need to generate profits out of which the banks' running expenses, their employees' salaries, and the dividends paid to shareholders had to be paid. Barclays Bank already employed 1,990 staff in 1910 and this reached 16,536 in 1939.

Increasingly it was only large banks that possessed both the financial strength and human expertise of the depth and breadth required to satisfy the needs of customers, cope with the increasing complexities of financial activity, and command the trust of the public. That trust in the large joint-stock banks was greatly enhanced when one of the most famous private banks, Barings, came close to failure in 1890.[72] In the Lend and Hold Model the bank provided its customers with a variety of services on a continuous basis, which deepened and broadened over time. This meant that these joint-stock banks expanded from providing such basic services as accepting deposits, making loans, and facilitating payments into those that were the preserve of more specialist banks. Within the financial system there were always new opportunities appearing. The drawback of size was that large banks were less responsive to new demands and so these were met by smaller banks often operating at the margin that the law permitted, or even beyond. However,

[72] Sayers, *Lloyds Bank*, p.108, 225; Ackrill and Hannah, *Barclays*, pp.29–31, 52, 70–80, 90, 139, 396.

once a new business area was proven the large banks moved in, using their resources of capital and manpower to make it theirs, including acquiring smaller competitors. This was the case with the finance of international trade before the First World War, foreign exchange dealing between the wars, and both large-scale project finance and small-scale hire purchase lending in the 1970s. Particularly after the reforms associated with Big Bang in 1986 the large banks expanded into many new areas.[73]

It was not simply the structure of banking that created resilience but also the way that banking was conducted. The Originate and Distribute Model worked well so long as the notes continued to circulate and demand for bills held up. The problem arose when there was a shortage of coin or even Bank of England notes to meet the demand for payment and maturing bills could no longer be replaced by new ones. That happened periodically and it was only when the way that banking was done changed that a stable system developed. That began with the Bank Charter Act of 1844, which restricted the ability to print notes. This was to the disadvantage of the smaller banks as it meant they could not expand their lending by printing more notes. Nevertheless, they could expand their lending by re-selling more bills, and there was a growing outlet for these in the mid nineteenth century with the formation of joint-stock discount houses and finance companies. They raised funds from investors and used these to purchase bills in competition with the Bank of England. That competition came to an abrupt end in 1866 with the collapse of the largest of these, Overend and Gurney, along with others among the new finance companies, while those that remained cut back on their bill purchases. Writing in 2009, Cottrell described what happened between 1855 and 1883 as 'London's First "Big Bang"'.[74]

What followed was a period of banking consolidation in which there emerged banks that adopted the Lend and Hold Model and so relied less and less on either the issue of bank notes or the re-selling of bills as the basis of their business. These banks increasingly attracted savers by paying generous rates of interest on their deposits while offering a high degree of security because of their joint-stock structure. They also attracted borrowers because of the flexibility of the loans they made compared to bills that were for fixed amounts over fixed periods at fixed terms. When these joint-stock banks reached a particular scale of operations, as they did sometime between the Overend and Gurney crisis of 1866 and the Baring Crisis of 1890, they

---

[73] M. Hollow, *Rogue Banking: A History of Financial Fraud in the Inter-War Britain* (Basingstoke: Palgrave Macmillan, 2015), pp.6, 21, 25, 36–43, 63; N. Ferguson, *High Financier: The Lives and Time of Siegmund Warburg* (London: Penguin Books, 2010), pp.41–2, 87–9, 101, 120–4; T. Gourvish, 'Project Finance and the Archives of Entrepreneurship: The Channel Tunnel, 1957–1975', Green, Pohle-Fraser, and Fraser (eds), *Human Factor*, pp.45–6.

[74] P.L. Cottrell, 'London's First "Big Bang"? Institutional Change in the City, 1855–83', in Y. Cassis and P.L. Cottrell (eds), *The World of Private Banking* (Farnham: Ashgate, 2009).

were able to match savers and borrowers internally without recourse to the Originate and Distribute Model. In the Lend and Hold Model the bank made a loan directly to a borrower by placing the agreed amount to the credit of their account. The borrower could then draw on that account by signing cheques, which were cashed by those receiving payment. By monitoring the state of the account the bank was in a position to assess the risks it was taking in making the loan. The expectation was that the balance in the account would vary as the borrower made and received payment. No longer was a bank liable to be faced with a sudden liquidity crisis, when it had to meet a spike in note redemptions, as that risk now rested with the Bank of England through its increasing monopoly over note issue in England and Wales.

By 1914 more than half the loans made by British commercial banks were given on the strength of no more than a personal guarantee.[75] The exposure to maturing bills still remained but this was now a declining element in a bank's business being replaced by loans and advances. By aggregating loans and advances with bills in their accounts this change in the risk profile of banks has been lost, leading to the assumption that the way in which they operated remained the same. However, it was this change that made British banking such a success in the fifty years before 1914 and provided it with the resilience to meet the challenges it faced between the beginning of the First World War and the end of the Second in 1945.

That did not mean that banks had no need for the facilities of the London money market. Even large banks still needed to ensure that they remained sufficiently liquid so that they could meet withdrawals, especially as they no longer had the facility of doing this by issuing their own notes as the Bank of England increasingly monopolized note issue throughout England from the mid nineteenth century onwards. Maintaining liquidity to meet exceptional demand would tie up a significant proportion of a bank's funds in a store of coins or Bank of England notes that would, normally, never be required. The solution to this problem was to maintain an account at the Bank of England, which could be drawn upon for either coin or that bank's notes when required. In addition to the coins and notes kept to meet immediate customer needs this account at the Bank of England provided the next layer available to a bank to meet liquidity demands. However, this money at the Bank of England did not generate any return. What did generate a return was to lend excess funds in the money market by making it available to those banks that needed to top up on liquidity. Within this money market, bills continued to circulate generated through international trade, representing manufactures and commodities in transit between producers and consumers, but there was also a growing volume of bills representing payments that banks expected to receive in the near future.

---

[75] Capie and Woods, *Money over Two Centuries*, p.116.

This move to the Lend and Hold Model over the course of the nineteenth century also changed the relationship between the Bank of England and other banks. Before 1826 the Bank of England provided discount facilities for the London private banks, as they were not seen as competitors because they did not issue notes. After 1826 this relationship changed with the formation of the joint-stock banks. Those in London could not issue notes but their size made them potential competitors. Those outside London could issue notes and they were also potential competitors because the Bank of England began opening provincial branches. The solution adopted by the Bank of England was to favour the bills issued by those banks that did not issue notes, which was a growing number after the restrictions imposed on note issuing after the 1844 Bank Charter Act. Increasingly the Bank of England was left with a monopoly over note issue in England and Wales. It also engaged more directly with the bill brokers, buying bills from them and lending them money as they represented a way of meeting the challenge of the joint-stock banks and their Lend and Hold Model. However, as bill brokers became discount houses, and especially when they took the joint-stock form after 1855, they also became potential competitors. Only with the demise of Overend and Gurney in 1866 did that threat to the business of the Bank of England largely disappear. Unlike the large joint-stock banks that increasingly adopted the Lend and Hold Model the Bank of England continued to focus on the original Originate and Distribute Model.

However, the role of the Bank of England within the market for bills was transformed over the course of the nineteenth century. Rather than acting as the principal market for bills, as it had been before 1826, it was relegated to a secondary position. As the joint-stock banks internalized the business of banking they dispensed with the bill of exchange. However, they still needed liquidity and they obtained it by keeping a cash deposit at the Bank which was used not only to make payments to other banks but also as a source of liquidity. In addition, they used the London discount market as a means not of reselling bills so as to generate funds that could be lent but as a means of either employing cash that was temporarily redundant or to make good a cash flow imbalance. That allowed the bank to operate without the need to maintain both a large capital and a large idle cash reserve as they could draw upon the collective liquidity of the banking system once their internal resources were exhausted. Faced with this situation the Bank of England was in the position of finding itself with large cash reserves, which it needed to employ. It did so by lending to the bill brokers/discount houses at high rates of interest which they were willing to pay because the bulk of their finance came directly from the banks at low rates of interest. Thus, it was the switch of the banks from the Originate and Distribute Model to the Lend and Hold Model that pushed the Bank of England into the position of lender of last resort rather than a process of gradual evolution or a deliberate policy decision to embrace this new role. By 1907 the Bank of England only provided discount facilities for seventy-four firms, mainly discount houses and bill brokers, compared to over 1,000 a century earlier. By 1907 it had become a specialist lender to money market intermediaries rather than a general purchaser of bills. This role allowed it to generate the profits it needed to pay dividends to its shareholders while avoiding the risks involved in longer-term lending.

It was not until the crisis created by the outbreak of the First World War that the Bank of England acted consciously as lender of last resort to the UK banking system. That emerged out of the role it played as the co-ordinator of the banking system's response to a crisis, which it had carried out in the rescue of Barings Bank in 1890, especially when its own position was threatened. Barings occupied a key role as an acceptor—guarantor—of the bills circulating in the discount market. If Barings had failed then the value of those bills held as collateral by numerous banks including the Bank of England, would be cast into doubt, hence the need for intervention. The intervention to save the Birkbeck Bank and the National Penny Bank also reflected self-interest as they were large holders of the National Debt, which the Bank of England managed on behalf of the government. In contrast a bank as large as that of the City of Glasgow was allowed to collapse in 1878 because that did not threaten the business of the Bank of England, whatever consequences it had for banking in general, especially in the West of Scotland. Similarly, the problems of the Liberator Building Society and its associated bank did not threaten the Bank of England and so it was also allowed to fail in 1892, only two years after the intervention to rescue Barings. What changed was the First World War and then the Governorship of Montagu Norman. Between the wars the Bank of England gradually emerged with the functions of a central bank with a remit far wider than the narrow business model it had long operated with.[76]

What happened prior to the 2007 crisis was that banking began to revert to the Originate and Distribute Model as it appeared to offer advantages over the Lend and Hold Model in an increasingly competitive banking environment. The saver benefited from a higher rate of return, the borrower from a lower rate of interest and more generous terms, the bank's employees from increased pay and bonuses, the shareholders from enhanced dividends and capital appreciation and the government from an expanded revenue from corporate and individual tax payments. Forgotten in all this was the reason why the Originate and Distribute Model had been replaced with the Lend and Hold Model, which was all to do with the careful management of risk-taking versus the returns obtained. Instead, the widely held belief that banks had long operated as a restrictive cartel, whose conservative behaviour had destroyed Britain's economy, encouraged political intervention to introduce much greater

---

[76] The development and operation of British banking between 1914 and 1945 is explored in chapter 4.

competition. Inspired by the belief that the Big Bang reforms had energized the City of London to regain its position as the key financial centre in the world, politicians believed the same could be done for banking, with positive consequences for the entire UK economy. The reforms of 1997/8 was Big Bang Stage 2, completing what had begun in 1986. The outcome was the 2007 crisis, which centred on those banks, beginning with Northern Rock, that had most embraced the Originate and Distribute Model and so suffered the fate of those banks in the past that had been seduced by its possibilities.[77]

CONCLUSION

As Richard Grossman noted, in his meticulous study of the evolution of banking across the industrialized world since 1800, there was no 'optimal banking structure'.[78] Calomiris and Haber reached a similar conclusion.[79] The reason was because the context within which banks operated was of crucial importance, forcing each banking system to adapt to meet differing challenges and opportunities. The mistake made in the past was to believe that there was a perfect model. Many believed that had been achieved by British banking before 1914 because of the stability it delivered both then and later. Subsequently there was admiration for the German model because of the contribution it was believed to have made to German economic growth both before 1914 and after 1945. There are also those who point to the dynamism of the US banking system combining as it does Wall Street investment banks with a global presence and small banks serving their local community. With hindsight each had its flaws and all were a product of time and space. High among the influences upon the structure of banking that emerged was the role of government. This could be relatively benign, as it was in Britain between 1844 and 1979, or highly interventionist, as in the USA both in the 1860s and the 1930s.[80]

What the financial crisis of 2007/8 does demand is that the British banking system that developed over the course of the nineteenth century and then survived virtually intact throughout the next century needs to be re-examined. No longer can the stability achieved and maintained by that banking system be taken for granted, as it was before the crisis of 2007/8. Furthermore, the analysis needs to go deeper than legislation, whatever its causes and

[77] The events surrounding the financial crisis of 2007/8 will be explored in the final chapters of the book.
[78] Grossman, *Unsettled Account*, p.64.
[79] Calomiris and Haber, *Fragile by Design*, p.485.
[80] Y. Cassis, 'Do Financial Crises Lead to Policy Change?', in Dimsdale and Hotson (eds), *British Financial Crises*, pp.178–83.

consequences, and explore such matters as banking practice, the relationship between banks and the role played by the Bank of England. Neither the Lend and Hold Model nor the Originate and Distribute Model can be regarded as the means through which banks conducted their business, with the other seen as either a conservative throwback to an earlier era or a dangerous innovation destined to lead to a crisis. The long-term perspective it introduces is an awareness of how the model changed over time and the implications that had both for individual banks and the system of which they were part. The same applies to the Bank of England. Over time it was forced to adapt to changing circumstances rather than setting the agenda for the rest of the banking system despite its size, influence, and longevity, though those who have written its history tend to put it centre stage.

2

Crises and Crescendo, 1694–1825

INTRODUCTION

In the classic account of English provincial banking by Leslie Pressnell, published in 1956, it was noted that the number of country banks peaked in 1810.[1] That year takes on even greater significance when the count of the total number of banks in the UK reveals it to be the date when it reached its maximum, before beginning a century of decline that would lead to the highly concentrated banking system of the twentieth century.[2] Within this process the timing of the transformation has long been attributed to legislation which favoured the creation of numerous individual banks in the eighteenth century and then consolidation in the nineteenth.[3] Taking their lead from those who first studied the development of British banking, later writers saw the process of consolidation as both inevitable and strongly influenced by legislation. As the scale of business increased so would the scale of banking and that spelt the end of the small partnership and its replacement by the joint-stock company.[4] In terms of legislation, the barriers placed on the growth of large banks before 1826 were emphasized, with their subsequent removal permitting the emergence of the joint-stock banks, which had flourished in Scotland where the legislation did not apply.[5] However, this legislative explanation does not fit a peak being reached in 1810, and long-term decline already taking place by 1826.

---

[1] Pressnell, *Country Banking*, p.11.
[2] See table in Appendix 1.
[3] S.E. Perry, 'The History of Companies' Legislation in England in its Practical Aspect, and its Effect upon our Industrial and Banking Development, *Journal of the Institute of Bankers*, 29 (1908), pp.481–96.
[4] H.E. Butson, 'The Banking System of the United Kingdom', in H.P. Willis and B.H. Beckhart (eds), *Foreign Banking Systems* (London: Pitman and Sons, 1929), p.1163.
[5] S.E. Thomas, *Banking and Exchange* (London: Gregg Publishing, 1930), p.5; J. Orbell, 'The Historical Structure and Functions of British Banking', in Orbell and Turton, *British Banking*, pp.13–14; L. Newton, 'The Birth of Joint-Stock Banking: England and New England Compared', *Business History Review*, 84 (2010), p.28.

The year 1810 did feature a financial crisis as a result of which a number of banks failed. During the boom that preceded a crisis, a bank expanded its lending because of the high demand for credit and the growing confidence in future prospects. When the boom ended and confidence collapsed, banks were left exposed as those holding its notes demanded coin, depositors withdrew their savings and borrowers defaulted on the repayment of their bills. Banks then faced an immediate liquidity crisis as they had insufficient cash to meet withdrawals of deposits and redemptions of notes. They also faced a solvency crisis as the value of assets shrank due to the bankruptcy of borrowers. The problem with the crisis of 1810 as an explanation is that financial crises had been frequent occurrences throughout the eighteenth century and continued into the nineteenth, and that of 1810 was of a lesser magnitude compared to many others.[6] On either side of 1810, those of 1793 and 1825 were regarded by contemporaries and in hindsight as much more significant.[7] Consequently, an explanation other than legislation or crisis needs to be sought in order to explain why 1810 was the peak year for the number of banks in the UK. Such a search requires a complete revision of British financial history, casting doubt upon many of the assumptions that have been made in the past.

THE FINANCIAL REVOLUTION REVISITED

A divide exists in British financial history between the study of high finance and low finance, especially for the period between the late seventeenth and the mid nineteenth century. High finance relates to the way the UK government raised funds through the money and capital markets and the activities of the Bank of England as the emerging central bank. Most of this activity was located in London. Low finance relates to the way that individuals and businesses obtained the credit and raised the capital they required. Most of this took place on a local basis.[8] Out of this emerges a perception of separate development. The City of London pursued a path that led, eventually, to its emergence as the leading financial centre in the world by the mid nineteenth

---

[6] Kindleberger and Aliber, *Manias, Panics, and Crashes*, p.158; Reinhart and Rogoff, *This Time is Different*, p.387; Thomas, *Banking and Exchange*, p.151; S. Hills, R. Thomas, and N. Dimsdale, 'The UK Recession in Context: What Do Three Centuries of Data Tell Us?', *Bank of England Quarterly Bulletin*, 50 (2010), pp.279-83; Grossman, *Unsettled Account*, pp.54-65.

[7] J.A. James, 'Panics, Payments Disruptions and the Bank of England before 1826', *Financial History Review*, 19 (2012), pp.290-1; Davies, *The Origins and Development of Cartelisation*, Table of Bank Failures.

[8] For an example see the chapters in R. Floud and P. Johnson (eds), *The Cambridge Economic History of Modern Britain* (Cambridge: CUP, 2004), v.1.

century. Elsewhere in Britain mechanisms were created and refined that allowed the Industrial Revolution to be financed, most notably the growing numbers of country banks providing the credit and capital required by the local community.[9] However, if the study of high and low finance is integrated, and the relationship between the City of London and the country is studied, a different interpretation of British financial history emerges. As Europe's largest city by the end of the seventeenth century, London possessed an important financial sector, which largely serviced London's own economy, met the needs of the King and the government, and provided the facilities required by the landed aristocracy, many of whom spent part of the year in London.[10]

London also provided financial services to the rest of Britain, and these were increasingly nationwide in their reach, varied in their nature, and intense in terms of the degree of contact. Nevertheless, London did not dominate the provision of credit and capital at this stage but, instead, occupied a strategic niche within the British financial system, as most financial requirements were met locally through informal networks.[11]

The establishment of the Bank of England in 1694 did represent the beginning of a major change in public finance, providing the government with a large and stable source of funding as long as they maintained interest payments. In 1946 the eminent historian, Clark, had observed that 'No department of the nation's life was more radically transformed between 1662 and 1760 than finance.'[12] It is to this period that the label, 'Financial Revolution' is attached, though that is very much the product of Dickson, a political historian, who confined himself to 'A study in the development of

---

[9] See, especially, P.J. Cain and A.G. Hopkins, *British Imperialism*, 2 vols. (London: Longman, 1993); B. Robson, 'Coming Full Circle: London versus the Rest, 1890-1980', in G. Gordon (ed.), *Regional Cities in the UK, 1890-1980* (London: Harper & Row, 1986).

[10] E.A. Wrigley, *Continuity, Chance and Change: The Character of the Industrial Revolution in England* (Cambridge: CUP, 1988), p.13.

[11] D. Keene, 'Medieval London and its Region', *London Journal*, 14 (1989), pp.99-101, 103-6; C.M. Barron, *London in the Later Middle Ages: Government and People, 1200-1500* (Oxford: OUP, 2004), pp.10-16. 45-6, 62-3, 76-117; Center for Medieval and Renaissance Studies (Blonquist, Prestwich, Bergier, Riu, Munro, eds), *The Dawn of Modern Banking* (Los Angeles: Yale University Press, 1979); Sir Peter Hall, *Cities in Civilization: Culture, Innovation, and Urban Order* (London: Phoenix Giant, 1998), pp.116-21; B.G. Carruthers, *City of Capital: Politics and Markets in the English Financial Revolution* (Princeton: Princeton University Press, 1999), pp.64-5; D.C. Coleman, 'London Scriveners and the Estate Market in the late 17th Century', *Economic History Review*, 4 (1951/2), p.230, E. Kerridge, *Trade and Banking in Early Modern England* (Manchester: Manchester UP, 1988), pp.47-84 C. Goodhart, 'Monetary Policy and Debt Management in the United Kingdom: Some Historical Viewpoints', in K.A. Chrystal (ed.), *Government Debt Structure and Monetary Conditions* (London: Bank of England, 1999), annex 2. See J. Alexander, 'The Economic Structure of the City of London at the End of the Seventeenth Century', *Urban History Yearbook* (1989).

[12] G. Clark, *The Wealth of England from 1496 to 1760* (Oxford: OUP, 1946), pp.178-9.

public credit,' and did not explore developments in banking.[13] The finance of the British state was revolutionized between 1694 and 1750, and this left in its wake a fully funded national debt, a powerful public bank, and an active securities market. This did have indirect implications for the banking system though none were foreseen at the time. The privileges given to the Bank of England made it a very powerful competitor for the bankers operating then and changed the way banking developed in Britain over the following century. Similarly, the existence of a large and permanent mass of securities, possessed of an active market, provided a safe, convenient, and profitable home for temporarily idle funds, as they could be purchased or sold quickly, cheaply, and easily. This made the City of London an increasingly attractive financial centre as funds released because of the seasonal nature of trade, the cyclical nature of economic activity, or the vagaries of individual circumstances could be easily employed rather than remain idle. Conversely, the existence of such funds in London attracted those seeking finance because it was readily available there at low rates of interest.[14]

However, all these developments took a long time to come to fruition. Also, to attribute these developments to political intervention ignores the gradual emergence of the City of London as a financial centre over the course of the seventeenth century. Developments in the City of London were driven both by domestic talent and the arrival of successive waves of Europeans, skilled in financial and commercial techniques. Included among these were a group from the Netherlands who were well established in London before the revolution that brought a Dutch king to the throne in 1688. The arrival of William of Orange from the Netherlands in 1688 is claimed by many to have

---

[13] P.G.M. Dickson, *The Financial Revolution in England: A Study in the Development of Public Credit, 1688-1756* (London: Macmillan, 1967). For the most relevant references see, pp.9-12, 33-9, 123, 154, 197, 236, 249, 256, 263-7, 278-85, 297, 311-12, 321, 336-7, 427, 449-52, 458, 484, 489, 492, 503-5, 515-16. Interestingly Dickson did not even list Pressnell's book on country banking in his bibliography though it had been published a decade earlier. For the approach of a more recent political historian to the subject see J. Brewer, *The Sinews of Power: War, Money and the English State, 1688-1783* (London: Unwin Hyman, 1989), p.88 cf, pp.89, 100, 114, 124, 135, 251.

[14] K.G. Davies, 'Joint-Stock Investment in the Later 17th Century', *Economic History Review*, 4 (1951/2), pp.288-96; S. Banner, *Anglo-American Securities Regulation: Cultural and Political Roots, 1690-1860* (Cambridge: CUP, 1998), pp.20-2, 28, 39; W.R. Scott, *The Constitution and Finance of English, Scottish and Irish Joint-Stock Companies to 1720* (Cambridge: CUP, 1912), v. I, pp.44, 155, 161, 345, 443, 460; Carruthers, *City of Capital*, pp.76-80, 82-5, 103-5, 108, 150, 155-8, 162-84, 193-4, 201-4; J. Carswell, *The South Sea Bubble*, rev. ed. (Stroud: Alan Sutton, 1993), pp.69-71, 77-9, 85, 87, 122, 129-31, 133-6, 140, 147, 164, 202; D. Stasavage, *Public Debt and the Birth of the Democratic State: France and Great Britain, 1688-1789* (Cambridge: CUP, 2003), p.92; H.I. Root, *The Fountain of Privilege: Political Foundations of Markets in Old Regime France and England* (Berkeley: University of California Press, 1994), pp.175-86. See A.M. Carlos and L. Neal, 'The Micro-foundations of the Early London Capital Market: Bank of England Shareholders during and after the South Sea Bubble, 1720-25', *Economic History Review*, lix (2006).

revolutionized the British financial system. However, though Amsterdam was the leading financial centre at the time, those in London were well aware of developments there long before the arrival of a King from that country. The major innovation in finance came not from William of Orange and his retinue but from those in London who were behind the creation of the Bank of England in 1694. It was not that the formation of a large joint-stock bank was novel, for similar institutions had been formed in other parts of Europe. What was novel was the intention of those promoting the Bank of England as a joint-stock company, to lend its entire capital of £1.2 million to the British government in perpetuity, and receive in return a guaranteed interest of 8 per cent per annum. Whereas individuals lending to the king had limited influence to reverse the decision if a default took place, which was a regular occurrence, because their power was so greatly inferior, that of the Bank of England was great. In its dealing with government the Bank of England collectively represented the numerous wealthy and powerful individuals who bought its shares, attracted by the interest promised by the government on its loan, the limit placed on their liability, and the ability to dispose of their investment when they wished. In essence, the creation of the Bank of England crystallized in one institution all the advances in finance that had taken place in Amsterdam, as it combined a public bank, a funded debt, and a joint-stock company with readily transferable securities.[15]

What the Bank of England had done was to convert a complex array of floating loans into a fully funded debt. Other joint-stock companies then did the same, notably the East India and South Sea companies, before the government created its own Consolidated Debt (consols) in 1749. The result was that, whereas in 1691 the UK government had a national debt of £3.1 million, which was entirely unfunded, by 1750 that had risen to £78 million of which 95 per cent was funded. Eventually this debt reached £840 million by 1820, in the wake of the wars with France that lasted from 1793 to 1815. Of that debt 95 per cent was also funded.[16] These changes were important for the government as they provided it with a large and stable source of funding as long as they maintained interest payments. Its immediate effect on the British financial system was, however, limited. The money raised by the government

---

[15] See chapters by Neal and Gelderblom/Jonker in W.N. Goetzmann and K. Geert Rouwenhorst (eds), *The Origins of Value: The Financial Innovations that Created Modern Capital Markets* (Oxford: OUP, 2005), pp.169–75. This revolution in finance in London in the 1690s has been carefully documented and analysed by Anne Murphy, revealing London's long-established Anglo-Dutch financial links, the willingness to copy developments in finance wherever they were taking place, and the dynamism of London's financial community as a continuous process of trial and error created new solutions to new problems. See A.L. Murphy, *The Origins of the English Financial Markets: Investment and Speculation before the South Sea Bubble* (Cambridge: CUP, 2009).

[16] B.R. Mitchell, *British Historical Statistics* (Cambridge: CUP, 1988), p.600.

either capitalized existing debts or was spent on new military campaigns, not on promoting economic growth. The Bank of England operated as the government's bank confining its activities to London. The one brief flurry of corporate enterprise, funded through the issue of transferable securities, also came to nothing with the collapse of the South Sea bubble in 1720. Nevertheless, the term, 'Financial Revolution' was quickly applied to the entire financial system by those searching for an explanation for why the Industrial Revolution took place in England in the eighteenth century. As Hartwell noted in his 1971 book, *The Industrial Revolution and Economic Growth*, 'Dickson, in a massively documented volume, has established that a "financial revolution" took place in England between 1688 and 1756, laying the modern bases of both public and private credit.' To Hartwell the changes introduced from 1688 onwards left Britain with a functioning banking system by 1750.[17] However, this claim of a 'Financial Revolution,' was disputed by those who documented, instead, the continuance of traditional forms of finance especially the importance of informal networks, re-invested profits and the circulation of bills of exchange as the main source of credit. One such was Holderness in 1976, who dismissively referred to the 'so-called financial revolution'.[18] This divide has remained ever since and helps explain why the question of whether improved financial services was a cause or a consequence of economic growth in the eighteenth century remains unresolved.[19]

What is required to resolve that question is to recognize that, important as was the formation of the Bank of England for public finance, it was developments in banking that were crucial for an Industrial Revolution that relied much more on credit than capital until the mid nineteenth century. What is usually forgotten is that long before the Bank of England emerged as a central bank it also operated as a bank in competition with other banks. In return for the loan obtained from the Bank of England in 1694 the government granted it the exclusive right to operate as a joint-stock bank in England and Wales and to issue its own currency in the form of bank notes. This gave the Bank of England an unrivalled position within the emerging banking community given the way that banking was conducted at this time.[20] When making a loan to a customer a bank issued its own notes, which would then be used by the borrower to make payments. These notes would circulate, being used as a means of payment, until presented at the bank of issue, where they would be

---

[17] R.M. Hartwell, *The Industrial Revolution and Economic Growth* (London: Methuen, 1971), pp.34, 117, 124.
[18] B.A. Holderness, *Pre-Industrial England: Economy and Society, 1500–1750* (London: J.M. Dent, 1976), pp.133, 179, 219–20, 230.
[19] N.F.R. Crafts, *British Economic Growth during the Industrial Revolution* (Oxford: Clarendon Press, 1985), pp.74–7. This book provides an authoritative judgement from a non-protagonist in the debate which remains valid today.
[20] For the early years of the Bank of England see Clapham, *The Bank of England*, v.1.

exchanged for coins minted on behalf of the state. There was a shortage of coins in the eighteenth century and the notes issued by banks provided an alternative means of payment. A bank then had to maintain a stock of coins ready to pay out in return for its own notes for, if it could not do so there would be a reluctance to accept such notes in future, making it impossible for the bank to operate. In return for these notes the borrower signed a bill of exchange promising to repay the bank the amount borrowed at a specified date in the future.[21]

A bill of exchange was an acknowledgement of a debt. Merchants gave it to manufacturers or farmers, when making a purchase which they could not pay for until they had sold the goods that they had bought. These bills represented a promise to pay at a future date. If the holder of the bill could not wait for payment, which was often the case as they had commitments to meet, the bill could be sold to another who could wait, but at a discount to its face value. That discount was the profit to be made by those purchasing the bill. These bills offered bankers an opportunity to employ the funds at their disposal profitably, as they could buy bills at a discount with their own notes and then wait repayment of the full value. What changed in the eighteenth century was that it was the banks that issued these bills to those whom they were lending money. The borrower signed to acknowledge the debt they had incurred and returned it to the bank. Bank bills were more widely acceptable to other purchasers, if the bank itself wanted to sell them, which they might do so to release funds for the repayment of its notes or to make additional loans to its customers. The name of a bank was much more familiar to the public and to other bankers than that of a merchant or other borrower, because their notes already circulated as a means of payment. A further refinement was for a bank with a reputation that virtually guaranteed repayment, even if the borrower defaulted, to put its name to a bill or, in the terminology of the time, accept it, in return for a commission payment. This made these bills even more acceptable to potential purchasers. Over time bankers emerged that specialized in this type of business such as the Barings and later the Rothschilds. What developed in the eighteenth century was thus an Originate and Distribute Model with bankers making loans through the issue of bank notes and then selling on the resulting bills, which were bought as investments by those with spare funds, including other banks.[22]

---

[21] This lack of coinage was noted by those who pioneered the study of the Industrial Revolution. A. Toynbee, *Lectures on the Industrial Revolution of the Eighteenth Century in England* (London: Longmans, Green, 1884), new ed. (1908), p.32. See Dawes and Ward-Perkins, *Country Banks of England and Wales*, v.1, p.19.

[22] S. Moshenskyi, *History of the Weksel: Bill of Exchange and Promissory Note* ([n.p.], Xlibris Corporation, 2008), p.167; P. Temin and H.-J. Voth, *Prometheus Shackled: Goldsmith Banks and England's Financial Revolution after 1700* (Oxford: OUP, 2013), pp.30, 42, 72, 91–4, 129, 147; S. Pollard and D.W. Crossley, *The Wealth of Britain* (London: Batsford, 1968), pp.50, 123,

Backed by its holding of government debt and the regular receipt of the interest that produced, the notes the Bank of England issued became more highly valued than those of a partnership. This was the case even though the Bank operated with limited liability, which meant the owners of the shares had no responsibility for the losses the bank might make beyond the value of their holding. In contrast, a banking partnership operated with unlimited liability, which meant that it could call on the entire wealth of its partners to back its note issue.[23] This unlimited liability of the partners in a bank might have operated to their advantage if they had been able to expand the number involved. However, in 1708 the Bank of England's position within banking was further enhanced when the number of partners in a banking partnership which could issue bank notes was capped at six.[24] The significance of this restriction on banking in England can be judged from the way that insurance companies developed. The Phoenix Insurance Company, for example, was established in 1782 as an extended partnership trading under a deed of settlement and operating with unlimited liability. Possessed of numerous partners, whose wealth and connections gave the public confidence in the service provided, it prospered. It was the cap on the number of partners that a bank could have that prevented similar companies being formed to undertake a banking business.[25] As the privileges possessed by the Bank of England did not extend to Scotland, what happened there can also be used to assess the impact made on England by the establishment of the Bank of England. Though part of the United Kingdom since 1603 Scotland retained its own parliament until 1707 and thereafter operated a separate legal system based on Roman, not Common, law. Scotland did establish its own joint-stock bank, the Bank of Scotland, in 1695 but this lost its exclusive right to operate on a joint-stock basis in 1716. In 1727 the Royal Bank of Scotland was given a charter while the British Linen Company, set up in 1746, was also given banking privileges. In addition, the restriction placed on the number of partners that a banking partnership could have was never extended to Scotland, allowing the formation of banking companies as extended co-partnerships there from the mid eighteenth century onwards. As a result, in the eighteenthth century Scotland

---

149-51; Clark, *The Wealth of England*, pp.63, 78-9, 178, 184; P.J. Corfield, *The Impact of English Towns, 1700-1800* (Oxford: OUP, 1982), pp.19, 71-3, 96-7; N. Ferguson, 'The Rise of the Rothschilds: The Family Firm as Multinational', in Cassis and Cottrell (eds), *World of Private Banking*, pp.10-11.

[23] For a recent statement on the importance of the banking privileges acquired by the Bank of England see Calomiris and Haber, *Fragile by Design*, pp.95-7.

[24] H.A.L. Cockerell and E. Green, *The British Insurance Business, 1547-1970* (London: Heineman, 1976), pp.61-70; C. Trebilcock, *Phoenix Assurance and the Development of British Insurance, 1782-1870* (Cambridge: CUP, 1985), pp.616-19; 665, 703-18, 736, 742.

[25] Cockerell and Green, *The British Insurance Business*, pp.61-70; Trebilcock, *Phoenix Assurance*, pp.616-19; 665, 703-18, 736, 742.

possessed a different banking system to England., comprising three joint-stock banks with limited liability and numerous extended co-partnerships with unlimited liability. In contrast, England possessed one very large joint-stock bank with limited liability, the Bank of England, and numerous small partnerships with unlimited liability.[26]

In England the Bank of England confined its activities to a single office in London, refraining from opening any branches until 1826. This was in common with other banks because transport was very slow in the eighteenth century, with speeds no better than five miles an hour. Such delays in communication made it difficult to manage a business of any kind on any other than a very local basis. This was especially the case with banks involved in making loans because of the risk of default. The solution was to confine the business to a small group who were well known to the banker because they lived locally.[27] Consequently, the impact made by the Bank of England was greatest in London and that was where it was able to monopolize the note issue and dominate the market for bills. London had an insatiable demand for goods produced elsewhere in the UK as well as providing manufactures and services in return. London was also the country's largest port, handling both imports and exports, both for its own economy and that of the rest of the UK.[28] All this generated a vast supply of bills of exchange, which were available to the Bank of England for purchase. The result of the Bank of England's activities was to alter the way banking was conducted in London. The banking partnerships located there had now to compete with the Bank of England for business, without the ability to issue notes to those who borrowed from them. One response was to become customers of the Bank of England themselves, selling bills to it in exchange for notes which they used when making loans. This arrangement was of mutual advantage. The Bank of England operated from a single office from which it handled an extensive banking business on behalf of its single largest customer, namely the government, which not only borrowed extensively but also received a large income from taxes and spent extensively on administration and the military establishment. This meant that the Bank of England used most of its staff to handle the government's banking business, the needs of other customers took second place. By acting through the

---

[26] See C.W. Munn, 'The Emergence of Joint-Stock Banking in the British Isles: A Comparative Approach', in R.P.T. Davenport-Hines and G. Jones (eds), *The End of Insularity: Essays in Comparative Business History* (London: Frank Cass, 1988).

[27] E.E.A. Pratt, *A History of Inland Transport and Communication* (London: Kegan Paul Trench Trubner, 1912), pp.49, 55; D. Marshall, *Industrial England, 1776–1851* (London: Routledge and Kegan Paul, 1973), p.23.

[28] H.J. Dyos and D.H. Aldcroft, *British Transport: An Economic Survey from the 17th Century to the 20th* (Harmondsworth: Penguin, 1974), pp.24–9, 47, 62. See E.A. Wrigley, 'A Simple Model of London's Importance in Changing English Society and Economy, 1650–1750', *Past and Present* 37 (1967).

other banks located in London, once they switched to using its notes, the Bank of England gained both a distribution network and additional manpower in direct contact with potential customers located throughout London. The Bank of England was thus able to expand the circulation of its notes and grow its business in bills, becoming the purchaser of those issued by the other London banks when they made loans, rather than relying on its own customers' needs. This meant that the Bank of England could expand its banking business and so pay the dividends that its shareholders demanded. From the perspective of the other banks the arrangement with the Bank of England meant they no longer had to keep a large store of coins to meet note redemptions, as customers were happy to use Bank of England notes, especially as that institution gained a reputation for stability and reliability. In the Bank of England the other banks had a ready buyer for their bills as well as a source of liquidity. In this way the Bank of England became the bankers' bank during the course of the eighteenth century. The result was to encourage the formation of ever more banks in London. In 1754 there were only around thirty-four banks in London whereas twenty years later there were 148 and 236 by 1799.[29]

Even more dramatic from the 1750s onwards was the establishment of banks outside London. There were only around twelve of these in 1750 compared to 650 by the peak in 1810. What emerges from Pressnell's authoritative examination of country banks between 1750 and 1844 is the importance of the links between them and London. It was through a connection with a London banker, known as a correspondent link, that the country banker was able to provide a wide range of financial services, such as the ability to lend money to customers, employ idle funds, and access the national and international payments system. Country banks were not the autonomous products of local supply and demand, but were key components of a developing network of nationwide financial intermediation. 'These connections between London and the provinces meant that the many hundreds of country firms formed a system of unit banking, but not one of isolated banks... The various parts of the banking structure, if not yet closely integrated, were certainly not independent of each other; at most, they were loose-jointed.'[30]

Unlike the London banks, those in the country did not face competition from the notes issued by the Bank of England. Thus they were able to operate by creating their own bank notes and giving these to borrowers when making a loan. These notes then circulated in the locality of the bank before being

[29] Hilton Price, *A Handbook of London Bankers*, Table of Banks; D. Hancock, *Citizens of the World: London Merchants and the Integration of the British Atlantic Community, 1735–1785* (Cambridge: CUP, 1995), pp.258–72.
[30] Pressnell, *Country Banking*, pp.76–7 cf, pp.1–6, 11–15, 36, 41, 45, 49, 60–3, 70, 75–80, 83, 90, 95, 100, 105–7, 116, 126, 224, 260, 288, 344, 365, 401, 439, 442–3, 509–10, 548. Pressnell's book does not appear in the bibliography of Dickson's book, though pre-dating it by ten years, providing further evidence of the divide between the study of high and low finance.

returned to it and exchanged for coin. Linked to a London banker these country bank notes were also made payable there, greatly widening their circulation. These country bank notes were also made exchangeable for Bank of England notes, which greatly increased the amount that could be issued as that was no longer limited to the holding of coins that each bank maintained. What developed from 1750 onwards was a process in which the country bank made a loan by issuing its own notes. The loan was accompanied by a bill of exchange on a London bank, which the borrower signed as an acknowledgement of the debt that had to be repaid. These bills were then sent to London, using the increasingly efficient postal service, where they could then be discounted through a London banker, so releasing funds that the country banker was then able to use to make further loans. If the country banker had no immediate use for the money it could be left on deposit at their London correspondent, and receive interest of 4 per cent per annum until needed. The London bank then employed the money in London. In this way, through the links that were established between London and provincial banks, including those in Scotland, Wales, and Ireland, the Bank of England became the bankers' bank for the entire UK.[31] If the total number of banks is taken as a measure of when a financial revolution occurred in Britain then the timing is located towards the end, not the beginning, of the eighteenth century, which makes it contiguous with the Industrial Revolution rather than a precursor.

It was over the course of the eighteenth century that the Bank of England recognized that other London banks, and their extensive national connections, complemented the role it played and so allowed them to open accounts with it. By opening accounts at the Bank of England these London banking partnerships were able to make and receive payments between each other using Bank of England notes as the means of payment, so minimizing the amount of coin they had to keep. Developing from this co-operation between the banking partnerships in London was the growth of the London money market. Due to the small size of each of these banks, there was a strong possibility that any one of them would either be short of funds, and so unable to make a loan to a customer, or possessed of excess funds for which it had no immediate use. Collectively, however, there could be equilibrium and so the practice developed through which these banks would borrow from or lend to each other, with bills of exchange acting as the circulating medium and payments made using Bank of England notes. Out of that arose specialist bill brokers from the 1770s, copied from those who already operated in Amsterdam. These brokers maintained contact with the various banks buying bills from some and selling

---

[31] Clapham, *The Bank of England*, v.1, pp.18, 113–30, 149, 161, 166–7, 204–13, 245, and Appendix E; Temin and Voth, *Prometheus Shackled*, pp.91–4; Crick and Wadsworth, *A Hundred Years*, pp.12, 25; Sayers, *Lloyds Bank*, pp.116–28; Ackrill and Hannah, *Barclays*, pp.1–16; L. Moffit, *England on the Eve of the Industrial Revolution* (London: P.S. King, 1925), p.246.

them to others. By selling a bill to a bank a bill broker received Bank of England notes in return, which could then be used to buy bills from another bank. By 1813 there were nineteen bill brokers in London with one of the most prominent being Thomas Richardson, who was doing about £7–8 million of business a year by 1810.[32]

The existence of this market in bills meant that these small banking partnerships in London could, collectively, provide an alternative source of demand for bills and so compete with the Bank of England. The Bank of England chose the bills it would buy carefully in order to minimize the risks it took. This was expressed in a preference for bills that had a short time to run, as that meant there was only short delay before repayment in full. It also preferred bills that had been used to finance trade, as that meant that they were backed by collateral, which could be sold in the event of a default. These preferences meant that there were other bills in circulation, especially those providing temporary credit, which the Bank of England did not purchase but were available at better rates of discount. By applying the spare funds that accumulated with them to purchasing these bills, the London banks could develop a profitable business buying and selling bills between each other, assisted by the activities of the specialist bill brokers. In 1773 the London bankers set up their own Clearing House at which they met to settle transactions between each other generated by their sale and purchase of each others' bills. The Bank of England was excluded from membership of this Clearing House until 1854.[33] As these London banks developed an expanding correspondent network to the banks that were being established elsewhere in the UK, from the 1750s onwards the effect was to create a national money market with the links between the London banks and then to the Bank of England at its nucleus.

This money market maximized the mobilization of savings and the provision of credit, both of which were essential for the growth of the economy. Though industrialization was financed through informal sources and internally generated funds, access to the credit provided by banks, through the use of bills of exchange, provided manufacturers with the short-term funds required to buy in raw materials and pay their workers while awaiting payment from the merchants who had purchased their products. This included the cotton textile industry whose development in Lancashire from

---

[32] K.F. Dixon, *The Development of the London Money Market, 1780–1830*, London University Ph.D (1962), pp.24, 32–3, 37, 156–63.

[33] Clapham, *The Bank of England*, v.1, pp.18, 113–30, 149, 161, 166–7, 204–13, 245, and Appendix E; Temin and Voth, *Prometheus Shackled*, pp.91–4; Crick and Wadsworth, *A Hundred Years*, pp.12, 25; Sayers, *Lloyds Bank*, pp.116–28; Ackrill and Hannah, *Barclays*, pp.1–16; Dixon, *The Development of the London Money Market*, pp.24–37; Dawes and Ward-Perkins, *Country Banks of England and Wales*, v.1, pp. 4–5, 19; Williams Deacon's Bank, *Williams Deacon's, 1771–1970* (Manchester: Williams Deacon's Bank, 1971), p.18.

the 1750s onwards was central to the Industrial Revolution. Banks were also involved in infrastructure finance. In the 1790s banks provided the companies building the new canals with short-term loans to finance construction, in anticipation that they would be repaid when they were complete and all the shares had been issued and paid up.[34] Recognition of the importance of the links between banks placed the City of London at the very centre of the system that provided the credit that businesses required.[35] Though most financial arrangements remained both local and personal, the specialist financial services that the City of London provided became an integral part of the British financial system over the course of the eighteenth century.

Contributing to the creation of an interdependent financial system was the use made of the National Debt by the banks. Though the National Debt was created to finance the government's military ambitions, once in existence it also played an important role in the way that banking developed in Britain over the course of the nineteenth century. What the National Debt possessed, whether in the form of consols or Bank of England, East India, and South Sea stock, was a market through which those holding it could easily buy and sell. This made the National Debt a liquid asset in contrast to investments in land, property and mortgages, and so one that was ideal for a financial institution that had a need to access money at short notice. That was the case with fire and marine insurance companies as they could be faced with a sudden call upon their resources, unlike life insurance companies where the use of mortality statistics made their business more predictable.[36] As Fairman, the accountant for Royal Exchange Assurance, explained in the 1790s, 'The regular payment of the interest on the government funds, and the number of persons in this

---

[34] S.D. Chapman, 'Fixed Capital Formation in the British Cotton Manufacturing Industry', in J.P.P. Higgins and S. Pollard (eds), *Aspects of Capital Investment in Great Britain, 1750-1850: A Preliminary Survey* (London: Methuen, 1971), pp.71-97; S. Shapiro, *Capital and the Cotton Industry in the Industrial Revolution* (Ithaca, N.Y.: Cornell UP, 1967), pp.60-1, 84-99, 152-5; Dyos and Aldcroft, *British Transport*, pp. 99-101.

[35] I.S. Black, 'The London Agency System in English Banking, 1780-1825', *The London Journal*, 21 (1996), pp.112, 127; I.S. Black, 'Geography, Political Economy and the Circulation of Finance Capital in Early Industrial England', *Journal of Historical Geography*, 15 (1989), p.381; I.S. Black, 'Money, Information and Space: Banking in Early Nineteenth-Century England and Wales', *Journal of Historical Geography*, 21 (1995), pp.403, 410; Ball and D Sunderland, *An Economic History of London, 1800-1914* (London: Routledge, 2001), p.42; S.D. Chapman, *Merchant Enterprise in Britain: From the Industrial Revolution to World War I* (Cambridge: CUP, 1992), pp.30, 76, 83, 181-2; J. Langton, 'The Industrial Revolution and the Regional Geography of England', *Transactions: Institute of British Geographers*, 9 (1984), pp.162-3, 511; D. Gregory, 'The Production of Regions in England's Industrial Revolution', *Journal of Historical Geography*, 14 (1988), pp.55-6, 173; D. Barnett, *London, Hub of the Industrial Revolution: A Revisionary History, 1775-1825* (London: Tauris, 1998), pp.13-17, 32-9, 127-32; L. D. Schwartz, *London in the Age of Industrialisation: Entrepreneurs, Labour Force and Living Conditions, 1700-1850* (Cambridge: CUP, 1992), p.14, 154, 233, 261.

[36] Cockerell and Green, *The British Insurance Business*, pp.61-70; Trebilcock, *Phoenix Assurance*, pp.616-19; 665, 703-18, 736, 742.

country preferring the interest they afford to the hazardous profits of trade, occasion continual purchasers for those shares in them which are brought to market for sale. The facility, also, and trifling expense, with which transfers are made in these funds, are inducements to prefer vesting money in them to laying it out on mortgages or other private security, which, though probably yielding a greater interest, is frequently attended with trouble and uncertainty.'[37]

With the expansion in the size of the National Debt during the eighteenth century, matched by the sophistication of the securities market in which its various securities were traded, banks, like insurance companies, had available to them assets which could easily, quickly, and cheaply be bought and sold while also yielding a reasonable rate of return. The ability of banks to expand the business that they could do was restrained by the obligation to redeem notes or repay depositors in coin if requested. The stock of gold and silver, out of which these coins were minted, was limited and annual production low until the discoveries in California, Australia, and later South Africa from the mid nineteenth century onwards. The use of bank notes provided an alternative, but only if the public could trust them. These notes entered circulation when banks made loans to customers. These loans could either be backed by collateral lodged by the borrower, such as a mortgage, gold coin, securities or other assets, or supported with none, being based on the expectation that the borrower would repay. Unlike the notes it had in circulation, which were liabilities, to a bank a bill was an asset, as it expected to be repaid what it was owed. A bill became a liability, however, if it was re-sold, as the bank would have added its name to it. Thus, a bank had to be in the position of not only redeeming its notes but it could also be called upon to meet the amount due on a bill that it had re-sold if the borrower defaulted. Securities, which could be easily bought and sold (as was the case with the government's own debt or quasi-official debt like Bank of England, East India Company, and South Sea stocks) provided a mechanism through which a bank could always employ idle balances and access coin or Bank of England notes.

As the availability of liquid assets grew, so a bank was able to expand the business that it could do by issuing notes and selling bills, as it was in a position to meet redemptions. No longer was a bank's ability to lend constrained by the capital it possessed and the deposits it received, as it could securitize its loans through the use of bills and then sell these on.[38] This was to the advantage of the saver as they now found a home for any temporarily idle funds by depositing money in a bank, so expanding the supply of finance. It was advantageous to the borrower as the bank could offer more generous terms as it was in a position to lend more, secure in the knowledge that any

---

[37] W. Fairman, *The Stocks Examined and Compared*, 3rd ed. (London: [n.p.], 1798), p.2.

[38] There is an analogy here to the securitization of loans by banks prior to the financial crisis of 2007/8.

sudden redemption of its notes or withdrawal of deposits could be met by selling bonds. It also encouraged more people to become bankers because of the ability to generate increased profits at a lower level of risk. Through there was always the possibility that a borrower would default, making a bank insolvent, by investing in bonds a bank could reduce though never eliminate the risk of a liquidity crisis. No bank could withstand a panic in which note holders and depositors demanded coin and Bank of England notes, which could quickly exhaust its holdings of these and force it to stop payment. In turn, that would lead to a chain reaction as panic withdrawals were made at other banks rumoured to be facing the same difficulties, for example, those connected through correspondent links. It was the need always to be in a position to repay depositors and redeem notes in gold or Bank of England notes that prevented an excessive expansion of credit, and so dampened down bank formation.[39] Throughout the eighteenth century and into the nineteenth the possibility of bankruptcy was an ever-present one for all those involved in the money market, whether they were bill brokers in London or bankers in the country.[40] What the growth of the National Debt provided, once it was accompanied by an active market in which the securities could be traded, was, simultaneously, an encouragement to bank formation and a means through which the risks involved could be reduced.[41]

But these risks remained. This system of Originate and Distribute lacked a stability mechanism. As confidence in future economic prospects grew, businesses borrowed by selling more bills which were bought by banks through issuing more notes, whether produced by the Bank of England or the country banks themselves. In turn, this increased availability of credit contributed to further economic expansion until a crisis occurred, such as a bad harvest, which would undermine business confidence through rising food prices and shrinking demand. Those holding notes would then seek to exchange them for coin, perceiving that to be safer than notes, while those who had issued bills would be unable to repay as goods went unsold. Inevitably banks would fail because they would be unable to meet demands from holders of their notes for coin, whether they were solvent or not. Once the ensuing depression was over the cycle would begin again. The Bank of England contributed to this cycle. During a period of rising prosperity it was a willing buyer of bills using its own notes. In contrast, when a downturn in the economy began it sharply

---

[39] Grossman, *Unsettled Account*, pp.37–45, 57, 67, 136, 146–7, 174; Dawes and Ward-Perkins, *Country Banks of England and Wales*, v.1, pp.2–6, 7, 25; A.H. John, 'Insurance Investment and the London Money Market of the 18th Century', *Economica*, ns 20 (1953), pp.140–6; Pressnell, *Country Banking*, pp.36, 45, 76–83, 95, 105–7, 116, 126, 224, 260, 288, 401.

[40] Pressnell, *Country Banking*, pp.536–8.

[41] A comparison of the number of banks, taken from the Tipping Points Project Banking Database, and the nominal value of the Funded National Debt, taken from Mitchell, *British Historical Statistics*, pp.600–1.

contracted its purchases, especially when a crisis threatened, in order to protect its own liquidity. It was only the largest borrowers, like the government or the East India Company that could borrow from the Bank of England without having to issue bills, and so they could be assured of the credit they required to operate, whatever the conditions. In contrast, other banks were dependent upon the willingness of the Bank of England to continue to buy their bills even in a crisis, and that depended upon the relationship that they maintained, with some being favoured and others not. The result was that banking remained a risky business throughout the eighteenth century as all were vulnerable to either a sudden liquidity crisis, whether real or generated by rumour, or a solvency crisis due to the failure of a major customer, given the small number of customers each bank had.[42] The only bank that could operate a Lend and Hold business was the Bank of England but even it was dependent for its survival upon the solvency of its largest customer, the British government.

THE CRISIS OF 1810

There was thus established an important connection between high and low finance and between the City and the provinces in the second half of the eighteenth century. According to Flandreau, Galinard, Obst, and Nogues, between 1688 and 1789 London became the hub of a global bill market that operated as both a means of transfer and a source of credit, and did so through a network of correspondent bankers that was simultaneously international and domestic.[43] Forming part of an increasingly dense and specialized financial cluster located around the Royal Exchange in London this bill market fused internal and external financial transactions and made a key contribution to the development of British banking in the eighteenth century.[44] This process was then greatly intensified by the huge increase in government borrowing to finance military expenditure during the French Revolutionary and Napoleonic wars, 1793 to 1815. Between 1790 and 1815 annual government expenditure grew

---

[42] Temin and Voth, *Prometheus Shackled*, pp.42, 72, 91–4, 129, 147; Crick and Wadsworth, *A Hundred Years*, p.13; Clapham, *The Bank of England*, v.1, pp.166–7, 204–13, 245.

[43] M. Flandreau, C. Galinard, C. Obst and P. Nogues, 'The Bell Jar: Commercial Interest Rates between Two Revolutions, 1688–1789', in Atack and Neal (eds), *The Origin and Development of Financial Markets and Institutions*, pp.162, 177, 199.

[44] Orbell and Turton, *British Banking*, pp.1–5; P. Gauci, *Emporium of the World: The Merchants of London, 1660–1800* (London: Hambledon Press, 2007), pp.32, 50, 68, 145, 161; D. Keane, 'The Setting of the Royal Exchange: Continuity and Change in the Financial District of the City of London, 1300–1871', in A. Saunders (ed.), *The Royal Exchange* (London: Guardian Royal Exchange, 1991), pp.254, 265.

from £16.8 million to £112.9 million while revenue only rose from £17 million to £77.9 million despite the introduction of an income tax. The deficit was met through an enormous expansion of government borrowing both in the form of long-term debt and short-term Exchequer bills, which had major implications for bank formation.[45]

The outbreak of war in 1793 had led to a financial crisis in which many banks collapsed, as depositors and note holders demanded gold because of the uncertain conditions. Even the Bank of England was under pressure and there were those who doubted whether the notes it issued were entirely safe. These conditions continued and intensified as the conflict continued.[46] The solution found by the government, desperate to increase its ability to borrow to meet military needs, was to suspend the requirement placed on the Bank of England to redeem its notes in gold. This decision was taken in 1797. With suspension of convertibility the Bank of England was under no obligation to repay its depositors or redeem its notes in gold and so could expand its note circulation without restraint as long as people were willing to hold the paper it had printed. Between 1796 and 1810 Bank of England notes in circulation more than doubled, from £10 million to £22.9 million. This provided all banks with a greater supply of notes, which could be used to make loans, whether they were London bankers using Bank of England notes or those outside issuing their own. Bankers also used the increased supply of notes to speculate in government debt, as did the bankers Edward Boldero and Stephen Lushington between 1797 and 1810. There was also a boom in company promotions between 1806 and 1808, such was the abundance of credit made available since the ending of convertibility in 1797.[47]

Of even more significance for the banking system was the increasingly active role played by the Bank of England in the discount market. Using its own notes, the Bank of England increasingly purchased bills of exchange in large amounts. Though it operated as the government's bank, and had invested its entire capital in government debt, the Bank of England was also a company answerable to shareholders who expected to be paid regular dividends. Operations in the discount market had always offered an easy and low-risk way of generating the profits used to pay these dividends, and so this type of business intensified after 1797. According to Clapham, during the period of

---

[45] Mitchell, *British Historical Statistics*, pp.575–88. For the rationale behind this interpretation see T. Congdon, *Central Banking in a Free Society* (London: IEA, 2009), p.55.

[46] The crisis of 1810 has been expertly researched by I.P.H. Duffy, *Bankruptcy and Insolvency in London during the Industrial Revolution* (New York & London: Garland Publishing, 1985) (originally an Oxford D.Phil 1973). This is a greatly undervalued source for the financial history of the period.

[47] J.H. Wood, *A History of Central Banking in Great Britain and the United States* (Cambridge: CUP, 2005), pp.9–11; Trebilcock, *Phoenix Assurance*, pp.624–5; J. Taylor, *Boardroom Scandal: The Criminalization of Company Fraud in Nineteenth-Century Britain* (Oxford: OUP, 2013), p.11.

suspension 'discounts grew outrageously' fuelling a huge expansion of banknote circulation both by the Bank of England and the country banks. The income generated by the Bank of England from the discounting of bills rose from £233,000 in 1796/7 to a peak of £914,000 in 1809/10 before falling back.[48] Between 1796 and 1810 the non-government securities held by the Bank of England more than quadrupled, rising from £5.2 million to £22.4 million. The effect was to encourage speculative bank formation, regardless of the risks involved, with the smaller banks possessed of little capital proving especially vulnerable to both liquidity and solvency crises. The rapid expansion in the number of banks was most apparent outside London, where wealthy individuals now had a greater need to access the payments system, whether to meet tax demands or to invest in government debt and receive the interest generated. There were an estimated 250,000 holders of the National Debt by 1815. In the absence of a nationwide banking system, with even the Bank of England having no branches, a local banker provided access through their links to a London agent. In turn, contact with a London banker meant more and more of their bills were being used to provide credit, and these bills could be easily discounted in London where the Bank of England was a willing buyer. It was not until the return to convertibility in 1819 that the constraint of redeeming notes in gold was finally restored. By then the growth of the National Debt had ended, having peaked in 1818, and remained stable for the rest of the nineteenth century.[49]

However, relating the rise and fall of the number of banks to either the inconvertibility of notes into gold or the growth in government borrowing would place the peak in bank formation in 1819 and not the earlier date of 1810. That raises the question of whether something happened in 1810 that then suppressed bank formation while increasing exits through failure. The answer lies in the relationship between the Bank of England and the discount market. Discounts at the Bank of England rose from £12.8 million in 1808 to £14.6 million in 1809 and then to £19.9 million in 1810. Increasingly these bills were being used not only to obtain short-term credit, as with a commercial transaction or a temporary shortfall in liquidity, but also to finance capital

---

[48] Clapham, *The Bank of England*, v.2, pp.11, 21, 90–7.Appendix C and D.
[49] Pressnell, *Country Banking*, pp.13, 45, 60, 63, 70, 90, 95, 100, 116, 224, 260, 288, 548; D. Laidler, 'Two Views of the Lender of Last Resort: Thornton and Bagehot', Paper Presented at a Conference in Paris (2002), pp.4–11; Mitchell, *British Historical Statistics*, pp.656–7; Ackrill and Hannah, *Barclays*, p.51; M. Hart, J. Jonker, and J. L. Van Zanden, *A Financial History of the Netherlands* (Cambridge: CUP, 1997), pp.55–62; J. de Vries and A. Van der Woude, *The First Modern Economy: Success, Failure and Perseverance, 1500–1815* (Cambridge: CUP, 1997), pp.12, 124, 129, 141–4, 154–5, 683; J.C. Riley, *International Government Finance and the Amsterdam Capital Market, 1740–1815* (Cambridge: CUP, 1980), pp.7–8, 19, 45, 50, 61–5, 77, 84–5, 105, 114, 123–7, 174, 178, 183–6, 194, 205–16, 243, 281; C. Wilson, *Anglo-Dutch Commerce and Finance in the 18th Century* (Cambridge: CUP, 1941), pp.79–83, 97, 111, 116–17, 191, 195.

expenditure through the ability to have them renewed or replaced. The inflation fuelled by the huge rise in government expenditure and the growth in the money supply, encouraged businesses to take on capital expenditure in the expectation that they could profit from the rising prices. Unfortunately, the volatile conditions created by war made the period also one of frequent business failures with the annual number of bankruptcies trebling between the 1780s and 1811/20. After each of these crises optimism nevertheless returned; the Bank of England continued to increase its operations in the discount market, and the number of banks grew again. That was not the case after the 1810 crisis and the explanation lies with the action taken by the Bank of England. According to Duffy, 'It may be suggested that...having allowed trading to become excessive by its liberal discounting, the Bank aggravated the subsequent depressions by sharply restricting its accommodation when the crises set in.' The detail of what happened begins with the failure of the West India merchant, Thomas Coles and Sons, on 6 July 1810, which was followed immediately by their City bankers, Brickwood and Company. A number of provincial banks for which Brickwood and Company was the London correspondent, subsequently collapsed, namely Bowles and Company in Salisbury and Rowton and Marshall in Chester. The fact that there was a delay and not all those provincial banks connected to Brickwood and Company failed, indicates the devolved nature of the correspondent banking system. Whether located in London or in the provinces, the partners of individual banks managed their business either conservatively or speculatively, if the former, making them resilient in a crisis or highly exposed if the latter. Bank failure in 1810 was not a generalized affair but was dependent on individual circumstances and connections, unlike what was to happen after the end of hostilities.

Nevertheless, what took place in 1810 provided a warning to the Bank of England of the danger it was in through its exposure to the market for bills. The Bank's response was to reduce its purchases of bills, fuelled by concerns that they would not be repaid on maturity. Bills and notes discounted by the Bank of England halved from £4.03 million for the week of 2–8th July 1810 to £1.98 million for the week of 9–15th July. The Bank of England did increase its lending from the 19th of July 1810 but then cut it back again as new concerns mounted after the huge losses became known that had led on 28 September 1810 to the suicide of Abraham Goldsmid, a major dealer in bills and bonds. By then fears in the City about particular banks and merchants increasingly left the Bank of England as the sole purchaser in the discount market. This forced the Bank to recognize its own exposure to the risk of widespread defaults. The result was a decision to permanently reduce its purchase of bills and only accept those considered the most secure. This can be deduced from the value of the bills and notes discounted at the Bank of England. These had risen from £18.6 million on the 6th of June 1810 to £21.5 million on the

4th of July, then fell back to £19 million on 29th August 1810, remained at much that level in September and early October, rose briefly to £20.1 million on the 10th of October, then dropped to a low of £15.1 million on 28th November, before experiencing a modest rise to £16.9 million by 24th December. What the Bank of England had done was to fuel a monetary expansion prior to July 1810 and a monetary contraction afterwards through its activities in the London discount market.[50] The non-government securities held by the Bank of England fell from a peak of £22.4 million in 1810 to £17.6 million in 1811, £16.5 million in 1812, and £13.7 million in 1813 before rising to £15.9 million in 1814 and £18.8 million in 1815. There then began a steep decline that took the total down to £4.6 million by 1820. The level of 1810 was never to be reached again until 1866 when it stood at £23 million.[51]

The role played by the Bank of England in the discount market had important implications for the English financial sector through the contraction, expansion, and then contraction of credit. Annual bankruptcies rose from a yearly average of twenty in the 1780s to thirty-two in the crisis years of the 1790s. They had then dropped to twenty-five in 1800-9 but rose to almost forty between 1810-19, before reaching fifty in 1820-5. As monetary conditions switched between inflation and deflation, reflecting government expenditure, which was increased and then cut back, the number of banks expanded when profits were easy to generate and shrank when losses mounted. During the periods of easy credit and rampant inflation, banks could obtain ample funds to lend while, in nominal terms, assets grew in value and liabilities remained constant. When credit became difficult to obtain and deflation set in, banks were faced with the reverse position. Liabilities rose in real terms while the value of assets fell in real and even in nominal terms as businesses collapsed and property prices declined. This pushed many banks to the brink of collapse, as they were not in a position to meet note redemptions and withdrawals since those who had borrowed from them were unable to repay what they owed. The result was numerous bank exits, whether through failure or voluntary liquidation driven by low profitability, and little by way of replacements.[52]

---

[50] Duffy, *Bankruptcy and Insolvency*, pp.179-80 cf. 2, 44, 168-9, 179-80, 188-93, 215-19, 231, 234-50, 255, 268, 296, 300-4, 310-14, 380; Dawes and Ward-Perkins, *Country Banks of England and Wales*, v.1, p.2; Hills, Thomas, and Dimsdale, 'The UK Recession in Context', pp.279-83; S.R. Cope, 'The Goldsmids and the Development of the London Money Market during the Napoleonic Wars', *Economica*, ns 9 (1942), pp.200-5.

[51] Mitchell, *British Historical Statistics*, pp.656-7.

[52] James, 'Panics, Payments Disruptions', pp.306-7; Pressnell, *Country Banking*, pp.536-8; Reinhart and Rogoff, *This Time is Different*, pp.76-7; Perry, 'The History of Companies' Legislation', p.482.

POST 1810

Individual bank failure continued to be a problem for English banking even after the end of the Napoleonic wars and the post-war depression. The cause lay with the longstanding restriction on the number of partners that a bank was able to have if it was to be allowed to issue notes in England and Wales. For a bank it was vital to maintain the appearance of stability but this remained difficult as long as it was reliant on so few partners to provide the capital. The change in fortune of a single partner, or even rumours to that effect, could prompt a rush by depositors to close their accounts and by note holders to redeem what they held. Trust could evaporate within moments, forcing a bank to close.[53] The problem with a limit of six was that it was insufficient to spread the risk that if a bank should fail, all partners would be left liable to the full extent of their wealth. Potential investors in banks with a limit of six partners were reluctant to commit funds unless personally involved in the management or related to those who were conducting the business. For that reason many English banks had many fewer than six partners. Though the possession of limited liability was an advantage in attracting investors to participate in a bank, it was not essential, as the experience of banks in Scotland and insurance companies in England showed. Until the limit on the number of partners was repealed in 1826 the effect was to keep the size of the individual banking unit in England small.[54]

As a consequence, the inevitable result of a return in confidence, accompanied by increased government borrowing, was growth in the number of banks followed by a contraction once the boom was over. However, the total number of banks never returned to the peak reached in 1810 before the repeal of the restriction on the number of partners and the permission given for joint-stock banking in England permitted the development of larger banks. The explanation for that lies with the behaviour of the Bank of England. Throughout the period from 1810 until 1826 it prioritized its own interests, followed by those of its largest client, the British government, over those of its other customers, including fellow bankers. Between 1816 and 1818, for example, it used its notes to purchase the Exchequer Bills issued by the government to raise finance rather than the bills brought to it by other banks for discounting, and so depressed bank formation. With the Payments Act of 1819, the Bank of England had, once again, to redeem its notes in gold coins. By 1822 it was also required to end the circulation of low-denomination notes began in 1797. Faced with the need to contract its note issue and resume

---

[53] Duffy, *Bankruptcy and Insolvency*, pp.300–4.
[54] Perry, 'The History of Companies' Legislation', pp.481–3; J.F. Dunn, 'Banking in 1837 and in 1897 in the United Kingdom, India and the Colonies: A Comparison and a Contrast', *Journal of the Institute of Bankers*, 18 (1898), p.378.

convertibility the Bank of England cut back discounting on government bills and called in loans so as to accumulate gold. The country banks had followed suit. The result was a severe credit contraction causing a number of banks to fail and discouraging new bank formation. However, in 1822, the government decided to extend the life of the low denomination notes in circulation, meaning that the Bank of England was left highly liquid and so resumed its liberal discounting policy. The result was a sharp increase in the availability of credit, encouraging new bank formation, which helped fuel a speculative boom beginning in 1823 followed by the inevitable collapse towards the end of 1825. As in previous such cycles the Bank of England's first response was self-preservation, as it had, like many other banks, become increasingly illiquid through investing in high-yielding mortgages rather than low-yielding government debt. This meant that it restricted its purchase of bills, so exposing those banks that had become dependent on its liberal discounting policy to fund their lending and lacked adequate reserves. The result was a series of bank failures from October 1825 onwards. The most spectacular was Pole, Thornton, and Company in December as this involved forty-three correspondent banks. Faced with a collapse of this scale, which would have repercussions for the Bank of England itself, the Bank provided Pole, Thornton, and Company with an emergency loan of £400,000 so it could continue in business but only on condition that it was reformed and recapitalized. Only when the Bank resumed discounting and increased its note circulation did the crisis abate. It was in the wake of this crisis in 1825 that the Bank lost its monopoly in 1826, because there was a widespread recognition that its actions in the face of a crisis were driven by its own interests and they had the effect of destabilizing the entire monetary and financial system.[55]

CONCLUSION

The year 1810 was the date when the number of individual banks in Britain peaked. Rather than being a random event, the fact that this happened then rather than earlier or later is highly significant. The actual peak was a product of the liberal lending policy adopted by the Bank of England from 1797 until 1810. That policy ended in 1810, removing the stimulus that had been given to speculative bank formation. The peak of 1810 was only partly a response to an increased demand for banking facilities driven by industrialization. That was

---

[55] B. Hilton, *Corn, Cash, Commerce: The Economic Policies of the Tory Governments, 1815-1830* (Oxford: OUP, 1977), pp.33-6, 48-55, 88-9, 159, 203-15, 234, 303; Taylor, *Boardroom Scandal*, pp.21-3, 45, 50-5; Wlliams Deacon's Bank, *Williams Deacon's, 1771-1970*, pp.50-2, 71-83; Clapham, *The Bank of England*, v.2, pp.83-5.

an underlying factor because the risks involved in banking kept the business personal and local, regardless of the artificial constraint imposed by the limitation of the number of partners to a maximum of six. Instead, the actual peak was driven by the actions of the Bank of England, no longer restrained after 1797 by the necessity of having to meet the need to convert its bank notes into gold, as that drove the number of banks to new heights. It was in 1810 that the Bank of England ceased to be such a liberal purchaser of bills, making it more difficult for banks to re-discount their bills and so expand or even maintain their existing business. The result was a contraction of credit, which was accentuated when the wars drew to a close and inflation turned to deflation. This led to a decline in the number of banks required as the business done became concentrated in the most resilient and the most competitive. Nevertheless, the number of banks could have reached new peaks, once prosperity returned, as was evident in the expansion of the 1820s and 1830s. The reason it did not, despite the continuing demand for banking facilities, was due to the ending of the cap on the number of partners. This happened in 1826 and allowed individual banks to expand to meet demand as they could access additional capital more easily.

The identification of 1810 as a tipping point, changes the narrative for British banking. Rather than the Glorious Revolution of 1688 and the legislation of 1826 being major discontinuities, supporting an interpretation that there was a major divide between the City of London and the rest of the British financial system over that period, the conclusion reached is that continuity rather than change prevailed throughout. Evidence for that is derived from the rise and fall in the number of banks as that was neither begun by the political revolution of 1688 nor ended by legislation in the nineteenth century. What took place in the eighteenth century was the gradual development of the British banking system within the parameters set by contemporary conditions and the activities of the Bank of England. Contemporary conditions acted against the emergence of a small number of dominant banks because of the slowness of communication, the problems of managing nationwide enterprise, and the risks involved in making loans at a time of recurring economic volatility. It was for entirely sound reasons that the Bank of England chose to focus its business on one location as that gave it direct control over its lending. Instead, what emerged was a banking system based on the Originate and Distribute Model. Individual banks were simply too small to operate a Lend and Hold Model but could provide the credit that an industrializing economy required by making loans through the issue of bank notes and receive in return bills which could be sold either to the Bank of England or to other banks. In this way the ability of the British economy to finance economic growth from the mid eighteenth century onwards was both mobilized and maximized while a payments system was provided that facilitated internal and external trade.

The character of the system that did gradually emerge was the product of the privileges that the Bank of England enjoyed. These gave it a special position within the emerging field of British banking and this had implications for the entire banking system. These were felt most in London where other banks stopped issuing their own notes and instead used those of the Bank of England. The effect was to make them customers of the Bank of England rather than rivals. These other banks re-discounted the bills they received, when making loans, at the Bank of England, and extended those facilities nationwide through the development of correspondent arrangements with the banks that were springing up across the country from the mid eighteenth century onwards. Banking as a business was also attracting an increasing number of entrants because some of the risks involved were being reduced through the use of securities. Such securities provided banks with an asset that was both remunerative and could be easily and quickly sold to raise the cash required when customers asked for notes to be redeemed in coin or withdrew their deposits. Risks remained in banking, especially in the frequent crises when the Bank of England prioritized its own survival, and the interests of its largest customer, the British government, and so cut off credit from the banks that were in the habit of selling bills to it.

What makes 1810 a tipping point for British banking was much less what happened beforehand, though that is important because the conditions created by the suspension of convertibility in 1797 and the enormous expansion in government debt fuelled a rapid growth in bank numbers. It was also not due to 1810 itself, as that involved a relatively small number of bank failures. Instead, it was the sequence of events that followed 1810, which made it emerge as the tipping point. None of these were directly related to the tipping point that took place in 1810 though they built upon what took place that year, particularly the changed attitude of the Bank of England to the provision of liberal credit. In the years after 1810 the conditions favourable to bank formation gradually disappeared as the end of the rise in government borrowing, the switch from inflation to deflation, the return to convertibility, and, finally, the ending of the cap on the number of partners in a bank as well as the Bank of England's monopoly of joint-stock banking in England. Even before these legislative changes took place in the mid 1820s the environment within which British banks operated had begun to change. In the long run, the rise and fall in the number of individual British banks was an inevitable process driven by the internal dynamics of banking as a business. However, the precise timing of the change, the actual numbers involved, and the eventual structure of the banking system that emerged, were all products of unique forces leading to a unique outcome.

3

Consolidation and Competence, 1825–1914

INTRODUCTION

Between 1825 and 1914 the composition, structure, and operation of the entire British banking system was transformed. Whereas in the first two-thirds of the nineteenth century British banking remained exposed to the frequent financial crises that took place, in the last third it developed a resilience that made it the envy of the world. The tipping point in the UK appeared to be the crisis of 1866. In that crisis the leading discount house, Overend and Gurney, collapsed causing shock waves to reverberate throughout the banking system as its reputation for security and reliability was regarded as second only to the Bank of England. After that crisis no other had the same consequences for the banking system until the outbreak of the First World War almost fifty years later. Even in terms of the stability of individual banks the last major collapse experienced before the First World War was that of the City of Glasgow Bank in 1878. Though banks continued to fail, or have near-death experiences, as with Barings in 1890, that did not destabilize the British banking system. It was not that the period was devoid of global financial crises, with those of 1873 and 1907 being of sufficient magnitude to destabilize the financial systems of other countries, but that their impact on the British banking system was limited. This was despite the fact that the City of London emerged as the dominant financial centre in this period, becoming the hub of international financial transactions. That alone should have made the British banking system vulnerable to shocks from abroad, let alone Britain's position as the leading trading nation and the central role that British investors played in the provision of international finance. British banking was also heavily exposed to international events through the existence of a specialist group that provided banking services around the world and the activities of the merchant banks and their finance of global trade and investment. No country's banking system was more exposed to external financial fluctuations in the fifty years before the First World War than that of the UK, with the government delegating monetary policy to the Bank of England and adhering to the fixed exchange-rate regime operating under the Gold Standard. However, that was also the time when the British banking system became most resilient. Not only did the banking system develop ways of working that minimized the risk of liquidity crises but also individual institutions became adept at managing their assets and liabilities in such a way as to make the risk of insolvency ever more remote. Dimsdale and Hotson see this period as the beginning of a Golden Age for British banking.[1]

It was also during the course of the nineteenth century that the British banking system became a source of pride for the British people. Using novels as a guide, the tipping point in public perception appears to have taken place around 1890. Before, all banks, with the single exception of the Bank of England, were regarded as identical and so prone to a bank run if rumours spread that it was in financial difficulties. This was as true of the run on the carefully managed Berkeley's Bank as with the one on the fraudulent Cavendish's Bank in Harriet Martineau's early 1830s novel. Both failed as a result.[2] Similarly, in Mrs Gore's, *The Man of Business or Stokeshill Place*, which appeared in 1837, the Westerton Bank failed with debts of £150,000, after one of its partners had defrauded it and fled the country. 'A country bank is the depository of all the little savings of the poor... Many will lose their all, many will be ruined, many will be driven out of their farms and houses.' In this case, the remaining partner was a wealthy landowner who had to forfeit his entire property to meet the demands of the creditors, including those with deposits and holding notes, so avoiding this outcome.[3] Though bankers were seen as both wealthy and powerful, banks were not considered safe, being exposed to fraud committed by the partners and embezzlement by the employees.[4] This view was not confined to the private banks, for doubts also extended to the security of the new joint-stock banks, as seen in a short story by Wilkie Collins, dating from 1859.[5] Also in 1859 in the novel by Charles Lever, the Irish banker, Davenport Dunn, arranged to have rumours circulated stating that the Ossory Bank in Kilkenny was in difficulty. These rumours led to a run on the bank as holders of its notes and those with deposits rushed

---

[1] N. Dimsdale and A. Hotson, 'Introduction', in Dimsdale and Hotson (eds), *British Financial Crises*, p.7.
[2] H. Martineau, *Berkeley the Banker* (London: Fox, 1832-4) 2 vols, v.1, pp.2, 8, 13-14, 38-9, 65-7, 82, 132-41, 156-7; v.2, pp.24-5, 131, 138-9.
[3] Mrs Gore, *The Man of Business or Stokeshill Place* (London: J. and C. Brown, 1837), pp.120, 185, 264-9, 294-9, 326-7, 326-7.
[4] Mrs Gore, *The Money Lender* (London: [n.p.], 1854), p.31; E. Robinson, *The City Banker or Love and Money* (London: Skeet, 1856), pp.8-9, 22-5, 337-47, 420-1; C. Lever, *That Boy of Norcott's* (London: Smith, Elder, 1869), p.222.
[5] W. Collins, 'The Biter Bit', in R.C. Bull (ed.), *Great Tales of Mystery* (London: Weidenfeld & Nicolson, 1960), p.38. Originally in *The Queen of Hearts* (London: Hurst and Blackett, 1859).

to convert them into coin. There is a vivid description of a huge crowd assembling in front of the bank in a desperate attempt to withdraw savings and convert the bank's notes into gold before the bank closed its doors forever. However, having made preparations for such an event, by secretly shipping in cash over the previous days, the bank was able to pay everybody and the crowd melted away. The bank's reputation was enhanced, and Dunn emerged a hero. When new fears about the financial state of the bank circulated again they were not believed, even though they were true. Despite being a joint-stock bank Dunn had used the bank as a vehicle for his speculative investments and this led to its eventual failure.[6]

It was the actions of the individual banker rather than banks in general that caused banks to fail in the novels of the nineteenth century, regardless of whether they were private or joint-stock. In Mrs Henry Wood's 1863 bestseller, *The Shadow of Ashlydyat*, the tale revolved around the demise of the 'old-established and most respected... sound and wealthy' banking-house of Godolphin, Crosse, and Godolphin in Prior's Ash. Its collapse was caused by one of the partner's robbing it to fund his extravagant lifestyle and gambling addiction. What finally brought the bank down was the panic withdrawals and redemptions by depositors and note holders which, as in the novel by Charles Lever, constituted one of the most dramatic incidents in the book. Rumours, vague at best, and therefore all the more dangerous, had been spreading in Prior's Ash and its neighbourhood. Some said the Bank had had a loss; some said the Bank was shaky; some said Mr George Godolphin had been lending money from the Bank funds; some said their London agents had failed; some said that Thomas Godolphin was dead. The various turns taken by the rumour were extravagantly marvelous: but the whole, combined, whispered ominously of danger. Only let public fear be thoroughly aroused, and it would be all over. It was a train of powder laid, which only wants one touch of a lighted match to set it exploding. Remittances arrived on the Saturday morning, in the ordinary course of business. Valuable remittances. Sufficient for the usual demands of the day: but not sufficient for any unusual demands... Saturday morning rose busily, as was usual at Prior's Ash. However stagnant the town might be on other days, Saturday was always full of life and bustle. Prior's Ash was renowned for its grain market; and dealers from all parts of the country flocked to attend it. But on this morning some unusual excitement appeared to be stirring the town; natives and visitors. People stood about in groups, talking, listening, asking questions, consulting; and as the morning hours wore on, an unwonted stream appeared to be setting in towards the house of Godolphin, Crosse, and Godolphin. Whether the reports might be true or false, there would be no harm just to draw their

---

[6] C. Lever, *Davenport Dunn or the Man and the Day* (Leipzig: Tauchnitz, 1859) v.2, pp.169, 190–216; v.3 150–1, 160–1, 174–5.

money out and be on the safe side, was the mental remark made by hundreds. Could put it in again when the storm had blown over—if it proved to be only a false alarm. Under these circumstances, little wonder that the Bank was unusually favoured with visitors. One strange feature in their application was, that they all wanted to draw out money: not a soul came to pay any in. George Godolphin, fully aware of the state of things, alive to the danger, was present in person, his words gracious, his bearing easy, his smile gay as ever. Only to look at him eased some of them of half their doubt. But it did not arrest their cheques, and old Hurde [the chief clerk] (whatever George might have done) grew paralysed with fear.

Once all the cash the bank held had been paid out the shutters were closed leaving the rest with nothing. 'the Godolphins were reduced to beggary. Worse off were they than any of their clamorous creditors, since for them all had gone: houses, lands, money, furniture, personal belongings.' The bank did re-open but as the branch of a joint-stock bank.[7]

This continuing distrust of individual bankers also comes across in the 1863 novel by Charles Reade, *Hard Cash*. The story is actually set in the late 1840s, in the aftermath of the railway mania, and concerns a country banker, Richard Hardie, in the small town of Barkington. Hardie had made large losses during the railway mania, through unwise speculations. To cover these he raided the funds of the bank and this led to rumours that it was insolvent, leading to its collapse. This came as a great shock, leaving customers stunned. On the day the bank closed 'the scene at the bank door was heart-rending: respectable persons, reduced to pauperism in that one day, kept arriving and telling their fellow-sufferers their little all was with Hardie, and nothing before them but the workhouse or the almshouse: ruined mothers came and held up their ruined children for the banker to see: and the doors were hammered at, and the house as well as the bank was beleagured by a weeping, wailing, despairing crowd.' Faced with ruin, customers of the bank fled abroad, hanged themselves, went mad, ended up in prison for debt, died of shock or despair, were forced into the workhouse or had to depend on charity.[8] This theme of the instability of banks and the implications this had for their customers, emerged in another of Charles Reade's novels, *Foul Play*, written with Dion Boucicault and published in 1868. The fate of the City merchants, Wardlaw and Son, lay with its bankers as it was dependent upon the credit they provided to finance its business. 'If the banks in question were run upon, and obliged to call in all their resources, his credit must go; and this, in his precarious position, was ruin.'[9] In contrast to the risks posed by individual bankers there was growing

---

[7] Mrs H. Wood, *The Shadow of Ashlydyat* (London: Richard Bentley and Sons, 1863), pp.9, 17, 66–7, 170, 181, 199–204, 226, 236–43, 256–7, 273–8, 286–302, 328–30, 474–5.
[8] C. Reade, *Hard Cash: A Matter of Fact Romance* (London: [n.p.], 1863), pp. 8–9, 93, 105, 126–32, 167, 213–28, 249–53, 358, 415–17, 549, 563, 569, 604–5, 610–13.
[9] C. Reade and D. Boucicault, *Foul Play* (London: Bradbury, 1868), pp.1–3, 36–7, 53, 106–13, 310–11, 408–12.

trust in the security provided by the joint-stock banks by the mid 1860s. This can be seen in Charlotte Riddell's most famous novel, *George Geith of Fen Court*, which was published in 1866. The accountant, George Geith, had switched his account to the prestigious privately run Norton's Bank and lost all his money when it failed. The losses were all borne by its depositors, while the owner retired to his estate in Devon, which was in the name of his wife. His account had been with the new joint-stock bank, the Merchant's and Tradesman's, and his money would have been safe there as it did not fail.[10]

Even the failure of a joint-stock bank, Rivers and Company, was attributed to the actions of the partners in the private bank which had preceded it, in Mrs Oliphant's 1872 novel, *At His Gates*. The partners had only converted their bankrupt business into a joint-stock company in order to avoid personal liability when it finally collapsed, leaving one of the newly installed directors, a financially naïve but commercially successful artist, to take the blame. This story is loosely based on what happened to Overend and Gurney, which had been converted into a company in 1865 and then failed in 1866.[11] In the 1872 novel, *Ready-Money Mortiboy*, by Besant and Rice, the focus was again on private banks, in this case located in the town of Market Basing, namely Melliship's and Mortiboy's. Both were subjected to bank runs once rumours spread that they were in trouble, even though it was only Melliship's, which had been poorly managed, that was insolvent and did fail as a result. Mortiboy's, which was well managed and solvent, came close to being forced to close before the run abated.[12] Similarly in 1883, Mrs Oliphant, in her novel, *Hester*, featured the privately owned Vernon's Bank, which had to survive a series of runs over the years, even though it was solvent on each occasion. Eventually it was converted into a company.[13]

However, by the later 1880s even bankers were being portrayed not as risk-takers whose actions could bring down a bank but more like company employees carrying out their duties as instructed. In Jerome K. Jerome's *Three Men in a Boat*, which came out in 1889, it was remarked that 'George goes to sleep at a bank from ten to four each day, except Saturdays, when they wake him up and put him outside at two.'[14] In novels set after 1890 it was no longer banks that were exposed to runs because they were either badly managed or subject to fraud. Instead, writers now picked other types

---

[10] C. Riddell [writing as F.G. Trafford], *George Geith of Fen Court* (London: R. Bentley, 1866), pp.257, 339. See also C C. Riddell, *Joy after Sorrow* (London: Hutchinson, 1873), pp. 134, 317.

[11] Mrs Oliphant, *At His Gates* [serialized in *Good Words for 1872* (London: Strahan and Co)], pp.39–41, 112, 177, 190, 250.

[12] W. Besant and J. Rice, *Ready-Money Mortiboy: A Matter-of-Fact Story* (London: Chatto & Windus, 1872), pp.1–2, 117–18, 121–4, 143, 192–3, 318, 323, 394, 423, 444.

[13] Mrs Oliphant, *Hester: A Study in Contemporary Life* (London: Macmillan, 1883), pp.1–8, 15–17, 20–1, 136–9, 154–5, 285, 420, 436–9, 458–9.

[14] J.K. Jerome, *Three Men in a Boat* (London: Arrowsmith, 1889), pp.11, 17.

of savings and loans institutions. In 1893 the famous Victorian journalist, W.T. Stead, based a short story, *Two and Two Make Four*, around the collapse of Jabez Balfour's financial conglomerate in 1892, which centered on the Liberator Building Society.[15] George Gissing's 1897 novel, *The Whirlpool*, featured the Britannia Loan, Assurance, Investment, and Banking Company, Limited.[16] Similarly, Conrad's novel, *Chance*, which appeared shortly before the First World War, told the story of the Orb Deposit Bank and the Sceptre Trust, both of which collected money from thousands of small depositors and invested it in high-yielding but increasingly risky investments.[17] In contrast banks were regarded as safe and bankers as trusted and dependable individuals, as in Henry Seton Merriman's 1898 novel, *Roden's Corner*. One of the central characters was Joseph Wade. He was proud of being a banker and aspired to nothing else, as that occupation had brought him both wealth and respect. 'I am a banker, and I am content to be a banker in the evening and on Sundays, as well as during bank-hours.'[18] A similar view of the banker as a wealthy and respected individual emerges from Jackson's novel, *Nine Points of the Law*, which appeared in 1903.[19]

CONSOLIDATION

What is evident from the output of novelists is the degree to which the perception of banks and bankers had changed by the end of the nineteenth century compared to the beginning or even in the middle. This transformation was largely the product of the consolidation that had taken place within commercial banking. The thousand small privately owned banks that existed at the beginning of the century had been converted into a small number of large joint-stock banks by the end. The main obstacle to consolidation has traditionally been seen to be legislation, which was repealed in 1826, as this removed the cap on the number of partners and permitted joint-stock banking. However, the law was not the only obstacle to consolidation. Even more significant were the risks that banks ran when operating as a commercial business. All banks faced sudden liquidity crises, while defaults among

---

[15] W.T. Stead, 'Two and Two Make Four: A Christmas Story for the Times', in *The Review of Reviews*, viii, July–December 1893, pp.550–5.
[16] G. Gissing, *The Whirlpool* (London: Lawrence and Bullen, 1897), pp.14–15, 38, 40–4, 48, 52, 64, 118.
[17] J. Conrad, *Chance* (London: Methuen, 1914), pp.6, 68–71, 78–81, 84–5, 209, 228–9, 362, 377, 385, 433–4.
[18] H. Seton Merriman, *Roden's Corner* (London: Nelson, 1898), pp.94, 191–2, 121–42, 192–5, 220–1, 245, 269, 332, 341–2.
[19] W. Scarborough Jackson, *Nine Points of the Law* (London: Lane, 1903), p.36.

borrowers led to solvency ones. The smaller the bank the more vulnerable it was to these crises as it lacked the resources to meet either the sudden redemption of notes, the withdrawal of deposits or the losses from borrowers not repaying their loans. The method widely used to limit these risks was to instil a sense of loyalty among customers, so that they would not rush to redeem its notes and withdraw their deposits while remaining committed to repaying loans. By conducting banking on the basis of personal relationships, and using local knowledge to avoid bad loans, banks hoped to limit the risks that they ran. Conversely, repeated bank failures were attributed by many to the relatively small size of English banks. The result in 1826, after a rash of bank failures, was to end the limit on the number of partners and the prohibition on joint-stock banking. As a concession to the Bank of England the restriction was not lifted for banks operating within 65 miles of the centre of London, though that happened in 1833. Freed from the curb on the number of partners banks could, if they wished, grow in scale and expand their activities beyond the close confines of their head office. Between 1810 and 1840 the number of UK banks whose operations were limited to the business of a single office fell from 800 to 542 and continued to fall, being down to 398 by 1875. Whether organized as partnerships or as companies, banks could now expand by opening branches or amalgamating into a single business, so allowing consolidation.[20]

Despite the lifting of the restrictions in England the result was not a sudden transformation of banking. Banking remained a risky activity and careful management remained essential if failure was to be avoided.[21] Business failure in general remained a frequent occurrence in the nineteenth century. There were between 1,100 and 2,000 formal bankruptcies a year between 1800 and 1861 and these excluded the large number of insolvencies handled privately with creditors agreeing to receive only a proportion of what they were owed.[22] Faced with these realities, banks continued to keep their business local and intimate, and thus relatively small, with branches clustering around the head office. This continued to leave banks vulnerable if a few of their major

---

[20] Perry, 'The History of Companies' Legislation', *Journal of the Institute of Bankers*, 29 (1908) pp.481–3; Dunn, 'Banking in 1837 and in 1897', *Journal of the Institute of Bankers*, 18 (1898) p.378; M. Anderson, J.R. Edwards, and D. Matthews, 'A Study of the Quoted Company Audit Market in 1886', *Accounting, Business and Financial History*, 6 (1996), pp.363–87.

[21] R.W. Barnett, 'The Effect of the Development of Banking Facilities upon the Circulation of the Country', *Journal of the Institute of Bankers*, 2 (1881), p.79; Dunn, 'Banking in 1837 and in 1897', pp.374–5; Macdonald, 'The Economic Effects', p.37; E.W. Sykes, 'The Growth of London as the Financial Centre of the World, and the Best Means of Maintaining that Position', *Journal of the Institute of Bankers*, 23 (1902), p.365; Perry, 'The History of Companies' Legislation', pp.481–96; H.F.R. Miller, 'An Examination of the Bank Charter Act of 1844 with a View to Amendment', *Journal of the Institute of Bankers*, 40 (1919), pp.276–7.

[22] V. Markham Lester, *Victorian Insolvency: Bankruptcy, Imprisonment for Debt, and Company Winding-Up in Nineteenth-Century England* (Oxford: Clarendon Press, 1995), pp.242–3.

customers defaulted on their loans, withdrew their deposits or demanded repayment in coin rather than notes. Where risks in banking remained high, and the business involved complex negotiations, strong personal relations, and bespoke solutions, small privately owned banks long continued, as was the case in investment banking.[23] Even among joint-stock commercial banks the average number of branches per bank long remained low. In 1850 it ranged from six in England and Wales to twelve in Ireland and twenty-five in Scotland, where they had been longer established. Even by 1875 the average was still only eleven in England compared to thirty-four in Ireland and eighty-four in Scotland. The real transformation came between 1875 and the First World War. By 1913 the average number of branches was 157 in England, 156 in Scotland and seventy-nine in Ireland.[24] By 1897, F.E. Steele could reflect that, 'A banking system which consisted for the most part of a large number of comparatively small and unconnected institutions, each applying its limited resources to the service of a narrow area, may have answered very satisfactorily the requirements of previous generations, but the altered commercial conditions of the present day have both demanded a re-adjustment and rendered it inevitable.' The result of this readjustment was 'a banking system composed of a few homogenous institutions of world-wide reputation, conducted on a comparatively uniform system, efficiently and economically worked and rigidly inspected.' This new system was 'likely to prove at least as stable when the time of trial comes as the ruinous and heterogeneous mixture of banks, large and small, private and joint-stock, of good and indifferent repute, which served a previous generation, but, which, mainly as a result of the impact of amalgamation, is rapidly becoming extinct.'[25]

---

[23] P. Wardley, 'The Anatomy of Big Business: Aspects of Corporate Development in the Twentieth Century', *Business History*, 33 (1991), p.278; N. Ferguson, *The World's Banker: The History of the House of Rothschild* (London: Weidenfeld & Nicolson, 1998), p.808; A.D. Morrison and W.J. Wilhelm Jr, *Investment Banking: Institutions, Politics, and Law* (Oxford: OUP, 2007), pp.101, 158, 272; V.P. Carosso, *Investment Banking in America* (Cambridge, Mass.: Harvard UP, 1970), pp.86–7, 242, 273; Keane, 'The Setting of the Royal Exchange: Continuity and Change in the Financial District of the City of London, 1300–1871', in A. Saunders (ed.), *The Royal Exchange* (London: Guardian Royal Exchange, 1991), p.260.

[24] Munn, 'The Emergence of Joint-Stock Banking', pp.78–9; L. Newton, *Change and Continuity: the Development of Joint-Stock Banking in the Early Nineteenth Century* (Reading: Henley Business School, 2007), pp.27–52, 1–20; Newton, 'The Birth of Joint-Stock Banking', pp.27–52, Davies, *The Origins and Development of Cartelisation*, pp.13–26; Dawes and Ward-Perkins, *Country Banks of England and Wales*, pp.7, 33, 45; Wood, *History of Central Banking*, pp.61–7; Butson, 'The Banking System', in Willis and Beckhart (eds), *Foreign Banking Systems*, p.1242; M. Collins, *Money and Banking in the UK: A History* (London: Routledge, 1988), p. 52; Capie and Webber, *A Monetary History*, v.I, pp.432, 576–8; Williams Deacon's Bank,*Williams Deacon's, 1771–1970*, pp.140–9.

[25] F.E. Steele, 'Bank Amalgamations', *Journal of the Institute of Bankers* (1897), p.115, 123; See Dick, 'Banking Statistics'; Attfield, 'The Advantages'; Dunn, 'Banking in 1837 and in 1897'. See also R.W. Barnett, 'The History of the Progress and Development of Banking'; R.W. Barnett, 'The Effect of the Development of Banking Facilities upon the Circulation of the Country',

In the second half of the nineteenth century it became increasingly possible to manage a bank operating an extensive branch network when its business was confined to the relatively routine task of accepting deposits and making short-term loans. From the 1840s, rapid transport using the railway, and near instant communication by means of the telegraph, allowed the staff in head offices to control the activities of employees located in evermore distant branches. This meant that trust could be replaced by supervision and control, and so limit the ability of staff to take risks, for whatever reason, that might endanger the survival of the bank. The railways also provided an example of how a large business with an extensive footprint could be managed. The result was to tilt the balance away from the merits of local ownership and local engagement towards the benefits of a national organization.[26] One of the benefits of a national organization was that it was better able to meet the greater financial requirements of business, as these grew in size, again from the mid ninteenth century onwards. It was not only railways that became giant enterprises but so did other types of business such as in manufacturing.[27] The outcome was a merger movement that created a small number of dominant banking companies by the beginning of the twentieth century. These mergers peaked between 1888 and 1902 when 191 individual banks disappeared as a result of 117 mergers. This process of consolidation was driven from a number of directions though the outcome was always the creation of larger and larger commercial banks. Both the City and Westminster Bank and the National and Provincial Bank expanded nationwide from a London base. In contrast, both the Midland Bank and Lloyds originated in Birmingham and expanded nationally from there, including acquiring a number of London banks. Between 1865 and 1914, Lloyds took over some fifty banks. Finally, Barclays was the product of a friendly merger between closely connected private banks under increasing pressure from the joint-stock banks. Whatever the route, the result was consolidation, as can be seen from the share of deposits controlled by the five largest banks that emerged, Barclays, Lloyds, Midland, National Provincial, and Westminster. Their share grew from 15 per cent in 1870 in England and Wales (20 per cent UK) to 43 per cent (UK 35.5 per cent) in 1910. By 1913 there

Journal of the Institute of Bankers, 2 (1881); R.W. Barnett, 'The Reign of Queen Victoria: A Survey of Fifty Years of Progress', *Journal of the Institute of Bankers*, 6 (1887).

[26] D. Williams, 'Trading Links: Patterns of Information and Communication, the Steamship and the Modernization of East-West Commerce', in P.L. Cottrell, M. Pohle-Fraser, and I. L. Fraser (eds), *East Meets West: Banking, Commerce and Investment in the Ottoman Empire* (Aldershot: Ashgate, 2008); R.C. Michie, 'The City of London and the British Regions: From Medieval to Modern', in W. Lancaster, D. Newton, and N. Vall (eds), *An Agenda for Regional History* (Newcastle-upon-Tyne, Northumbria UP, 2007), pp.201–15; L. Hannah, 'The Twentieth Century Transformation', in Green, Pohle-Fraser, and Fraser (eds), *The Human Factor*, p.191.

[27] A.G. Kenwood and A.l. Lougheed, *Technological Diffusion and Industrialisation before 1914* (London: Croom Helm, 1982), pp.176–9, 187.

were only 104 commercial banks in Britain operating a network of 8,910 branches and holding over £1 billion in deposits. London-based banks controlled 4,716 branches and £0.7 billion in deposits, or 58 per cent of all branches and 64 per cent of all deposits. Of these the Midland Bank operated 846 branches, Lloyds 673, and Barclays 599.[28] The degree of change at the level of the individual bank can be seen in the case of Lloyds Bank. In 1865 Lloyds was a Birmingham-based bank operating from seven offices and handling the business of 2,041 customers. In 1914 it was a London-based bank operating from 879 offices and handled the business of 333,090 customers.[29]

To many this changed structure of the British banking system is a central explanation for the stability it exhibited from the late nineteenth century onwards, despite individual failures such as the City of Glasgow Bank in 1878. The suggestion is that a banking system consisting of a few large banks operating through numerous branches was more stable than one comprising numerous small banks.[30] Such a view is especially prevalent among those who contrast the British branch-banking structure with that of the contemporaneous unitary banking system in the USA, noting 'the inherent instability of financial institutions that could not diversify risk by pooling the risks of different regions or respond to difficulties by shifting resources across branches of an interconnected network.'[31] The great strength of the branch banking system was its size and diversification. Diversification made it resilient to localized difficulties and the problems of individual borrowers, while size allowed funds to be easily and quickly moved to where they were required, so providing a defence against a liquidity crisis that would destroy any single bank. Each branch could draw on a central pool of funds to meet sudden withdrawals or requests for credit.[32] However, the changes that took place in British banking, especially in the last quarter of the nineteenth century, involved much more than the replacement of a large number of individual units with single organizations operating through a branch network. The pre-existing correspondent network had long linked separate banks, facilitating both emergency assistance and the movement of funds into strong national networks.[33] The metamorphosis of a close network of

---

[28] F. Capie and G. Rodrik-Bali, 'Concentration in British Banking, 1870-1920', *Business History*, 24 (1982), p.281-91; Shepherd, *The Growth and Role of UK Financial Institutions*, Appendix A 1.1; Davies, *The Origins and Development of Cartelisation*, pp.26-31.
[29] Sayers, *Lloyds Bank*, p.108; Orbell and Turton, *British Banking*, pp.329, 373.
[30] Grossman, *Unsettled Account*, pp.3, 63, 72-6.
[31] Calomiris and Haber, *Fragile by Design*, p.201.
[32] Capie and Webber, *A Monetary History*, pp.130, 153, 432, 576-7; Collins, *Money and Banking*, p.55; P.W. Matthews and A.W. Tuke, *History of Barclays Bank Ltd* (London: Blades, East & Blades, 1926), p.1; R. Reed, *National Westminster Bank: A Short History* (London: National Westminster Bank, 1983), p.14; A.R. Holmes and E. Green, *Midland: 150 Years of Banking Business* (London: Batsford, 1986), pp.56, 100.
[33] P.L. Cottrell, 'Commercial Enterprise', in R. Church (ed.), *The Dynamics of Victorian Business: Problems and Perspectives to the 1870s* (London: Allen and Unwin, 1980), pp.239-41.

Quaker banks into the single organization called Barclays did not take place until 1896.[34] It was not until the 1890s that it became clear that the use of these correspondent links could no longer allow individual banks to compete against the power of an integrated branch network. It was in 1890 that the Manchester and Salford Bank, established in 1836, took over the London bank, Williams Deacon, which had acted as its correspondent from the very beginning, in order to gain the benefits of an integrated operation.[35]

Consequences of Scale

What this indicates is that a single banking organization could deliver benefits that were denied to a looser federation. In this, size alone was not the only element. Large joint-stock banks operating sizeable branch networks proved as vulnerable in a crisis as the smaller partnerships of the past.[36] Despite the reputation for stability that British banking acquired after 1866 there were continuing bank failures. These included banks of all types and sizes, covering partnerships and joint-stock companies, with and without branches, and operating throughout the UK and abroad. In Ireland these included the collapse of the Tipperary Bank in 1856, which probably prompted the Davenport Dunn novel, as well as the Munster Bank in 1885. In Scotland there was the failure of the Western Bank of Scotland in 1857 and the City of Glasgow Bank in 1878, both of which were large joint-stock banks with extensive branch networks. In England a great variety of banks failed. In the mid nineteenth century these ranged from such large joint-stock banks as the North of England Joint Stock Banking Company in 1848 and the Royal British Bank in 1856 to the long-established private bank of Strahan, Paul, and Bates in 1855. In the mid 1860s there was a rash of failures involving joint-stock banks such as the Leeds Banking Company, the Oriental Commercial Bank, The English Joint Stock Bank, Agra and Masterman's Bank, and Barned's Banking Company. Failures continued in the late nineteenth century and into the twentieth, including some sizeable banks. The Co-operative Credit Bank, which failed in 1876, had a network of sixty branches, the West of England and South Wales District Bank, which collapsed in 1878, had forty-two branches, while the Charing Cross Bank, which failed in 1910, had forty branches. In all of these cases there were specific reasons for failure. These included poor judgement by the management, thefts by owners and staff, or simply bad luck, with otherwise sound banks being overwhelmed by a liquidity crisis through association with a bank that had failed, or even with one that did

[34] Ackrill and Hannah, *Barclays*, pp.56–63.
[35] *Williams Deacon's, 1771–1970*, pp.96, 141–7.
[36] Cottrell, 'Commercial Enterprise', p.248.

Consolidation and Competence, 1825-1914   81

not. The English Bank of the River Plate collapsed in the wake of the Baring Crisis of 1890, as that centred on the problems experienced in Argentina.[37]

Many of these failures, however, were associated with the business model that these banks were employing, for a common cause was a lack of liquidity. This was especially the case with the numerous failures of building societies throughout this period. These societies provided mortgages secured on housing property and financed their lending through the collection of deposits from their members. In the event of members making sudden large withdrawals, these building societies were unable to meet the demand and so were forced to close even though they were, in many cases, solvent. One solution adopted by a number of the larger societies, like the Woolwich, was to make arrangement with banks and insurance companies to provide them with cash in a crisis, up to an agreed limit and in exchange for a fee. Those without such arrangements remained vulnerable to a liquidity crisis whether occasioned by genuine fears or ill-founded rumours.[38] What this suggests is that the stability of the British banking system, as a whole, after 1870 was related not only to size or even structure but the changes in the way that they did business.

The most noticeable change from the mid nineteenth century onwards was the declining use of bank notes by banks. Faced with yet another financial crisis, despite the legislative changes made in 1826 and 1833, the government took the opportunity in 1844, when renewing the Bank of England's charter, to limit the ability of banks to expand note issue in times of prosperity only to equally quickly contract it when economic conditions deteriorated. The effect had been a regular cycle of destabilizing speculative booms and busts. Though the effects of the Bank Charter Act on note circulation were not immediate they did lead to a long-term reduction. No new banks could be formed that had the right to issue notes while those that did have such privileges gradually lost them when merging or re-locating to London. Especially after 1844 it was the Bank of England alone, plus the Scottish and Irish banks, that were able to print money. The result was the gradual elimination of note issue other than by the Bank of England particularly after 1870.[39]

Banks in London had long operated without relying on the ability to issue their own notes. Instead, they had acted as the distribution arm of the Bank of England. They gave borrowers Bank of England notes in exchange for bills and

---

[37] Taylor, *Boardroom Scandal*, pp.47-9, 97, 103, 108-16, 122, 126, 136, 138-50, 169, 177-84, 187, 215, 223-31, 239, 241, 265; Hollow, *Rogue Banking*, p.23; Turner, *Banking in Crisis*, pp.50-1; D. Sunderland, *Financing the Raj: The City of London and Colonial India, 1858-1940* (Woodbridge: Boydell Press, 2013), p.134.

[38] B. Ritchie, *We're with the Woolwich*, pp. 17, 31, 39, 41, 57; Shepherd, *The Growth and Role of UK Financial Institutions*, p.14.

[39] D. Ziegler, *Central Bank, Peripheral Industry: The Bank of England in the Provinces, 1826-1913* (Leicester: Leicester UP, 1990), p.5, 7, 16, 38; Cameron, 'Banking and Industrialisation', pp.108-10.

then either held these bills until maturity, sold them to the Bank of England, or traded them on the inter-bank money market. Through their correspondent links they undertook the same business for banks outside London, but these banks could issue their own notes. However, this business model was disrupted in the wake of the legislation of 1826 and 1833. The Bank of England regarded the newly formed joint-stock banks as rivals in a way that had not been the case with the small banking partnerships that had existed in the past. As a result, it initially refused to buy bills from those located in London and those outside that issued notes. This forced these banks to find an alternative way of operating. The solution that had been devised in London was to make loans without the use of notes. Those customers who were made loans were allowed to draw on their account with the bank up to an agreed limit through issuing cheques when making payments. These cheques could then be paid into the bank. The problem with that arrangement was the small scale of banking as cheques would have to be cashed at the bank in which the issuer had an account. The solution, also devised in London, was to make cheques payable at any bank, using the Bankers' Clearing House to settle inter-bank debts. Through the correspondent network these facilities were extended nationwide. The effect was to give those banks that were members of the Clearing House an advantage over those that were not, as customers of those banks could use cheques to make and receive payments. For that reason the private banks long resisted granting the joint-stock banks membership of the Clearing House. They did not achieve that until as late as 1854. With membership of the Clearing House, the joint-stock banks could compete more effectively against those banks that still had the right to issue notes, as payments were made and received through the use of cheques that were accepted by any bank. A bank with the privilege of issuing its own notes was able to operate on the basis of lower reserves of coin and Bank of England notes, in the expectation that most customers would be content to use those they provided. To be competitive those banks without such privileges had to devise an alternative way of operating and this is what they did, especially after 1854. No longer was banking being conducted as in the past on the basis of note circulation.[40]

The other major change was the gradual elimination of the bill of exchange when making a loan. This did not mean that bills were no longer generated, as they continued to have a use in particular transactions, but increasingly banks made loans to customers based on either collateral or personal guarantee. Again, the demise of the bill of exchange was sparked by the initial refusal of the Bank of England to buy those issued by the joint-stock banks because of the threat they posed to its business. In the face of this refusal the joint-stock banks searched for an alternative method of doing business. The solution was

[40] Clapham, *The Bank of England*, v.1, pp.170, 351.

found through scale, which the Bank had already demonstrated itself in the eighteenth century, when it made loans to its largest customers without the use of bills. If a bank could attract deposits from savers and match these with the borrowing requirements of its customers then there would be no need to discount bills. Instead, the borrower could be charged interest on the loan, which could then be monitored by the bank and adjusted to meet changing conditions. This was the Lend and Hold Model. However, banks had to attract deposits if they were going to apply such a model and this the joint-stock banks proceeded to do from the 1830s onwards by offering attractive rates of interest to savers. However, attractive rates of interest were not sufficient unless the joint-stock banks could also offer depositors security that their savings would not be lost. The Bank of England had long been able to offer that security and so attracted savings while paying little or no interest on its deposits. It took decades before the emerging joint-stock banks could command the trust of the public so as to attract the deposits of savers. As a result it was some time before these new banking practices became standard. When they did, all benefited. Those with savings earned a higher rate of return than the private banks had been willing to provide while their deposits were increasingly perceived as safer. At the same time borrowers were provided with more flexible arrangements at, often, lower rates of interest compared to the use of bills of exchange and the discount that was included when issued. Both these developments were coming together by the 1870s and then accelerated in the following decades.

The effect of all these changes was to provide banks with an incentive to become larger and larger, which was reflected in the acceleration in the mergers between banks towards the end of the 19th century. The Originate and Distribute Model served a unitary banking system well as it made it possible to expand the amount of business done by a small bank as it acted as the intermediary between the borrower and the lender through the medium of notes and bills. In contrast, the Lend and Hold Model required a bank to reach a sufficient scale so that it could match the borrower and lender internally, and so dispense with both notes and bills. The changeover can be seen from the balance sheets of those banks that separated out loans made via bills and those by way of overdrafts and advances. In 1830 the Leicestershire Banking Company operated on the basis of £14,000 in capital and reserves and £27,000 in deposits. With those funds it had lent £13,000 to customers, putting an equivalent of notes in circulation, but had accepted £34,000 in bills. In contrast, in 1890 its capital and reserves totalled £564,000 and it had another £1,953,000 in deposits while the circulation of its own notes was only £39,000. Loans now stood at £1,483,000 compared to £449,000 in bills. A similar pattern can be observed from the balance sheets of the Midland Bank, which became one of the largest in the world by 1914. In 1850 the Midland had £138,000 in capital and reserves plus £112,000 in deposits but only £34,000 had been lent directly to customers compared to £239,000 in bills. By 1880 the position had already altered dramatically with the £510,000 in capital and reserves being dwarfed by £2,015,000 in deposits while the £619,000 in bills was now half the £1,329,000 in loans. What this shows is the importance of scale in the operation of the Lend and Hold model. Deposits then continued to grow over the next thirty years, reaching £73,415,000 by 1910, compared to the rise in capital and reserves to £7,579,000. Bills remained significant, standing at £6,686,000 but were now dwarfed by loans of £41,088,000.[41] By then, most of the bills held by the Midland Bank were generated by international trade or its role as London correspondent for banks from around the world, rather than being the product of domestic lending.[42]

As bills have often been grouped with loans and advances when analysing a bank's assets, this transformation of banking from an Originate and Distribute Model to a Lend and Hold Model over the course of the nineteenth century has tended to be ignored. Nevertheless, what collective evidence there is supports that from the Leicestershire and Midland banks. It indicates a substantial decline in the use of bills from the 1860s onwards, especially for the large London-based banks. In particular, the use of the bill of exchange for domestic lending peaked in 1873 and then entered a period of continuous decline. The change can be traced between 1880 and 1914 through the researches of Collins and May. What can be noted first is the rise in the size of the average loan, which grew from £2,680 in 1880/4 to £19,816 in 1910/14, reflecting the ability of ever larger banks to service the needs of businesses that were, themselves, ever larger. Also notable was that an increasing proportion of loans were made based on no more than the personal guarantee of the borrower. In 1880/4 64.6 per cent of loans were made to those providing collateral whereas in 1910/14 the figure was only 27.3 per cent. By then the Lend and Hold Model was deeply ingrained in British banking practice.[43]

Related to the operation of the Lend and Hold Model was the need for trained and experienced staff to assess potential borrowers and then monitor the account of those provided with funds in such a way as to anticipate any failure to repay. The larger the banks became, the more they were able to recruit such staff, train them in the ways of banking and then supervise their

---

[41] Crick and Wadsworth, *A Hundred Years*, pp.35, 42, 82, 269, 275, 326, 336-7, 347; Sayers, *Lloyds Bank*, pp.108, 161-5, 234; Ackrill and Hannah, *Barclays*, pp.90, 139.

[42] For the international role played by the City of London before 1914 see R.C. Michie, 'The City of London and International Banking in the Nineteenth and Twentieth Centuries: The Asian Dimension', in S. Nishimura, T. Suzuki, and R. Michie (eds), *The Origins of International Banking in Asia: The Nineteenth and Twentieth Centuries* (Oxford: OUP, 2012), pp.13-54.

[43] M. Collins and M. Baker, *Commercial Banking and Industrial Finance in England and Wales, 1860-1913* (Oxford: OUP, 2003), pp.74-5, 125, 181-95; Shepherd, *The Growth and Role of UK Financial Institutions*, pp.111-17; Capie and Woods, *Money over Two Centuries*, pp.3, 49-50, 64-5, 105-6, 116, 329-32; Cottrell, 'London's First "Big Bang"'?, pp.65-81; R.A. Church, *The Great Victorian Boom, 1850-1873* (London: Macmillan, 1975), p.54.

behaviour. By 1914 the Midland Bank employed 5,000 people and the London County and Westminster over 3,000. These staff were distributed between the head office in London and the numerous branches and so had opportunities for both mobility and progression that kept them loyal to the bank. Following on from an apprenticeship, employees moved within the bank as their careers developed, rising from a position as a clerk through a role as accountant and then inspector and/or branch manager ending, finally, for some in a management position with a larger branch or heading a section within the London head office. There was also a career track within the head office involving greater specialization such as in the handling of securities and investments. As the banks grew as businesses, these career opportunities expanded and promotion became quicker and easier to achieve, though progress was counted in terms of decades rather than years. It was no coincidence that the establishment of Institutes of Bankers coincided with the development of these large joint-stock banks. An institute was formed in Scotland in 1875 and in England in 1879, and they supplemented the practical training of bankers by providing written instruction and examinations. No longer was banking a career to be followed by the sons of bankers who learnt their trade by working in the family bank. It was now a desirable profession with a defined career path that offered opportunities at home and abroad for those who were clever, and willing to study and work hard.[44]

Contributing to the growing professionalism of banking in the late nineteenth century was the external scrutiny to which banks and their staff became subjected. In the wake of the City of Glasgow Bank collapse in 1878, legislation had been passed permitting joint-stock banks to acquire limited liability, so protecting their shareholders from responsibility from unlimited losses. This was quickly taken up by the joint-stock banks who chose to appoint chartered accountants to undertake the annual audits in the expectation that such a move would enhance the degree of trust placed in them not only by shareholders but also depositors. By 1884, sixty-nine banks had taken advantage of this dispensation, with the most prominent London ones making use of an elite group of chartered accountants located in the City, while those based elsewhere relied on local firms. The strategy was a successful one with joint-stock banks increasingly gaining the public's trust in comparison to the private banks.[45] However, there was a fundamental change after 1890. By

---

[44] Dunn, 'Banking in 1837 and in 1897', p.376; L. Hannah, 'The Twentieth Century Transformation', in Green, Pohle-Fraser, and Fraser (eds), *The Human Factor*, pp.190-6; C.W. Munn, 'The Development of Joint-Stock Banking in Scotland, 1810-1845', in A. Slaven and D.H. Aldcroft (eds), *Business, Banking and Urban History* (Edinburgh: John Donald, 1982), p.121; *Williams Deacon's, 1771-1970*, p.93; M. Heller, *London Clerical Workers, 1880-1914: Development of the Labour Market* (London: Pickering and Chatto, 2011), pp.33, 100-1, 118, 162, 173, 248.

[45] D. Matthews, *A History of Auditing: The Changing Audit Process in Britain from the Nineteenth Century to the Present Day* (London: Routledge, 2006), pp.6-15, 23, 60-9, 85;

1891 not only did all joint-stock banks in England publish accounts but so did nearly half of private banks. What forced the change was the near collapse of Barings Bank in 1890. As a private partnership, Barings had no reason to either publish a balance sheet or employ professional auditors. What its near collapse revealed was the degree to which those outside the bank were ignorant of the true state of affairs, making all realize that the same judgement could be passed on all banks that did not publish their accounts and employ professional accountants, who had slowly gained a reputation for impartiality and accuracy when auditing the accounts of railways and other utilities. The result was to force all banks to do so, which made it easier to both arrange mergers and takeovers as there was now an accurate estimate of the value of each business.[46] As Dunn noted in 1898, 'a large bank, conducted on the principle of limited liability, with vast resources, issuing audited balance sheets and subjected to a rigorous system of inspection, inspires confidence and support.'[47]

The impact made by the Baring Crisis on the private banks can be gauged from what took place among those that came together to form Barclays Bank. In the wake of the Baring Crisis of 1890, customers of private banks became concerned about the safety of the money they had deposited. Barings itself did not accept deposits from the public because its focus was on the finance of international trade, through guaranteeing payment on the bills of exchange issued by merchants and others, and issuing stocks and bonds on behalf of governments and companies. Nevertheless, the sudden exposure of its problems did spread alarm as, like all banks, it traded on its 'good name' in order to gain the trust of its customers. Even before 1890 a number of private banks had seen that trust in their 'good name' could be enhanced if they employed a firm of professional accountants to audit their accounts and draw up the annual balance sheet. One such was the long-established bank of Bassett, Son and Harris of Leighton Buzzard. They had commissioned Price

R.L. Watts and J.L. Zimmerman, 'Agency Problems, Auditing, and the Theory of the Firm: Some Evidence', *Journal of Law and Economics*, 36 (1983), pp.613–33; D. Edwards, M. Edwards, and D. Matthews, 'Accountability in a Free-Market Economy: The British Company Audit, 1886', *Abacus*, 33 (1997), pp.1–25; Anderson, Edwards, and Matthews, 'A Study of the Quoted Company Audit Market', pp.363–87; R.H. Parker, 'Regulating British Corporate Financial Reporting in the Late Nineteenth Century', *Accounting, Business and Financial History* 1 (1990), pp.52–67; T.A. Lee and R.H. Parker (ed.), *The Evolution of Corporate Financial Reporting* (Sunbury-on-Thames: Thomas Nelson, 1979), pp.18, 153–7, 197–9.

[46] J. Dick, 'Banking Statistics', p.293; Steele, 'Bank Amalgamations', p.116; Macdonald, 'The Economic Effects', p.374; J.M. Henderson, 'The Joint-Stock Companies Acts, 1862–1900, in Relation to Banking', *Journal of the Institute of Bankers* (1906), pp.63–4; Perry, 'The History of Companies' Legislation', *Journal of the Institute of Bankers*, 29 (1908), pp.494–6; F. Shewell Cooper, 'Company Law in Relation to Bankers', *Journal of the Institute of Bankers* (1921), p.92; R.W. Jones, 'Statutory Requirements Relating to the Balance Sheets of Limited Companies', *Journal of the Institute of Bankers* (1930), p.493.

[47] Dunn, 'Banking in 1837 and in 1897', *Journal of the Institute of Bankers*, 18 (1898), p.380.

Waterhouse to draw up a balance sheet in 1889. All that Price Waterhouse did was to check the accuracy of the accounts drawn up within the bank itself, as they noted at the bottom of the balance sheet. 'We have compared the above account with the Books of the Bank at the Head Office, and the Returns from the Branches, and have examined the Securities representing the Investments of the Bank, and certify that the above Account correctly sets forth the position of the Bank on the 20th June 1889.' This use of Price Waterhouse, and the publication of the audited accounts, was seen by the partners in private banks as one means of reassuring the public about the safety of the money deposited with them as well as the unlimited liability of the partners for any losses.[48]

In the wake of the Baring Crisis, which suggested that unlimited liability was insufficient to cover losses, the use of external auditors was thus an obvious and additional device that private banks could employ to reassure the public, and many rushed to do so. One such bank that took this course of action was Barclays. Customers were sent copies of the audited balance sheet for 1891 in the hope that it would reassure them that the bank was sound. A number replied indicating that such action was not required.[49] As A. K. Hitchens, of Hitchens, Harrison, and Company, City stockbrokers, observed, 'I am sure you have done the right thing in publishing the account and I want heartily (to) congratulate you on having such a strong statement and such satisfactory figures to show—of course this publication don't do much more than satisfy a more or less idle curiosity, but nowadays it don't pay to go against the stream and it is fortunate which one can go with it in such an entirely satisfactory manner.'[50] Much more revealing about the current mood of the time, was the reply from a fellow private banker, R. G. Hoare, writing from Newcastle, on the value to be attached to the balance sheet that Barclays had circulated:

> It is an additional evidence of the strength of your old private banks and how clear they are from the slightest blame of keeping too small reserves. I had heard that you were about to publish so I was not surprised, in fact so many have done it now that each additional one makes it more likely that others should follow. We are quite ready to do so if our neighbours do it, but at present I believe they are equally strong with ourselves against it, though I am afraid the appearance of your balance sheet may shake them. If ones' customers asked for a balance sheet I am quite willing to allow they have a right to be shown it, but we have never received the slightest hint of any such desire and I believe the rage for publicity is not fostered by the general public but only by the press. If legislation were imminent I then think it would be wise to forestall it but I don't at all believe

---

[48] Barclays Bank Archive: Balance Sheets of Bassett, Son and Harris 29 June 1889, 30 June 1891, 30 June 1893.
[49] George Forrester (Norwich) 27 July 1891; E. Backhouse 27 July 1891; George Main, Carlisle 16 July 1891.
[50] A.K. Hitchens, 25 July 1891.

that is so. One thing is shown by what has appeared is that private banks have allowed joint stocks to push them out of the field. This I believe has arisen from the lethargy of so many private bankers who are very wealthy and have driven away business because they did not care to be troubled with any investments inferior to balance sheet investments, and have been ruled by hard and fast lines, old fashioned, quite incapable of adaptation to present circumstances. I know this to be very markedly the case in some mutual friends of ours in this district. Publicity won't bring business back to them. In fact I confess I do not see what is to be gained by publishing. I can't help thinking that the strength of private banking is in the position, character and business qualities of the partners rather than in their wealth though, of course this latter is an element that must not be ignored. From all this if you have waded through it you will see that I at any rate want to say that you have yielded to the newspaper cry and I do not believe the real form of business will be any better or grow any bigger by publishing.[51]

However, it was the views of Hoare that reflected the past and the publication of externally audited accounts increasingly became standard practice for private banks in the 1890s. In 1892 the Bursar of Brasenose College, Oxford, wrote to their London bankers, Cocks, Biddulph and Co., to indicate that 'The college will learn with satisfaction that you are considering the question of issuing an annual balance sheet, as is now done by many of the leading Private Banks.'[52] Faced with a media demanding action from the private banks, they had little option but to emulate the well-established practice of the joint-stock banks. In competing for the deposits of savers the employment of professional auditors provided a degree of reassurance that the bank was sound without the need for some kind of statutory insurance scheme. In doing so it avoided the moral hazard that came with a universal guarantee that made no distinction between a conservatively run bank with large reserves and a risk-taking institution with none. With the external auditing of bank accounts by members of the Institute of Chartered Accountants, whether covering England, Wales, or Scotland, even a private bank quickly acquired the confidence of the public. Nevertheless, that was insufficient to allow private banks to compete with their joint-stock brethren when it came to the routine business of commercial banking. By the 1890s it was scale, not audits or unlimited liability, that determined who the public trusted to handle their banking, and the joint-stock banks possessed that.

---

[51] R.G. Hoare, 25 July 1891.
[52] Bursar, Brasenose College, to Cocks, Biddulph and Co., 1 March 1892.

CONCLUSION

What happened to the British banking system between 1826 and 1914 is that it learnt how to cope with crises and to meet the needs of an urban/industrial economy operating in a global economy with almost no barriers to the free movement of goods, services, capital, and people. The banking system achieved this position not as a result of direction from government but through a process or trial and error over an extended period of time. Crucial to this transformation was the structural change that banking underwent, though this was confined to the field of commercial banking. What emerged over the century, but especially in the fifty years before the First World War, were a small number of very large banks directed from head offices in the City of London but managing an extensive branch network covering England and Wales. These banks possessed the resilience to cope with both liquidity and solvency crises as they could move funds to wherever they were required and cover losses in one branch of the business from profits made in another. However, it was not structure alone that contributed to the resilience of these banks, for the scale of operations they achieved changed the way that they did business. Instead of holding to the Originate and Distribute Model perfected in the eighteenth century, these ever-larger banks adopted the Lend and Hold Model. In that model they dispensed with a reliance on bank notes and bills and, instead, sought to match the savings of depositors with the loans made to borrowers, generating their profits from the interest-rate differential between what they paid and charged. It took many years before this Lend and Hold Model was standard practice but it had become so by the late nineteenth century, helping to drive the amalgamation movement that produced a few giant banks over the period from 1870 to 1914. A vital ingredient in the Lend and Hold Model were staff who knew what its requirements were and how to manage it. The very scale that these banks achieved allowed them to cultivate and train such people. Consolidation led to competence and competence encouraged greater consolidation as it was the largest banks that commanded the trust of the public and so drew in their custom, whether it was to make deposits, borrow money, or use the payments system they provided through the use of cheques and inter-bank clearing.

4

Choice and Connections, 1825–1914

INTRODUCTION

Despite the success achieved by British banking in the years between 1866 and 1914 it did generate a degree of criticism at the time. Some traced back to the banking system that emerged before the First World War, the subsequent problems experienced by the British economy. Central to these criticisms was the emergence of a small number of very large banks in the late nineteenth century, and their dominant position within the British financial system. To Davies, these constituted an oligopoly possessed of sufficient power to stifle competitive behaviour.[1] These banks were portrayed, variously, as being centralized businesses increasingly remote from the needs of their customers; huge bureaucratic organizations that fostered an overly conservative culture among their staff; so large that they encouraged reckless risk-taking by their employees secure in the knowledge that they could not fail; or so central to the financial system that no government could allow them to collapse regardless of their performance. More generally, these banks ranked high among the explanations for the decline of the British economy from a position of industrial supremacy in the mid nineteenth century to that of a minor player by the end of the twentieth.[2] Throughout these criticisms there is a fundamental contradiction. On the one hand, the emergence of these dominant banks made the British banking system ultra risk-averse while, on the other hand, it made it ultra risk-orientated. This contradiction exists in the work of Rondo Cameron. He had been impressed by the superiority of the Scottish banking system before 1850 because its 'combination of a relatively small number of substantial banks, each with a large number of branches, provided the benefits of competition without the constant threat of bankruptcy.'

---

[1] Davies, *The Origins and Development of Cartelisation*, pp.26–31.
[2] For a flavour of the criticisms see G. Ingham, *Capitalism Divided? The City and Industry in British Social Development* (London: Macmillan, 1984), pp.153, 169; W.P. Kennedy, *Industrial Structure, Capital Markets and the Origins of British Economic Decline* (Cambridge: CUP, 1987), pp.56, 79, 110, 120, 139–41, 148–9.

In contrast, when the UK possessed the same system after 1870, he concluded that it was overly conservative in prioritizing stability over risk-taking. The difference in judgement was attributed to the centralization of control in London, though that did not apply to Scotland, which retained an independent banking system.[3] It is this centralization of the control of the large banks in London that was the theme of Carnevali's criticism of the British banking system, centering on its failure to meet the financial needs of smaller businesses.[4]

The crisis of 2007/8 has forced a radical re-appraisal of some of the earlier criticisms, because many have traced its causes to excessive risk-taking by the large British banks. This has necessitated a search for what might have changed over the last 150 years. Hence Turner's argument that the explanation for the ultra-conservative behaviour lay in the constraints imposed on risk-taking by the exposure of the owners to unlimited liability and then contingent liability in the event of losses. That era, which lasted until the end of the 1930s, was followed by the imposition of external controls, which also prevented banks from pursuing their natural inclination towards taking risks. When these controls were removed from the 1980s onwards so also was the restraint on risk-taking. Risk-taking was further encouraged by the belief of those working for these large banks that they had become too big to fail. Any losses arising from their mistakes would be borne by tax payers while the benefits would accrue to themselves. However, that thesis does not fit the evidence. The banks most engaged in risk-taking were the merchant banks, and these were partnerships and so exposed to unlimited liability. In contrast, it was the joint-stock commercial banks, some possessing limited liability dating from 1694 (Bank of England) and 1695 (Bank of Scotland), which were among the more conservative, and that was the accusation levelled against the large banks that emerged in the late nineteenth century. Neither does there appear to be a direct connection between those running a bank and those owning it, once the transition was made from a partnership to a joint-stock company. With the average number of shareholders in one of the five largest banks in 1900 having reached 8,365, doubling to 17,102 in 1910 and tripling to 53,305 by 1921, the possibility that they could directly influence the actions of the management was remote. These banks faced the same dilemma as in any large joint-stock company in which the interests of the owners were at variance with those of the individual employee and ways had to be devised so as to create an effective compromise.[5]

---

[3] Cameron, 'Banking and Industrialisation', pp.106-9.
[4] Carnevali, *Europe's Advantage*, pp.1, 9-16, 197.
[5] Turner, *Banking in Crisis*, pp.6-10, 45, 204-7; Turner, 'Holding Shareholders to Account', in Dimsdale and Hotson (eds), *British Financial Crises*, pp.139-55.

One reason for the inherent contradiction in the criticisms made of the British banking system in the pre-1914 era and subsequently, is the tendency to generalize from a study of only one component. The performance of the large joint-stock banks has long been used as a proxy for the entire banking system. Added to that has been the attention paid to the merchant banks located in the City of London. However, the British banking system was both large and diversified. This reflected the advanced state of the British economy and the position of the City as a leading international financial centre. It was a magnet for banks from throughout the world while it continually spawned the creation of specialist banks.[6] Each of these different types of banks have usually been regarded as occupying their own distinct niche within the financial system, with this functional specialization being used as part of the explanation for the stability of the system as a whole. In particular, it meant that the large commercial banks avoided the risks associated with property finance, in which loans to purchase houses were funded through short-term deposits.[7] However, this focus on single components of the banking system ignores both the strong relationships that existed between them and the continually shifting boundaries in the business that each had done. Banks were competitive businesses and so were continually exploring new avenues that could generate profits. This meant that they invaded the territory of rivals if to do so appeared to present profitable opportunities. Conversely, banks also developed specialities that attracted other banks as customers. Building societies, for example, competed with commercial banks for business but looked to and received assistance from them in a liquidity crisis, precisely because of the illiquid nature of the assets that they held.[8] Without knowing the choice available to those seeking to make use of the services provided by banks, and the connections that existed between banks, it is impossible to reach a judgement about the performance of the entire system.

The need to facilitate payments was only one of the reasons that banks needed to maintain close connections with each other. Regardless of the size of even the largest bank, the variety of business that each was engaged in meant that they could easily find themselves with an excess of funds or facing a temporary deficit, depending upon whether their customers were withdrawing savings and borrowing money or making deposits and repaying loans. As banking was a competitive business, no bank could refuse a withdrawal, a deposit, a loan, or a repayment from a valued customer, regardless of their current state of funds. The solution was to lend to another bank what they had

---

[6] R.C. Michie, 'The Emergence and Survival of a Financial Cluster in Britain', in *Learning from Some of Britain's Successful Sectors: An Historical Analysis of the Role of Government*, BIS Economics Paper 6 (2010), pp.89–111.

[7] Offer, 'Narrow Banking', in Dimsdale and Hotson (eds), *British Financial Crises*, p.158.

[8] Hollow, *Rogue Banking*, p.63; B. Ritchie, *We're with the Woolwich*, pp.39–41, 57, 86.

in excess at any one time and borrow what they needed at another. The London money market provided a means of doing that. As Warren observed in 1903, 'this stream of credit flows to London, and as demand throughout the country is not sufficiently strong to attract it all back again, a large fund of loanable capital accumulates in the hands of the London banks, and flows from there to the bill brokers, who employ it in discounting bills of exchange.'[9] In London it was possible to employ funds remuneratively for very short periods of time, so ensuring the liquidity that banks operating the Lend and Hold Model required, while generating the returns their shareholders demanded.[10] As Crump observed in 1877, 'The advantages the community enjoy through the agency of banks is that they collect money from those who do not want it and lend it to those who do, to the profit of all.'[11] Simple as the basics of banking were, it only worked if those who lent money to the banks, whether individuals, businesses or other banks, could withdraw it when they wanted. For that reason banks had to be ready at all times to meet such withdrawals, and the ability to lend to and borrow from each other provided them with a means of doing so, without the necessity of each bank maintaining large cash reserves that would, normally, never be required and so would remain idle.

COMPETITION

Although the level of concentration within British commercial banking grew over the course of the nineteenth century, competition intensified. In particular, the formation of new joint stock-banks challenged the business being done by the established partnerships, forcing them to pay interest on deposits and offer more generous terms to borrowers. The degree of competition was particularly marked in the formative years of joint-stock banking between the 1830s and the crisis of 1866. Even with the steep fall in the number of commercial banks after 1870, evidence suggests that the level of competition between them either remained the same or even grew, despite contemporary comment that the reverse would happen. Before the transformation of communications and transport in the mid nineteenth century, competition between commercial banks had been limited. Each bank served a particular geographic area bounded by the distance between it and the customers it served. Even in London there was a distinction between those banks that

---

[9] H. Warren, *The Story of the Bank of England* (London: [n.p.], 1903), p.135.
[10] Holmes and Green, *Midland*, p.81.
[11] A. Crump, *The Key to the London Money Market*, 6th ed. (London: Longmans Green, 1877), p.11.

served the wealthy residents of the West End and those that met the business needs of those to the East, in the City. Banks also served different types of customers ranging across class, ethnicity, and business interests. With the revolution in transport and communications from the 1840s onwards, the ability of banks to compete with each other grew, as the barriers imposed by distance were lowered and eventually disappeared. The last relic of those barriers was the continued existence of separate banking systems in Scotland and Ireland.[12]

Also driving competition was the increased reliance placed on the Lend and Hold Model as the mainstay of the business done by the large joint-stock banks. Such banks were professionally managed and answerable to shareholders, forcing them to generate profits sufficient to meet not only costs, including salaries, but also pay the dividends that investors expected. As Fraser told the Institute of Bankers in 1907, 'The small banks dotted about England in isolated detachment, with no cohesion, confined in space and operations, are replaced by the branches of a homogenous whole, with centralized control of directors and managers, who place all deliberations on a purely business footing.'[13] The Lend and Hold Model required the managers and staff of each bank to maintain close links to their customers, constantly monitoring behaviour, and making fine judgements about whether or not to grant a loan and the terms and conditions to apply. On that judgement rested the loyalty of the customer or their decision to move their account to a rival, and was vital to the success of the bank.[14] The most profitable part of a commercial bank's business was the loans it made directly to its customers because this involved a higher degree of risk than investing in bills and securities. Whereas bills and securities could be easily sold, if a liquidity crisis arose, the money lent on no more than a personal guarantee was neither quickly recoverable nor supported with collateral if the borrower defaulted.[15] Over the period 1870–1914 losses

---

[12] Dunn, 'Banking in 1837 and in 1897', pp.376–80; Macdonald, 'The Economic Effects', pp.371–5; Munn, 'The Development of Joint-Stock Banking in Scotland', pp.118–21; Capie and Woods, *Money over Two Centuries*, pp.3, 49–50; Dimsdale and Hotson, 'Financial Crises and Economic Activity in the UK since 1825', in Dimsdale and Hotson (eds), *British Financial Crises*, pp.38–9; Ackrill and Hannah, *Barclays*, p.66; Shepherd, *The Growth and Role of UK Financial Institutions*, Appendix A 1.1.

[13] D. Fraser, 'A Decade of Bank Amalgamations, 1897–1906', *Journal of the Institute of Bankers*, 29 (1907), p.35.

[14] Dick, 'Banking Statistics', pp.187–215; D.D. Fraser, 'Some Modern Phases of British Banking, 1896–1911', *Journal of the Institute of Bankers*, 34 (1913), pp.96–8. For some well-researched examples of the relations between banks and their customers see K. Watson, 'Banks and Industrial Finance: The Experience of Brewers, 1880–1913', *Economic History Review*, 49 (1996); F. Capie and M. Collins, *Have the Banks Failed British Industry? An Historical Survey of Bank/Industry Relations in Britain, 1870–1990* (London: Frank Cass, 1992).

[15] Dick, 'Banking Statistics', pp.187–215; Fraser, 'Some Modern Phases', pp.96–8; *Williams Deacon's, 1771–1970*, p.165. For a forensic investigation of surviving commercial-bank balance sheets from the 1860–1913 period see Collins and Baker, *Commercial Banking*.

from bankruptcy varied from a high of £12.5 million in 1884 to a low of £2.4 million in 1872 but generally ran at about £4–5 million per annum. Lending to small firms, especially in retailing and manufacturing, was a highly risky business as in the event of business failure few assets remained to repay creditors, including banks.[16]

Although the bankers' preference was for loans of short-term duration, measured in months not years, to retain customers banks were forced to make longer-term loans. An estimated 13 per cent of loans made to industrial firms, for example, were for over three years. Banks got to know the requirements of their business customers through a careful monitoring of the individual accounts, which allowed them to make accurate assessments of their needs and the risks involved. With losses on loans before 1914 running at a mere 0.2 per cent of the amount lent, banks appear to have trained their staff well to balance risk and return. Over time, bankers learnt that they could safely lend around 60 per cent of their available funds directly to customers, while keeping the rest in short-term loans or investments in readily realizable assets such as bills and securities. In this way a bank was able to provide the finance that borrowers required while being in a position to meet any withdrawal or request for credit.[17] Drummond Fraser's detailed examination of the collective balance sheets of British joint-stock banks for 1911/14, (replicated at Table 4.1.) reveals that on the assets side of the balance sheet they maintained

Table 4.1. Joint-Stock Banks: Assets and Liabilities, 1911/14

	1911/14
Deposits	£483 m.
Cash	£74 m.
Money at Call	£61 m.
Investments	£70 m.
Bills + Advances	£320 m.
Cash as % of Deposits	15.3%
Money at call as % of Deposits	12.6%
Investments as % of Deposits	14.5%
Bills + Advances as % of Deposits	66.3%
Cash + Money at Call + Investments as % of Deposits	42.4%

Source: The data for 1911/14 is taken from the tables in Sir D. Drummond Fraser, 'British Home Banking'.

[16] Markham Lester, *Victorian Insolvency*, pp.216–18, 267, 271, 279, 314.
[17] Collins and Baker, *Commercial Banking*, pp.74–5, 125; E. Nevin and E.W. Davies, *The London Clearing Banks* (London: Elek, 1970), p.136; P. Ollerenshaw, *Banking in Nineteenth-Century Ireland: The Belfast Banks, 1825–1914* (Manchester: Manchester UP, 1987), pp.81–94, 185; Holmes and Green, *Midland*, p.81; Sayers, *Lloyds Bank*, p.312; C.W. Munn, 'The Emergence of Central Banking in Ireland', *Irish Economic and Social History*, 10, 1983, p.28.

three levels of defence against a liquidity crisis. The first was cash that amounted to 15.3 per cent of deposits and was there to meet the everyday needs of the bank, such as withdrawals by customers. With rapid communications and fast transport it was not considered necessary to keep a higher ratio because any exceptional needs in one location could be met by re-distributing cash around the network, as directed from the head office. The next line of defence was money at call, which came to 12.6 per cent of deposits. This money was lent out at short notice in the London money market and so could quickly be accessed if a need arose, such as sudden demand from customers for additional finance or in the event of a crisis. Finally, there were investments in marketable securities such as the UK National Debt and selected bonds issued by other governments and large corporations. These amounted to another 14.5 per cent of deposits. This meant that the joint-stock banks could call on the equivalent of 42.4 per cent of deposits before reaching the largely illiquid part of their assets, which included the loans made to their customers by way of advances or bills.

This lending was largely financed out of deposits, which could be quickly withdrawn, rather than capital and reserves, which were permanent. The ratio of capital to assets fell from around 40 to 50 per cent in the mid nineteenth century to 10 per cent by the First World War.[18] As a result the need for liquidity was well understood by those who managed these banks, and was placed at the forefront of the decisions they made. Steele told his fellow bankers in 1897, 'It is beyond doubt that the fall of one of our huge modern banks would be infinitely more disastrous than the failure of a small bank here and there under the old regime but there are reasons that such disasters are more remote than ever... a banking system composed of a few homogenous institutions of world-wide reputation, conducted on a comparatively uniform system, efficiently and economically worked and rigidly inspected, is likely to prove at least as stable when the time of trial comes as the ruinous and heterogeneous mixture of banks, large and small, private and joint-stock, of good and indifferent repute, which served a previous generation, but, which, mainly as a result of the impact of amalgamation, is rapidly becoming extinct.' This sentiment was echoed by Sykes in 1902. 'Most bankers nowadays realize the danger of locking up large sums in advances to single individuals or firms. The class of business which is now most sought after is that of loans for short periods of security which is easily and promptly realizable. The practice of advancing money on unmarketable security is equally foolish with that of locking it up for a long period of time. The essential qualification for a banker's

---

[18] For a detailed examination of bank lending in this period see Collins and Baker, *Commercial Banking*.

security is not ultimate safety, but immediate convertibility, and this fact is now accepted in theory, if not in practice, by our chief bankers.'[19]

The successful operation of the Lend and Hold Model required a bank to get close to its customers so as to understand their collective behaviour, whether it involved the likelihood of withdrawing their deposits or the possibility that they would be unable to repay their loans. That had been achieved in the past through limiting a bank's business to customers in its immediate vicinity or connected through family, religion, or other close ties. However, these conditions no longer applied in the integrated urban/industrial economy that Britain became over the course of the nineteenth century. The solution adopted by the joint-stock banks was to open more and more branches and offices as that put the bank in direct contact with potential savers or borrowers. Through locating a branch or an office in the midst of a community, a bank was better placed to compete with a rival, without taking undue risks. The manager and staff employed had not only been trained by the bank in its way of doing business, and remained answerable to head office, but they also became part of the community in which they were located.[20] As the number of commercial banks in England and Wales fell, the number of offices from which they did business expanded. Between 1883 and 1911 the number of commercial banks was estimated to have fallen from 327 to 55 whereas the number of bank offices more than doubled from 2,382 to 6,053. This growth in the number of offices far outpaced population growth with the ratio of people per office halving from 11,135 to 5,960. Tables 4.2. to 4.4. show that this aggressive expansion in the number of offices in England and Wales was far greater than in either Scotland or Ireland, where the trend towards concentration was much less pronounced.

Table 4.2. Number of Banks

Year	England and Wales	Scotland	Ireland
1883	327	10	12
1891	268	10	11
1896	206	10	11
1911	55	9	9

Source: Sir D. Drummond Fraser, 'British Home Banking', p.453

---

[19] Steele, 'Bank Amalgamations', pp.115–23; Sykes, 'The Growth of London', p.377. See also Attfield, 'The Advantages', pp.450–73; Dunn, 'Banking in 1837 and in 1897', pp.374–80; W.A. Cole, 'The Relations between Banks and Stock Exchanges', *Journal of the Institute of Bankers*, 20 (1899), pp.409–19; W. Fowler, 'Banking Reserves', *Journal of the Institute of Bankers*, 21 (1900), p.251; Macdonald, 'The Economic Effects', pp.371–5; Perry, 'The History of Companies' Legislation', p.496.
[20] Steele, 'Bank Amalgamations', p.123.

Table 4.3. Number of Bank Offices

Year	England and Wales	Scotland	Ireland
1883	2,382	898	542
1891	3,249	982	583
1896	3,858	1,007	637
1911	6,053	1,235	842

Source: Sir D. Drummond Fraser, 'British Home Banking', p.453

Table 4.4. Ratio of Bank Offices to Population

Year	England and Wales	Scotland	Ireland
1883	11,135	4,160	9,520
1891	8,915	4,107	8,072
1896	7,962	4,157	7,117
1911	5,960	3,854	5,204

Source: Sir D. Drummond Fraser, 'British Home Banking', p.453

One result of this expansion of branches and offices was that even in the countryside credit was generally far more available in the UK than in other European countries because the commercial banks were well placed to assess the risks involved. Even through the problems experienced by British agriculture from 1873 onwards in the face of growing imports of wheat and then meat, British commercial banks remained willing to lend to landowners providing land as collateral and to farmers based on their profit record.[21]

It would also be a mistake to believe that the joint-stock commercial banks competed only among themselves. Despite the dominant position that these banks achieved in certain areas of banking in the fifty years before 1914, new bank formation continued apace, providing a significant level of competition in terms of the market for both savings and loans. This competition was felt both for savings and loans. In addition to the existence of informal social networks, there were numerous mutual organizations that both collected savings and made loans. There were an estimated 33,600 friendly societies in 1913, for example. In addition, the savings bank movement grew strongly throughout the nineteenth century, taking a number of different forms. In the first half of the century the pace was driven by the trustee savings banks, which had the philanthropic mission of encouraging thrift among the working class. By 1829 there were 476 of these with the peak of 645 being reached in 1861, before a slow decline took the number down to 202 in 1913. This decline was a

[21] Kenwood and Lougheed, *Technological Diffusion*, pp.43–4.

result of competition from other savings banks sponsored by particular organizations. The biggest was the Post Office, which developed its own savings bank from 1861. This meant that every branch of the Post Office could offer a savings account on which interest was paid. An Army savings bank had been started in 1842 and a Naval one followed in 1866. The railway companies also operated their own savings banks for their employees. By 1910 the Great Western Railway Savings Bank had 6,385 depositors holding £0.5 million and receiving interest of 3.5 per cent. These savings banks provided strong competition for the commercial banks in the market for individual savings, backed as they were by large and powerful organizations and offering attractive rates of interest. Even the security of the funds placed in the trustee savings banks was secure as it was invested in the National Debt. As a result deposits in savings banks tripled from £80 million in 1880 to £256 million in 1913.[22]

Another group of institutions competing strongly with the commercial banks for savings were the building societies. These collected money from their members and used it to finance house purchases until all involved owned their own homes. The society was then closed, or terminated. These terminating societies were increasingly replaced by permanent ones, in which the membership continually renewed itself, as that provided a permanent organization and the employment of trained staff. These societies attracted savers by offering high rates of interest. The Woolwich paid 10 per cent in 1885 and 9 per cent in 1886. The number of these permanent building societies stood at 701 in 1876, reached a peak of 2,809 in 1891, fell back to 2,158 in 1894, recovered to 2,527 in 1897, and then began a slow and steady decline reaching 1,550 in 1913. What these fluctuations in the 1890s indicated was the degree of instability associated with building societies as they were exposed not only to thefts by those appointed to supervise their affairs but also regular liquidity crises as savers tried to withdraw their money during a financial crisis or merely as a result of rumours. As the money had been largely lent to those constructing or buying houses these loans could not be easily recalled by the building society. Property was a notoriously difficult asset to dispose of quickly. In 1892 the property empire created by Jabez Balfour, and centred on the Liberator Building Society, collapsed leaving numerous savers with large losses. In this case the value of the assets had been greatly inflated so as to create an illusion that the money being invested by savers was secure. In the wake of these losses the government was forced to introduce legislation to regulate the affairs of building societies and place them on a more secure

---

[22] A. Offer, 'Narrow Banking, Real Estate, and Financial Stability in the UK, c.1870–2010', in Dimsdale and Hotson (eds), *British Financial Crises*, p.161; Horne, *A History of Savings Banks*, pp.386–91; Shepherd, *The Growth and Role of UK Financial Institutions*, pp.7–8, 166, Tables A2.3, A3.3; Pratt, *A History of Inland Transport*, p.432.

footing. However, there continued to be serious doubts associated with the security of all building societies and similar institutions. Deposits in building societies stood at £50 million in 1880 and had only risen to £60 million in 1913.[23] What the slow growth in the deposits placed with building societies, when compared with savings banks, indicates is the importance of security in the competition for savings rather than the rate of interest paid. The Charing Cross Bank had been founded in 1886 and attracted substantial deposits by offering generous rates of interest compared to the commercial banks. It was only able to pay these by investing in highly risky securities, and this gamble came to an end in 1910 when the bank collapsed leaving shareholders and depositors with losses of over £2 million.[24] In contrast the joint-stock banks were increasingly able to offer security to savers, and so attracted their deposits.

The competition that commercial banks faced in attracting savings was not confined to rival domestic institutions. From the 1870s and 1880s US land mortgage companies established offices in the City of London and used them to sell high-yielding debentures to UK investors. These debentures were backed by mortgages on US farms in Kansas, Texas, and Louisiana. Farmers borrowed at 6 per cent and the debentures paid 5 per cent, which was a higher rate than the commercial banks paid on deposits. Financing lending on illiquid property using short-term borrowing from savers was, however, a risky enterprise. When trust evaporated in these mortgage companies to service the interest on the debenture bonds, which it did in 1892/3, investors requested repayment rather than reinvesting, as they had in the past, leaving the mortgage companies unable to refinance their property portfolios. The result was a crisis in 1893 when a number of the land mortgage companies were forced to suspend payment of interest and repayment of debentures, leading them to close their UK operations. A similar fate overcame those Australian banks and building societies that had collected deposits in Britain by offering attractive interest rates. By 1892 they had collected around £30 million in Britain. When the Australian property bubble burst in April 1893, and when the Commercial Bank of Australia suspended payment, many British depositors were unable to recover their deposits as both solvent and insolvent banks closed.[25] The profits to be made through lending on mortgage was used by both British building societies and foreign banks and other institutions, as a way of generating the higher returns necessary to pay the

---

[23] Shepherd, *The Growth and Role of UK Financial Institutions*, Table A 2.4, A 3.3. See Price, *Building Societies*; B. Ritchie, *We're with the Woolwich: The Story of the Woolwich Building Society 1847–1997* (London: James & James, 1997), pp.18, 31, 39–41, 51–7.
[24] Hollow, *Rogue Banking*, p.23.
[25] A.G. Bogue, *Money at Interest: The Farm Mortgage on the Middle Border* (Lincoln, NE: University of Nebraska Press, 1955), pp.87–90, 132–6, 160, 189–203, 267, 276; N. Cork, 'The Late Australian Banking Crisis', *Journal of the Institute of Bankers*, 15 (1894), pp.180–200.

higher interest rates that attracted savers away from the commercial banks throughout the period 1870-1914. From time to time the result was a classic liquidity squeeze forcing some lenders to halt interest payments and even default on what they owed.[26] The large losses experienced by some did lead to a temporary decline in the competition for savings, as in the 1890s, but it resumed once confidence returned.

It was not only in the market for savings that the commercial banks faced strong competition. They also faced a competitive environment when it came to lending. Like the banks themselves, as the scale of enterprise grew, so businesses were able to move funds internally. By doing so they could dispense with the credit previously obtained from banks. When the firm of wholesale grocers, Joseph Travers and Sons, was converted into a company in 1889 the capital that it raised allowed it to provide extensive credit facilities to its trade customers. Other businesses went so far as to form their own bank, such as the department store, Whiteley's, for the use of their customers. The Prudential Insurance Company even acquired in 1868 an existing financial institution, the British Mutual Investment Loan and Discount Company, which it proceeded to convert into the British Mutual Banking Company and use as an in-house bank. Instead of its agents paying the insurance premiums they collected into the branches of banks, they were deposited with the British Mutual Banking Company to be used for the benefit of the Prudential itself.[27] For those businesses organized as companies, there also existed the possibility of selling either stocks or bonds to investors, with the issue handled by a merchant bank or some other intermediary, instead of borrowing from a bank. It was only the larger businesses that could choose this route but a growing number were converting themselves from partnerships into companies in this period, so opening up this opportunity. There were also vibrant financial communities located in all major cities through which finance could be arranged informally, while reinvested profits provided a major source of funds once a business was established.[28]

---

[26] A. Offer, 'Narrow Banking, Real Estate, and Financial Stability in the UK, c.1870-2010', in Dimsdale and Hotson (eds), *British Financial Crises*, p.162.

[27] Joseph Travers & Sons, *Chronicles of Cannon Street: A Few Records of an Old Firm* (London: Joseph Travers and Sons, 1958), pp.29, 53, 59; L. Dennett, *A Sense of Security: 150 Years of Prudential* (Cambridge: Granta Editions, 1998), pp.72, 386; Cottrell, 'London's First '"Big Bang"?' in Cassis and Cottrell (eds), *The World of Private Banking*, p.83.

[28] S.D. Chapman, *The Rise of Merchant Banking* (London: Allen & Unwin, 1984), pp.15-16, 29, 43, 49, 70-81, 103, 106, 121-5, 137, 170-2; V.P. Carosso, *The Morgans: Private International Bankers, 1854-1913* (Cambridge, Mass: Harvard UP, 1987), pp.7-9, 51, 149, 159, 162, 221-2, 390, 395-6, 403, 461, 596, 606, 612; J. Orbell, *Baring Brothers and Co. Ltd: A History to 1939* (London: Baring Brothers, 1958), pp.39, 43, 51-3, 65, 69; P. Ziegler, *The Sixth Great Power: Barings 1762-1929* (London: Collins, 1988), pp.132, 164, 199-202, 281, 287; C. Fohlin, 'Bank Securities Holdings and Industrial Finance before World War I: Britain and Germany Compared', *Business and Economic History*, 26 (1997), p. 465.

An indication of the complex world that British banks increasingly operated in can be seen in the relations that existed between domestic and overseas banks through their use of the City of London as a financial centre. By the First World War, London was the key hub in a global cable network that linked all of the world's financial and commercial centres, making it the Clearing House for world information flows.[29] For that reason alone banks needed a link to London in order to participate in the international payments system and access the network which handled the constant ebb and flow of money around the world. Though it appeared that banks from different countries occupied geographically distinct spheres, their participation in these systems and networks led them to compete and co-operate both at the same time. This blurred the distinction, for example, between British domestic and overseas banks. Following on from the success of joint-stock banks within the UK, others were formed specializing in the provision of banking for specific countries and regions. The number of British banks whose operations were exclusively abroad rose from fifteen in 1860 to twenty-five in 1913, while their branch network expanded from 132 to 1,387.[30] Over time, these British overseas banks met increasing competition from joint-stock banks formed locally, including a number by British expatriates. These local banks were at a disadvantage in competing with British overseas banks because they lacked the direct access to the international payments system centred in London and the facilities provided by the London money market. The British overseas banks had such links because their head offices were in London.[31] A number of foreign and colonial banks opened branches in London to establish similar contacts.[32] Between

---

[29] E.M. Winter, 'London's Global Reach? Reuters News and Network, 1865, 1881, and 1914', *Journal of World History*, 21 (2010), pp.271-96.

[30] For an overview of British overseas banking see G. Jones, *British Multinational Banking, 1830-1990* (Oxford: O.U.P, 1993). See also G. Tyson, *100 Years of Banking in Asia and Africa* (London: National and Grindlays Bank, 1963), pp.2, 15, 19, 24-5, 32, 44; Sir Compton Mackenzie, *Realms of Silver: One Hundred Years of Banking in the East* (London: Routledge & Kegan Paul, 1954), pp.9-10, 25, 62; S. Muirhead, *Crisis Banking in the East: The History of the Chartered Mercantile Bank of India, London and China, 1853-93* (Aldershot: Ashgate, 1996), pp.6-8, 180-4.

[31] A.S.J. Baster, *The International Banks* (London: P.S. King, 1935), p.4; A. Teichova, G. Kurgan-Van Hentenryk and D. Ziegler (eds), *Banking, Trade and Industry: Europe, America and Asia from the Thirteenth to the Twentieth Century* (Cambridge: CUP, 2011); Nishimura, *The Decline of Inland Bills of Exchange*, pp.379-92; O. Checkland, S. Nishimura, and N. Tamaki (eds), *Pacific Banking, 1859-1959: East Meets West* (Basingstoke: Macmillan, 1994), pp.17, 36, 47-8, 175; S. Kinsey and L. Newton, *International Banking in an Age of Transition: Globalisation, Automation, Banks and their Archives* (Aldershot: Ashgate, 1998); Newton 'The Birth of Joint-Stock Banking', p.83, Cottrell, 'London's First "Big Bang"?', p.106, 121, 124, 126; Muirhead, *Crisis Banking*, pp.180-4; Mackenzie, *Realms of Silver*, pp.9-10, 25, 62; G. Tyson, *100 Years of Banking*, p.57; F.H.H. King, *The History of the Hongkong and Shanghai Banking Corporation* (Oxford: OUP, 1988), v.1, pp.100-1, 279, 300.

[32] M. Pohl and K. Burk, *Deutsche Bank in London, 1873-1914* (Munich: Piper, 1998), pp.14, 19, 24, 41, 43, 55; N. Tamaki, *Japanese Banking: A History 1859-1959* (Cambridge: CUP, 1995), pp.17, 29, 46, 70-2, 107, 129, 131, 155-6.

1898 and 1911, for example, the number of foreign banks with offices in London doubled from thirteen to twenty-six.[33] A simpler, cheaper, and less risky alternative was for a foreign bank to establish a correspondent relationship with a British bank having a London head office. By 1912 a total of 1,211 banks from around the world had done so.[34] A correspondent arrangement with a British domestic bank allowed foreign banks to compete with British overseas banks as they could now offer the same range of services, including access to the international payments system and inter-bank money market located in London. The business became so important the major UK deposit banks even set up specific branches in the City to handle it. For example, Lloyds Bank established its 'foreign' branch in London in 1898.[35] Conversely, these correspondent links allowed British domestic banks, like the Midland, to compete with both the older British merchant banks and the British overseas banks. At the beginning of the twentieth century the Midland Bank's 'foreign' branch was at the centre of a very extensive web of connections totalling around 850, and these included numerous foreign banks. By then, according to Van Beck of the Midland Bank, in 1906, 'the London City and Midland Bank Ltd is not only one of the three largest but probably far and away the largest lender of call money on the security of bills.'[36] By 1913 it was estimated that though the merchant banks still controlled 40 per cent of the provision of international trade finance conducted in London, the British overseas and foreign banks had taken 35 per cent of the business while the domestically focused British joint-stock banks did 25 per cent of it.[37] Not content with invading the business of international trade finance, the joint-stock commercial banks also became involved in the securities business. Instead of simply buying securities through stockbrokers, joint-stock banks like the Midland began to participate in the consortiums handling the issue. In this way they cut out the commission fees they had traditionally paid to brokers while receiving

---

[33] W.F. Spalding, 'The Establishment and Growth of Foreign Branch Banks in London, and the Effect, Immediate and Ultimate, upon the Banking and Commercial Development of this Country', *Journal of the Institute of Bankers*, 32 (1911), pp.435-55.

[34] For an excellent description of what a correspondent agreement involved see E. S. Furniss, *Foreign Exchange: The Financing Mechanism of International Commerce* (New York: Houghton Mifflin, 1922), pp.314-27. For some Japanese examples see Tamaki, *Japanese Banking*, pp.17, 29, 46, 70-2, 107, 129, 131, 155-6.

[35] C. Rozenraad, *The History of the Growth of London as the Financial Centre of the World and the Means of Maintaining that Position* (London: Effingham Wilson, 1903), p.31.

[36] Van Beck (Midland Bank, London) to J.E. Gardin (National City Bank, NY) 24 July 1906, 20 October 1906, 2 May 1907, 9 September 1908; Holmes and Green, *Midland*, p.132.

[37] Y. Cassis, 'Private Banks and the Onset of the Corporate Economy', in Cassis and Cottrell (eds), *World of Private Banking*, pp.45-7; A.I. Bloomfield, *Short-Term Capital Movements Under the Pre-1914 Gold Standard* (Princeton: Princeton UP, 1963), pp.35, 46; Collins, *Money and Banking*, p.149.

a discount on the issue price from the merchant banks as well as any underwriting privileges.[38]

The development of these relationships between banks can be studied in detail through the arrival of Australian banks in London. Such relationships had developed from the 1840s onwards, but were transformed when the telegraph linked the UK and Australia in 1872. This led immediately to payments by telegraphic transfers, rather than the use of bills of exchange that accompanied the cargoes or were sent on faster ships. With telegraphic transfers, an Australian bank had to have facilities to make and receive payments in London. The British overseas banks that had been established to operate in Australia had this, because their head office was in London, but the banks that had been set up in Australia did not. Opening a branch in London was both expensive and involved risks, as it could not be easily supervised from such a distance, which was a perennial problem for British overseas banks, causing failures through bad loans in some cases. The alternative was to establish a correspondent relationship with a bank already operating in London, which was familiar to the many British bankers who had been recruited to staff these Australian banks. The most obvious candidates for such correspondent arrangements were the domestic joint-stock banks, as they had no conflict of interest, compared to the merchant banks or the overseas banks. An account would be opened with a correspondent bank at which deposits would be kept, often with no interest received, but services would be provided such as the ability to have payments made and received and bills discounted. Thus, at the same time as the development of branch banking in Britain removed the need for bills, as it made possible a Lend and Hold Model, the transformation of international communications was creating a need for bills as a means through which banks could transfer funds between each other. These bills were used not simply as a means of financing the expansion of international trade but to equalize the supply and demand of funds over space and time between the different components of the global banking system. The Commercial Bank of Australia, for example, opened a correspondent link with the City Bank, a London bank, in 1873. This link provided them with a local credit facility and the means of making and accepting payment. This correspondent link was followed in 1882 with the opening of their own branch in London, such was the value placed on the connection to London. From these branches the Australian banks competed with their British counterparts for deposits and in providing

---

[38] Cassis, 'Private Banks', in Cassis and Cottrell (eds), *World of Private Banking*, pp.45–7; J. Siegel, *For Peace and Money: French and British Finance in the Service of Tsars and Commissars* (Oxford: OUP, 2014), pp.116–19; Kenwood and Lougheed, *Technological Diffusion*, p.160.

services for those wanting to make and receive payments between the UK and Australia.[39]

THE LONDON MONEY MARKET

The London money market had long played a central role within British banking. Writing in his classic account of the London money market, *Lombard Street*, based on his personal experience of country banking, Bagehot noted that, 'All country bankers keep their reserve in London. They only retain in each county town the minimum of cash necessary in the transaction of the current business in that country town. Long experience has told them to a nicety how much this is, and they do not waste capital and lose profit by keeping more idle. They send the money to London, invest a part in securities, and keep the rest with the London bankers and the bill brokers.'[40] By 1873, when this was written, such a view of British banking was becoming anachronistic. As the scale of individual banks grew so did the opportunity to complete transactions and employ money internally, and so by-pass both the London-based payments system and the London money market. Payments between customers of the same bank, as well as lending and borrowing, could all take place within a single bank managed from a London head office and conducting its business from hundreds of branches. By 1913 a small number of banks managed a network of 8,910 bank branches and commanded £1,032 million in deposits and operated on the basis of the Lend and Hold rather than Originate and Distribute Model.[41]

---

[39] G. Blainey and G. Hutton, *Gold and Paper, 1858-1982: A History of the National Bank of Australasia* (Melbourne: Macmillan Australia, 1983), pp.45, 47, 75, 86, 90-100; N.M. Chappell, *New Zealand's Banker's Hundred: A History of the Bank of New Zealand, 1861-1961* (Wellington: Bank of New Zealand, 1961), pp.107-8, 193; S.J. Butlin, *Australia and New Zealand Bank: The Bank of Australasia and the Union Bank of Australia Limited, 1828-1951* (London: Longmans, 1961), pp.85, 192-4, 221, 240, 255, 306, 316; D.T. Merrett, *ANZ Bank: A History of the Australia and New Zealand Banking Group Limited and its Constituents* (London: Allen & Unwin, 1985), p.27; R.J. Wood, *Commercial Bank of Australia* (Melbourne: Hargreen, 1990), pp.93-6, 122-3, 137-8; R.F. Holder, *Bank of New South Wales: A History* (Sydney: Angus & Robertson, 1970), pp.143, 153, 196, 528, 571.

[40] W. Bagehot, *Lombard Street: A Description of the Money Market* (London: H.S. King, 1873).

[41] Capie and Webber, *A Monetary History*, pp.130, 576-7; Thomas, *Banking and Exchange*, p.5; J. Orbell, 'The Historical Structure and Functions of British Banking', in Orbell and Turton, *British Banking*, pp.1-5; Davies, *The Origins and Development of Cartelisation*, pp.13-14; Newton, 'The Birth of Joint-Stock Banking', p.28; Newton, *Change and Continuity*, pp.1-20; Pressnell, *Country Banking*, pp.2, 11; S. Nishimura, *The Decline of Inland Bills of Exchange*, pp.72-9; J.W. Lubbock, *On the Clearing of the London Bankers* (London: [n.p.], 1860), p.5; W. Howarth, *The Banks in the Clearing House* (London: Effingham Wilson, 1905), pp.118, 129, 173; Capie and Webber, *A Monetary History*, pp.221, 280, 291, 310; W.T.C. King, 'The London

Nevertheless, a system was still required through which separate banks could settle payments between customers of different banks, and that was most easily located in London as that was where most transactions were generated, involving not only business done on the domestic account but also internationally. The correspondent network funnelled transactions to London, which acted as the central clearing house for all inter-bank business that could not be settled locally.[42] Reflecting the growing rather than falling importance of a link to London after the mid nineteenth century was the effort made by the major Scottish and Irish banks to open branches there, despite the costs involved. In turn, they were followed by a small number of foreign and colonial banks, though correspondent links continued to provide the main point of access.[43] But access to London meant far more than the ability to make and receive payments. It also provided banks with the ability to either lend or borrow money between each other. This can be seen in the activities of the Scottish banks in London. These banks had long used London to make and receive payments as well as to buy and sell bills and conduct other financial transactions such as investment in securities. This had been done through the use of London banks as correspondents. However, in the mid nineteenth century these correspondent arrangements were increasingly replaced with branches, despite the expense and risks that involved. By 1878 all the major Scottish banks had London offices, which were integrated into their Lend and Hold method of doing business.

The London office was where these Scottish banks maintained their liquid reserves. By using London as the home for their liquid funds these banks could ensure that they were also not idle funds in the way that cash kept at each branch was. In London liquid reserves could always be employed with their level kept to a minimum as additional funds could be quickly and easily borrowed. In 1881/4, for example, the Union Bank of Scotland's London branch had lent out £0.8 million to bill brokers, £0.4 million to stockbrokers, and invested £1million in the National Debt. Though low yielding these were all highly liquid funds, which could be immediately converted into cash if required. The importance of the London branch to the Scottish banks is

Discount Market', in *Current Financial Problems and the City of London* (London: Institute of Bankers, 1949), pp.39, 273; Collins, *Money and Banking*, p.106.

[42] G.W. Pownall, 'The Proportional Use of Credit Documents and Metallic Money in English Banks', *Journal of the Institute of Bankers*, 2 (1881), pp.642-59; F.E. Steele, 'On Changes in the Bank Rate of Discount, First, their Causes; and Secondly, their Effects on the Money Market, on the Commerce of the Country, and on the Value of all Interest-Bearing Securities, *Journal of the Institute of Bankers*, 12 (1891), pp.477-89; Spalding, 'The Establishment and Growth', pp.435-55.

[43] Collins, *Money and Banking*, p.106; Nevin and Davies, *The London Clearing Banks*, p.75; N. Tamaki, *The Life Cycle of the Union Bank of Scotland, 1830-1954* (Aberdeen: Aberdeen UP, 1983), pp.13, 53, 84, 106; Ollerenshaw, *Banking in Nineteenth-Century Ireland*, pp.81-94.

revealed from the use made of it by the Bank of Scotland. Between 1880 and 1914 between 20 per cent and 30 per cent of the Bank's capital and deposits were employed in London. Through its London branch the Bank of Scotland was able to constantly adjust the balance between its assets and liabilities and so maintain the equilibrium that was essential for the successful implementation of the Lend and Hold Model. This can be seen in the net balance between loans made and deposits held at the Bank of Scotland's London office. In 1870, for example, loans exceeded deposits from January to May, were equal in June, September, and November, while in July, August, October, and December deposits exceeded loans. Overall, however, the result was equilibrium as spare funds were lent out and any shortfall covered by borrowing, allowing the bank to operate the Lend and Hold Model securely. By 1910 loans always exceeded deposits but the values fluctuated. The peak difference was reached in January of that year at £3.5 million and reached a low in June at £2.6 million. By then the Bank of Scotland's London branch was fully integrated into the London money market with its business not only driven by its role within the bank of which it was part but also as a profit centre in its own capacity. The London branch of the Bank of Scotland had become the London correspondent for a number of foreign banks, including the large and rapidly growing Canadian Bank of Commerce, which meant that it accepted deposits from these banks and employed them in the London money market, as well as providing them with payment and other services.[44]

A similar development took place in the relationship between the Australian and New Zealand banks and the City of London. The seasons were a major influence on the Australian and New Zealand economies, where wool, meat, and wheat production were of major importance. Banks were in the position of being either short of funds or with an unemployable excess depending on the timing and state of the harvest. This severe seasonal imbalance made the operation of a Lend and Hold Model difficult but access to London, obtained through either a correspondent link or a branch, made it possible to achieve equilibrium. Those Australian and New Zealand banks that opened branches in London were able to accept deposits not for the purpose of accessing additional funds but to use as a liquidity reserve. Safe in the knowledge that they had these reserves in London that could be lent out until needed, these banks could employ more of the deposits they collected at home in making loans there. Those Australian and New Zealand banks that possessed this liquidity reserve in London were able to survive the crisis of 1893 as they possessed the shock-absorbing buffer required to meet sudden redemptions.

---

[44] C.W. Munn, *Clydesdale Bank: The First One Hundred and Fifty Years* (London: Clydesdale Banking Company, 1988), pp.72-3, 83, 142-3; R. Saville, *Bank of Scotland: A History, 1695-1995* (Edinburgh: Edinburgh UP, 1996), pp.337, 400-1, 427, 437-41, 457-8, 464-5; Tamaki, *The Life Cycle of the Union Bank of Scotland*, pp.132-6, 181, 187-9.

In contrast, those banks that had raised money in London and then used it in Australia or New Zealand to finance property purchases lacked the reserves required to survive the liquidity crisis when the speculative boom burst. After the crisis the surviving Australian and New Zealand banks used London as a source of liquidity while matching deposits and loans domestically.[45]

Over the 1870-1914 period banks from all over the world recognized that a presence in London had become a vital part of the way that they did business. When the Hong Kong and Shanghai Banking Corporation (HK) was being formed in 1864 it was not considered essential to have a London office, let alone a branch there. What they did require was a presence in London through which payments could be routed and the means of obtaining credit or employing funds on a temporary basis. They obtained these by signing a correspondent agreement in 1865 with the London and Westminster Bank. That bank would accept bills on behalf of the HK bank up to £0.1 million without collateral and a further £0.5 million if backed by acceptable bills. In return the HK bank would maintain a minimum deposit of £10,000. However, such was the business done by the HK bank that it kept exceeding the borrowing conditions set by the London and Westminster. When the London and Westminster would not offer better terms, because of the risks involved, the HK bank switched to another London bank, the London and County, where it received more generous terms, namely up to £1.5 million if covered by bills, which was raised to £2.5 million in 1879. However, the HK bank required even more than the London and County could deliver and so began to accept deposits at the branch it had opened in London. By 1878 these had reached £0.5 million and stood at £4 million in 1888. With these funds the HK bank was now in direct control over liquid reserves in London, which could be used to cover either a temporary shortfall caused by the seasonal nature of its business or to meet a liquidity crisis.[46] Banks from elsewhere in Europe also gravitated to London as that provided them with access to the international payments system and the ideal location to keep liquid reserves at a time when the operation of the Gold Standard removed most of the exchange risk from the international movement of funds. One of the first acts of the newly formed Deutsche Bank was to open an agency in London in 1873. The turnover at the London branch of Deutsche Bank rose from £7.7 million in 1874 to £1,063 million in 1913. The Dresdner Bank opened a London branch in 1895 and Disconto-Gesellschaft in 1899. By 1913 these three German banks were doing an extensive business in London not

---

[45] Blainey and Hutton, *Gold and Paper*, pp.45, 47, 75, 86, 90–100; Chappell, *New Zealand's Banker's Hundred*, pp.107–8, 193; Butlin, *Australia and New Zealand Bank*, pp.85, 192–4, 221, 240, 255, 306, 316; Merrett, *ANZ Bank*, p.27; Wood, *Commercial Bank of Australia*, pp.93–6, 122–3, 137–8; Holder, *Bank of New South Wales*, pp.143, 153, 196, 528, 571; Cork, 'The Late Australian Banking Crisis', p.200.

[46] King, *History of the Hongkong and Shanghai Banking Corporation*, v.1, pp.100–1, 279, 300.

only on behalf of their own parent banks but also for all German banks and their clients. This included the finance of German international trade and the constant borrowing and lending activity required to maintain a safe level of liquidity for the German banking system.[47] French banks made similar use of London despite the rival attractions of Paris because only in London could they access the international payments system and obtain the liquidity their banking system also required.[48] Especially for countries in which agriculture remained a dominant activity, matching the supply of and demand for credit over the year was a complex task and one that could easily give rise to a sudden liquidity crisis. A link to London became an essential component in balancing this supply and demand without the necessity of either tying up funds in the form of cash or taking large risks by operating with inadequate reserves. For that reason both Indian and South African banks also turned to London after 1870, either indirectly through a bank already located there or indirectly via an office or branch.[49]

As Fuller and Rowan reported in 1901, when noting the growing presence of foreign banks in London, 'the London money market is the money market of the world, and... immediate access there is little short of necessary to their success.'[50] Central to the operation of this money market was the continued use of the bill of exchange. As global trade expanded rapidly from the mid nineteenth century onwards there was an enhanced need for an international payments system that could cope with the receipts and payments that such trade generated as well as the credit required. Merchants needed to obtain credit so as to carry stocks of both goods for export and imports for sale to customers. Bills denominated in £sterling and payable in London provided the international means of payment required, building on the role they already played for Britain's own extensive imports and exports. An estimate for 1913 suggested that around half of world trade was financed using sterling bills, including most of the USA's exports and imports. The result was that around two-thirds of the bills circulating in London at any one time, totalling £0.5 billion, were on foreign account. By then the bill on London had become the universally accepted means of payment.[51] As one Canadian banker reflected,

---

[47] Pohl and Burk, *Deutsche Bank*, pp.14, 19, 24, 41, 43, 55.

[48] J.T. Madden and M. Nadler, 'The Paris Money Market', *Bulletin of the Institute of International Finance, New York* (1st June 1931), pp.3-4, 15.

[49] Sunderland, *Financing the Raj*, pp.24, 108-12, 132-3, 165, 178; Muirhead, *Crisis Banking*, pp.7, 180-4, 206, 216; J.A. Henry and H.A. Stepmann, *The First Hundred Years of the Standard Bank* (London: O.U.P, 1963), pp.17, 43, 101, 110, 116, 133, 141.

[50] F.J. Fuller and H.D. Rowan, 'Foreign Competition in its Relation to Banking', *Journal of the Institute of Bankers*, 22 (1901), pp.51-69.

[51] Thomas, *Banking and Exchange*, p.381; E. Brett, 'The History and Development of Banking in Australasia', *Journal of the Institute of Bankers*, 3 (1882), pp.19-35; Nevin and Davies, *The London Clearing Banks*, pp.105-6; W.F. Spalding, *Eastern Exchange Currency and Finance*, 4th ed. (London: Pitman, 1924), pp.2, 106-7, 429; E.L. Stewart Patterson, *Domestic and Foreign Exchange* (New York: Alexander Hamilton Institute, 1917), pp.138-42; M. Escher, *Foreign*

concerned about the disruption caused by the outbreak of the First World War, 'The bill on London is a better currency than gold itself, more economical, more readily transmissible, more efficient... by means of the bill on London not only the vast commerce of Britain herself, but also a substantial share of the purely foreign traffic of the world is financed and liquidated.'[52]

However, these bills were far more than instruments of trade finance. According to George Peel writing in 1928, before 1914, 'A draft on London is the real cash of international commerce and finance.' because London was 'the monetary centre of the universe.'[53] The financial journalist, Hartley Withers, explained in 1910 how the bill of exchange had been transformed from an aid of commerce to a vital instrument of finance: 'Out of the bills of exchange, originally drawn against merchandise actually shipped, grew the finance bill drawn sometimes in anticipation of produce or merchandise to be shipped, sometimes against securities, and sometimes against the credit of the parties to it.'[54] By drawing a ninety-day bill on its London correspondent and then selling it, a foreign bank obtained a short-term loan at the cost of the discount and the commission paid to the London bank. Conversely, by buying such a bill a foreign bank employed spare funds for the duration of a bill or for however long it held it, profiting from the difference between the discount at the purchase date and that on sale or maturity. Such operations were only made possible by the extensive banking network in place by the late nineteenth century, with London at its hub.[55] In turn, these bills could be circulated in the London money market until they reached their expiry date, providing banks with both a medium of exchange and a means through which funds could be lent and borrowed. Through either a physical presence or via the extensive correspondent network, all the leading banks in the world had access to the facilities provided by the London money market.[56] It was estimated that by

---

Exchange Explained (New York: Macmillan, 1917), pp.10–11; G. Clare, *A Money-Market Primer and Key to the Exchanges* (London: Effingham Wilson, 1893), pp.92, 145; H.T. Easton, *Money, Exchange and Banking* (London: Pitman, 1908), pp.52, 72; King, 'The London Discount Market', pp.12–14; E. Seyd, *The London Banking and Bankers' Clearing House System* (London: Cassell, Petter & Galpin, 1931); W.M. Scammell, *The London Discount Market* (London: St Martin's Press, 1968), pp.162, 193; G.A. Fletcher, *The Discount Houses in London: Principles, Operations and Change* (London: Macmillan, 1976), pp.17–34.

[52] G.I.H. Lloyd, 'The London Money Market and the War Crisis', *Journal of the Canadian Bankers Association*, 22 (1914/15), p.67.

[53] G. Peel, *The Economic Impact of America* (London: Macmillan, 1928), pp.11, 29, 286–7.

[54] Withers, *The English Banking System*, p.55.

[55] E.F. Foster, *Seasonal Movements of Exchange Rates and Interest Rates under the Pre-World War I Gold Standard* (New York: Garland Publishing, 1994), pp.27–31, 41.

[56] A.S.J. Baster, *The Imperial Banks* (London: P.S. King, 1929), p.269; Baster, *International Banks*, p.245; F.H.H. King, *The Hongkong Bank in Late Imperial China 1864–1902* (Cambridge: CUP, 1987), pp.43, 98; F.H.H. King, *The Hongkong Bank in the Period of Imperialism and War, 1895–1918* (Cambridge: CUP, 1988), pp.135, 539, 544; Chapman, *The Rise of Merchant Banking*, pp.15–16, 29, 43, 49, 70–81, 103, 106, 121–5, 137, 170–2; Carosso, *The Morgans*, pp.7–9, 51, 149,

1913, 60 per cent of the bills in circulation were finance bills.[57] A large proportion of these finance bills were now being used to finance investment through the connection to the securities market. As Cole explained in 1899, 'nearly the whole of the 'professional' speculation on the Stock Exchange is carried on with bank money, which can be borrowed on negotiable securities with ease and cheapness, and in larger proportion to value than on any other descriptions of security; so that a dealer can, under favourable circumstances, keep on buying and borrowing on his purchase to a remarkable extent.' In addition to the large dealers there were specialist money brokers who were located within the London Stock Exchange and acted as intermediaries between banks and smaller brokers so as to facilitate borrowing and lending. The stocks and bonds they bought and sold were those regarded by bankers as 'quasi-money' because of their ease of transfer, not just domestically but also internationally. Many were US railroad bonds that were actively traded on both the London and New York stock exchanges as well as other markets located in Continental Europe. With currency instability eliminated through adherence to the Gold Standard, a profit was to be made by borrowing short-term funds from banks, available in London at low rates of interest, and investing the proceeds in higher yielding stocks and bonds, in the knowledge that if one bank called in the loan another bank would provide one, or funds could easily be obtained by selling the securities. In turn banks were confident that they could borrow the funds they needed to finance such operations by selling finance bills in the London money market.[58]

Increasingly the funds in use in the London money market were drawn from banks elsewhere in the world, as they came to recognize that the London money market was a place where otherwise idle balances could be employed remuneratively. As F.E. Steele told the Institute of Bankers in 1891, 'London has become practically the recognized banking and financial centre of the world.' Bankers from around the world not only drew on London for funds and but employed funds there.[59] In 1914 the deposits employed by the foreign and colonial banks in London were estimated to be almost twice the size of those under the control of UK domestic banks. The result was to concentrate in London a vast supply of money available for short-term lending such as the finance of international trade or the holding of easily realizable securities.

159, 162, 221–2, 390, 395–6, 403, 461, 596, 606, 612; Orbell, *Baring Brothers*, pp.39, 43, 51–3, 65, 69.

[57] R. Roberts, *Saving the City: The Great Financial Crisis of 1914* (Oxford: OUP, 2013), pp.30–1; Bloomfield, *Short-Term Capital Movements*, pp.35, 46; E.G. Peake, *An Academic Study of Some Money Market and Other Statistics* (London: P.S. King, 1923), pp.7, 21, 24, 37, 39.

[58] Cole, 'The Relations between Banks and Stock Exchanges', pp.409–19. See also E.E. Gellender, 'The Relations between Banks and Stock Exchanges', *Journal of the Institute of Bankers*, 20 (1899), pp.492–7.

[59] Steele, 'On Changes in the Bank Rate of Discount', pp.477–89.

Overall, the amount of foreign money employed in London rose from an estimated £30–40 million in the early 1870s to around £1.9 billion in 1913.[60] The result was to place the London money market at the very centre of the mechanism which not only allowed banks from both within the UK and around the world to debit and credit each other as payments were made by their customers, but also to borrow and lend between each other as the supply of and demand for the funds at their disposal waxed and waned.[61] As the Canadian banker, L. D. Wilgress, observed on the eve of the First World War, 'The London money market is the most important and influential in the world. London is the world's financial centre, and is the clearing house for international payments... in times of strain especially, London is the only place where money can be found at all times for loans.'[62]

What this meant for the British banking system was that even the domestically focused joint-stock banks played a key international role through their correspondent relationships and their participation in the London money market. This explains the increasingly high level of liquidity maintained by UK banks. The ratio of cash/near cash to total assets grew from 23 per cent of all bank assets in the mid 1860s to 40 per cent in the early 1890s, at which level it remained until the First World War. This ratio was much higher for London-based banks than for provincial banks which has been used as evidence to suggest that as the process of consolidation proceeded, one result was to distance these London-based banks from their customers in the manufacturing areas of the north. However, this conclusion can be queried on a number of grounds. The first is timing. The process of consolidation continued apace until the First World War, whereas the trend towards more liquid assets did not. The second is that a comparison with Scottish banks, which did not participate in the nationwide amalgamation movement, reveals that they maintained the same ratios as the London-based banks. In 1896, whereas those banks that confined their operations to London had a ratio of money at call and short notice, relative to deposits, of 12 per cent, those with provincial branches had a ratio of 11.6 per cent, which was identical to that for Scottish banks. In 1911 the ratio of cash, including deposits at the Bank of

---

[60] Capie and Webber, *A Monetary History*, p.221; *Report and Proceedings of the Sub-Committee of the Committee for Imperial Defence or Trading with the Enemy*, Cabinet Office (1912): Evidence of A.C. Cole; R.S. Sayers, *Gilletts in the London Money Market, 1867–1967* (Oxford: OUP, 1968), pp.2, 36–7, 45–7, 50, 60, 80.

[61] H. Withers, *The English Banking System* (Washington: Government Printing Office, 1910), p.55; J. Atkin, *The Foreign Exchange Market of London: Development since 1900* (London: Taylor & Francis, 2005), pp.9–10, 84–5; Baster, *The Imperial Banks*, pp.140–4, 216; Baster, *International Banks*, pp.76, 258, K.E. Born, *International Banking in the 19th and 20th Centuries* (Leamington Spa: Berg, 1983), p.117; R.J. Truptil, *British Banks and the London Money Market* (London: Jonathan Cape, 1936), pp.142, 149, 155, 178–80.

[62] L.D. Wilgress, 'The London Money Market', *Journal of the Canadian Bankers' Association* 20 (1912/13), pp.210–12.

England, and money at call and short notice, stood at 28 per cent for banks in England and Wales compared to 26.9 per cent for Scottish banks.[63] What has to be recognized is that UK banks could not rely on a stable depositor base to fund their lending. Instead, they were dependent upon the fluctuating balances of their business customers, including other banks. For this reason, access to the London money market retained its importance as it could be used both to employ spare balances and to access temporary funds present across the entire banking system. The banks could continue to develop the Lend and Hold Model rather than revert to the Originate and Distribute one, because access to the money market allowed them to make use of customer balances that could move from positive to negative depending upon the state of business over time, including within the day as well as month to month and year to year. Success in this business meant very careful money-market management, which is what the British banking system perfected in the late nineteenth century. Such was its success that British banks proved resilient in crises, such as that of 1893, when many of their domestic and foreign rivals succumbed. In turn, that success encouraged both emulation and the increasing use of the London money market by foreign banks as it provided them with the same opportunity to even out the fluctuations in depositor balances they were exposed to from business customers. This access was mainly provided through correspondent links with banks that already had an established presence in London.

THE BANK OF ENGLAND

The depth and breadth of the London money market meant that British banks could be confident that it would provide them with the liquidity they needed to continue operating on a limited capital base and the use of short-term funds for longer term investment, whether that was at the retail level with the Lend and Hold Model, or the wholesale one where the Originate and Distribute Model was used. However, in using the London money market, given the international role it performed, especially after 1870, British banking was constantly exposed to financial crises from around the world.[64] If each bank

---

[63] Dick, 'Banking Statistics', pp.187–215; Fraser, 'Some Modern Phases', pp.96–8. For a forensic investigation of surviving commercial bank balance sheets from the 1860–1913 period see Collins and Baker, *Commercial Banking*.

[64] C. Rozenraad, 'The International Money Market, *Journal of the Institute of Bankers*, 24 (1902), pp.278–80; F. Schuster, 'Foreign Trade and the Money Market', *Journal of the Institute of Bankers*, 25 (1904), p.58; D.M. Mason, 'Our Money Market and American Banking and Currency Reform', *Journal of the Institute of Bankers*, 30 (1909), p.203; Spalding, 'The Establishment and Growth', pp.435–55.

had to operate in the expectation that it could be faced at any moment with a high level of withdrawals by depositors, or a request for an alternative form of money from those holding its notes, it would have to increase its capital base and maintain very large reserves of cash. This would mean that it was not in a position to provide abundant credit or pay a high rate of interest to depositors. It would also mean that banking was not an attractive business because it generated low profits relative to the risks run. Normally, however, the level of liquidity across the entire banking system was roughly constant. If a bank was in a position to access the latent liquidity of the entire banking system, even in exceptional times, then it could continue to operate on less capital, maintain lower reserves, provide more credit, pay a higher rate of interest, and generate more profits. The London money market provided this to a large degree as it acted as a mechanism through which banks could lend and borrow between each other, so equalizing the supply of liquidity across the entire system. There still existed the risk that the money market would freeze, especially in a crisis, thus depriving all banks of access to this latent liquidity. The survival of those banks with the lowest reserves would then be threatened, as they could not survive mass withdrawals by those from whom they had borrowed. Fear spread by rumours would then bring down other banks whether they lacked reserves or not. What was required was a lender of last resort, which would make good any shortfall in liquidity, both on a daily basis, guaranteeing that banks could always access the funds they required, and ensure in exceptional circumstances that the money market would always function. Without such a lender, the London money market would be vulnerable to crises, whether home-grown or externally generated. Such a lender would not only serve the UK banking system because it would also act as lender of last resort to the global banking system, given the extensive connections that existed between British and foreign banks through the correspondent network.[65]

Key to providing this facility of a lender of last resort to the London money market throughout the century before the First World War were the activities of the bill broker or discount house. These intermediated between the banks, borrowing money from one and buying bills from another, regardless of whether the bill was generated through commercial or financial transactions, because, according to J. H. Tritton in 1901, 'a bill of exchange records a debt, transfers it...as often as may be required, and discharges it when duly paid at maturity.' The role of the bill broker was 'to discover each morning in his rounds which banks are full of money, and therefore lenders. And which are poor and therefore taking money off the market.' Adjustments to the rate

---

[65] Grossman, *Unsettled Account*, pp.96–102, 147–8; King, 'The London Discount Market', pp.9, 30, 42, 48, 99, 117, 175, 183; C.A.E. Goodhart, *The Business of Banking, 1891–1914* (London: Weidenfeld & Nicolson, 1972), p.31; Capie and Webber, *A Monetary History*, pp.310–13.

of interest paid on the money borrowed and the discount to face value at which bills were sold, reflected the constantly changing balance between supply and demand.[66] According to Straker, writing about bill brokers in 1904, 'Their business demands great knowledge and discrimination as to the standing of parties, and they are practically bound to buy at the prevailing market price all good bills offered to them, or they lose their connection and business.' For the same reason they had to accept the money that banks offered to them. In contrast, 'when dealing with their brokers, the banks can buy or refrain from buying, as suits their books.'[67] According to Cole, in the same year, 'money in the City is lent indifferently in the discount market, on the Stock Exchange, and in the produce markets. It is merely a question of which market offers the best rate of interest, taking into account the security and the duration of the loan.'[68] The solution adopted by the bill brokers was to turn to the Bank of England to make up the difference between the bills they were committed to buying and the funds that the banks were willing to lend them. In return for collateral in the form of bills, the Bank of England would lend the brokers the money they required, though at a rate of interest higher than that charged by the banks, and potentially higher than that they were receiving on the bills that they had bought. In this way the Bank of England discouraged the bill brokers from relying on money borrowed from it to finance their holdings of bills and other securities.[69]

This relationship between the bill brokers and the Bank of England evolved in the first half of the nineteenth century, but it was neither sufficiently close nor fully developed to avoid regular liquidity crises resulting in multiple bank failures, as in the 1820s, 1830s, 1840s, and 1850s, as well as that associated with Overend and Gurney in the 1860s. For many the key to the success achieved by the British banking system after the 1860s lay with the changed role played by the Bank of England. It was in this period that it became lender of last resort to the London money market and so helped to eliminate the liquidity crises that had plagued the British banking system since the early eighteenth century. In addition, the Bank of England acted in emergencies, co-ordinating a collective response from the banks when a major player came close to failure with potentially damaging consequences for the whole banking system. This was most clearly demonstrated in 1890 when it was the Bank of

---

[66] J.H. Tritton, 'The Short Loan Fund on the London Money Market', *Journal of the Institute of Bankers* 23 (1902), pp.96-114; J.H. Tritton, 'Bills of Exchange and their Functions', *Journal of the Institute of Bankers*, 23 (1902), pp.213-16.

[67] F. Straker, 'The Daily Money Article', *Journal of the Institute of Bankers*, 25 (1904), pp.5-13.

[68] A.C. Cole, 'Notes on the London Money Market', *Journal of the Institute of Bankers*, 25 (1904), p.134.

[69] For the early development of the London money market see Dixon, *The Development of the London Money Market*, pp.7-8, 14, 18, 32-3, 37, 92, 98, 156, 160.

England that led the rescue of the merchant bank, Barings. Less than twenty-five years before, in contrast, the Bank of England had not intervened to help the discount house Overend and Gurney when in difficulty, and its collapse sparked a major financial crisis. The Bank of England also refused to assist the City of Glasgow Bank when in trouble in 1878, demonstrating its ability to act judiciously and only help those banks that were illiquid, not insolvent. In that way the issue of moral hazard was avoided as banks could not rely on the unconditional support of the Bank of England to prevent their collapse because of the wider damage it would create, regardless of the degree of risk-taking they had indulged in while pursuing a profit-maximizing strategy. Instead, banks were made aware that the assistance of the Bank of England was dependent upon the pursuit of a banking strategy that blended the need to balance risk and return and so ensure survival. The arrival at this position after 1866 is depicted as a long process of trial and error through which the Bank of England slowly assembled the strategy and the tools required. Such a view is particularly prevalent in the USA where it is contrasted with the absence of an emerging central bank until the founding of the Federal Reserve in 1913. Until then the US banking system was seen as lacking both support and co-ordination leaving it exposed to frequent liquidity crises and the collapse of systemically important banks.[70] As George Peel, put it in 1928, 'until the Federal Reserve act was passed in 1913, the banking system of the United States was a disorganized chaos of some 30,000 institutions.'[71] Of course he had no way of knowing that the greatest crisis in US financial history was imminent with the Wall Street Crash of 1929, followed by an avalanche of bank failures in the early 1930s.

What is absent in this interpretation of British banking history is the degree to which the Bank of England was forced to adopt a strategy of becoming lender of last resort, because that was the only option left open to it in the face of the rise of the large joint-stock banks and the use of the Lend and Hold Model. What the Bank of England gained after the 1844 Bank Charter Act was a monopoly over the monetary circulation in England and Wales. In 1845 the circulation of bank notes was divided into £20.7 million from the Bank of England and £7.7 million from other banks. In contrast, by 1913 the total for

---

[70] Allen and Gale, *Understanding Financial Crises*, p.2; Grossman, *Unsettled Account*, pp.96–102; Capie and Woods, *Money over Two Centuries*, pp.3, 49–50, 329–32; N. Dimsdale and A. Hotson, 'Introduction', in Dimsdale and Hotson (eds), *British Financial Crises*, p.7; Capie, 'British Financial Crises', in Dimsdale and Hotson (eds), *British Financial Crises*, p.16; C. Goodhart and G. Illing, 'Introduction', in Goodhart and Illing (eds), *Financial Crises*, p.1; M.D. Bordo, 'The Lender of Last Resort: Alternative Views and Historical Experience', in Goodhart and Illing (eds), *Financial Crises*, p.117, A.J. Schwarz, 'Earmarks of a Lender of Last Resort', in Goodhart and Illing (eds), *Financial Crises*, pp.450–1; J. Hughes, *The Vital Few: American Economic Progress and its Protagonists* (New York: Houghton Mifflin, 1966), pp.441–53.

[71] Peel, *The Economic Impact of America*, pp.29–30.

the Bank of England had risen to £28.7 million whereas that for other banks had virtually disappeared, being down to £0.1 million. In contrast, in both Scotland and Ireland banks retained the right of note issue. In Scotland the total grew steadily from £3.3 million in 1845 to £7.6 million in 1913 while in Ireland the expansion was more modest, rising from £6.9 million in 1845 to £8.3 million in 1913 though it had dropped to as low as £4.5 million in 1850 and £5.7 million in 1880. What the Scottish and Irish data show is the ability of banks in those parts of the UK to expand lending in response to demand by issuing notes, and the necessity of cutting back in a crisis, with consequences for financial stability. It was in Ireland and Scotland that the most notable bank failures took place after 1866 with that of the City of Glasgow in 1878 and the Munster Bank in 1880. In contrast, this option of lending by issuing notes was not available in England after 1844 and, as this took effect it contributed to the growing stability of the banking system.[72]

What the Bank of England lost over the same period was its ability to dominate lending in the UK. This can be seen in the distribution of deposits. By 1870, when Bank of England deposits stood at £25.7 million, those of the trustee savings banks had reached £38.3 million, those of the recently established Post Office Savings Bank stood at £15.1 million, while the commercial banks had accumulated a massive £427.5 million. By 1913, the gap had become even greater. By then deposits at the Bank of England had reached £54.9 million but this was less than the trustee savings banks with £68.7 million, the Post Office Savings Bank with £187.2 million and the commercial banks with £1,064.1 million, while there also existed a plethora of other banks and financial institutions that collected deposits such as the building societies, benefit clubs, merchant banks, discount companies, finance houses, overseas banks, and the branches and agents of foreign banks. Under these conditions the Bank of England lacked the resources to operate as anything other than the lender of last resort. Even taking the Bank of England's deposits and its bank note circulation together for 1870 only produces a total of £49 million compared to the £427.5 million of deposits alone held by the commercial banks, creating a difference of £377.5 million. In 1913 the gap was even more apparent. The combined circulation and deposits of the Bank of England stood at £83.6 million compared to the commercial bank deposits of £1,064.1 million, creating a difference of £970.5 million.[73]

In the era in which all banks, apart from it, were small and private, the Bank of England had no direct rivals, being the sole English joint-stock bank. Under those circumstances the Bank of England was inclined to act as lender of

---

[72] Mitchell, *British Historical Statistics*, p.868.
[73] Mitchell, *British Historical Statistics*, pp.658–9, 663, 671–2, 868; Clapham, *The Bank of England*, v.2, pp.115, 134–48, 177, 183–7, 220, 250–61, 276–6, 280, 299, 321–2, 357, 373, 403–7, Appendices C, D, and E.

last resort to a private bank in difficulty, but only on a highly selective basis and without any consistency. After the cap on the number of partners was removed, and a growing number of banks were organized on a joint-stock basis, the Bank of England faced growing rivalry that threatened its position as the dominant bank. This made it reluctant to act as lender of last resort, and so prop up potential rivals.[74] The level of competition the Bank of England faced intensified from the late 1850s onwards with the formation of joint-stock discount houses and other finance houses. Using the joint-stock form these discount houses and related financial companies were able to raise a large capital, which they employed by buying bills, threatening the Bank's dominance of the discount market. As a result, it was openly hostile to their activities and refused to deal with them. A number of these joint-stock discount houses did overreach themselves in the early 1860s, by buying bills directly from borrowers who subsequently defaulted, and they collapsed, receiving no assistance from the Bank of England. However, a new group of joint-stock discount houses were formed in 1863-5, and these included conversions of existing partnerships. One of these conversions in 1865 was Overend and Gurney, the largest discount house at the time. With the appearance of so many heavily capitalized joint-stock discount houses at the same time, the market for bills became overcrowded and highly competitive. To survive in business, these discount houses took greater and greater risks, buying bills that had been issued not to obtain temporary funds but to finance investment such as railway infrastructure. There was no possibility that such bills could be repaid after ninety days as they would have to be renewed until the investment was completed and more permanent funding obtained, such as through the sale of stocks and bonds to investors. This left the likes of Overend and Gurney exposed to a liquidity crisis as it was funding the purchase of these bills not only from its capital but also using short-term funds borrowed from banks on which it paid attractive rates of interest. However, when concerns began to circulate that some of the borrowers were likely to default, as they could not obtain this replacement funding, those who had lent to the discount houses tried to withdraw their money. The run on Overend and Gurney began in January 1866 but came to a head on the 9th of May 1866 when it became known that the Bank of England had refused assistance. Overend and Gurney then suspended payment to those it owed money on the 10th of May, though it was not the first joint-stock discount house to be forced to do so, just the largest and best known. What this suspension also meant was that those borrowers who had expected to re-finance their operations by issuing new

[74] Newton, *Change and Continuity*, pp.4, 20; Wood, *History of Central Banking*, pp.111-13; R. Sylla, 'Comparing the UK and US Financial Systems, 1790-1830', in Atack and Neal (eds), *The Origin and Development of Financial Markets and Institutions*, pp.234-5; Collins, *Money and Banking*, p.40; Newton, 'The Birth of Joint-Stock Banking', pp.27-52.

bills to replace those that were maturing, could not do so. Instead, they defaulted on the payment of their bills, and their failure then spread the panic to those banks that were known to be large holders of these bills, causing a run on them by those that held their notes or had deposits with them. It was only after Overend and Gurney had collapsed that the Bank of England stepped in to buy bills and make loans, so alleviating the liquidity crisis while re-establishing its dominance of the discount market. In the aftermath of the Overend and Gurney crisis, banks became wary of trusting any financial institution, other than the Bank of England, with those funds that were temporarily idle but constituted their liquid reserve. Instead, they spread it around a number of bill brokers and discount houses while also keeping a balance with the Bank of England. This meant that the Bank of England was no longer threatened by a major rival but it still needed to generate profits so as to pay dividends to its shareholders.[75]

Another major development that took place after 1866 provided the Bank of England with a means of generating these profits, and that was the use made of it by the joint-stock banks. In 1854, both the Bank and the joint-stock banks had become members of the London Clearing House. What this provided was a mechanism for settling the balances that built up between the banks through debiting and crediting the accounts they opened at the Bank of England. It was to cover these balances that the banks maintained deposits at the Bank of England on which they received no interest. What developed after 1866 was a situation in which the major British banks kept accounts at the Bank of England through which they made and received payments from each other. These accounts required them to maintain positive balances at the Bank out of which they could meet any shortfall and on which they received no payment. In 1844, out of the Bank's total deposits of £13.6 million only £1million came from banks. The rest came from individuals, businesses, and the government. By 1913 deposits had grown to £54.9 million and of these £24.6 million was owed to banks or almost half the total, helping to make it the bankers' bank.[76] As a result it had available to it the collective liquidity of the British banking system, apart from that kept as cash in each branch and head office. As Fowler

---

[75] J.E. Lander, *Operations in the London Money Market, 1858-67* (Ph.D., University of London, 1972), pp.5, 11, 13, 53, 66, 71–2, 83–9, 113, 116, 122–32, 144–8, 159, 182–6, Appendices B and E; Taylor, *Boardroom Scandal*, p.137; G. Elliot, *The Mystery of Overend Gurney: A Financial Scandal in Victorian London* (London: Methuen, 2006), pp.154–8, 171–85, 226; Cottrell, 'London's First "Big Bang"?' in Cassis and Cottrell (eds), *World of Private Banking*, pp.66, 71–3, 90–3; Capie, 'British Financial Crises', in Dimsdale and Hotson (eds), *British Financial Crises*, pp.11–18; Dimsdale and Hotson, 'Financial Crises and Economic Activity in the UK since 1825' in Dimsdale and Hotson (eds), *British Financial Crises*, pp.38–40; M. Flandreau and S. Ugolini, 'The Crisis of 1866', in Dimsdale and Hotson (eds), *British Financial Crises*, pp.81–5; G. and P. Cleaver, *The Union Discount: A Centenary Album* (London: Union Discount, 1985), pp.12–26; Sayers, *Gilletts*, pp.6–8; Sayers, *Lloyds Bank*, p.183.

[76] Mitchell, *British Historical Statistics*, pp.658–9, 663, 671–2, 868.

noted in 1900, 'The one reserve system has been adopted and holds its own so far, as involving so great economy of loanable money, and being so convenient to all concerned in the management of our banking system.'[77]

This gave the Bank of England access to a cheap but volatile source of funding. Bankers' balances at the Bank of England fluctuated during the course of the day as well as over the year, as each bank made and received payments through its own business and the global correspondent network of which it was the key hub. In 1870 these balances were as low as £5.2 million and as high as £16.1 million while in 1913 they went from a low of £21.4 million to a high of £40.7 million. The Bank of England increasingly used these funds to lend money to the discount houses at premium rates, when they needed to cover the margin between their borrowing and lending. By 1907, the Bank of England only provided discount facilities for seventy-four firms, mainly discount houses and bill brokers, compared to over a thousand a century earlier.[78] One of those was the discount house Gilletts, for example, which became a specialist dealer in money after 1870. However, Gilletts only turned to the Bank of England for funds when no other was available, because alternative sources were always cheaper.[79] The activities of the India Office in London between 1860 and 1914 are particularly revealing about the role played by the Bank of England. The India Office maintained a minimum balance of £0.5 million at the Bank of England so as to be in a position to meet commitments. As it received no interest on this deposit it employed any additional funds it had elsewhere in the City. The India Office lent out money directly to banks, discount houses, and stockbrokers on a staggered basis so that re-payments occurred daily, though the loans could be renewed at the prevailing interest rate. Borrowers provided collateral in the form of bills, bonds, and stocks. This was all arranged through the stockbrokers, Nivisons, who operated as rivals to the discount houses. At the beginning of each day Nivisons were told by the India Office the amount of new money available for lending and the loans that were to be renewed. They used their expertise and knowledge of the money market to determine the interest rate and who to lend to. These loans provided an alternative source of liquidity to that available from the Bank of England.[80]

What developed after 1866 was a new set of relationships between banks, including the Bank of England. The joint-stock banks moved steadily towards a Lend and Hold Model and so no longer generated the same volume of bills. Their use of the discount market was to either employ their liquid funds or

---

[77] Fowler, 'Banking Reserves', p.246. See also W.J. Aitchison, 'On the Ratio a Banker's Cash Reserve Should Bear to his Liability on Current and Deposit Accounts, as Exemplified by the London Clearing Joint-Stock Banks', *Journal of the Institute of Bankers*, 6 (1885), pp.300–8.

[78] Clapham, *The Bank of England*, v.2, pp.275–6, 280, 299, 321–2, 353–7, 373, 403–7, Appendices C, D, and E.

[79] Sayers, *Gilletts*, pp.53–5.   [80] Sunderland, *Financing the Raj*, pp.24, 69, 146, 190–206.

borrow to meet a temporary shortfall as part of a strategy in which assets and liabilities were matched so as to minimize the risk of a crisis. The Bank of England played a key role in this by acting as lender of last resort to the discount houses, who intermediated between the banks.[81] The discount houses were aware of the quality of collateral that the Bank of England required when acting as lender of last resort on a daily basis, and this acted as a restraint on the type of bills they would accept from banks, and thus on the banks themselves. Between 1857 and 1890, for example, the Bank of England refused to discount bills not having more than fifteen days to run. This was an attempt to restrict its lending to what were considered legitimate productive purposes such as the finance of trade and prevent the loans it made being invested in stocks and bonds, which it regarded as speculation. Commercial bills normally ran for ninety days while finance bills covered the settlement period of the London Stock Exchange, where sales and purchases had normally to be completed at the end of a specified fourteen-day period. The attempt was not successful and was eventually abandoned in 1890 as finance bills grew in popularity. The change reflected a growing flexibility by the Bank of England as lender of last resort to the London money market. The discount houses also acted as the Bank of England's informants as they were aware of those that needed to borrow, those able to lend, and the rumours circulating as they walked around the City twice daily on their visit to those banks that were their clients. What this meant was that the bill brokers operating in the London money market could rely on the support of the Bank of England to balance their commitments in terms of the money they had borrowed and lent between the banks. It also meant that they could look to the Bank of England for assistance in a crisis.[82]

It was to fulfil this role that the Bank of England co-ordinated the support that saved the merchant bank, Barings, from collapse in 1890 rather than concerns about the bank itself and the role it played in the issue of securities on behalf of foreign governments and companies. Barings was heavily engaged in guaranteeing bills of exchange as this improved their quality and so made

---

[81] Capie and Woods, *Money over Two Centuries*, pp.3, 49–50, 64; Grossman, *Unsettled Account*, pp.72, 96, 111–12, 125, 147–8, 178–81; Wood, *History of Central Banking*, pp.111–13; Collins and Baker, *Commercial Banking*, pp.108, 179–81; Singleton, *Central Banking in the Twentieth Century*, p.37; Y. Cassis, 'Management and Strategy in the English Joint Stock Banks, 1890–1914', *Business History*, 27 (1985), p.301; M. Collins and M. Baker, 'Financial Crises and Structural Change in English Commercial Bank Assets, 1860–1914', *Explorations in Economic History*, 36 (1999), pp.429–30; J. Armstrong, 'Hooley and the Bovril Company', *Business History*, 28 (1986), p.24; M. Collins, 'English Bank Lending and the Financial Crisis of the 1870s', *Business History*, 32 (1990), p.210.

[82] Aitchison, 'On the Ratio a Banker's Cash Reserve Should Bear to his Liability', pp.477–89; Steele, 'On Changes in the Bank Rate of Discount', pp.477–89; Dunn, 'Banking in 1837 and in 1897', p.384; Tritton, 'The Short Loan Fund', p.100; Sykes, 'The Growth of London', p.376; Straker, 'The Daily Money Article', pp.5–13.

them more acceptable within the London money market. If Barings had failed, the guarantee it provided would have become worthless, creating doubt and confusion in the mind of those holding the bills it had accepted. This was the predicament the Bank of England faced in 1890 when the growing volume of bills that Barings had guaranteed made it aware that a potential crisis was developing. It was not only the Bank of England that would be affected if Barings was allowed to fail, for doubts might emerge about all bills in circulation between the banks. As Barings was able to show that it was solvent, the risk of incurring a loss in providing Barings with financial assistance was limited, and so the Bank of England was able to carry the large joint-stock banks with it in organizing a rescue. What this reflected was a closer way of working between the various banks operating in London by this time. In contrast, neither the City of Glasgow Bank in 1878 nor the Liberator Building Society in 1892 posed a threat to the security of bills and the operation of the inter-bank money market and so could be allowed to fail.[83]

This role played by the Bank of England, as lender of last resort, was the last piece in the complex arrangements that brought stability to the British banking system in the course of the 1826–1914 period. All had been achieved without government intervention, other than the removal of the laws that had restricted the growth of large-scale banking. This lack of government intervention in shaping the British banking system even extended to the Bank of England itself because it remained a joint-stock company throughout, owned not by the British government but by investors and so answerable to them. Hence the reason it guarded its position as lender of last resort so jealously, as that was one of the ways it could generate profits in competition with either joint-stock banks possessed of huge deposits, extensive branch networks and strong businesses, or private banks specializing in international finance, whether involving the issuing of stocks and bonds or the provision of trade credit. This independence from government intervention was a source of pride among bankers who contrasted it with the situation in other countries. In 1906 H.G. Brown noted that, 'in England, banks, whether owned by individuals or companies, are allowed to conduct their business practically free from

---

[83] 'The Financial Crisis of November 1890', *Journal of the Institute of Bankers*, 12 (1891), p.5; Cottrell, 'London's First "Big Bang"?' in Cassis and Cottrell (eds), *World of Private Banking*, p.98; J. Orbell, 'Private Banks and International Finance in the Light of the Archives of Baring Brothers', in Cassis and Cottrell (eds), *World of Private Banking*, p.147; Capie, 'British Financial Crises' in Dimsdale and Hotson (eds), *British Financial Crises*, p.16; Flandreau and Ugolini, 'The Crisis of 1866', in Dimsdale and Hotson (eds), *British Financial Crises*, pp.87–93; R. Roberts, '"How We Saved the City": The Management of the Financial Crisis of 1914', in Dimsdale and Hotson (eds), *British Financial Crises*, pp.96–8; Turner, 'Holding Shareholders to Account', in Dimsdale and Hotson (eds), *British Financial Crises*, p.151; Sayers, *Lloyds Bank*, pp.183–4, 208, 312; Sayers, *Gilletts*, pp.36–7, 46–8, 52–5; Roberts, *Saving the City*, pp.30, 83–6.

special interference or restrictions.'[84] In particular, comparisons were made between the UK banking system and that of the USA, which were all in favour of the former. In 1909, J.A. Schearme referred to the US banking system as 'decentralized and headless', suggesting that was the reason for its chronic instability.[85] In the same year S.E. Perry claimed that the 'complex American system for the regulation of banks, bristling with legal restrictions, elaborate reports and provisions for their strict supervision by a state bureau, has no counterpart in this country.'[86] However, it was not simply the absence of a lender of last resort that made the US banking system so unstable. The barriers to size imposed by the legislation of the 1860s made it impossible to operate a Lend and Hold Model without incurring the risks of both liquidity and solvency crises.

The Bank of England did not act as lender of last resort to the UK banking system until the crisis created by the outbreak of the First World War. What had developed after 1866 was a changed relationship between the Bank of England and the rest of the British banking system, driven by the steady move of the joint-stock banks towards a Lend and Hold Model. This pushed the Bank of England to the position of marginal provider of liquidity to the discount houses, which was of major importance not only for British domestic banks but also the global banking system because of their direct and indirect connections to it. That still left the Bank of England with a role to play co-ordinating action in a crisis but, again, it did so to protect its own interests. That was the case in 1890 with Barings because of its key role as an acceptor—guarantor—of the bills circulating in the discount market. In contrast Overend and Gurney posed a threat to the Bank of England and so was allowed to fail. The problems of the City of Glasgow Bank and the Liberator Building Society were both irrelevant to the Bank of England, and so they too could be allowed to fail. What changed was the First World War and then the Governorship of Montagu Norman. Between the wars the Bank of England gradually emerged with the functions of a central bank with a remit far wider than the narrow business model it had long operated with.[87]

[84] H.G. Brown, 'The Position of Foreign Companies in England', *Journal of the Institute of Bankers*, 27 (1906), p.164.
[85] J.A. Schearme, 'English and American Banking Methods: A Comparison and Contrast', *Journal of the Institute of Bankers*, 30 (1909), pp. 498-500.
[86] S.E. Perry, 'English and American Banking Methods: A Comparison and Contrast', *Journal of the Institute of Bankers*, 30 (1909), p.551.
[87] This is dealt with in chapter 5.

CONCLUSION

What happened to the British banking system between 1826 and 1914 is that it learnt how to cope with crises and to meet the needs of an urban/industrial economy operating in a global environment with almost no barriers to the free movement of goods, services, capital, and people. It was only in the fifty years before the First World War that the banking system achieved a way of working that balanced risk-taking with resilience through careful attention to the asset and liability side of the balance sheet and the facilities it could call upon in London, notably access to an unrivalled international payments system and a money market of depth and breadth unmatched by any other. The sense of what had been achieved is evident in the statements made by British bankers as they exported their model of operation to other countries around the world, and their inability to comprehend why everyone did not copy what they had achieved. For those reasons they found incomprehensible the few criticisms levelled at them by those who regretted the passing of the private bank and the local bank. It seemed little more than nostalgia for a simpler and more rural past and was out of keeping with the complex global economy within which bankers had to survive and prosper. On the eve of the First World War, British bankers had confidence in the system they had created, and could point to its ability to surmount successive financial crises as proof that their faith was not misplaced. According to Richard S. Grossman the high costs of bank collapses mean that bank stability should be highly valued but it was also important to have an efficient banking system and that was achieved through competition which could lead to instability.[88] Balancing stability and competition had defeated British bankers before 1866 but over the next fifty years they accomplished the task. In the years that followed the stability would, unfortunately, be taken for granted and the limits on competition magnified in importance.

[88] Grossman, *Unsettled Account*, pp.130–1.

5

Complications and Co-operation, 1914–1945

INTRODUCTION

The thirty years between the outbreak of the First World War in 1914 and the end of the Second in 1945 were ones in which the British banking system was subjected to enormous challenges. The environment within which British banks operated became increasingly complicated compared to the past, whether it was in the domestic economy, overseas countries, or international finance. In addition to the disruptive effects of the two world wars there was also a global financial crisis that began with the Wall Street Crash in 1929 and did not end until 1932, if not later. It left a deep and prolonged global economic depression in its wake. This meant that for half the period between 1914 and 1945 the British banking system was operating under either wartime conditions or under severe financial stress. Internationally, evidence of the difficult environment within which banks had to operate can found in the unstable monetary conditions. The UK government suspended Britain's participation in the international Gold Standard between 1919 and 1925 and then again from 1931 onwards. Domestically, this period was one in which Britain's major manufacturing industries as well as coal mining experienced very volatile trading conditions, pushing many businesses into losses in the 1920s and 1930s. Throughout, the London money market faced a major challenge from other financial centres, especially New York. These conditions tested the resilience of the British banking system. What is remarkable is how well all components of the banking system performed, continuing to function normally throughout the entire period, and doing so with only limited government support, unlike the position in most other countries. With few exceptions, most countries experienced a severe banking crisis at some stage between 1914 and 1945. One of those exceptions was the UK, along with the likes of Australia and Canada, which possessed similar banking systems in terms of structure and operation. In many ways the period from 1914 to 1945 was when the British banking system was most tested. The result was a vindication of what had emerged before 1914.[1]

WAR

To many, the First World War was a watershed, dividing a world in which banking systems evolved relatively free of political intervention to one in which governments played a major role.[2] That was certainly the direction of travel in the UK though the level and pace of change was neither direct, nor rapid, nor transformative. Unlike the USA or Germany in the 1930s there was no radical government intervention prompted by the fear that the entire banking system was on the verge of collapse. The only outward indication that something had changed was the action by the post-war Labour government to take the Bank of England into state ownership in 1946.[3] The absence of visible signs of change belied the gradual transformation that had taken place in the previous thirty years.

The outbreak of the First World War caught the British banking system completely unprepared. Only prompt action by the Bank of England, the commercial banks, and the Stock Exchange, supported by the Treasury, averted a crisis that threatened the entire financial system with collapse. The exposure of banks to mass withdrawals by worried depositors meant that they were extremely vulnerable in the event of a panic caused by the prospect of a major European conflict. To cover such an eventuality, but not on this potential scale, banks had relied on the London money market. The crisis created by the threat of a major war froze the money market as all banks wanted to borrow or sell bills and securities and none were willing to lend or buy. The closure of the London Stock Exchange on the 31st of July 1914 was a signal to those holding bills, stocks, and bonds that they could no longer sell them and so repay borrowed funds. On the 30 July 1914, there was around £350 million in bills circulating in the London discount market, with two-thirds being on account of foreign banks, including those from Germany. As the possibility of a military conflict grew real there was a run on banks as retail depositors sought to change Bank of England notes for gold while at the wholesale level loans were called in and no new ones made. It was those financial institutions catering for small savers such as the building societies

---

[1] For the context within which British banks operated in this period see Reinhart and Rogoff, *This Time is Different*; Cassis, *Crises and Opportunities,*; Kindleberger and Aliber, *Manias, Panics, and Crashes.*

[2] See P. Krugman (ed.), *Currency Crises* (Chicago: University of Chicago Press, 2000), p.18.

[3] R.S. Sayers, *The Bank of England, 1891–1944* (Cambridge: CUP, 1976), pp. 578–9.

and the 'penny' banks that were worst affected, forcing them to stop all lending and limit withdrawals. However, the large joint-stock banks were also exposed because they operated on low reserves of cash, relying on the money market to make good any deficit.

The UK government's response was an Act that came into force on the 3rd of August 1914 that temporarily suspended payment on bills of exchange. This moratorium prevented banks from calling in their loans, which stabilized the situation. Prompt action by the Bank of England, acting as both lender of last resort and crisis manager, then prevented the emerging liquidity crisis becoming a solvency crisis bringing down the entire banking system. The Bank of England agreed to buy all bills outstanding including those it would not normally have accepted. By 27th November 1914 the Bank of England had bought £120 million out of the estimated £350 million in circulation, and continued to advance money to allow additional bills to be paid off. It had the resources to do this as the bankers' balances it held rose from an average of £25 million in July to a peak of £109 million by early December. Its safe haven status drew money to it and away from banks perceived at being at risk. When the banks re-opened there was no run as preparations had been made to ensure that they were able to meet any demands. Faced with the prospect of a financial panic that could have brought down the entire banking system, and so inflict widespread damage on the economy, the Treasury, Bank of England, and the commercial banks devised a scheme that would meet the demand for cash. By guaranteeing that payments would be made, and by expanding the money supply, sufficient confidence and liquidity was provided to persuade those owed money from pressing for payment. Those actions overcame the immediate crisis and so prevented a widespread panic in which the public would have rushed to withdraw their savings, fearing that banks were on the verge of collapse.[4] The result was a large increase in the issue of notes and a general expansion of credit, which satisfied the immediate demand and averted a serious crisis.[5]

All around the world moratoria had been enacted suspending payment. Spalding reflected in 1915 what this meant. 'for a period following the outbreak of war the credit system of the principal markets of the world had broken down'.[6] In the UK the combination of the moratorium on payments, the issue of Treasury-backed paper currency and the action by the Bank of England had averted a potentially catastrophic banking crisis that no

---

[4] D. Lloyd George, *War Memoirs* (London: Odhams, 1933), v.1, chapter entitled 'How We Saved the City'.

[5] For this episode see J. Peters, 'The British Government and the City/Industry Divide: The Case of the 1914 Financial Crisis', *Twentieth Century British History*, 4 (1993) and T. Seabourne, 'The Summer of 1914', in Capie and Wood (eds), *Financial Crises*.

[6] W.F. Spalding, 'The Foreign Exchanges and the War', *Journal of the Institute of Bankers*, 36 (1915), p.320.

peacetime financial system could cope with.[7] The discount house, Smith St. Aubyn recorded the unfolding crisis in brief but stark detail in their daily Business Diary. On 1st August 1914 they reported that, 'The Joint Stock banks panicked, and it was only at ¼ to 1 that we were able to get anything. A truly fearful Saturday... The worst day we have ever had since the business began... The whole market absolutely broke.' Holding a portfolio of bills they could not sell and unable to replace the loans being called in by the banks, the discount houses faced bankruptcy and looked to the Bank of England for support. On the 7th of August, Smith St. Aubyn recorded that, 'A moratorium declared for one month, which saved the whole financial situation. We re-opened for business but did nothing.' By the beginning of September 1914 Smith St. Aubyn observed, 'Things getting on to a more workable condition.'[8]

This close co-operation between the Treasury, the Bank of England, and the banks continued for the duration of the war. Reflecting this closer relationship with the government, forged during the war, was the creation of two bodies to represent different branches of banking. The first to be formed in 1914 was the Accepting Houses Association. This grouped all the leading merchant banks. In 1919 the British Bankers' Association was formed, to represent the joint-stock banks. Co-operation between these organizations and the government not only helped to avert subsequent financial crises, caused by shocks on the military front, but also ensured that the government obtained the funds necessary to finance the continuing war effort, whether its own or that of its allies.[9] For the duration of the war the British government's own funding requirements, as orchestrated by Cunliffe, Governor of the Bank of England, took priority. On the 24th of November 1915, Smith St. Aubyn reported that, 'All the clearing banks have been ordered to charge 4½ for call, notice and evening money, with what object is not clear except that Cunliffe hopes to get more money from the Banks at 4½ to lend to the government at 5%.' Such a situation continued to the end of the war, as revealed in this comment from the 8th of January 1917: 'Bank of England (Cunliffe) is up to his old Tricks and is offering to take any money from the Bankers at 5%. Even foreign bankers are lending "through" their bankers.'[10] Much of this borrowing took place through the issue of short-dated Treasury Bills. The value of Treasury Bills

---

[7] Roberts, *Saving the City*, pp.30–2, 48–68, 83–6, 129–43, 151–68; Roberts, '"How We Saved the City"' in Dimsdale and Hotson (eds), *British Financial Crises*, pp.100–13; Sayers, *Lloyds Bank*, p.216; B. Ritchie, *We're with the Woolwich*, p.59.

[8] Smith St. Aubyn: Business Diary 1 August 1914, 7 August 1914, 2 September 1914, 24 November 1915, 8 January 1917; E. Sykes, 'Some Effects of the War on the London Money Market', *Journal of the Institute of Bankers* 36 (1914), pp.73–8.

[9] Siegel, *For Peace and Money*, p.7; Ackrill and Hannah, *Barclays*, p.99. See Roberts, *Saving the City*.

[10] Smith St. Aubyn: Business Diary 1 August 1914, 7 August 1914, 2 September 1914, 24 November 1915, 8 January 1917.

outstanding rose from £15.5 million in July 1914 to £1.1 billion in January 1919.[11] The effect of this was to crowd out other borrowers.

Internationally, those banks that had relied on the London money market were forced to look elsewhere, either to their own resources or New York, while the London branches of enemy nations, like Germany, were closed down completely.[12] Even British overseas banks, with London head offices, reduced their dependence upon the London money market and relied more on local sources of credit.[13] It was not only banks operating outside the UK that suffered as a result of the enormous escalation of government borrowing during the First World War. By 1919, lending by domestic banks to their individual and business customers had fallen to about half its pre-war level, or 32 per cent of the funds available, as the government absorbed the nation's savings. It was banks that took up most of the government's short-term borrowings, as well as lending to their customers so that they could buy the long-term bonds issued by the government. The National Debt, which stood at £706.2 million in 1914, had risen to £7,481.1 million in 1919, or a tenfold increase.[14]

During the First World War, the British banking system had to respond to the needs of the British government rather than operate within a commercial environment where each bank competed for business. The result was to create a climate of co-operation, under the authority of the Bank of England, which contributed to the successful mobilization of funds for the war effort but reduced the incentive to compete actively for depositors and borrowers. The experience of co-operation between the Treasury, the Bank of England, and

---

[11] S. Broadberry and P. Howlett, 'The United Kingdom during World War I: Business as Usual?', in S. Broadberry and M. Harrison (eds), *The Economics of World War I* (Cambridge: CUP, 2005), p.218.

[12] J. Inouye, *Problems of the Japanese Exchange, 1914-1926* (Glasgow: Macmillan, 1931) [English translation by E. H. de Bunsen from the Japanese original written in 1926], p.4; G. Odate, *Japan's Financial Relations with the United States* (New York: Columbia University, 1922), pp.32-6; Tamaki, *Japanese Banking*, pp.119, 131, 155-6; H. van B. Cleveland and T.F. Huertas, *Citibank, 1812-1970* (Cambridge: Mass.: Harvard UP, 1985), p.74; A.C. Whitaker, *Foreign Exchange* (New York: Appleton, 1919), p.627; Further Papers Relating to the Measures Taken by His Majesty's Government for Sustaining Credit and Facilitating Business, 1914: Public Statements 5 September 1914, 3 November 1914; Letter from Treasury to Bank of England, 30 September 1914; Enemy Banks (London Agencies): Report by Sir William Plender 16 December 1916, p.12.

[13] A.K. Bagchi, *The Evolution of the State Bank of India, v.2, The Era of the Presidency Banks, 1876-1920* (Delhi: State Bank of India, 1997), pp.450-3, 519, 535, 549; Mackenzie, *Realms of Silver*, p.228; Tyson, *100 Years of Banking*, pp.157, 178; D. Joslin, *A Century of Banking in Latin America* (London: OUP, 1963), pp.217, 228; King, *The History of the Hongkong and Shanghai Banking Corporation*, v.2, pp.569-70; G. Jones, *The History of the British Bank of the Middle East* (Cambridge: CUP, 1986), v.1, pp.41, 158, 179, 248, 259-63, 286, 354; Sunderland, *Financing the Raj*, pp.71, 202-6.

[14] For government war finance see A.W. Kirkaldy (ed.), *British Finance During and After the War, 1914-21* (London: British Association for the Advancement of Science, 1921); E.V. Morgan, *Studies in British Financial Policy 1914-25* (London: Macmillan, 1952).

the major banks forged during the war remained as a legacy long after the end of hostilities in November 1918.[15]

CONGRATULATIONS AND CRITICISMS

At the beginning of the war no less a person than the economist, John Maynard Keynes, was fulsome in his praise for the British banking system, after it had coped with the instability created by the outbreak of hostilities. In November 1914 he noted that, 'I believe our banking system, and indeed the whole intricate organism of the City, to be one of the best and most characteristic creations of that part of the genius and virtue of our nation which has found its outlet in "business".'[16] Such an opinion prevailed throughout the war years as the banks continued to function normally despite all the obstacles created by a military conflict of growing intensity and cost. Similarly, the stability exhibited by the British banking system during the world financial crisis of 1929–32, occasioned a great deal of self-congratulation, as in 1931: 'None other than the British banking system could have withstood so successfully such a financial upheaval as we have recently witnessed, and this undoubtedly has been due to the deeply rooted belief in the integrity and prudence of our banks.'[17] With problems apparent in the banking systems of other countries, this self-congratulation continued throughout the 1930s, as in 1935: 'The strength of the British banks has been amply demonstrated during the last few years of crisis and depression. During that period there has not at any time been any hint of failure or even of real anxiety for their safety.'[18] In particular, during both the 1920s and the 1930s British banking was favourably compared to that of the USA. The US central bank, the Federal Reserve, was regarded as structurally inferior to the Bank of England, while the system of branch banking that existed in the UK was regarded as so obviously superior to the unitary banking system of the USA, especially in terms of resilience in the face of crises, that there was a lack of comprehension over why it had not been adopted there. The only explanation as to why the British

---

[15] Roberts, *Saving the City*, pp.167–8.
[16] J.M. Keynes, 'The Prospects of Money, November 1914', *Economic Journal*, 24 (1914), p.633.
[17] H.E. Evitt, 'Exchange Dealings under Current Conditions', *Journal of the Institute of Bankers*, 52 (1931), p.456.
[18] C.W. Taylor, 'The Case against the Nationalisation of the Banks', *Journal of the Institute of Bankers*, 56 (1935), pp.374, 385–6.

system of banking had not been universally adopted appeared to be that each country chose a banking system to suit its own needs.[19]

This self-congratulation was partially defensive because growing criticisms of the British banking system emerged soon after the end of the war and the brief post-war boom. To many between the wars the difficulties experienced by British manufacturing industry were attributed to a lack of support from the banks.[20] British banks were judged not against their ability to remain resilient in the face of crises, maintain a reliable payments system, or provide a secure home for savings. Instead, they were judged on the single criteria of the level of finance that they provided for UK manufacturing industry, and there they were found wanting. A number of public inquiries were established to inquire into whether there was a case against the banks. The most extensive was the Committee on Industry and Trade that conducted a series of industry-based investigations between 1924 and 1928. In its final report in 1929, the conclusion it reached was that, 'It has been shown that the root cause of this incapacity (to re-equip) is not any defects on the part of the British banks or other financial institutions, which are undoubtedly able and willing to supply industry with all necessary facilities on reasonable terms of security. Nor does it arise from any indisposition of the public to subscribe new capital for industrial concerns provided that there is a prospect of obtaining a reasonable return. This is abundantly shown by the ease with which such industries as are earning good profits are able to secure all the capital they need. The tap root of the mischief is the continued non-profitability of so many industrial concerns, which makes them unable to give security to the banks or offer an attractive investment to the public.'[21]

This was not a popular verdict in the face of the continuing economic problems, manifesting themselves in the persistence of high levels of unemployment. The result was another inquiry, to be conducted by the Committee on Finance and Industry. Among its members was the eminent economist John Maynard Keynes, who was highly influential in driving both its agenda and the conclusions it reached. Its report was issued in 1931, in the midst of a global financial crisis, and provided the verdict that met public approval. While praising 'the short-term money market' and the

---

[19] E.C. Gibson, 'A Critical and Historical Account of the Working of the American Federal Reserve Banking System', *Journal of the Institute of Bankers*, 48 (1927), pp.464-7; T.E. Gregory, 'The Practical Working of the Federal Reserve Banking System of the United States', *Journal of the Institute of Bankers*, 50 (1929), pp.556-65 and 51 (1930), pp.3-15, 77-9; F.W. Gray, 'Impressions of New York Banking', *Journal of the Institute of Bankers*, 50 (1929), p.283; P. Barrett Whale, 'English and Continental Banking', *Journal of the Institute of Bankers*, 52 (1931), pp.204-9, 388-9.

[20] T. Johnston, *The Financiers and the Nation* (London: Methuen, 1931); see 'Introduction' by Sydney Webb at p.vii.

[21] Committee on Industry and Trade, *Final Report*: Cmd 3282 (London: H.M.S.O., 1929), pp.298-9.

contribution of banks to the 'the financing of trade and commerce' the report was highly critical of the banks in terms of their support for British manufacturing. 'Coming back now to the more general question of the relations between finance and industry, and in particular to the provision of long-dated capital, we believe that there is substance in the view that the British financial organization concentrated in the City of London might with advantage be more closely co-ordinated with British industry, particularly large-scale industry, than is now the case; and that in some respects the City is more highly organized to provide capital to foreign countries than to British industry.'[22]

Out of this report came the term the 'Macmillan Gap', named after the chairman of the committee, Lord Macmillan. Though referring specifically to the lack of provision within the financial system for the needs of medium-sized businesses, the Macmillan Gap was taken to represent the gulf between banking and industry in Britain. With many industrialists facing difficult trading conditions between the wars, resulting in low profitability or persistent losses, it was only natural that they would blame banks for refusing to provide them with the funds to keep going or to invest in the new equipment that might make them more competitive, so providing ample evidence that the financial system was failing to deliver. In contrast, few appreciated the predicament that banks were in, faced with the necessity of balancing the interests of their depositors, whose money it was they were lending, and those of the industrialists who came to them for loans, at a time when their businesses were losing money and had little prospect of becoming profitable in the near future. One person who did appreciate the predicament that British bankers faced at the time was a fellow banker from Germany, Jacob Golschmidt. He gave evidence to the Macmillan Committee and made his opinions clear. When asked, 'Do I understand that the German banker, like the English banker, does not like to have his money tied up permanently in industry?' he replied, 'No, the German banker dislikes that as much as any banker anywhere else in the world.'[23] However, his was not the opinion that the Macmillan Committee based their conclusions upon. A reason for the critical stance the Macmillan Committee adopted is found in its own report, when it confessed that, 'It may be that we are too far removed in this country from the days of great banking failures and panics, and the ruin following from the destruction of confidence, to esteem at its proper worth the enormous value of an impregnable banking system.'[24]

One important reason why public opinion was so ready to blame banks for manufacturing industry's economic woes was the link to the concentration of power that had taken place within British banking. No longer was the control

---

[22] Committee on Finance and Industry (1931), pp.161–75.
[23] Committee on Finance and Industry (1931), Q 7285.
[24] Committee on Finance and Industry (1931).

of banks spread over the country, keeping them in touch with the specific financial needs of each community. Instead, it rested in a small number of London head offices. From that it seemed an obvious conclusion to draw that banks directed from London were not interested in serving customers located elsewhere in the UK. It was no mere coincidence that London and the South-East enjoyed continuing prosperity whereas it was the North that was experiencing economic distress. Here a contrast was drawn with Germany where the level of concentration was much less. A.W Kirkaldy, writing in 1921, was one among a number who made this observation: 'The German banking system, with its tentacles stretching into every important trade, particularly of a developmental character, has much for commendation from a national standpoint. To it has been largely due the extraordinary development of the trade, manufactures, and business of Germany in recent pre-war years.'[25] This unfavourable comparison between the UK's banking system and that of other countries has become embedded in the literature seeking to explain Britain's economic performance in the twentieth century.[26]

CONCENTRATION

It was certainly true that banking in England and Wales had become dominated by those with London head offices through a process of mergers that largely ended in 1922. Specialist financial institutions had always been located in London, such as the merchant and overseas banks, but now commercial banking was in this position. Between 1910 and 1920 the number of banks fell from 112 to 75. No longer was this a process of the large joint-stock banks acquiring the remaining private banks, or even smaller joint-stock banks. Instead, it involved mergers between equals to create very large banks. In 1918 Lloyds Bank with £174 million in deposits and 888 offices merged with Capital and Counties Bank with £60 million and 473 offices. By 1920 five London-based banks accounted for 79 per cent of all deposits and 79 per cent of all branches compared to only 37 per cent of deposits and 33 per cent of branches in 1910. Legislation to prevent future bank amalgamation had been dropped in 1918 but the banks voluntarily agreed to submit all future proposals to the Treasury for approval. As a result, once the final round of mergers was completed there was no further consolidation until after the Second World War, though there was a small degree of mopping-up caused

---

[25] Kirkaldy (ed.), *British Finance*, p.115, cf. p.120.
[26] Carnevali, *Europe's Advantage*, pp.9–16. See S. Pollard, *The Development of the British Economy, 1914–1980*, 3rd ed. (London: Edward Arnold, 1983), pp.8–9, 35–6. This was long the standard text used for the study of the British economy in the twentieth century.

Table 5.1. Number of Banks

Year	England and Wales	Scotland	Ireland
1911	55	9	9
1924	19	8	8

Source: Sir D. Drummond Fraser, 'British Home Banking', p.453

by exceptional circumstances. The result was that five very large banks dominated British commercial banking throughout the inter-war years. These were Barclays, City and Westminster, Lloyds, London City and Midland, and National and Provincial, and they were known as the Big Five.[27]

Though this situation was the product of a long-term trend there had been a sudden acceleration during and immediately after the First World War. Drummond Fraser's careful study for the Institute of Bankers, published in 1925, documented the change that had taken place within joint-stock banking between 1911 and 1924, as in Table 5.1, and it was this position that was to prevail for the rest of the inter-war years. For 1911 he counted 55 joint-stock banks operating in England and Wales but only 19 by 1924.

It was widely believed that a consequence of this concentration was to make British bankers become increasingly conservative in their behaviour, as they were now immune from failure. As early as 1914, H.V. Burrell observed that, 'With English bankers the first consideration had been absolute safety. To that we largely owe our comparative freedom from serious financial crises, especially in recent years.'[28] Evidence for the continuance of this attitude can be found in the answers given to the Committee on Finance and Industry by those running Britain's largest banks. They expressed their fears, time and again, that mounting debts among business customers could turn into defaults, bringing their banks close to insolvency and prompting mass withdrawals among depositors as this became widely known. This was a fate that could only be avoided by pursuing a policy of restricting loans only to those customers most likely to be in a position to repay, no matter the hardship to do so would inflict.[29] As W.N. Goschen, chairman of the National Provincial Bank, put it, 'I think when an industry has reached such a point that it has exhausted all its capital and credit that it is entitled to have there is

---

[27] Capie and Rodrik-Bali, 'Concentration', pp.286–7; Capie and Woods, *Money over Two Centuries*, p.64; Turner, *Banking in Crisis*, p.45; Davies, *The Origins and Development of Cartelisation*, pp.26–31; Sayers, *Lloyds Bank*, pp.265, 274.

[28] H.V. Burrell, 'The Opening of Foreign Branches by English Banks', *Journal of the Institute of Bankers*, 35 (1914), p.41.

[29] Committee on Finance and Industry (1931): Minutes of Evidence Q 1530, 1537, 1934, 2257, 2271, 2511, 2536, 3607, 3651–3, 3695, 3706, 6760, 7976, 7980, 8351, 8365, 8372, 8382, 8400, 8494, 8548, 8576, 8694, 8696, 8742, 9267.

only one thing—to disappear.'[30] Such a blunt response could hardly have endeared him to a committee looking for ways of solving the problem of mass unemployment!

A detailed examination of the actual business done by these banks also indicates a tendency towards risk aversion rather than risk-taking. As these banks were highly vulnerable to the risks posed by the sudden withdrawal of deposits they were careful to maintain not only a substantial cash margin, ready to meet the everyday requirements of their customers, but also a further margin of liquid funds that could be quickly called upon. Before the First World War these banks kept 15.3 per cent of their deposits as cash with another 12.6 per cent as money at call, making a total of 27.9 per cent that was immediately accessible. This meant that they were always in a position to meet withdrawals unless faced with a total panic that would bring down every bank, as happened with the outbreak of war. Faced with a quadrupling of deposits between 1911/14 and 1921/4 the banks increased the amount kept as cash by a similar amount, so maintaining almost the same ratio at 14.6 per cent. However, the ratio of money at call to deposits did drop by 50 per cent being only 6.4 per cent in 1921/4, with the difference being made up by increased investments. This might give the appearance of increased risk-taking as a greater share of deposits were placed in long-term investments rather than lent out short term. Such a reading of the collective balance sheets would be inaccurate because the main rise in investments was holdings of UK government debt, especially Treasury Bills. These Treasury Bills possessed an active market in London into which they could be easily, quickly, and cheaply sold for cash, and so provided banks with a ready source of liquidity if required. (See Table 5.2.)

Table 5.2. Joint-Stock Banks: Assets and Liabilities, 1911/14 and 1921/4

	1911/14	1921/4
Deposits	£483 m.	£1,601 m.
Cash	£74 m.	£233 m.
Money at Call	£61 m.	£102 m.
Investments	£70 m.	£342 m.
Bills + Advances	£320 m.	£1,015 m.
Cash as % of Deposits	15.3%	14.6%
Money at Call as % of Deposits	12.6%	6.4%
Investments as % of Deposits	14.5%	21.4%
Bills + Advances as % of Deposits	66.3%	63.4%
Cash + Money at Call + Investments as % of Deposits	42.4%	42.3%

Source: The data for 1921/4 is taken from the tables in Sir D. Drummond Fraser, 'British Home Banking'.

[30] Committee on Finance and Industry (1931): Minutes of Evidence Q1934, cf. Q2257, 2271, 7980, 8382, 8494.

A comparison between 1921/4 and 1938 indicates that the position reached as a result of the changes caused by the First World War remained unaltered for the rest of the inter-war years. As deposits continued to rise so did the amount held as cash. What did not recover was the proportion placed in call money as this remained at the level reached during and after the First World War. Instead, it was the proportion invested that grew, both in total and as a proportion of all assets, reaching £644 million and 28.3 per cent of deposits in 1938. Again, a high proportion of this was in Treasury Bills or long-dated government debt, into which much of the short-dated securities had been concentrated in the early 1930s. All these securities possessed a very active market, including on the London Stock Exchange, and this provided banks with highly liquid assets, which could be either sold or used as collateral for inter-bank loans. Taken collectively the total kept by banks as cash, money at call, and investments remained virtually constant between 1911/14 and 1921/4 and had then increased by 1938, by which time it reached 50.5 per cent of deposits. This made British banks highly liquid and so resilient in the face of the economic, financial, and monetary challenges they experienced from the outbreak of the First World War in 1914 through the Wall Street Crash in 1929, the departure from the Gold Standard in 1931, the depression of the 1930s, and the approach to war evident by 1938.[31] (see Table 5.3.)

This evidence indicates that British banks continued to follow very conservative banking practices between 1914 and 1945, maximizing liquidity over returns. Such a strategy was entirely in keeping with the highly uncertain conditions within which they operated. As Billings and Capie have concluded, 'The increased concentration arising from the amalgamation process which

Table 5.3. Joint-Stock Banks: Assets and Liabilities, 1921/4 and 1938

	1921/4	1938
Deposits	£1,601 m.	£2,348 m.
Cash	£233 m.	£362 m.
Money at Call	£102 m.	£160 m.
Investments	£342 m.	£664 m.
Bills + Advances	£1,015 m.	£1,263 m.
Cash as % of Deposits	14.6%	15.4%
Money at Call as % of Deposits	6.4%	6.8%
Investments as % of Deposits	21.4%	28.3%
Bills + Advances as % of Deposits	63.4%	53.8%
Cash + Money at Call + Investments as % of Deposits	42.3%	50.5%

Source: The data for 1921/4 is taken from the tables in Sir D. Drummond Fraser, 'British Home Banking'. That for 1938 from the tables in Crump, 'Evolution of the Money Market'.

[31] Shepherd, *The Growth and Role of UK Financial Institutions*, Appendices A1.1, A3.3; Crick and Wadsworth, *A Hundred Years*, p.347.

created the Big Five Clearing banks had produced powerful and resilient institutions.'[32] However, neither the conservative behaviour of bankers nor their resilience should be confused with a refusal to support individual businesses in financial difficulty. Instead, it was the result of these banks being sufficiently large to train staff in identifying potential risks among those to whom they lent money and then monitor their adherence to the rules governing their behaviour. It was also a product of being sufficiently diversified to be able to withstand multiple losses among those to whom they had lent money, when these did occur. The example of Williams Deacon's Bank, which was not one of the Big Five, illustrates the risks that banks did experience between the wars. This bank came close to collapse because it was heavily exposed to the losses being made by customers operating in the Lancashire cotton textile industry, and its inability to cover these with profitable activities elsewhere in the UK. In contrast the five largest banks possessed the scale and spread to cover such losses, as in the case of the Midland. By the end of 1929 the Midland Bank had around £2m locked up in loans to firms in Lancashire cotton textile manufacturing and to the equally troubled South Wales coal and steel industry. Conversely, the Midland Bank was conducting a profitable business in both London and the West Midlands. Barclays Bank was in a similar situation, having acquired the Union Bank of Manchester in 1919, as that exposed it to the problems of the cotton textile industry in the 1920s and 1930s. The losses Barclays made on loans to firms in the cotton textile industry were covered by profits generated in the more prosperous areas of the business, especially London and the South East. Gross bad debts written off by Barclays between 1920 and 1939 totalled £18 million. Large banks also had the resources and the incentive to take over any smaller bank that was on the verge of failure, because it removed competitors and expanded their own business, while enhancing public trust in the banking system as a whole. The specialist army bank, Cox and Co., was rescued by Lloyds in 1923 while Williams Deacon's was acquired by the Royal Bank of Scotland in 1930.[33]

The suggestion that the increased concentration of British banks can be related to the problems of British manufacturing industry between the wars also fails to explain why those parts of the British Isles, such as Scotland, that did not participate in the process also experienced severe economic difficulties. Drummond Fraser's study allows comparisons between England and Wales and other parts of the UK and Southern Ireland, which became independent

---

[32] Billings and Capie, 'Financial Crisis, Contagion and the British Banking System', p.211.
[33] Holmes and Green, *Midland*, pp.174-87; S.E. Thomas, *British Banks and the Finance of Industry, 1897-1960* (London: P.S. King & Son, 1931), pp.14, 100, 154, 242-7, 255; Truptil, *British Banks*, p.107; A.W. Tuke and R.J.H. Gillman, *Barclay's Bank Ltd, 1926-1969* (London: Barclays Bank, 1969), pp.40-8; W.A. Thomas, *The Finance of British Industry, 1918-1976* (London: Methuen, 1978), pp.91-108; *Williams Deacon's, 1771-1970*, pp.156-9; Ackrill and Hannah, *Barclays*, pp.71-2, 125, 451; Turner, *Banking in Crisis*, p.160.

in 1922, in terms of concentration. What his data reveals in Table 5.1. is that there was little in the way of increased concentration in either Scotland or Ireland, with the number of banks dropping from 9 to 8 in each case. Though a few of these banks were acquired by London-based banks, they continued to be run out of head offices located in these countries. Between 1917 and 1923 the Midland acquired the Belfast Bank, the Clydesdale Bank and the North of Scotland Bank; Westminster took control of the Ulster Bank, Lloyds the National Bank of Scotland, and Barclays the British Linen Bank. All were kept separate from their English operations as that allowed them to retain note circulation powers in Scotland and Ireland. Nevertheless, there was a degree of integration allowing money to be moved between branches across the combined groups. The result was not to impose London controls but to allow business customers in Scotland and Ireland to tap the greater pool of finance available in London.[34] (See Table 5.1.) Only a highly metropolitan view of British banking could ignore the continuing autonomy of the Scottish and Irish banking systems, and the implications that had for the link drawn between industrial distress and the structure of banking. All of the UK experienced economic difficulties between the wars and those of central Scotland were very similar to those of Northern England, which was hardly surprising as they had very similar structures, with a high dependency on export-orientated manufacturing industry.

COMPETITION

Banking was not a single product market. Banks competed with each other for different types of customers by offering a variety of specialist products and services. On the one hand there was the market for savings while on the other there was that for loans while, in between, were the services that banks provided ranging from the ease of cash withdrawals and the use of cheques to access to foreign currency and payment systems. In the market for savings the large joint-stock banks chose not to compete aggressively amongst themselves, including agreeing a standard rate of interest payable to depositors in 1921. One result of this interest-rate cartel was that deposits in the commercial banks grew only modestly, from £2.4 billion in 1919 to £3 billion in 1938. In contrast, deposits in savings banks doubled from £353 to £835 million while those in building societies increased tenfold, from £71 million to £711 million, over the same period. What this indicates is the degree of competition there

[34] Turner, *Banking in Crisis*, p.44; Munn, *Clydesdale Bank*, p.158, 161, 189.

was for savings. The building societies, in particular, were able to generate growing public confidence as they grew in size and scale, including through mergers. This was despite occasional runs as in 1929 when banks provided them with liquidity support. As a result of the higher rates of interest that they paid compared to the banks, building societies attracted those who did not require to borrow and were willing to use cash rather than cheques.[35]

The building societies also competed with the joint-stock banks in the field of loans. It was the building societies that provided the finance required by those who wanted to buy their own homes, and the demand for such loans grew strongly between the wars. The Rent and Mortgage Restriction Act introduced in 1915 greatly reduced the supply of rented accommodation. In 1914, 90 per cent of housing was privately rented but that had fallen to 65 per cent by 1938, by which date owner-occupation had risen to 25 per cent of the total. By operating a mutual model, through which the savings of one group met the borrowing needs of another, building societies were able to use short-term deposits to finance long-term mortgages with housing as collateral. Though the model was expanded to cover a wider range of savers between the wars the result remained the same. By acting as a member-owned co-operative, building societies were able to rely on a pool of fairly stable deposits to finance long-term investment in housing. This meant that building societies were able to capture the market for housing finance. Building society lending rose from £22 million in 1920/1 to £137 million in 1937/8.[36] Rather than compete for savings with the likes of the savings banks and the building societies for savings, or even among themselves, banks focused on providing other services to savers. This they were able to do successfully when dealing with businesses and the wealthy. Both these groups alternated between periods when their accounts were in credit and debit, and so needed access to occasional loans as well as investment advice. These groups also made extensive use of payment facilities such as cheques, as well as requiring other services like access to foreign exchange. It was these services that the larger banks provided while the alternatives did not.[37]

The large banks did experience a growing demand for loans between the wars. High levels of personal taxation, introduced during the First War, combined with low profitability in the established industries after the end of

---

[35] Ackrill and Hannah, *Barclays*, pp.96–104, 139; Shepherd, *The Growth and Role of UK Financial Institutions*, Appendices A1.1, A3.3; B. Ritchie, *We're with the Woolwich*, pp.64–8, 72–6; N. Crump, 'The London and New York Markets in the Autumn of 1925', *Journal of the Institute of Bankers*, 47 (1926), pp.307–16.

[36] Cleary, *The Building Society Movement*, p.151; B. Ritchie, *We're with the Woolwich*, pp.17, 39–41, 57, 67.

[37] Collins, *Money and Banking*, p.214; Financial News, *The City, 1884–1934*, p.56.

the post-war boom, meant that many business people, and those with inherited wealth, no longer received the income they had once enjoyed. As a result they turned to banks to cover periods of exceptional expenditure, whether for business or personal purposes. Informal sources of finance and the re-investment of earnings, had been very important sources of venture capital in the past, but were now less readily available. This put increased pressure on banks to provide funds to those starting up new businesses or expanding existing ones, which was always risky because of the high failure rate among start-up firms and during periods of transition. Despite the risks, banks did provide these funds. Loans to customers by British banks grew from 48 per cent of total funds in 1923/4 to 52 per cent in 1928/30, despite the continuing problems experienced in traditional British industries. It was only in the 1930s that such lending fell back as the world economic depression had a devastating effect on the export markets for major sectors of British manufacturing. Even by 1936/8, bank advances had risen to only 41 per cent of available funds, or considerably below previous levels. The continuing depressed state of many industries reduced their need for finance as well as making banks reluctant to lend more because of continuing losses and poor prospects.

In contrast, there were expanding and profitable businesses, such as those in electrical and light engineering, that did offer the joint-stock banks attractive opportunities, but here they faced strong competition. The decline of opportunities in international finance, which became acute in the 1930s, drove many established merchant banks to diversify into domestic finance. The result of the 1931 financial crisis, in particular, was to create an environment that was positively hostile to international investment, especially for those whose focus lay outside the Empire. This left merchant banks with little choice but to look elsewhere for business if they wanted to survive. In the 1920s, for example, most of the new issues for domestic, industrial, and commercial companies had been left to stockbrokers, including both members and ex- or non-members of the London Stock Exchange, whereas in the 1930s the larger and more established merchant banks joined in. For example, the merchant banking firm Schroders opened an office in Birmingham in 1936 to improve its relationship with those companies operating in the West Midlands, where the thriving motor industry was located. In addition, specialist finance houses were also set up, such as Charterhouse Industrial Development Corporation in 1934. These venture funds were the product of those who were quick to spot the new opportunities created by matching investors with those entrepreneurs seeking to tap additional sources of funds outside the close social web of contact that had sufficed in the past. No longer was international investment attractive to investors, especially in the 1930s, while the rent controls imposed during the war had rendered the private provision of rented accommodation unprofitable. The result was to encourage investors to search out domestic opportunities, which encouraged domestic, industrial and commercial companies to issue stocks and bonds through merchant banks, finance houses, and stockbrokers, rather than borrow from their bank.[38]

Rather than be by-passed, the joint-stock banks even worked in co-operation with the specialist finance houses, because of the potential profits to be made. When the business empire created by the financier Clarence Hatry failed in 1929, the losses of £13.8 million he had incurred mainly fell on banks. When making loans the banks had accepted securities as collateral, and these either fell dramatically in value or became worthless once Hatry's activities were exposed. Such securities had been used to finance long-term business development indicating that banks were willing to provide long-term loans but only through the buffer of securities. The banks were able to absorb the losses that they made through Hatry as it was only one small part of their lending, and a highly profitable one until the collapse. Once a company proved to be successful the securities could be sold at a far higher price than the bank had paid for them. In this way banks devised ways of making long-term loans to new businesses, while limiting the risks they were taking, as the securities they received in return could be disposed of once the business was established. Also, when the businesses collapsed, there was no direct connection to the banks, as they were only shareholders not creditors, and so they escaped reputational damage that might provoke a run.[39]

Evidence of the competitive pressures being experienced by the joint-stock banks between the wars can be found in their investment in labour-saving technology as that cut operating costs. The introduction of calculating machines resulted in significant productivity gains, for example, through the reduction in the amount of time devoted to routine tasks.[40] However, the most visible sign of the effects of competition was the rapid expansion in

---

[38] F. Lavington, *The English Capital Market* ([n.p.]: Methuen, 1921), pp.212–21; Thomas, *British Banks*, pp.222–41; Thomas, *Finance of British Industry*, pp.50, 91–102; L. Hannah, *The Rise of the Corporate Economy* (London: Methuen, 1976), pp.58–61, 75, 99, 105; A.T.K. Grant, *A Study of the Capital Market in Post-War Britain* (London: Macmillan, 1937), pp.157, 169, 182, 199–200, 214, 223, 227, 275–6; Holmes and Green, *Midland*, p.182; S. Tolliday, *Business, Banking, and Politics* (Cambridge, Mass.: Harvard UP, 1987), p.183; B. Ellinger, *The City: The London Financial Markets* (London: P.S. King & Son, 1940), pp.163, 191, 226, 289–322, 337, 347, 357–9, 365–72, 381; J. Kinross, *Fifty Years in the City: Financing Small Business* (London: Murray, 1982), pp.47–8, 71–81; Financial News, *The Stock Exchange: An Investors' Guide* (London: Financial News, 1933), p.22, 48, 62; A. Vallance, *The Centre of the World* (London: Hodder & Stoughton, 1935), pp.173–6; O.R. Hobson, *How the City Works* (London: News Chronicle, 1940), p.36; Truptil, *British Banks*, pp.102, 128, 136, 162–3, 167, 265–6; S. Diaper, 'Merchant Banking in the Inter-War Period: The Case of Kleinwort, Sons & Co.', *Business History*, 28 (1986), pp.67, 72; Committee on Finance and Industry (1931), Minutes of Evidence Q1530, 2511, 3950.

[39] Hollow, *Rogue Banking*, pp.25–6, 36–43, 62–3.

[40] B. Batiz-Laso and T. Boyns, 'The Business and Financial History of Mechanization and Technological Change in Twentieth-Century Banking', *Accounting, Business and Financial History*, 14 (2004), p.226; P. Wardley, *Women, Mechanization, and Cost-Savings in Twentieth-Century British Banks and Other Financial Institutions* (Helsinki: WEHC, 2006), pp.4–5, 15–18.

Table 5.4. Number of Bank Offices

Year	England and Wales	Scotland	Ireland
1911	6,053	1,235	842
1924	9,044	1,563	1,083

Source: Sir D. Drummond Fraser, 'British Home Banking', p.453

Table 5.5. Ratio of Bank Offices to Population

Year	England and Wales	Scotland	Ireland
1911	5,960	3,854	5,204
1924	4,201	3,184	3,693

Source: Sir D. Drummond Fraser, 'British Home Banking', p.453

the size of the branch network. By expanding the size and density of the network they could acquire more customers through invading the territory of their rivals.[41] Whereas in 1911, according to Drummond Fraser, there were 6,053 bank offices in England and Wales, or one for every 5,960 people, by 1924 the number had grown by almost 3,000 and the ratio had fallen to 4,201. As the comparison with Scotland and Ireland made clear, the density of banking provision in England and Wales was growing closer to that of those countries even though the more urban nature of its population reduced the need for multiple branches and offices. (See Tables 5.4. and 5.5.)

Put another way the number of branches reached 2.6 per 10,000 people in England and Wales in 1937, which was a considerable advance over the 1.83 in 1913. As a result of these extensive branch networks, the big banks built up strong customer loyalty, each one conscious that a nearby branch of a rival bank was available as an alternative, if the service it provided fell off. Detailed examination of the relationship between banks and their customers between the wars reveals that loans to long-standing businesses in difficulty were extended and renewed time and again in the expectation that an improvement would take place. Refusing to maintain such assistance created the possibility the customer would move his account to another bank. In every case the bank manager, with or without advice from head office, had to make a judgement on whether it was better to continue the loan and risk a default or call it in and see the customer move to a rival.[42]

What can be concluded was that the competitive pressures experienced by banks between the wars forced them to improve the service they provided and

---

[41] C.W. Taylor, 'The Case against the Nationalisation of the Banks', pp.385–6.

[42] Billings and Capie, 'Financial Crisis, Contagion and the British Banking System', pp.196–7. For a few examples see D.M. Ross, 'The Unsatisfied Fringe in Britain, 1930s–80s', *Business History*, 38 (1996); Capie and Collins, *Have the Banks Failed British Industry?*

respond to the needs of their customers. Conversely, concerns about the wider economic environment within which their business customers were operating, encouraged caution because of the possibility that borrowers would default, leaving the bank with large losses, leading to a liquidity, if not a solvency crisis. There were numerous examples of bank failures abroad, especially during the world financial crisis between 1929 and 1932. Between the Wars, some British banks also failed, making all bankers aware how fragile was the basis of trust upon which they operated. The largest was Farrow's Bank, which collapsed in 1920.[43] A survey of new bank formation covering the period from 1930 to 1942 revealed the degree of mortality among new banks, once those associated with existing ones were excluded. This survey identified 160 new companies that included the words 'bank', 'bankers', or 'banking', in their title. Of these 160, a total of 141 were offshoots of either existing banks or banking families, leaving 19 that were completely new. Of these 19 a total of 8 had ceased business completely by 1944 while another 6 were doing little or nothing. Only 5 had managed to survive in business.[44]

Actual bank failures at home and abroad, and the significant mortality among new banks, did not however undermine public confidence in the large banking companies. The reason for that was because the public could distinguish between different types of banks, and so failure was not contagious. Such conclusions can be drawn from a careful reading of inter-war novels. It was the smaller banks, such as those still privately owned, mutual savings societies, or City finance houses that were at risk of failure, not the large banking companies. Such banks were more exposed to thefts by employees or collapse due to risk-taking. In J.S. Fletcher's 1920 novel, *The Middle Temple Murder*, both the privately owned Market Milcaster Banking Company, and the mutually controlled Hearth and Home Mutual Benefit Society, were robbed by their own staff. The loss experienced by the Market Milcaster Bank was met by the partners, but the collapse of the Hearth and Home left 'thousands of honest working folk in terrible distress if not absolute ruin'.[45] Similarly, in his 1933 novel, *The Mystery of the London Banker*, it was the long-established private City bank, Champernowne Brothers, that had been systematically robbed by one of its trusted employees.[46] Even the large joint-stock banks were not immune from the fraudulent actions of their staff but they were large enough to cover the losses and so avoid adverse publicity by simply dismissing the employee. This was the case in C.S. Forester's 1926 novel, *Payment Deferred*, involving a foreign exchange trader who worked for

---

[43] Hollow, *Rogue Banking*, pp.25–6, 36–43, 62–3.
[44] *Journal of the Institute of Bankers*, 'Memorandum', pp.51–2.
[45] J.S. Fletcher, *The Middle Temple Murder* (London: Ward Lock, 1920), pp.126–37, 198–200.
[46] J.S. Fletcher, *The Mystery of the London Banker: Being Entry Number Seven in the Case-Book of Ronald Camberwell* (London: George Harrap, 1933), pp.9, 38–9, 224.

County National Bank in its head office in the City.[47] Though featuring a bank brought near to collapse because of a bank run, Stanley J. Weyman's 1922 novel, *Ovington's Bank*, not only set the story a century earlier in 1825, but also emphasized how carefully the bank was run. Ovington's Bank was 'solvent, amply solvent, if time be given us to realize our resources'. But customers, 'would rush in at the first alarm, like a flock of silly sheep, and thrusting and pushing and trampling one another down, would run, each bent on his own safety, blindly on ruin'.[48]

There was also an ingrained view between the wars that British banks and bankers were superior to all others, as can also be deduced from the way they were portrayed in contemporary novels. In R.H. Mottram, *Our Mr Dormer*, published in 1927, there was a fictional eulogy to the British banker, based on the history of Barclays. 'It was not that the English were liked. It was not that they were sought or admired. But their word was trusted. When they wrote on a piece of stamped paper 'Pay to the order of Mr.— "so many" pounds,' they meant it. In ninety-nine cases out of a hundred the money was forthcoming.' Under such circumstances the public could be reassured that whatever else was happening in the world British banks could be totally relied upon.[49] Mottram continued the story of his fictional bank with two further novels, namely *The Boroughmonger* in 1929 and *Castle Island* in 1931. In all these novels there is expressed a nostalgia for the days when banking was conducted on a local and personal basis by people whose life revolved around the bank that they either worked for or owned. That is then contrasted with the impersonal world of the large joint-stock bank operating through branches run from a remote London head office. Nevertheless, an overwhelming sense of stability and permanence pervades these joint-stock banks, despite Mottram's antipathy.[50] In the 1934 novel, *The Bank Manager*, by E. Phillips Oppenheim, James Huitt, the manager at the Aldwych branch of Barton's Bank was regarded as a perfect banker as he was something of a robot. 'I cannot imagine anyone ever making him act upon impulse, saying or doing an incorrect thing.' This made it all the more surprising when it emerged that he had been robbing his bank's customers and, once they became suspicious, killing them.[51] Ronald Fraser, in his 1942 novel, *Financial Times*, had the chairman of the London and South Kensington Bank express

---

[47] C.S. Forester, *Payment Deferred* (London: Bodley Head, 1926) [reprinted London: Penguin, 2011], pp.43, 82.

[48] S.J. Weyman, *Ovington's Bank* (London: John Murray, 1922), pp.8–22, 61–2, 90–1, 250, 256, 327, 350, 461–2.

[49] R.H. Mottram, *Our Mr Dormer* (London: Chatto & Windus, 1927), p.278.

[50] R.H. Mottram, *The Boroughmonger* (London: Chatto & Windus, 1929), pp.76–9; R.H. Mottram, *Castle Island* (London: Chatto & Windus, 1931), pp.262, 291, 295.

[51] E. Phillips Oppenheim, *The Bank Manager* (London: Hodder & Stoughton, 1934), pp.3–4, 7, 32–9, 297, 314.

the view that Titian Woollacombe would make a successful banker because he saw in him someone who had 'a total absence of feelings for the hopes and anxieties of common men'.[52] It was not only the Big Five banks that had captured the trust of the public, it also extended to the City's merchant banking elite, as can be seen in Vincent Seligman's 1934 novel, Bank Holiday. 'the British Public stolidly continue to place unlimited confidence in their financial institutions, no doubt because they enjoy that reputation for sound and conservative finance.'[53] The impression generated by these novels was that the British public had confidence in the leading banks, whether they were the large joint-stock ones or the established merchant banks. While remaining competitive, such banks as these were careful to preserve that confidence, and so maintain a balance between risk-taking and risk-averse behaviour.

MONEY MARKET

Helping to maintain the public's trust in the British banking system between the wars was the role played by the London money market. As Barrett Whale, an expert on British and German banking, wrote in 1931, 'At the centre of every developed banking system, there is a highly concentrated money market, around which the head offices of all the leading banks and financial houses are clustered. In this market the banks are able to employ funds in a manner which is both safe and highly liquid.'[54] For this market to operate there had to be complete trust between the participants in terms of their ability to repay the money that they borrowed. That trust was not universal, being confined to the largest UK banks, the long-established merchant banks, and those for whom they acted as correspondents, including British overseas banks and selected smaller UK and foreign banks, but only after careful vetting. Beyond this core there existed numerous other banks, including the building societies, but they did not have access to the facilities of this money market, leaving them vulnerable to liquidity crises.[55] This money market provided those banks that were trusted by their peer group with a means of not only employing idle balances, so enhancing profitability, but also making good temporary shortages, and so avoid a liquidity crisis leading to a solvency one.

G.J. Scott, the manager of the London office of the Union Bank of Scotland, described the relationship between such banks and the money market as it

[52] R. Fraser, *Financial Times* (London: Jonathan Cape, 1942), pp.42–3.
[53] V. Seligman, *Bank Holiday* (London: Longmans, Green, 1934), pp.1–10, 41, 76, 104.
[54] Barrett Whale, 'English and Continental Banking', p.207.
[55] N.F. Hall, 'The Control of Credit in the London Money Market', *Journal of the Institute of Bankers*, 59 (1938), p.64.

existed in 1921. The first task of the manager was to estimate what money the bank had available and was likely to receive during the day—bills the bank held and were due to mature. The next was to estimate all the payments that had to be made—bills that were due to mature but the bank had sold. Having done that, the manager knew whether he wanted to borrow or lend, and for how long, when the bill broker called round. This was the sharp end of the Lend and Hold Model. Money could be lent out in the morning for repayment at the end of the day or overnight with repayment in the morning. If the banker was short, loans were called in. The same judgement was carried out in every bank, leading to the bill broker borrowing from one bank and lending to another as he made his rounds in the morning and afternoon. 'The advantage of buying from the broker is that you can get any maturity that you wish, and to whatever extent you wish; whereas, if a bank is only discounting bills for its own customers, it has to take them as and when offered, consequently the bank may have large maturities at one time with considerable blanks in between the dates of maturity of its bills as a whole.' As Scott reported, 'It is a matter of considerable surprise to the uninitiated to watch how easily these sums, which total huge amounts, are rearranged from day to day.'[56] When Spring-Rice reported in 1929 the procedure remained the same. 'The bank manager at his office in London, having before him a statement from his near and far distant branches, knows what his cash position is each morning. Part of his knowledge must be guesswork, but it is guesswork based on long experience. He has to meet his liabilities for bills maturing, his own acceptances, and be ready to make advances to his customers, as well as the cheques which experience tells him are likely to be drawn on him that day.' Depending on this calculation, he decided whether to lend or call-in loans. It was this access to the London money market, and the centralization of the ebb and flow of funds in London, that meant that the British banking system could 'work with perfect safety on a proportion of cash smaller than elsewhere.'[57]

The First World War had changed the London money market.[58] During the war, UK Treasury Bills replaced commercial and financial bills as the medium through which banks borrowed and lent among themselves.[59] Over the course of the war Treasury Bills in circulation in the London money market rose from

---

[56] G.J. Scott, 'The Bill-Broker in the Bank Parlour', *Journal of the Institute of Bankers*, 42 (1921), pp.58–62.

[57] D. Spring-Rice, 'The Financial Machinery of the City of London', *Journal of the Institute of Bankers*, 50 (1929), pp.8–15, 78.

[58] Roberts, *Saving the City*, pp.167–8; Roberts, '"How We Saved the City"' in Dimsdale and Hotson (eds), *British Financial Crises*, pp.110–13; S. Cochrane, *Assessing the Impact of World War I on the City of London*, University of Oxford Department of Economics Discussion Paper Series 456 (Oxford: University of Oxford, 2009), pp.5–8.

[59] F. Whitmore, *The Money Machine* (London: Pitman, 1930), p.35; Hall, 'The Control of Credit', pp.64–70; N. Crump, 'The Evolution of the Money Market', *Journal of the Institute of Bankers*, 59 (1938), pp.291–301.

between £1 and £2 million to around £1.1 billion, displacing all other bills. Though the value of Treasury Bills in circulation gradually fell in the 1920s it was still around £0.7 billion towards the end of the decade, with each week a new issue of around £40 million being offered to the market as existing ones matured.[60] The dominance of the London money market by Treasury Bills led many foreign banks to make use of alternative financial centres when they needed to borrow, with New York being the principal beneficiary.[61] In the 1920s there was some revival in the use of commercial bills but not to the extent that they challenged Treasury Bills.[62] Around two-thirds of the bills circulating in the London money market in the 1920s were Treasury Bills, while the value of commercial bills had fallen by half.[63] Nevertheless, the London money market continued to offer British banks a very attractive venue.[64] Leaving the Gold Standard in 1919 did undermine the international appeal of the London money market, as it added an exchange risk to the holding of funds in London, but that was removed by the return to gold in 1925.[65] Writing in 1926, Phillips was of the opinion that London still had 'incomparably the best organized money market in the world, with resources at its command equal to any call, no matter how large that may be made upon it'.[66] A similar view was expressed by Greengrass in 1930, 'here credit is more freely given and, more important still, more cheaply given than anywhere else abroad.' He went on to claim that 'The London money market is the most important and influential in the world. London is the world's financial centre, and is the clearing house for international payments.'[67]

In addition to the facilities provided by the money market for borrowing and lending on a short-term basis, another development took place in London in the 1920s that helped to meet the new risks that banks were incurring.

---

[60] Spring-Rice, 'The Financial Machinery', p.8.
[61] Nevin and Davies, *The London Clearing Banks*, p.161; Scammell, *London Discount Market*, pp.196–8; Fletcher, *Discount Houses*, pp.45–7, 253; H.W. Greengrass, *The Discount Market in London: Its Organization and Recent Development* (London: Pitman, 1930), p.27; Truptil, *British Banks*, pp.177, 199.
[62] C.W. Phelps, *The Foreign Expansion of American Banks: American Branch Banking Abroad* (New York: Ronald Press, 1927), pp.98–101; Sayers, *Gilletts*, pp.78, 80, 95, 101–2.
[63] Whitmore, *Money Machine*, p.35; Sir D. Drummond Fraser, 'British Home Banking', p.439; Crump, 'The London and New York Markets', pp.307–15; Spring-Rice, 'The Financial Machinery', pp.10–15.
[64] The Times, *The City of London* (London: The Times, 1928), p.169; Financial News, *The City, 1884–1934* (London, Financial News, 1934), p.62; Greengrass, *Discount Market*, p.37; Truptil, *British Banks*, pp.176–80; Sayers, *Bank of England*, pp.112, 124, 132, 138–9; Scammell, *London Discount Market*, p.31.
[65] R. Wilson, *Capital Imports and the Terms of Trade: Examined in the Light of 60 years of Australian Borrowing* (Melbourne: [n.p.], 1931), p.36; Blainey and Hutton, *Gold and Paper*, pp.197, 206, 212.
[66] H.W. Phillips, *Modern Foreign Exchange and Foreign Banking* (London: Macdonald & Evans, 1926), p.63.
[67] Greengrass, *Discount Market*, pp.4, 30.

Before the war British trade and international investment was conducted on the basis of the UK£, removing any risk due to currency fluctuations. With Britain's departure from the Gold Standard in 1919, and even after the return in 1925, the exclusive reliance on the UK£ fell. Many exporters and importers were required to receive payment or pay in other currencies, especially the US $, and so turned to their banks for a way of minimizing the exchange risks they now ran as a result. What the banks did was shoulder these exchange risks, as part of the process of providing credit to their business customers. In turn they looked to the London money market for a way of covering the currency risks they now ran. Given the degree of currency volatility in the 1920s it was no longer possible for a bank to leave a credit or debit outstanding for up to three months in a currency other than that in which its assets and liabilities were denominated.[68]

The solution was found in the foreign exchange market, as this allowed banks to match assets and liabilities across a range of currencies, through either direct dealing between each other or by the use of an emerging group of foreign exchange brokers.[69] By the early 1920s London had developed the broadest, deepest, and most sophisticated market for foreign exchange trading in the world.[70] As with London's money market, the foreign exchange market was also used by banks to borrow and lend between each other. By buying 'forward' and selling 'spot', a bank obtained the use of the money for the intervening period. Conversely, by selling 'forward' and buying 'spot', the bank employed the money for that period. The difference in price between the forward and the spot price represented the interest paid or received and was thus equivalent to the discount at which bills had been sold in the past. It was not only British banks that relied on the service provided by the London foreign exchange market, for it was extensively used by banks from around the world. As Miller reported in 1925, 'London acts to a great extent as the world's financial clearing house, and a large portion of the payments between other nations are settled through London.'[71] The use of this foreign exchange

---

[68] Financial News, *The City, 1884–1934*, pp.31, 50, 56; S.W. Dowling, *The Exchanges of London* (London: Butterworth, 1929), pp.208–12; Greengrass, *Discount Market*, pp.35, 110; W.L. Fraser, *All to the Good* (London: New English Library, 1963), pp.64–5; Collins, *Money and Banking*, p.209. See Westminster Bank, *The Financial Machinery of the Import and Export Trade* (London: Westminster Bank, 1925).
[69] Correspondence between Brown Shipley and Brown Brothers, 30 August 1922, 5 February 1924, 30 July 1924; M. Anson and T. Gourvish, *Leopold Joseph: A History, 1919–2000* (London: [n.p.], 2002); Y. Cassis, *Capitals of Capital: A History of International Financial Centres, 1780–2005* (Cambridge: CUP, 2006), p.177.
[70] E.H. Lever, *Foreign Exchange from the Investor's Point of View* (London: Institute of Actuaries, 1925), pp.84–5, S.E. Thomas, *The Principles and Arithmetic of Foreign Exchange* (London: Macdonald & Evans, 1925), pp.180–3.
[71] H.F.R. Miller, *The Foreign Exchange Market: A Practical Treatise on Post-War Foreign Exchange* (London: E. Arnold, 1925), p.147 cf. pp.9, 65, 96–7, 120, 126; Bank of England, Memoranda on London Foreign Exchange Market, 27 April 1928, 9 March 1929; Bank of

market by foreign banks, as with the broader money market, was largely channelled through the London offices of British banks. In 1929 the Midland Bank employed 773 in its 'foreign' branch in the City, to provide money market and foreign exchange facilities for its banking customers from around the world, including maintaining numerous accounts in both sterling and foreign currencies on their behalf. In that year it received 76,326 telegrams and sent 100,348, or approximately 1,000 every working day.[72]

These developments in London's money and foreign exchange markets contributed to making British banks better able to cope with the risks they faced in the 1920s. The risks were magnified towards the end of the decade with banking crises in the USA, Germany, and Austria as well as Britain's own economic and monetary problems.[73] These difficulties were not resolved until Britain abandoned the Gold Standard on 21st September 1931, leaving the currency to take the strain rather than the banking system.[74] Though this crisis damaged London's money and foreign exchange markets these continued to operate, providing banks with a mechanism for accessing liquidity at a very difficult time.[75] However, the monetary stability discouraged foreign banks from using the London money market, as the Bank of England acknowledged in 1931, 'People would like to take advantage of higher interest rates ruling here

---

England, Sterling Dollar Exchange 18 July 1928; 'The Changing Character of the London Foreign Exchange Market', *Bankers Magazine* (July 1938), p.406; W.F. Spalding, *Dictionary of the World's Currencies and Foreign Exchanges* (London: Pitman, 1928), pp.55, 89, 125; J. Sangway, *Clare's Money Market Primer and Key to the Exchanges* (London: Pitman, 1936), p.212.

[72] Midland Bank Overseas: Description of Operations, August 1930; Lloyds Bank Ltd: Foreign Business Regulations, 1925; District Bank: Foreign Dept Minute Book, 8 June 1918.

[73] Bank of England, Memorandum 20 February 1931 cf. 11 March 1931, 21 September 1931; Lloyds Bank Colonial and Foreign Department, Correspondence and Memoranda 3 October 1929, 27 January 1932, 1 March 1932, 5 April 1932; Wilson, *Capital Imports*.

[74] Smith St. Aubyn: Business Diary 13 July 1931, 19 August 1931, 9 September 1931, 25 September 1931, 27 March 1933; Lloyds Bank Colonial and Foreign Department, Correspondence and Memoranda 3 October 1929, 27 January 1932, 1 March 1932, 5 April 1932; N. Dimsdale and N. Horsewood, 'The Financial Crisis of 1931 and the Impact of the Great Depression on the British Economy', in Dimsdale and Hotson (eds), *British Financial Crises*, p.135.

[75] Evitt, 'Exchange Dealings', 457–8; P. Einzig, 'London as the World's Banking Centre', *The Banker*, xxvii (September 1933), p.184. See H. Clay, 'Finance and the International Market', *The Banker*, xx (October 1931), pp.30–2; P. Einzig, 'The Future of the London Foreign Exchange Market', *The Banker*, xx (November 1931), p.110; L.T. Conway, *The International Position of the London Money Market, 1931–1937* (Philadelphia: [n.p.], 1946), pp.20, 57–61; W.K. Duke, *Bills, Bullion and the London Money Market* (London: Pitman, 1937), pp.14, 86; Madden and Nadler, 'The Paris Money Market', p.13; Bank of England, Memoranda on Foreign Exchange 24 March 1932, Report on the Exchange Equalisation Account, 13 July 1937; War Measures: Foreign Exchange and Gold. Memorandum by Sir F. Phillips, 24 June 1938, Note of a telephone conversation with George Bolton in Ottawa 14 November 1938, H.C. Note 16 November 1938, Foreign Exchange Market Reports 26 January 1939; *Financial News* 9 August 1939; *Wall Street Journal*, 27 July 1934, 22 October 1934, 25 October 1935; Smith St Aubyn: Business Diary 3 August 1934, 17 August 1934, 28 September 1934, 3 September 1938; Hobson, *How the City Works*, p.38.

but are afraid that when they want to withdraw it they will lose more in the rate of exchange than they make on the differences of interest.' As confidence returned, foreign banks slowly resumed their use of the London money market, largely through their correspondent contacts, but not to anything approaching the extent of the past.[76] Barings's acceptance business fell from £5.5 million in 1930 to £1.6 million in 1939. What business that remained was done by the large joint-stock banks as they had the staff required to deal with the complications created by government controls.[77]

In the aftermath of the 1931 crisis, with international trade badly depressed and international finance almost at a standstill, the operation of the money market became entirely dependent upon the circulation of Treasury Bills. Commercial bills outstanding in London fell from £752 million in 1928/9 to £275 million in 1936/7. In contrast, outstanding Treasury Bills reached £834 million by May 1938. In the 1930s the discount house, Smith St. Aubyn, dealt in little more than Treasury Bills and did so in a routine way, requiring none of the judgement and skills that had underpinned their business in the past. Instead, as part of a consortium they submitted a monthly tender to the Bank of England to buy Treasury Bills using money borrowed from the banks to finance their purchases. These bills were then traded between the banks allowing those with spare funds to employ them and those with a shortage to cover the deficit.[78] Leaving the Gold Standard also led to a revival in the foreign exchange market as currency volatility returned after the partial interlude provided by the years between 1925 and 1931. As in the 1920s the money market and the foreign exchange market continued to provide British banks with a means of covering the risks they ran, whether it involved a sudden shortage of liquidity or potential foreign exchange losses. These markets also provided the London offices of British banks with a profitable business, acting on behalf of foreign banks, though a growing number of these did open their own branch. By 1938 a total of eighty-five foreign banks had London offices.[79]

---

[76] Bank of England, Memoranda 20 February 1931, 24 March 1932; Committee on Financial Questions, Report on Sterling Policy, March 1932 and Fourth Report of Committee on Economic Information: Survey of the Economic Situation, July 1932 in S. Howson and D. Winch, *The Economic Advisory Council, 1930-1939: A Study in Economic Advice during Depression and Recovery* (Cambridge: CUP, 1977), pp.255-8, 272-80; King, *History of the Hongkong and Shanghai Banking Corporation*, v.3, pp.165, 366; Sunderland, *Financing the Raj*, pp.67, 83.

[77] P. Bareau, 'Eclipse of the Merchant Banker', *The Banker* (August 1942), pp.83-4.

[78] Smith St. Aubyn: Business Diary, 1929-1939; Cleaver, *The Union Discount*, p.66; Sayers, *Gilletts*, pp.78-82, 87, 95, 122-34.

[79] Crump, 'The Evolution of the Money Market', pp.291-301; Collins, *Money and Banking*, pp.206, 213, 232, 252; Nevin and Davies, *The London Clearing Banks*, p.132; Ellinger, *The City*, pp.163, 191, 226, 310, 337, 347, 357-9, 365-72, 381; Financial News, *The City, 1884-1934*, pp.48, 62; Vallance, *Centre of the World*, pp.173-6; Hobson, *How the City Works*, pp.36, 71; Truptil, *British Banks*, pp.102, 128, 136, 162-3, 167, 265-6; Diaper, 'Merchant Banking', pp.67, 72; S.N. Broadberry, *Market Services and the Productivity Race, 1850-2000* (Cambridge: CUP, 2006), p.270.

Without the facilities provided by the London money market even the largest British banks would have lacked the resilience necessary to meet the challenges of the inter-war years. What the money market provided, to those banks trusted by their peers, was access to liquidity when it was required. This can be seen in the case of the Midland Bank. In the inter-war years domestic bills were, again, of major importance for the Midland Bank having been in steady decline over the fifty years before the First World War. In 1920, with capital and reserves at £21,720,000 and deposits at £371,842,000, loans had risen to £189,720,000 but bills had increased even more dramatically, reaching £57,672,000. A similar picture emerges for 1930 with capital and reserves at £28,496,000, deposits at £399,606,000, loans at £203,583,000 with bills now standing at £83,923,000. The explanation was the huge increase in government borrowing through the issue of Treasury Bills caused by the First World War, as these were extensively held by UK banks. Holding these bills made banks like the Midland very liquid as they possessed a ready market provided by the discount houses backed by the Bank of England as lender of last resort.[80] In addition, the development of the foreign exchange market provided banks with the ability to provide their business customers with credit in different currencies. This was important to both exporters as they increasingly received payment in a foreign currency while their outgoings were in UK£s. The reverse predicament faced importers. They were committed to making a payment in foreign currency for the goods received but were unsure how much sterling to set aside. Without the money market and the foreign exchange market the risks that banks faced between the wars could have endangered their survival, especially during the periodic bouts of international currency turmoil that took place throughout the 1920s and 1930s.

THE BANK OF ENGLAND

The changes that took place in the London money market during the First World War and, again, after the 1931 crisis, increased the power the Bank of England possessed. As early as 1925, that informed observer of British banking, Drummond Fraser, noted that 'The Bank of England alone by buying or selling Government securities can increase or decrease the "cash" and thereby expand or contract the basis of bank credit.'[81] With Treasury Bills now dominating the London money market, the Bank of England was in a position to influence the lending decisions of banks through their need to maintain liquidity. Before the war, the bills in circulation in the London money market

---

[80] Crick and Wadsworth, *A Hundred Years*, p.347.
[81] Sir D. Drummond Fraser, 'British Home Banking', p.437.

were the product of the ebb and flow of international trade and finance. The London money market was where the world's banks employed their idle balances or accessed temporary funds. This meant that the Bank of England had very limited control, acting only as a marginal supplier of liquidity to the discount houses. That position changed with the war and there was no reversion to the previous position once hostilities were over. Though the Bank of England continued to operate through the discount houses, rather than in direct contact with the banks, it could now dictate access to liquidity by expanding or contracting the supply of Treasury Bills or instructing the government broker, Mullins, to buy or sell longer-dated government debt on the Stock Exchange. With the virtual demise of the commercial bill after 1931, as banks provided their business customers with short-term loans instead, the ability of the Bank of England to dictate to the London money market became absolute. This power of the Bank of England over the banks was a recurrent theme throughout the inter-war years, being commented upon by Crump in 1926 and 1938, as well as Gibson in 1927, Spring-Rice in 1929, and Hall in 1938.[82] The Bank of England had moved from a position of acting as lender of last resort to the London money market to one where it was able to influence the workings of the market itself.

The way the market worked remained nevertheless the same because the Bank of England continued to operate through the discount houses or bill brokers and not by providing liquidity directly to banks, as was the case with the other central banks, such as the Federal Reserve in the USA.[83] As Spring-Rice put it in 1929, 'It is the knowledge that the discount market is able as a last resort to borrow from the Bank of England which makes the banks as a whole ready to lend freely to the discount market, and thus ensure a maximum economy in the use of their funds.'[84] It was through the discount market that the Bank of England continued to act as lender of last resort to the UK banking system. What had changed was the relationship between the discount houses and the Bank of England. With the issue and circulation of Treasury Bills squeezing out other alternatives in the 1920s, and then having the field to themselves in the 1930s, the discount houses were converted from acting as independent intermediaries into becoming the Bank of England's agents in the money market. As a result, the Bank of England took a protective attitude towards the discount houses, notably in the 1930s. Faced with a position in which banks were buying up government debt directly, including Treasury Bills, in the face of weak demand for credit from their customers, the Bank of

[82] Crump, 'The London and New York Markets', p.311; Gibson, 'A Critical and Historical Account', p.467; Spring-Rice, 'The Financial Machinery', pp.10–11; Hall, 'The Control of Credit', pp.64–70.

[83] See Crump, 'The London and New York Markets'; Gibson, 'A Critical and Historical Account'.

[84] Spring-Rice, 'The Financial Machinery', pp.10–11.

England introduced a policy in the 1930s that forced them to operate through the discount houses. Banks agreed not to buy new issues of Treasury Bills other than through the discount houses, and to lend the discount houses the amount that they required. Instead of the discount houses using their expertise to evaluate the bills they were offered by each bank, they now bought Treasury Bills from one bank and sold them to another, using funds borrowed from the banks to finance their purchases. If these funds were insufficient they turned to the Bank of England to make up the difference, alerting it to where the problems lay. The object of such a policy was to ensure that the Bank of England was always aware of what was happening in the money market not only by monitoring the state of the accounts that banks kept with it but also through the reports received from the daily rounds of the bill brokers. These kept the Bank of England informed about which banks were in a position to lend, those that had to borrow, and those whose credit was considered strong or weak among their peers.

What the Bank of England was no longer able to do was to act as international lender of last resort to the global banking system in a world in which the UK£ was challenged by other currencies, such as the French Franc and, especially, the US$, and the fixed exchange rates of the past could no longer be relied upon. This is what happened in the 1931 financial crisis, which also exposed the absence of an alternative in the shape of either the Federal Reserve or the Bank of France.[85] The domestic power of the Bank of England increased after the 1931 crisis with Britain's departure from the Gold Standard. Instead of the value of the UK£ being fixed, it was left to fluctuate. In 1932, however, the Exchange Equalization Account was established at the Bank of England, and with this account the Bank of England was entrusted with foreign-currency reserves and given responsibility for stabilizing the value of the UK £ against other leading currencies, notably the US$. It even hired staff from the London foreign exchange market to handle this intervention. Whereas in the 1920s, the Bank of England had not intervened in the operation of the foreign exchange market, though it did monitor its growth, it now had the means and the authority to become involved. Though the Bank did not develop the same relationship with those involved in the foreign exchange market as it had with the discount market, it now took much greater note of what happened there. It did not act as lender of last resort to the foreign exchange market even though it was used by banks to borrow and lend among each other. Unlike the discount market, where the bill brokers bought and sold bills using both their own capital and borrowed funds, intermediaries in the foreign exchange market only facilitated transactions between banks, and took no positions themselves. In that way the banks remained dependent upon the discount

---

[85] Capie and Woods, *Money over Two Centuries*, pp.163, 334.

houses and their relationship to the Bank of England to access lender-of-last-resort support.[86]

Throughout the 1920s and 1930s the Bank of England remained a highly informed lender of last resort because it did not only act in times of crisis or when a particular bank was in trouble, but daily and on the basis of inside knowledge and advance warning. In this way the Bank of England could take pre-emptive action to avert a banking crisis, as it did in the case of Williams Deacon's in 1930. If Williams Deacon's had been allowed to fail it might have destabilized the entire banking system, as it was a relatively large bank, though not one of the Big Five. What the Bank of England did was provide liquidity support until a solution was found. That solution involved Williams Deacon's takeover by the Royal Bank of Scotland, which already possessed a small retail network in England. It was also the Bank of England that was responsible for the orderly demise of the British Overseas Bank in the 1930s.[87] What the cases of Williams Deacon's and the British Overseas Bank reveal is the growing extent of the Bank of England's engagement with the British banking system between the wars, moving beyond the position of acting solely as lender of last resort to the London money market. Through informal discussions and meeting, and using the increased power the Bank of England now possessed, its Governor sought to influence the strategy and behaviour of the banking system as a whole. Reflecting the role played by the Governor was the fact his became a permanent appointment while his Deputy was chosen from among the permanent officials of the Bank. Driving this intervention of the Bank of England in the internal affairs of the large banks was an acute sense of concern that the unstable economic and monetary conditions could destabilize the entire banking system, leading to a crisis it would be unable to prevent.[88]

One consequence of this intervention was a deliberate attempt by the Bank of England to prevent banks from becoming any bigger and more complex once the merger movement of the wartime years and the immediate post-war

---

[86] Vallance, *Centre of the World*, pp.189, 191; Collins, *Money and Banking*, p.221; Grant, *A Study of the Capital Market*', p.63; Scammell, *London Discount Market*, p.244; Diaper, 'Merchant Banking', p.61; Sayers, *Bank of England*, pp.426, 468, 561, 570; Dowling, *Exchanges of London*, p.234; Greengrass, *Discount Market*, p.166; Ellinger, *The City*, pp.59, 70, 339, 363–4, 389–95, 399, 401; R. Saw, *The Bank of England, 1694–1944* (London: Harrap, 1944), p.103.

[87] Hall, 'The Control of Credit', pp.64–70; Financial News, *The City, 1884–1934*, pp.31, 62; Cleaver, *The Union Discount*, pp.50–66, 558–9; Ellinger, *The City*, pp.191, 373, 383; Hobson, *How the City Works*, pp.36–44; King, 'The London Discount Market', p.15; Truptil, *British Banks*, pp.246, 261, 309; Collins, *Money and Banking*, pp.212–20, 245–55, 268–72; Nevin and Davies, *The London Clearing Banks*, pp.146, 160–1; Sayers, *Bank of England*, p.541; Scammell, *London Discount Market*, pp.221, 244; Fletcher, *Discount Houses*, pp.45–9, 253; Williams Deacon's Bank, *Williams Deacon's, 1771–1970*, pp.156–61.

[88] Sayers, *Bank of England*, pp.243–9, 275–8, 298, 314, 333–4; Fletcher, *Discount Houses*, pp.39–40; Ellinger, *The City*, p.30; Truptil, *British Banks*, pp.79–80; Saw, *Bank of England*, p.103; Greengrass, *Discount Market*, pp.151–2; Tuke and Gillman, *Barclay's Bank*, pp.12–13; Holmes and Green, *Midland*, p.165; Collins, *Money and Banking*, p.212.

period had run its course. It was for this reason that the Bank of England's preferred solution to the Williams Deacon's crisis was its takeover by the Royal Bank of Scotland rather than its absorption by one of the Big Five, which would have been the easiest and simplest course of action. The Bank of England was also concerned that the largest British banks were becoming too complex, which would complicate its role as lender of last resort. What was acceptable to the Bank of England was the way that British banks acted as correspondents for other banks, as those arrangements limited their exposure to the risks being taken by others. A correspondent arrangement was not an open-ended contract but one bounded by commitments and limitations and was also terminable. However, the Bank of England became alarmed whenever the large banks began to diversify into other financial activities and doing so increased their direct exposure to risks. In response, it used its power to prevent this taking place. One example of its success in this strategy was the pressure it exerted to prevent the takeover of British overseas banks by British domestic banks. These British overseas banks were vulnerable to growing competition because they had long relied on the competitive advantages provided by access to the London money market and the international payments system. These advantages were undermined by the war and never regained fully. However, they did represent potentially attractive takeover targets for British domestic banks, with which they had longstanding correspondent arrangements. A number of British banks did acquire some of the smaller British overseas banks, as in the case of Barclays, but the Bank of England intervened to prevent mergers involving the larger ones. As early as 1919 the Bank of England blocked Lloyds's attempt to merge with the National Bank of India. From the point of view of the Bank of England it was much easier to monitor the financial health of banks whose business was simple and easy to understand. That was best achieved if the banks were prevented from combining different types of financial activity. In both the cases of Barclays and Lloyds the international banking activities they built up between the wars were maintained as separate organizations so as to reduce the risk of contagion from any losses incurred. From the perspective of the Bank of England separation contributed to the firewalls that helped prevent contagion at a time of financial stress.[89]

Fear that Britain's economic problems would destabilize the entire banking system also led the Bank of England to become actively involved in industrial reorganization between the wars. Their concern was that the failure of

[89] Sayers, *Bank of England*, pp.243-9, 275-8, 298-314, 333-4; Saw, *Bank of England*, p.103; Tuke and Gillman, *Barclay's Bank*, pp.12-13; Holmes and Green, *Midland*, p.165; Collins, *Money and Banking*, p.212; Fletcher, *Discount Houses*, pp.39-40; Truptil, *British Banks*, p.79-80; Greengrass, *Discount Market*, p.151-2; A.K. Bagchi, *The Evolution of the State Bank of India*, v.2, pp.574, 582, 586; Mackenzie, *Realms of Silver*, p.260; Tyson, *100 Years of Banking*, pp.154, 189, 201, 206, 210-11; Jones, *Multinationals and Global Capitalism*, p.174.

numerous firms in a single industry would be sufficient to create a solvency crisis for a bank, causing it to collapse and so lead to a wider liquidity crisis that the Bank would be unable to stop. Direct intervention in the economy was an unprecedented step for a central bank as it went far beyond its role as lender of last resort or even rescuing a bank on the edge of collapse. This involvement nevertheless began in 1927/8 with the reorganization of firms in the steel and armaments industry, which led to the setting up of the Securities Management Trust and National Shipbuilding Security in 1929. This was followed by the formation of the Bankers' Industrial Development Company in 1930. In retrospect these interventions achieved little as the problems faced by certain sections of British industry were beyond the power of bankers to solve.[90]

The increased power over the banking system possessed by the Bank of England after 1914 also translated into greater potential government influence, given the close relationship that had long existed between the two and its intensification during the war. Though the Bank of England remained independent until 1946, it was increasingly regarded as being under government control.[91] Percy Arnold, writing in 1938, was one among many who believed that the Bank of England was now a servant of government.[92] In his Mansion House speech of 1936, Montagu Norman, the Governor of the Bank of England, made it clear that the Bank of England was very responsive to the wishes of government policy, 'I assure ministers that if they will make known to us through the appropriate channels what it is they wish us to do in the furtherance of their policies, they will at all times find us willing with good will and loyalty to do what they direct us as though we were under a legal compulsion.'[93] As it was now the issue and circulation of Treasury Bills that was the major influence in the London money market, especially after 1931, the government was well placed to influence what went on there, through the Bank of England, and thus the banking system as a whole.[94]

However, that potential did not translate into actual government intervention in the British banking system. There were proposals from the Labour Party in the 1930s for the state to take direct control of the banks, but these came to nothing.[95] Neither was there any legislation to control banking as took

[90] R.G. Hawtrey, *The Art of Central Banking* (London: Longmans, 1932), p.299; Sayers, *Bank of England*, pp.314–30, 548; K. Rosenberg and R.T. Hopkins, *The Romance of the Bank of England* (London: Thornton Butterworth, 1933), pp.256–7; Ellinger, *The City*, pp.18–20; Vallance, *Centre of the World*, p.122.

[91] see M. Collins and M. Baker, 'Bank of England Autonomy: A Retrospective', in C.-L. Holtfrerich, J. Reis, and G. Toniolo (eds), *The Emergence of Modern Central Banking from 1918 to the Present* (Aldershot: Ashgate, 1999).

[92] P. Arnold, *The Bankers of London* (London: Hogarth Press, 1938), pp.14–15. See Hall, 'Control of Credit', p.66–70.

[93] quoted in Saw, *Bank of England*, p.103.

[94] Grant, *A Study of the Capital Market*, p.2.

[95] see A. Citizen, *The City Today* (London: New Fabian Research, 1938).

place in the USA after the Wall Street Crash. This lack of intervention has generated a substantial literature attributing it to the ability of banks and bankers, especially those located in the City of London, to influence government policy. However, evidence is lacking to support this verdict. Instead, the explanation appears to lie in the fact that the policies of successive governments were aimed at more direct means of improving the economic situation, ensuring the stability of the £sterling or financing the huge debt left by the war. In the absence of any banking crisis in Britain there was simply no need for governments to intervene. Like the public at large, governments between the wars had confidence in the British banking system and so were content to leave it alone. What influence they required could be obtained via the Bank of England and the co-operation of those who managed the Big Five banks. That was deemed sufficient to meet such policy priorities as ensuring that there were always sufficient funds to meet government expenditure, financing the National Debt, and managing sterling as an international currency.[96]

WAR AGAIN

The outbreak of the Second World War was long anticipated in financial circles, giving banks, including the Bank of England and the Big Five banks ample time to prepare. One area of banking immediately disrupted by the war was that related to foreign business, still an important activity for the large joint-stock banks and the established merchant banks. The account of what happened in the London branch of the Midland Bank that handled overseas business, reveals the sudden transformation: 'Normally, the dealing room at the Overseas Branch of the Bank was one of the liveliest in the building, filled throughout the day with the clamour of telephone conversations and the bargaining of expert dealers making and accepting contracts in half-a-dozen languages with their fellows in financial centres throughout the world. Very large sums were dealt hourly by verbal contract, a swift, trained judgement being essential to ensure a satisfactory currency "position" when the day's work was done. With the first shot of war this room was silenced, the special

---

[96] For the government's priorities between the wars see R. Middleton, *Government versus the Market: The Growth of the Public Sector, Economic Management and British Economic Performance, c.1890–1979* (Cheltenham: Edward Elgar, 1996); S. Howson, *Domestic Monetary Management in Britain, 1919–38* (Cambridge: CUP, 1975); D.E. Moggridge, *British Monetary Policy, 1924–31* (Cambridge: CUP, 1972); T. Balogh, *Studies in Financial Organization* (London: CUP, 1947); J.M. Atkin, *British Overseas Investment, 1918–31* (New York: Arno, 1977); S. Pollard (ed.), *The Gold Standard and Employment Policies between the Wars* (London: Methuen, 1970); S. Newton, *Modernization Frustrated: The Politics of Industrial Decline in Britain since 1900* (London: Unwin Hyman, 1988).

equipment left in a dusty stillness that has lasted the past six years. So too throughout the whole field of foreign business normal transactions were suspended.'[97] This position remained the same throughout the duration of the war as all operations involving the ebb and flow of funds between Britain and other countries was centralized in the Bank of England. Elsewhere the impact of the outbreak of war was much more a gradual process of increasingly intrusive controls as the hostilities dragged on year after year. By 1945, the whole practice of banking was governed by stringent government controls organized and supervised by the Bank of England in co-operation with the banks themselves.[98] These were designed to ensure the smooth working of an economy functioning for a single purpose, and that purpose was to wage war effectively and so achieve final victory.[99] As Pollard succinctly put it, during the war there was a 'subordination of finance to strategy'.[100]

In many respects banks were converted into agents of the state during the war. According to Ward-Perkins, writing in 1952, the position was that 'banking now approximates increasingly to a public service... The wartime economy had already harnessed the banking system securely to the Treasury Chariot, and the nationalization of the Bank of England and the statutory powers that were given it to direct the commercial bankers only formalized an existing state of affairs.'[101]

Rather than operate as businesses, competing for customers and making judgements on whether or not to grant loans, banks were used to distribute cash, make and receive payments, collect savings, and to provide loans to approved borrowers. There was little scope for discretionary behaviour by banks in an economy involving the central direction of labour; rationing of essential food, clothing, and other material; compulsory savings; state control of production; and the use of currency and capital controls to govern international financial transactions. During the war, for example, savings sought the safest haven. Though deposits in the joint-stock banks rose from £3 billion

---

[97] J. Wadsworth, *Counter Defensive: The Story of a Bank in Battle* (London: Hodder & Stoughton, 1946), p.31 cf, pp.9–10, 30, 100–1.

[98] Shepherd, *The Growth and Role of UK Financial Institutions*, pp.15–16, 103; Scammell, *London Discount Market*, pp.48, 103, 243–4; Nevin and Davies, *The London Clearing Banks*, pp.172–99; A.C. Drury, *Finance Houses: Their Development and Role in the Modern Financial Sector* (London: Waterlow Publishers, 1982), pp.37–42, 89, 227; Fletcher, *Discount Houses*, pp.73, 163–4; Holmes and Green, *Midland*, pp.233–40, 338; Collins, *Money and Banking*, pp.268–72, 293, 317–21, 424, 434, 440, 449, 450, 476.

[99] See S. Broadberry and P. Howlett, 'The United Kingdom: "Victory at all Costs"', in M. Harrison (ed.), *The Economics of World War II: Six Great Powers in International Competition* (Cambridge: CUP, 1998).

[100] Pollard, *Development of the British Economy*, pp.210–16. See N.J. Gibson, 'Money, Banking and Finance', in A.R. Prest (ed.), *The UK Economy: A Manual of Applied Economics* (London: Weidenfeld & Nicolson, 1966), p.52.

[101] C.N. Ward-Perkins, 'Banking Developments', in G.D.N. Worswick and P.H. Ady (eds), *The British Economy, 1945–1950* (Oxford: OUP, 1952), pp.208–15.

in 1939 to £5.8 billion in 1945, it was the savings banks that attracted the greatest inflow, rising from £0.8 billion to £2.5 billion over the same period. In contrast, deposits in building societies hardly grew, standing at £760 million in 1945 compared to £711 million in 1939.[102] One measure of the degree of control that the government was now capable of exerting can be seen through the size of the National Debt. This rose from £8.3 billion in 1938 to £25.9 billion in 1948, of which 25 per cent was in the form of short-term borrowing. This growth in the National Debt finally killed off what remained of the non-government element in the London money market, giving complete control to the Bank of England.[103]

The foreign exchange market was closed down for the duration of the war, with all such transactions routed via the Bank of England and the rigid controls it implemented.[104] Foreign banks largely abandoned the business they had done through their London correspondents either switching to local facilities or turning to New York. The discount market continued to function but only as an appendage of the Bank of England.[105] The discount brokers were nothing more than intermediaries between the Bank of England and the banks, moving money between the various components as directed. As was reported in *The Banker*, in 1947 the routine business that the discount houses did for the Bank of England did not require 'that keen judgement and expert knowledge which provided the original reason and justification for the intervention of Lombard Street intermediaries between borrowers and banks.' However, the control exerted by the Bank of England was not absolute as it did contain a number of gaps which both the discount houses and the banks were able to exploit. In order to generate profits, the discount houses started dealing in short-dated government bonds, using any money made available from the banks that was not otherwise tied up in lending to the government. The banks themselves also developed an inter-bank call loan market that by-passed the discount houses. That provided them with a greater

---

[102] Shepherd, *The Growth and Role of UK Financial Institutions*, Appendices A 1.1, A3.3.

[103] Nevin and Davies, *The London Clearing Banks*, p.161; Scammell, *London Discount Market*, pp.243–4; Fletcher, *Discount Houses*, pp.117, 124, 163–4, 253–6; M.C. Borer, *The City of London: Its History, Institutions and Commercial Activities* (London: Museum Press, 1962), pp.99–100; O.R. Hobson, 'Financial Control after the War', *Journal of the Institute of Bankers*, 63 (1942), p.9; W. King. 'The Market's Changing Role, pp.9–10, H.F. Goodson, 'The Functioning of the London Discount Market', pp.18–21, and C.W Linton, 'The Commercial Banks and the London Discount Market', p.37, all in *The London Discount Market Today* (London: Institute of Bankers, 1962).

[104] Fletcher, *Discount Houses*, pp.57–62; Sayers, *Bank of England*, pp.578–9; Scammell, *London Discount Market*, p.223; King, 'London Discount Market', pp.17, 22, 24; Nevin and Davies, *The London Clearing Banks*, p.182; Middleton, *Government versus the Market*, p.418; L.K. O'Brien, 'The Technique of the United Kingdom Exchange Control', in *The Pattern and Finance of Foreign Trade* (London: Institute of Bankers, 1949), pp.158–60.

[105] 'The City at War', *The Banker* (August 1941), pp.83–4, 96; Henry and Stepmann, *The First Hundred Years*, pp.178–92, 269.

degree of flexibility in the how and where they employed their funds compared to the rigidly-controlled discount market.[106] Despite the attempts by the banks and the discount houses to maintain even a small element of the commercial business that they had engaged in previously, an analysis conducted by the New-York-based Institute of International Finance in 1943 was very pessimistic about whether they would be successful. 'The outlook for the London money market in post-war years is problematical. The institutions laboriously developed over centuries are slowly disintegrating because of lack of business. The personnel skilled in selecting, grading, and handling foreign credits is being dispersed. It is doubtful whether the City of London will regain its dominant position in international trade and finance.'[107] It was not just internationally that the war was transforming the role and functions of British banks. According to Ward-Perkins, writing in 1952, another legacy of the prolonged period of direction and control that banks were subject to was to make them overly conservative. 'The so-called principles of British banking, which above all demand a high liquidity for banking assets, are based on sound historical experience. As the events of the great depression showed, the British banking system, hidebound though it might be, was at least sound. Perhaps, however, the pendulum has swung too far in the opposite direction and there will have to be a revision of banking attitudes.'[108]

CONCLUSION

Between the outbreak of the First World War in 1914 and the end of the Second in 1945, the British banking system faced a series of major challenges at home and abroad. Two world wars made a major and prolonged impact, as did the deep recession in the 1920s and long-lasting depression in the 1930s. Externally there was worldwide monetary and financial instability throughout both the 1920s and 1930s, punctured between 1929 and 1932 by the most severe crisis that the banks had ever experienced. This resulted in the imposition of government controls on the free movement of finance around the world. The British banking system appeared, however, to be largely unaffected. It avoided direct political intervention by maintaining prudent policies on lending and the use of the London money market with the support of the Bank of England as lender of last resort, even though there was popular clamour

---

[106] 'The Changing Discount Market', *The Banker* (March 1947), p.96.
[107] Institute of International Finance, 'Effects of the War on British Banking' (New York, IIF), no 124, pp.1-24 (1943).
[108] Ward-Perkins, 'Banking Developments', in Worswick and Ady (eds), *British Economy*, p.223.

for intervention because of a perceived failure to support manufacturing industry. This resilience exhibited by the British banking system, in contrast to failures elsewhere in the world, greatly enhanced its reputation for stability.

But beneath the appearance of an unchanging landscape for British banking a subtle transformation had taken place, as can be seen in what happened with the Bank of England. Beginning with the First World War, its power in relation to the British banking system greatly increased, compared to the years before 1914. This power was exercised in a number of ways. The most important was the role it played as lender of last resort to the London money market, acting through the discount houses. The reliance of the London money market on Treasury Bills, which were its responsibility, greatly enhanced its power within the market, becoming absolute during the 1930s. Added to the power it obtained by acting as lender of last resort was the practice of informal persuasion that had long existed but had grown enormously during the war years. These powers were used to influence bank strategy, such as discouraging any policy of diversification if it involved a greater exposure to risk. The spirit of co-operation also prevailed when forestalling potential crises, as with the intervention to save Williams and Deacon's from collapse. However, the Bank of England did appear to be acting on its own authority when it became involved in industrial re-organization, though that could be interpreted as an attempt to prevent a banking crisis by saving selected businesses from collapse. Such a policy was feasible in the 1920s, when the prospects of recovery still existed, but was not in the 1930s in the context of a world economic depression. Hence the abandonment of direct intervention by the Bank of England in the 1930s, even though the need might have appeared greater. Finally, during the Second World War the British banking system was converted into a utility providing routine services to a centrally-driven economy. Within that economy there was little or no requirement to respond to competitive pressures whether they related to the activities of the London money market or the decisions taken in bank head offices or branches. That was a situation totally at variance with the one that had existed before the outbreak of the Second World War.

6

Control and Compartmentalization, 1945–1970

INTRODUCTION

The period from 1945 to 1970 was a unique period in global financial history because of the absence of major crises. Between 1950 and 1970, in particular, the world economy experienced prolonged and steady growth in a low inflationary environment, and Britain shared in this, so creating a benign climate within which banks could operate.[1] Crises did occur in the British economy in these years, as it struggled to become and remain internationally competitive, but the domestic consequences were largely neutralized through government intervention, so limiting any destabilizing impact on the British banking system. Adjustments took place internationally, as with the devaluations of the UK£ in 1949 and 1967, so avoiding any shocks that might have created problems for banks through a collapse in confidence among depositors or loan defaults among borrowers.[2] Even when a bank failed, as happened on the 10th of December 1963 to Knowles and Foster, it had no impact on the rest of the banking system. It was a small privately-owned London merchant bank that did a lot of foreign business, and its collapse was largely attributed to a serious fraud committed in 1962.[3] However, this stability of the British banking system was not attributed to the prevailing conditions but to the inherent strengths it possessed. Those who had lived through all or some of the events since the outbreak of the First World War could reflect on the resilience exhibited by the British banking system, which was almost unique, and so regarded its stability as both internally generated and permanent.[4]

---

[1] Allen and Gale, *Understanding Financial Crises*, pp.2, 13; Reinhart and Rogoff, *This Time is Different*, pp.205, 243–4; Y. Cassis, *Crises and Opportunities*, pp.4, 31.
[2] C.R. Schenk, *The Decline of Sterling: Managing the Retreat of an International Currency, 1945–1992* (Cambridge: CUP, 2010), pp.19, 320.
[3] F. Capie, *The Bank of England, 1950s–1979* (Cambridge: CUP, 2010), p.204.
[4] Capie and Woods, *Money over Two Centuries*, p.333; Capie, 'British Financial Crises' in Dimsdale and Hotson (eds), *British Financial Crises*, p.21.

An alternative view of the British banking system nevertheless gained traction, building on the criticisms made both before the First World War and between the two wars. This view was that the British banking system had failed the economy from the late nineteenth century onwards. It chimed with the search for causes of Britain's post-war economic decline.[5] Increasingly a link was made between banking stability and a lack of competition, because of the dominance of the five large joint-stock banks.[6] In turn this lack of competition fostered a highly conservative attitude among British bankers, which meant that they were unwilling to take any risks and so did not provide British manufacturing industry with the finance it required. Such views were being expressed by the early 1950s and became more entrenched over the period.[7] As Channon reflected from the perspective of 1978, 'Among the clearing banks the long period of limited competition led not only to strategic stagnation, but to bureaucracy in their organizations.'[8] Such an interpretation of British banking between 1945 and 1970 was endorsed by the staff at the Bank of England, in a reflective article published in 1991. 'From the war until the 1960s the British banking sector was remarkably stable. It operated within a highly-structured financial system, with clear demarcations from other types of institution. This was reinforced both by its oligopolistic behaviour and by various forms of official controls, such as lending constraints imposed for monetary purposes and exchange controls. Both had the effect of restricting competition.'[9]

The questions that arise are threefold. The first is whether there *was* a lack of competition when the full array of banking provision is surveyed rather than a focus on the five largest joint-stock banks. The second is whether this lack of competition was an inevitable product of the dominant position occupied by these five large joint-stock banks. The third is whether the banking system did fail to provide the economy with the financial services it required and so contributed to Britain's relatively poor economic performance between 1945 and 1970. What there can be no doubt about is that the

---

[5] For a sample of critical views of British banking from different types of scholars writing after 1945 see T.L. Alborn, *Conceiving Companies: Joint-Stock Politics in Victorian England* (London: Routledge, 1998), pp.87, 130-7, 141-2; M. Collins and M. Baker, 'English Commercial Bank Stability, 1860-1914', *Journal of European Economic History*, 31 (2000); Carnevali, *Europe's Advantage*, pp.15-16.

[6] Davies, *The Origins and Development of Cartelisation*, pp.26-31.

[7] Ward-Perkins, 'Banking Developments', in Worswick and Ady (eds), *British Economy*, p.223; Sir George Erskine, 'Finance for Industry', *Journal of the Institute of Bankers*, 76 (1955), pp.161, 167; L. Hannah, 'The Twentieth Century Transformation', in Green. Pohle-Fraser and Fraser (eds), *The Human Factor*, p.200.

[8] D.F. Channon, *The Service Industries: Strategy, Structure and Financial Performance* (London: Macmillan, 1978), p.72.

[9] 'The Performance of Major British Banks, 1970-90', *Bank of England Quarterly Bulletin*, 31 (1991), p.508.

period was characterized by the use of anti-competitive practices, including agreements on the rate of interest, among the large banks. These practices were also condoned and even encouraged by the Bank of England and by the UK government, as they helped make the implementation of Government monetary policy more effective.[10] However, a product of these restrictive practices, and the controls that lay behind them, was the growth of alternatives to the large retail banks. These included building societies, offering higher rates of interest to savers and generous loans to homebuyers, and finance companies providing businesses with loans on more attractive terms. There was also a revival in the use of the domestic bill and the use of corporate structures and the issue of stock as methods of business finance. A myopic focus on the five largest banks omits these developments.

STRUCTURE AND OPERATION

English banking in 1945 was dominated by eight banks, of which five constituted a top group by a considerable margin, namely Barclays, Lloyds, National Provincial, Westminster, and Midland. This was the same structure that had emerged by 1922. There were few significant changes until the end of the 1960s. In 1962 the National Provincial bought the Manchester-based District Bank while in 1968/9 there were a number of significant mergers and disposals. Barclays bought the Liverpool-based Martins Bank which, like the District Bank, was suffering because of its northern orientation. In contrast, Barclays disposed of its Scottish bank, the British Linen Bank, to the Bank of Scotland, as it had never been fully integrated because of the separate note issue. More significantly, the National Provincial and Westminster merged so as to give them the same scale possessed by the other three large banks. However, a merger between Barclays and Lloyds was blocked, as a step too far. The Bank of England was concerned about the size of individual English banks and so put obstacles in the way of further consolidation. This was unlike the situation in Scotland, which retained a separate banking system and was regarded as having too many banks.[11]

However, consolidation in British banking did not necessarily involve mergers between retail banks. It also involved potential mergers between domestic and overseas banks to create global banks. The overseas banks faced growing difficulties after 1945 as the type of business they had relied

---

[10] B. Griffiths, 'The Development of Restrictive Practices in the UK Monetary System', *Economic and Social Studies*, 41 (1973), pp.8, 12, 15.

[11] Davies, Richardson, Katinaite and Manning, 'Evolution of the UK Banking System', pp.322–5, Capie, Capie, *Bank of England*, pp.327–9; Ackrill and Hannah, *Barclays*, p.171–7.

upon was in decline. These banks had thrived by serving expatriate business communities around the globe, meeting the needs of international trade when conducted by numerous separate enterprises, and providing financial services to colonial governments. Since the Second World War these expatriate communities were in decline as the countries of the British Empire asserted their independence and international trade was falling under the control of governments and multinational companies. In addition, the competitive advantage provided through a connection to London was no longer of the same value as so much of the borrowing and lending that banks conducted was confined to single countries because of exchange controls. In 1969, two of these London-based overseas banks, the Standard Bank of South Africa and the Chartered Bank, which was largely Indian-based, merged as a defensive measure. However, a merger with a British domestic bank, with whom these British Overseas Banks had longstanding correspondent relations, offered both the opportunity to prosper in a world in which international trade and finance was rapidly recovering and the scale of business was rising. The era of the global bank, possessing the scale and reach required to serve the global economy, was beginning to emerge. This was not to happen because the Bank of England opposed these merger moves. Its motivation was governed by the regulatory complications it would create. Its focus was entirely domestic and that was best served if the activities of the large joint-stock banks remained simple and were confined to the British economy. Even those banks such as Barclays, that had sizeable overseas operations from the past, had to maintain them as separate subsidiaries rather than create an integrated global bank. What was permitted by the Bank of England, but not until 1971, was the merger between Lloyds and the Bank of London and South America (Bolsa). Those British banks whose field of activity was Latin America were facing a particularly hostile environment. As a result, British banking missed an opportunity to match the US banks that were developing a global footprint in the 1950s and 1960s. As a result, British overseas banks were largely absorbed into local banking groups.[12]

Another potential avenue for consolidation within British banking was the combination of different types of financial activity within the same institution. This already existed in many countries in Continental Europe, most notably Germany and Switzerland, where the universal banks conducted the full range of financial services. Again, the Bank of England opposed such mergers because it would also complicate its regulatory role. With the joint-stock

---

[12] Jones, *Multinationals and Global Capitalism*, p.174; F. Bostock, 'The British Overseas Banks and Development Finance in Africa after 1945', in G. Jones (ed.), *Banks and Money: International and Comparative Finance in History* (London: Frank Cass, 1991), pp.157–65; Ackrill and Hannah, *Barclays*, pp.269, 311; 'Banking Mergers and Participations', *Bank of England Quarterly Bulletin*, 12 (1972), p.452; Capie, *Bank of England*, pp.329–31, 339.

banks focusing on the provision of credit it was through them that the Bank could influence money supply and so act in furtherance of the government's monetary policy. If the joint-stock banks were allowed to issue stocks and bonds and trade in bills, through merging with merchant banks, they would be better placed to evade the credit controls imposed upon them. These were areas that the joint-stock banks were keen to expand into because of the constraints under which they operated elsewhere in their business, such as attracting deposits and making short-term loans. Combining with a joint-stock bank would also benefit the merchant banks, as the capital and connections it would provide could open up new domestic opportunities and so compensate for the decline in the international business they had previously relied upon. In 1967 the Midland Bank did make a move in this direction, taking a one-third stake in Montagu Trust, a City merchant bank. The Bank of England opposed the deal but had not been consulted. Even without Bank of England opposition, British joint-stock banks faced a problem in expanding into investment banking. The London Stock Exchange restricted membership to partnerships and to those whose sole business was the buying and selling of securities. As a consequence, UK investment banks could not add the associated activities of dealing in stocks and bonds once issued, and so transform themselves into Wall-Street style investment banks or European-style universal banks. For that reason, even when Britain's accession to the European Economic Community on 1st January 1973 allowed different types of banks to combine, regardless of the wishes of the Bank of England, there was no rush to merge.[13] In this way British banks also missed out on the possibility of re-positioning themselves within the domestic banking world. Such an opportunity would not arise again until the 1980s.

The result was that throughout the 1945 to 1970 period the UK banking system was highly compartmentalized, being divided into different types of banks. This had long been the case but not to the extent it was after 1945, when it suited the administrative convenience of the Bank of England. As Shepherd observed in 1971, 'by the late 1950s, the UK financial institutional system had evolved into a carefully segmented type of market system in which each set of institutions had acquired a tacitly agreed monopoly over a certain section of the loan market, and in which each institution in turn endeavoured to avoid direct interest-rate competition with its competitors for its share of household savings.'[14] From the era of the individual banker onwards, banking had never been bounded by rigid lines of demarcation though specialization

---

[13] 'Banking Mergers and Participations', p.452; J. Padovan, 'New Influences in Merchant Banking', *Journal of the Institute of Bankers*, 98 (1977), p.126; Capie, *Bank of England*, pp.329-31, 339; T.M. Rybczynski, 'The Merchant Banks', *Economic and Social Studies*, 41 (1973), pp.117-20.

[14] Shepherd, *The Growth and Role of UK Financial Institutions*, p.16.

developed. Banks responded to challenges and seized opportunities and so adjusted their business model to suit the environment within which they operated, which is why it was so difficult to define a bank.[15] In contrast, rigid compartmentalization suited the government as its policies were driven by multiple agendas. By targeting different segments of the market for loans, ranging from businesses through consumers to those borrowing to finance house purchases, these policy objectives could be met whether the intention was to dampen consumer demand, boost investment or encourage home ownership.[16] The flaw in such an approach was that rigid compartmentalization could not be enforced indefinitely within a market economy. As Shepherd went on to note, 'From the late 1950s, however, the inter-locking market-sharing cartel arrangements tended to break down as foreign banks and domestic merchant banks, drawing on the growing pool of Euro-dollars, stepped up their intervention in the domestic market place.'[17]

If the definition of a bank is widened to include all the banks accepting deposits and/or making loans in Britain after 1945, the field widens far beyond five large joint-stock banks. What was true is that until 1970, though these five large joint-stock banks did compete with each other, they did not do so aggressively and also indulged in collusive practices. They were members of an interest-rate cartel until 1971 and so did not compete on the basis of price and did so instead on service, convenience, and established relationships.[18] This lack of competition was not solely a product of the banks and the existence of a group of five, and then four, dominant players. It was much more a product of the time, being a legacy of the close working relationship built up between the banks since 1914, honed during two world wars and fostered by the Bank of England. Through the control it exercised over these large banks, the Bank of England was able to manipulate the prevailing rate of interest and adjust the supply of credit as it sought to make government policy effective.[19] Faced with a banking system that was not fully meeting the needs of its customers because of the combination of restrictive practices and external credit controls, alternative financial providers appeared from the late 1950s onwards. One group were hire purchase companies. These borrowed money from the joint-stock banks, which they were unable to lend directly to customers because of government restrictions, and then re-lent it to

---

[15] Journal of the Institute of Bankers, 'Memorandum' pp.51–2; Blunden, 'The Supervision of the UK Banking System', pp.213–18; Capie, Bank of England, pp.591–8.
[16] Ackrill and Hannah, Barclays, p.208.
[17] Shepherd, The Growth and Role of UK Financial Institutions, p.16.
[18] Griffiths, 'The Development of Restrictive Practices in the UK Monetary System', pp.8, 12, 15.
[19] Gibson, 'Money, Banking and Finance', in Prest (ed.), The UK Economy, p.103; A. Cairncross, The British Economy since 1945: Economic Policy and Performance, 1945–1990 (Oxford: Blackwell, 1992), pp.24, 98; Ackrill and Hannah, Barclays, pp.117–39, 160–5, 208.

those wanting to purchase cars and other consumer durables, with re-payment being made on instalment. That was a relatively risk-free retail business as incomes were rising, unemployment was low, and goods could always be re-possessed and sold if the borrower defaulted. Unable to provide this finance themselves, in 1958 the joint-stock banks bought stakes in nine out of the twelve hire purchase companies.[20]

Another group were the finance houses, and these grew rapidly from the late 1950s onwards. Finance houses relied upon using short-term deposits to finance property development. Unlike cars and consumer durables, investment in property was both long-term and left the lender with assets that were not easily disposed of in the event of a default. But it was highly profitable, as past planning controls created periodic shortages of office space, so driving up rents. That was then followed by a rush to build once such controls were relaxed. Though these finance companies did attract deposits from the public they also relied heavily on funds borrowed from the banks, either obtained by way of loans secured on the property they were acquiring or building, and bills which the banks bought at a discount. In this way one effect of the restrictions on the ability of the joint-stock banks to lend was to revive the Originate and Distribute Model that had been in long-term decline.[21] Overall, by 1967 there were an estimated 125 alternative lenders, or quasi-banks, operating in Britain.[22]

The banks also experienced growing competition from the building societies. Banks had long left the field of retail deposits from small savers and the finance of house purchase to others. The result was to give building societies an established base from which they could rapidly expand after 1945 as rising affluence and increasing home ownership greatly expanded the market for their services. Building societies also profited enormously from the restrictions placed on banks. In the face of these restrictions banks prioritized their business customers, as that was where they had traditionally generated their profits. This left a gap to be filled in meeting the needs of the small saver and those wanting a mortgage. The result can be seen in what happened in the market for savings. In 1945 the joint-stock banks held £5.8 billion in deposits compared to £2.5 billion with the savings banks and only £0.8 billion in building societies. By 1966 the total held by the joint-stock banks had doubled to £11.4 billion and that in the savings banks had almost kept pace, reaching £4 billion. In contrast, the amount now in the hands of the building societies

[20] C.J. Montgomery, 'The Clearing Banks, 1952–77: An Age of Progress', *Journal of the Institute of Bankers*, 98 (1977), pp.89–91; Gibson, 'Money, Banking and Finance', in Prest (ed.), *The UK Economy*, pp.74–5, 103; Shepherd, *The Growth and Role of UK Financial Institutions*, pp.11, 15.

[21] Gibson, 'Money, Banking and Finance', in Prest (ed.), *The UK Economy*, pp.74–5, 103; Shepherd, *The Growth and Role of UK Financial Institutions*, pp.11, 15.

[22] Capie, *Bank of England*, pp.307–9.

had increased spectacularly, standing at £5.9 billion, and continued to grow fast. By 1970 building societies had reached parity with the banks in terms of the share of deposits they held. Riding on the back of the home ownership boom fostered by rising inflation and government incentives, the building societies had become a major force in British finance. With property prices rising every year while the value of fixed-interest bonds, such as those issued by the government, fell, home ownership was seen as a safe haven for savings, especially as rent controls, imposed during the First World War, and the expansion of publicly-provided accommodation destroyed the market for privately-rented accommodation. At the same time all the major political parties became committed to the creation of a property-owning democracy and so provided tax incentives to homeowners. Building societies had long dominated the provision of housing finance and so were ideally placed to benefit from these opportunities. In turn, the ability of borrowers to service their mortgages at a time of full employment and job security meant that the building societies were able to pay attractive rates to savers and provide them with a reasonable guarantee of security. The attractions of building societies for savers were also enhanced by mergers as these created large institutions operating nationwide branch networks. In this way the building societies came to resemble the joint-stock banks and could also ensure that when a smaller society got into financial difficulties its problems were dealt with by a rapid takeover by one of its larger brethren without any interruption to business, loss to savers or even publicity.[23] The government itself increased the competitive nature of the market for savings by creating the National Giro Bank in 1968, even though the complaints at the time focused on access to loans by business.[24]

When the survey of banks is widened it becomes apparent that the large joint-stock banks were restrained when competing with each other, mainly as a result of the controlled environment within which they operated. The effect of this was twofold. The first was to limit the absolute amount of their lending at times of monetary stringency due to the various credit limitations imposed by the Bank of England. The second was a tendency towards very conservative behaviour as they prioritized the supply of funds to established customers with a track record of servicing their loans, as opposed to those attempting to develop new businesses. In spite of this hostile environment and growing

---

[23] Shepherd, *The Growth and Role of UK Financial Institutions*, pp.32–3,Appendix 3.3. L. Williams, 'The Banks and their Competitors', *Journal of the Institute of Bankers*, 101 (1980), p.143; 'The Development of the Building Societies Sector', pp.502–10; Turner, *Banking in Crisis*, p.187; A. Offer, 'Narrow Banking, Real Estate, and Financial Stability in the UK, c. 1870–2010', in Dimsdale and Hotson (eds), *British Financial Crises*, pp.163–5; Nevin and Davies, *The London Clearing Banks*, pp.129, 187, 190–1, 216, 227, 274, 274, 284–5, 304. See B. Ritchie, *We're with the Woolwich*.

[24] Capie, *Bank of England*, pp.442–3.

competition the large joint-stock banks did nevertheless expand their lending both absolutely and relatively. By the end of the war these banks had become little more than collection agencies for the government, which absorbed most of the funds they gathered. In 1946 only 18 per cent of bank lending was in the form of loans to customers. The other 82 per cent went to the government, in one way or another. The banks then slowly increased their lending to non-government customers though business had, initially, only a limited need for loans. During the war businesses had accumulated large holdings of low-yielding government debt which they were able to dispose of and to re-invest the proceeds as more profitable opportunities arose. Also, the post-war years were ones of generally rising domestic prosperity, which generated increasing profits available for re-investment. The high rates of personal taxation prevailing between 1945 and 1970 encouraged the re-investment of these profits rather than payments to partners and shareholders, as capital gains were not taxed. Despite this, the joint-stock banks gradually re-asserted their position as an important source of funding for British business. Their lending to non-government customers reached 30 per cent of the total in 1956 and 52 per cent in 1968.[25]

The restrictions imposed on these joint stock banks by the government, and implemented by the Bank of England as part of their strategy for managing the post-war economy, did however restrict the ability of the joint-stock banks to meet the borrowing needs of their customers. These restrictions became particularly acute from time to time as the government intervened to reduce inflation or dampen demand for imports in order to protect the balance of payments.[26] One solution found was for these banks to lend their excess funds to the growing number of shadow banks, as these operated outside the controls imposed. In turn, these shadow banks then lent to both businesses and individuals. Another was the revival of the domestic bill market, which had fallen into abeyance with the Lend and Hold Model and the dominance of the government's own Treasury Bills. Companies and public bodies, such as local authorities, discovered that they could issue bills, which could be sold to the banks at a discount. In turn these bills could be bought and sold until maturity providing both investment opportunities and liquidity to banks.[27] These attempts to circumvent the controls imposed upon the banks came at a cost, as it made them less efficient lenders compared to the smooth operation

[25] Shepherd, *The Growth and Role of UK Financial Institutions*, pp.15–16; Collins, *Money and Banking*, pp.268–72, 293, 317–21, 424, 434, 440, 449, 450, 476.

[26] Committee on the Working of the Monetary System; Principal Memoranda of Evidence, v.2, p.59, Report, pp.42–52, 72–3, 109, 112–16, 197–8, Institute of Bankers, *The Bank of England Today* (London: Institute of Bankers, 1964), pp.2–3, 27.

[27] Scammell, *London Discount Market*, pp.48, 103, 243–4; Fletcher, *Discount Houses*, pp.73, 163–4; Drury, *Finance Houses*, pp.37, 41–2, 89, 227; Nevin and Davies, *The London Clearing Banks*, pp.172–5, 181–4, 198–9.

of the Lend and Hold Model that had been perfected since the mid-nineteenth century. However, the banks were relatively content with the situation as they occupied an assured position within the financial system. They had become accustomed to a world characterized by collusion and control. In this they were little different from other components of the post-war British economy that had either been taken into state ownership or subjected to intrusive controls that dictated behaviour.[28]

It was not only in the provision of credit that the actions of the government were distorting the financial system. Despite the end of the Second World War in 1945, government borrowing continued to rise. Part of this was the nationalization programme implemented by the Labour government, as the state took control of such businesses as the railways, utilities, and coal mining, providing previous owners with compensation in the way of national debt. There was also the inability of successive governments to balance income and expenditure, so they resorted to borrowing. The National Debt stood at £25 billion by 1950, £28 billion by 1960 and £33 billion by 1970. Allied to the need to service this high level of National Debt were high levels of taxation. These eroded the ability of individuals to save and so self-fund business expenditure, putting pressure on the banks to provide increased levels of financial support. Conversely, the tax system also encouraged companies to internalize financial flows so as to escape taxation.[29] The overall effect was to greatly distort the nature of the business that banks could do and their way of operating. No longer were banks left free to determine their own business model, whether it was Lend or Hold or Originate and Distribute, for they were now forced to adapt to the environment set by the government and implemented by the Bank of England. Out of this arose a variety of criticisms of the joint-stock banks voiced by those either in business, who could not obtain the funding they wanted, or outside observers noting the problems emerging in British manufacturing industry at this time and searching for causes.[30] These criticisms continued even in the face of various initiatives to solve the financing problems of British industry, such as the formation and operation of the Industrial and Commercial Finance Corporation.[31] In contrast, those who have searched for a direct connection between the inadequacies of finance and the poor performance of British manufacturing industry in the 1950s and 1960s have failed to find it when they cover the full array of providers. As Bowden concluded from one such study, 'The growth and role of the finance houses during the post-war decades provides an important counter to those

---

[28] Collins, *Money and Banking*, pp.231–4, 220, 365–8, 371, 373, 377, 405, 411, 420, 434, 503, 582.
[29] Thomas, *Finance of British Industry*, pp.143–7, 153–5, 184–90, 199, 218, 234–5, 310, 325; Working of Monetary System Report, pp.92–5, 108–9, 166.
[30] W.E. Alford, *British Economic Performance, 1945–1975* (London: Macmillan, 1988), p.56.
[31] Kinross, *Fifty Years in the City*, p.122; Carnevali, *Europe's Advantage*, pp.113–27.

critics who cite the absence of innovation in the provision of finance and the lack of constructive links between the City and industry as factors in the problems of British industry after 1945.'[32]

THE BANK OF ENGLAND

In contrast to the years before the First World War, in those after the Second the British banking system was not responsible for its own destiny. Instead, it had to operate within a framework set by the government and implemented by the Bank of England. Externally, these included exchange controls and severe restrictions on capital flows between Britain and other countries. Internally the banking system was subjected to a range of controls and directions as the government attempted to micro-manage the economy. The Bank of England was the instrument through which the government exerted these controls.[33] The role played by the Bank was already changing before its nationalization in 1946, due to the demands placed upon it by the government in both world wars and during the economically-troubled interwar years. Change continued after the Second World War when the Bank was entrusted with the implementation of British monetary policy as well as playing a role in the management of the British economy. This had the effect of shifting the Bank's focus away from acting as lender of last resort to the money market and crisis manager for the banking system to one of operational responsibility for the stability of the entire economy and it used the power it had over the banking system and the money market, at a time of exchange and capital controls, to achieve that. In conducting this role, the Bank interpreted its remit very narrowly and so focused almost exclusively on the joint-stock banks and the established merchant banks, ignoring smaller banks, the branches of foreign banks operating in London, the emerging finance houses and the building societies, leaving them forge their own future but fend for themselves if they encountered difficulties.[34]

Many at the Bank of England were aware that changes in the structure of banking in the 1950s were eroding their ability to implement government policy, but they did not want the government to go down the legislative route that had developed in the USA from the 1930s. There was a general belief

---

[32] S. Bowden, 'Competition and Collusion in the Finance Sector in the Post War Period', *Financial History Review*, 4 (1997), p.164.

[33] Schenk, *Decline of Sterling*, p.8; Gibson, 'Money, Banking and Finance', in Prest (ed.), *The UK Economy*, p.52; Capie, *Bank of England*, p.525-7.

[34] Singleton, *Central Banking in the Twentieth Century*, pp.113, 127-32, 167; Billings and Capie, 'Financial Crisis, Contagion and the British Banking System', pp.196-7; Dyer, 'The Secondary Banking Crisis', pp.46-8.

in the Bank that successful supervision could only be done by those who understood what was involved, and that meant them. As early as 1962 the Bank had argued that legislative intervention in the banking system was neither appropriate nor effective. Instead, an informal but close working relationship was what was required. 'Because it is only possible to assess the adequacy of a bank's liquidity in the light of the most detailed information about its liabilities and assets, together with an intimate knowledge of the bank's normal pattern of business, only the bank itself is able to judge whether its position is such as to give the most profitable use of its resources while providing ample means to meet all foreseeable demands for cash.'[35] Such an attitude was still prevalent in the 1970s. Sir George Blunden, head of banking supervision at the Bank of England, argued in 1975 that, 'We believe that each bank is a unique institution which must be judged individually. We do not accept the sort of system in force in some countries in which legislation lays down rigid standards and ratios with which all banks must comply at all times.'[36] Under this type of supervision the Bank of England acted both as the gatekeeper of the banking club and the authority that maintained standards of behaviour among those admitted. It had no responsibility for those excluded. This approach allowed financial institutions that were not recognized as banks to expand, free from the controls and regulations that could have prevented their development. The consequence was that banking remained competitive in the UK, as those that were already established could not exclude new entrants. Once one of these new financial institutions reached a stage where they were recognized as a bank by the Bank of England it was admitted to the club, and so entitled to support but also subject to control. This system appeared to achieve the best of both worlds for banking, namely competition and stability. The problem arose when the behaviour of the unrecognized banks threatened the entire financial system, including the stability of those admitted to the club and supervised by the Bank of England. Such a situation was inevitable if the controls imposed on the established banks limited their ability to provide all borrowers and savers with the service they required. Under these conditions new financial institutions would emerge to meet unsatisfied financial needs and by doing so their behaviour could threaten the stability of the entire system. Any regulator of the banking system was likely either to over-regulate thus preventing the growth of competition, or under-regulate and so contribute to instability as new financial institutions expanded by taking more risks than the established ones, with the inevitable crisis exposing those with a flawed business model. Only by staying closely in

---

[35] Bank of England, 'Bank Liquidity in the United Kingdom', *Bank of England Quarterly Bulletin*, 2 (1962), pp.249.

[36] Blunden, 'The Supervision of the UK Banking System', pp.189-4.

touch with banks could the regulator find the balance between over- and under-regulation.[37]

A key element in the relationship between the Bank of England and the banking system was the role it played as lender of last resort to the London money market.[38] The central element in this money market at the end of the Second World War was the discount market. In the discount market, banks borrowed from and lent to each other with discount houses acting as intermediaries. If the discount house could not match what they had lent with what they had borrowed they could cover the deficit by borrowing from the Bank of England but only at a high rate of interest and providing good quality bills as collateral.[39] The Bank of England was able to provide the funds required as it was in receipt of the money deposited by the British banks through which they settled imbalances between each other. According to Capie, when writing of the post-war period up to 1979, 'The concept of lender of last resort is best defined in terms of lending to the market as a whole rather than to an individual bank and so avoiding charges of cronyism.'[40] Thus the Bank of England did not have to differentiate between individual banks when deciding whether to lend or not. Instead, that task was devolved to the discount houses.[41] Through the power the Bank of England possessed as lender of last resort to the discount market it was able to influence short-term interest rates, whether to lower the government's borrowing costs or, more generally, as an aid to the implementation of monetary policy. The discount market was used, for example, by the Bank of England as a way of bridging the day-to-day shortfall between government receipts and payments through the issue or purchase of Treasury Bills. Once in circulation, Treasury Bills were the means through which banks could borrow and lend to each other as a sale and purchase represented a transfer of funds. The problem for the discount market was that the Bank of England manipulated it in the interests of government policy. What banks required was a regular supply of Treasury Bills and the ability to sell part of their holding if they were becoming illiquid or buy additional ones if they had a temporary surfeit of funds. It was this position that was increasingly undermined as the Bank of England used the discount

---

[37] Cairncross, *The British Economy since 1945*, pp.24, 98; Shepherd, *The Growth and Role of UK Financial Institutions*, pp.11–15.

[38] R.J. Clark, 'British Banking: Changes and Challenges', *Journal of the Institute of Bankers* 89 (1968), pp.468–78; Allen and Gale, *Understanding Financial Crises*, pp.2, 94–9, 154–5, 269, 282–313.

[39] Bank of England, 'Commercial Bills', *Bank of England Quarterly Bulletin*, 1 (1960–1), p.27.

[40] Capie, *Bank of England*, p.585.

[41] Hall, 'The Control of Credit', pp.63–72; Crump, 'The Evolution of the Money Market', pp.287–301; N. Crump, 'Finance and the Crisis', *Journal of the Institute of Bankers*, 59 (1938), pp.386–96; O.R. Hobson, 'Future of the City', *Journal of the Institute of Bankers*, 57 (1946), pp.91–9; W.T.C. King, 'War and the Money Market', *Journal of the Institute of Bankers*, 58 (1947), pp.47–61.

market as a tool of monetary policy. In response, banks turned away from the discount market and made increasing use of alternative or parallel money markets including direct inter-bank borrowing and lending. Money could be borrowed, usually for less than fourteen days, at attractive rates of interest in this sterling inter-bank market. Activity in the sterling inter-bank market grew from deposits of £131 million and advances of £191 million in December 1962 to deposits of £1,694 million and advances of £1,747 million in December 1970. By then it was larger than the discount market. The problem with these parallel markets was that they involved greater risks and lacked a lender of last resort because the Bank of England was not involved. The security attached to any loan rested on the counterparty to each deal rather than the collateral exchanged and the absence of the discount houses meant they could not look to the Bank of England for support.[42]

It was not only the British banking system that was affected by the relative decline of the discount market, as it had long been used directly or indirectly by banks from around the world. Even after the Second World War, London remained at the centre of global banking.[43] It was through a vast correspondent network centred in London that banks from around the world not only made and received payments but also borrowed and lent to each other, using the sale and purchase of UK Treasury Bills as the means of doing so. Though the UK£ was in steady decline as a reserve currency after the Second World War it long continued to be favoured by banks because of the continuing appeal of the London discount market. The problem was that the British government simultaneously exploited its ability to borrow easily and cheaply in its own currency and restricted the use of sterling as an international currency. In 1957 the British government placed restrictions on the international use of sterling to finance trade because of the strain it was putting on UK foreign exchange reserves. These restrictions were not lifted until 1963 and then re-imposed in 1968. The response by banks was to continue to use London as a location for both payments and lending and borrowing but to switch to the use of the US$ rather than the UK£, leading to the emergence of the Eurodollar market from 1955 onwards.[44]

The Bank of England supported this switch from the UK£ to the US$ as it was keen to see the City of London retain its position as an important

---

[42] Capie, *Bank of England*, pp.66, 102, 295-6, 304-5, 479-81; Cleaver, *The Union Discount*, p.96, Scammell, *London Discount Market*, pp.35, 100, 205, 221; Fletcher, *Discount Houses*, pp.201, 204, 228, Drury, *Finance Houses*, p.90; E.R. Shaw, *The London Money Market* (London: Heinemann, 1975), p.163.

[43] B.B. Boreham, 'The London Information Market', *The Banker* (August 1945), p.90; G.O. Nwanko, 'British Overseas Banks in the Developing Countries', *Journal of the Institute of Bankers*, 93 (1972), p.152; Bostock, 'British Overseas Banks and Development Finance in Africa after 1945', in Jones (ed.), *Banks and Money*, p.159.

[44] Schenk, *Decline of Sterling*, pp.88-9, 99, 110, 114, 117, 125, 133-4, 212, 216-23, 225-9, 320.

international financial centre and recognized that restrictions on the use of sterling made that difficult. In contrast to the restrictions placed on the use of the UK£ internationally, US$s were readily available. Legislation in 1933 and 1935 in the USA placed a ceiling on the rate of interest paid by banks on deposits, and one effect of this by the late 1950s was to encourage those holding US$s to deposit them in non-US banks as they paid higher rates of interest. However, with the UK£ subject to exchange controls, and its future value in doubt, it was not an attractive currency in which to hold bank deposits. The solution offered by the likes of the British overseas bank, BOLSA, from 1957 onwards, was to actively offer accounts denominated in US$s rather than UK£s. This was not seen at the time as a threat to the London discount market, and the Bank of England's role as lender of last resort, as that continued to be extensively used by all banks located in London.[45]

A consequence, nevertheless, of the rise of parallel money markets, especially the euro-dollar market, was to undermine the importance of the discount market during the 1960s.[46] The discount market continued to be used extensively by the British deposit banks, because of their largely domestic business and their close connections to the Bank of England. Other banks located in London increasingly deserted it as parallel markets became deeper, broader, and more sophisticated over time. Negotiable certificates of deposit, for example, were invented in the USA in 1961 as a way of evading the interest-rate ceiling. They were introduced in London in May 1966, denominated in US$, as a flexible means through which banks could borrow from and lend to each other and rapidly became popular. As a result the discount market quickly declined in importance among both the British overseas and the foreign banks located in London. In terms of inter-bank lending versus the discount market, these banks split their business 75 per cent/25 per cent in favour of the discount market in 1951 but by 1960 it had switched to a 53 per cent/47 per cent split in favour of the inter-bank market, followed by a rapid decline from then on. In 1974, when the data ceased to be published in the Statistical Appendix of the *Bank of England Quarterly Bulletin*, the ratio was 96 per cent /4 per cent in favour of the inter-bank market. Over that period the total value of lending involving overseas and foreign banks with head offices or branches in London had risen from £239 million in 1951 to £16,057 million in 1974.[47] This reflected the increasing appeal of London as a location for

---

[45] Capie, *Bank of England*, pp.137, 183–7, 209, 425, 780–3.

[46] R.S. O'Brien, 'The Euro-Currency Market', *Journal of the Institute of Bankers*, 92 (1971) (O'Brien was Chairman of Charles Fulton and Company, one of the largest of the inter-dealer brokers), pp.89–91; Montgomery, 'The Clearing Banks', pp.89–91.

[47] Source: *Bank of England Quarterly Bulletin Statistical Supplement, 1960–1980*. The data used is for the 31st of December of each year and excludes UK domestic banks. It only includes British overseas banks and those foreign banks with branches in London. These banks were permitted to accept deposits in London whereas those banks with only representative offices in

inter-bank borrowing and lending through a combination of restrictions in other centres and the facilities available in the City, especially the presence of so many other banks and the operations of the interdealer brokers.[48]

The same data is not available for UK-based banks until 1971 though what was produced for the period from 1951 onwards for the Scottish and Northern Irish banks does not indicate a similar switch to the inter-bank market away from the discount market over that period.[49] For the 1970s comprehensive data is available. In 1971 UK banks had balances with other banks of £519 million (26 per cent of the total) and still had £1,441 million committed to the discount market (74 per cent of total).[50] The decline in the use of the discount market by UK banks appears to have begun on the 29th of December 1958 when the UK£ was made fully convertible into other major currencies, including the US$. As a result it became much easier for banks in London to switch to the US$ for their interbank operations. The UK£ still remained an important currency as it was extensively used throughout the sterling area and for international trade. But on the 23rd June 1972, the UK£ was floated and the sterling area ceased to exist. It was from then that banks in London increasingly operated on the basis of the US$ when they borrowed from and lent to each other.[51]

The staff at The Bank of England had been monitoring the changes taking place in the London money market for some time, and assessing the implications it had for them. Firstly, the arrival of numerous foreign banks with branches of their own meant they no longer operated through correspondent links to British banks, which looked to the Bank of England for support through the discount houses. Instead, these banks dealt directly with each other. The Bank was also well aware of the growth of the alternative money markets through which these banks borrowed and lent among each other as these increasingly included the large UK deposit banks in these operations. Not only was the Bank of England collecting the relevant data but its staff also

---

London were not. What is included are the balances these banks had with other banks and their lending to the London money market. In 1975 lending to the money market ceased to be separately reported having become a very small proportion of the total.

[48] Weismuller, 'London Consortium Banks', p.201; B. Mitchell, 'An American Banker's View of the City', *Journal of the Institute of Bankers*, 95 (1974), p.186; Pringle, 'Foreign Banks in London', p.48; Capie, *Bank of England*, p.481.

[49] Source: *Bank of England Quarterly Bulletin Statistical Supplement, 1960–1973*. The data used is for the 31st of December of each year. It is compiled from the separate data produced for each category of UK domestic bank. It was not until 1971 that a return was produced for London banks' balances with other banks.

[50] Source: *Bank of England Quarterly Bulletin Statistical Supplement, 1972–1980*. The data used is for the 31st of December for each year. For the period 1971 to 1979 the data was compiled from the separate entries for each type of bank. The data includes both balances with other banks and lending to the money market.

[51] Capie, *Bank of England*, pp.610, 711, 730, 770.

produced regular reports on what was happening.[52] Following on from the convertibility of the UK£ in December 1958 they noted a significant increase in the volume of deposits from overseas being placed with British overseas banks and the London branches of foreign banks, especially those from the USA. Of this, approximately 40 per cent was held as foreign currency rather than sterling, and so was not employed in the discount market. The report observed, 'Most of the steep rise shown since 1958 has occurred in foreign currency deposits, predominantly in US dollars or "Eurodollars". These deposits are mostly made by banks in Western Europe, and are part of the greatly increased volume of short-term funds which now move readily from one international financial centre to another.' The reason given for this inflow in 1962 was because, 'There is available in London an exceptionally broad range of opportunities for the employment of funds overnight or for any longer period, and frequently offering yields that are higher than those readily obtainable in financial markets abroad.' When these opportunities involved the use of foreign currencies they were all matched between banks. Though recognizing that these foreign currency deposits could be very volatile, and thus pose a threat to the stability of banks, the Bank of England was not unduly concerned because UK deposit banks were little involved.[53] Nevertheless it steadily increased its coverage of foreign banks in London from December 1962 onwards.[54]

By 1964 the Bank of England knew that there had been a large increase in foreign currency deposits in London and that UK banks were becoming involved, as their correspondents did not want to hold UK sterling because of the risks of devaluation. They also knew that much of this money was flowing from the USA because of the restrictions imposed there on the rate of interest paid on deposits: 'Banks in London have been able to attract large sums in dollars by quoting better rates for deposits, including interest on money at call and very short notice—categories which earn nothing at all with New York banks—and have employed them at less than the US lending rate and still made a worthwhile return.'[55] Welcome as this business was in reviving the fortunes of the City of London as an international financial centre the Bank of England had growing concerns about its ability to act as lender of last resort to the London money market if a crisis should occur.[56] An

[52] Bank of England, 'Overseas and Foreign Banks', pp.18–20.
[53] Bank of England, 'Inflows and Outflows of Foreign Funds', *Bank of England Quarterly Bulletin*, 2 (1962), pp.93–9; Bank of England, 'Bank Liquidity', p.248.
[54] See Bank of England, 'New Banking Statistics', *Bank of England Quarterly Bulletin*, 15 (1975), pp.162–5; Bank of England, 'Developments in UK Banking and Monetary Statistics since the Radcliffe Report', *Bank of England Quarterly Bulletin*, 25 (1985), pp.392–7.
[55] Bank of England, 'UK Banks' External Liabilities and Claims in Foreign Currencies', *Bank of England Quarterly Bulletin*, 4 (1964), pp.100–6.
[56] Bank of England, 'The UK and US Treasury Bill Market', *Bank of England Quarterly Bulletin*, 5 (1965), p.327; Bank of England, 'The London Discount Market: Some Historical

unintended consequence of the international money market remaining centred on London rather than relocating to New York was that the central bank it looked to in an emergency was not the Federal Reserve but the Bank of England and that institution was no longer able to fulfil that role for a number of reasons. Firstly, the Bank of England's involvement in the London money market was driven by the needs of UK monetary policy and not the needs of the market as had been the case in the past. Secondly, the London money market had grown in both scale and reach becoming the central money market for the world's banks.[57]

There was always a counterparty risk as banks borrowed from and lent to each other. Traditionally that risk had been minimized in two ways. The first was the use of collateral in the shape of bills of exchange, whether commercial or Treasury. The other was the existence of a lender of last resort that provided a reservoir of liquidity to the money market, and so balanced supply and demand. What emerged from the late 1950s onwards was an inter-bank market that operated to a large degree without collateral and without a lender of last resort, and as it grew so did the counterparty risk run by each bank. The Bank of England had no direct involvement in the inter-bank market and its responsibility only extended to the commitments made by British banks in that market, rather than acting as the lender of last resort for all. This money market relied on the strength of the individual banks that participated in the inter-bank borrowing and lending. Those intermediaries that were involved did not take a position in the market as their role was only to match borrowing and lending between banks, charging a commission for doing so. This left the reputation of the individual bank as the sole guarantee that a loan would be repaid and that the interest rate charged was an accurate reflection of current market conditions. If a risk of serious default developed banks would refuse to lend to each other leaving the whole market to freeze. Under those conditions banks had no option but to rely on their own national central bank as there was no lender of last resort to the money market as a whole.[58]

What the developments in the London money market reveal is the process of continuous adaptation taking place within banking as solutions were sought for difficulties, including those caused by central bank intervention. The international banking community, which included those banks from the

---

Notes', *Bank of England Quarterly Bulletin*, 7 (1967), p.146; Bank of England, 'Overseas and Foreign Banks', pp.156-64.

[57] Bank of England, 'Eurocurrency Business', pp.31-7; Bank of England, 'Reserve Ratios', p.483; Bank of England, 'London Dollar', pp.446-9; Bank of England, 'Eurobanks', pp.351-9; Bank of England, 'Foreign Banks in London', pp.368-73; Bank of England, 'Japanese Banks', pp.518-21; Bank of England, 'The Role of Brokers', pp.221-5; Bank of England, 'International Bond Market', pp.521-7.

[58] Singleton, *Central Banking in the Twentieth Century*, pp.236-7; Grossman, *Unsettled Account*, pp.96, 168, 285, 286-9.

UK, needed a mechanism through which they could settle transactions between each other, employ idle balances, and access liquidity. Over the course of the second half of the nineteenth century that mechanism was developed in London and that was where it still was in 1945. However, the actions taken by the Bank of England in using the discount market for national policy objectives meant that the mechanism was increasingly not fit for purpose. The problem was that an alternative in New York was not available because of the actions of the US government, and no other centre had the capacity and connections. The result was that the location of this mechanism remained in London but it was no longer through the discount market. Instead, it took the shape of a variety of parallel money markets.[59] One of those was the foreign exchange market, but that was also subject to government controls. Even after the government permitted the re-establishment of the foreign exchange market in London in 1951 it continued to hamper its ability to regain lost business by, for example, banning forward dealing as this was seen as potentially destabilizing for the international value of the £. More generally, in the 1950s the British government actively discouraged the use of sterling as a currency by third parties, as in the finance of international trade. The reasoning behind such a policy was that the international use of sterling would allow speculators to build up holdings which, when sold, would undermine the status of the £ as a reserve currency. By 1971 less than 20 per cent of international trade was conducted in sterling compared to 40 per cent in the 1950s and 60 per cent before 1914.[60] To survive the decline of the UK£ the London foreign exchange market also increasingly switched to the US$ as a basis of operations.[61] The result was the growth of London's Eurocurrency markets from the late 1950s.[62]

[59] P. Einzig, *A Dynamic Theory of Forward Exchange* (London: Macmillan, 1961, 2nd ed. 1967), p.13; J. Fforde, *The Bank of England and Public Policy, 1941–1958* (Cambridge: CUP, 1992), pp.222–3, 727, 756–7; Sayers, *Gilletts*, pp.124–6, 138.

[60] Schenk, *Decline of Sterling*, pp.13, 84, 117, 123, 152–3, 206–40, 241, 277, 310, 380, 394–5, 397, 417, 423–51; P. Einzig, *A Dynamic Theory of Forward Exchange*, pp.41, 303; P. Einzig, *A Textbook on Foreign Exchange* (London: Macmillan, 1966), p.17; A. Ellis, *Heir to Adventure: The Story of Brown, Shipley and Company* (London: Brown, Shipley, 1960), pp.148–54; M. Ikle, *Switzerland: An International Banking and Finance Center* (Stroudsburg: Dowden, Hutchinson & Ross, 1972), p.30; *The Times* 13 October 1952, 19 October 1953, 13 September 1954, 29 December 1958, 31 December 1958, 2 February 1959, 14 March 1960.

[61] G. Burn, *The Re-emergence of Global Finance* (Basingstoke: Palgrave Macmillan, 2006), pp.6–7, 17, 23; C.R. Schenk, *Hong Kong as an International Financial Centre: Emergence and Development 1945–65* (London: Routledge, 2001), pp.82, 72–3, 82–7, 125–6, 135; Jones, *The History of the British Bank of the Middle East* v.2, pp.31, 56–9, 93–4, 225, 244–5, 292–9; P. Einzig, *A Dynamic Theory of Forward Exchange*, p.116.

[62] Developments in these years have received an authoritative treatment by a number of authors in S. Battilosssi and Y. Cassis (eds), *European Banks and the American Challenge: European Banking under Bretton Woods* (Oxford: OUP, 2002). See also C.R. Schenk, 'The Origins of the Euro-Dollar Market in London, 1955–1963', *Explorations in Economic History*, 35 (1998); W.M. Clarke, *The City and the World Economy* (London: Institute of Economic Affairs,

Such were the attractions of these alternative money markets that developed from the late 1950s onwards, and the diverse facilities they provided, that London not only retained its position as a centre for international banking but also enhanced it. One estimate suggests that the deposits held by foreign banks in London rose from £0.3 billion in 1955 to £12.5 billion in 1969, by which time they comprised over 40 per cent of all bank deposits in London.[63] In turn, these deposits were actively traded between banks, by-passing the discount market.[64] There was also a major change in the way banks from around the world accessed these London markets, as they increasingly opened branches to replace their correspondent links.[65] The number of foreign banks in London almost doubled between 1957 and 1969 while the deposits they handled exploded from £263 million to £12.5 billion.[66] The result was to diminish the international role played by Britain's domestic banks over the course of the 1960s, indicating the opportunity that had been missed through the failure to create global businesses through mergers with the overseas banks after 1945. These new opportunities also benefitted most of those banks that had a diversified business model like that of the European universal banks, or the US banks when operating in London and freed from domestic constraints. Again, the failure of the joint-stock banks to merge with the merchant banks after 1945 left both poorly positioned to prosper from the world that was emerging in the 1960s.

1965); R. Fry (ed.), *A Banker's World: the Revival of the City, 1957-1970* (London: Hutchinson, 1970); *The Future of London*; S.F. Frowen (ed.), *A Framework of International Banking* (Guildford: Guildford Education Press, 1979), chapters by Shaw.

[63] S. Bell and B. Kettell, *Foreign Exchange Handbook* (London: Graham and Trotman, 1983), pp.75-6; P. Einzig, *The Euro-Bond Market* (London: Macmillan, 1969), pp.65, 147, 195; E.W. Clendenning, *The Euro-Dollar Market* (Oxford: OUP, 1970), pp.7, 22-3, 186; P. Einzig, *The History of Foreign Exchange* (London: Macmillan, 1962), p.241; L. Gall et al., *The Deutsche Bank, 1870-1995* (London: Weidenfeld & Nicolson, 1995), p.754; Grady and Weale, *British Banking*, pp.26, 28, 85-6, 92, 119, 121, 130, 196.

[64] P. Einzig, 'Dollar Deposits in London', *The Banker*, cx (Jan 1960), pp.23-4; J.R. Colville, 'London, Europe's Financial Centre', *The Banker*, 1966, p.467 and 'Foreign Banks in London', *The Banker*, 1967, pp.943-5, 945; C. Kleinwort, 'The City in Britain's Invisible Earnings', *The Banker*, 121 (1971), pp.171, 175.

[65] H.H. Thackstone, 'Work of the Foreign Branch of a Commercial Bank', in *Current Financial Problems and the City of London* (London: Institute of Bankers, 1949), pp.122-3; 'Memorandum on Overseas Business of Lloyds Bank 16 December 1968' (Lloyds Bank Archives); J.R. Winton, *Lloyds Bank, 1918-1969* (Oxford: Oxford University Press, 1982), p.155; Grady and Weale, *British Banking*, pp.98, 110.

[66] Shaw, *London Money Market*, pp.7-8, 99-104, 114-17, 122, 191, 219; Committee to Review the Functioning of Financial Institutions, Report, pp.68-9; Collins, *Money and Banking*, pp.359-73; G. Burn, 'The State, the City and the Euromarkets', *Review of International Political Economy*, v. 6 (1999), p.236.

CONCLUSION

Though the banking system that operated in Britain between 1945 and 1970 looked unchanged from that that had existed before the Second World War, that was not the case. The environment within which it conducted these operations was one of controls and these governed the way that banking was conducted and the interaction between banks. The compartmentalization that had long been a feature of British banking was now one imposed from outside and policed by the Bank of England rather than being a product of competition and co-operation leading to specialization within ever-changing parameters. It was as if the British banking system had been frozen in time and that time was 1922. Even the nationalization of the Bank of England was seen as leaving the banking system unchanged despite it now being wholly answerable to the government. The problem with the situation that the British banking system found itself in between 1945 and 1970 was that the world within which it existed was a rapidly changing one with the restoration of global prosperity, the disappearance of empires, and the gradual removal of the barriers that had so impeded international trade and finance in the 1930s. This required banking systems to change, which did happen elsewhere in the world but not in Britain. The changes that were taking place in British banking between 1945 and 1970 were being driven by the controls imposed. These controls prevented banks from pursuing spatial and functional diversification even though these were obvious routes given the emerging business opportunities. Instead, the application of controls to particular parts of the banking system, while leaving others to develop as they wished, caused major distortions. Gaps emerged in the provision of financial services for either savers or borrowers, and these were filled by either new providers or the expansion of those components of the banking system that were left uncontrolled. At the same time those elements that were subject to controls devised ways to avoid them that were both less efficient and more risky than previous practice. A similar situation existed externally, for the world economy was passing through a very dynamic phase between 1945 and 1970, and this generated a demand for the services provided by banks. All over the world, banks were growing in scale and this allowed them to embrace the Lend and Hold Model developed in Britain over the course of the nineteenth century. This scale also meant that these banks no longer relied on correspondent connections to access the international payments system or participate in the inter-bank money markets, which gradually deprived British domestic banks of the central position they had once occupied in the global banking system. These large banks could now participate directly by establishing branches and subsidiaries in London. London was still the hub of the global payments system and it was there that new inter-bank money markets were being created to replace the discount market which had been converted into a tool of domestic monetary control.

Influencing so many of the developments, or non-developments, that took place in British banking between 1945 and 1970 was the Bank of England, now under the direct control of the government and acting as its executive arm when it came to monetary and financial matters. What suited the Bank of England was compartmentalization as this made regulation easier as well as the operation of its role as lender of last resort. But the effect was to rob British banking of the opportunities on the one hand to challenge the US banks and on the other, the European banks. The stability achieved between 1945 and 1970 came at a cost. The cost was not the one identified by contemporaries and later experts as a lack of finance for industry. Industry's problems lay elsewhere and not at the door of the banks. Instead, it was restrictions placed on what, with hindsight, became a major growth sector of all advanced economies in the second half of the twentieth century, namely financial services in general and banking in particular. British banks were prevented from responding to the challenges and opportunities that presented themselves both at home and abroad in the quarter century after the Second World War. As a result, they were condemned to remain in a time warp, being well positioned to respond to another world depression, as in the 1930s, but not to the remarkable growth that the global economy was actually experiencing. The Bank of England itself recognized that British banks were being eclipsed by rivals and so moved to a new policy agenda in 1970.

7

Convergence and Conversions, 1970–1997

INTRODUCTION

In contrast to the years before 1970 those after witnessed a series of major crises in the global economy that increased both in terms of frequency and severity, although until the crisis of 2007/8 British banking appeared remarkably stable.[1] That is something of an illusion however as it ignores those failures in the banking system that left untouched the large joint stockbanks. In 1974 there was the Secondary Banking Crisis in which a number of the newer banks that had developed from the late 1950s onwards got into severe financial difficulties. Almost twenty years later, in 1990/1, there was another crisis which also revolved around newer and smaller banks, a number of which failed and had to be liquidated. There were also a series of individual bank failures including the Johnson Matthey Bank in 1984, the Bank of Credit and Commerce International in 1991 and Barings Bank in 1995. A number of smaller building societies also got into difficulties in this period, such as Grays Building Society in 1978 and the New Cross Building Society in 1984. However, none of these individual or even collective failures led to a general banking panic or cast doubt on the stability of the entire system, which made it impervious to the effects of crises.[2] Whereas the stability of British banking between 1945 and 1970 can be attributed to the absence of destabilizing forces, a high degree of inertia and conservatism, and the existence of externally imposed controls, that combination did not apply to the era between 1970 and 1997. Also, unlike the years after 1997, the changes that took place did not culminate in a major crisis forcing the government to intervene to rescue a number of the largest banks so as to prevent a

---

[1] Reinhart and Rogoff, *This Time is Different*; Cassis, *Crises and Opportunities*, pp.4; Kindleberger and Aliber, *Manias, Panics, and Crashes*, pp.272, 278, 302–11.
[2] Goodhart, Hartmann, Llewellyn, Rojas-Suarez, and Weisbrod, *Financial Regulation*, p.29; B. Ritchie, *We're with the Woolwich*, p.112; Logan, 'The United Kingdom's Small Banks' Crisis', pp.1–3.

systemic collapse. The fact that not all banking systems succumbed in the crisis of 2007/8, even among countries closely integrated into the world economy, suggests that unique features were of significance when trying to identify the long stability of British banking between 1970 and 1997.[3]

STRUCTURE AND OPERATION

One of the major changes that took place between 1970 and 1997 was the ending of the compartmentalization of British banking that had been such a feature of the prevalent past situation, whether for organic or externally imposed reasons. A fundamental characteristic of British banking in 1970, for example, was the division between commercial banking, as conducted by the large joint-stock banks, and investment or merchant banking, which was the preserve of partnerships. Barclays, Lloyds, Midland, and NatWest, with their extensive branch networks, collected savings, provided credit, and were central to the payments system. Merchant banks like Barings, Kleinworts, Morgan Grenfell, Rothschilds, and Schroders focused on the provision of long-term loans to business, the issuing of stocks and bonds on behalf of governments and companies, and the management of investments for individuals and institutions. This separation made British banking different from the universal banking model found in many countries in Continental Europe, most notably Germany and Switzerland. In that model a single bank conducted the full range of financial services. It also made British banking both different from and similar to that of the USA, where nationwide deposit banks were not permitted because of legislation dating from the 1860s, and the Glass-Steagall Act had banned the combination of commercial and investment banking in the 1930s.[4]

On Britain's accession to the European Economic Community on 1st January 1973, British deposit banks were allowed, if they wished, to own merchant banks, so bringing them into line with Continental practice. However, British deposit banks faced a problem in expanding into investment banking. The London Stock Exchange restricted membership to those whose sole business was the buying and selling of securities. As a consequence, UK investment banks could not add the associated activities of dealing in stocks and bonds once issued, and so transform themselves into universal banks.[5] That position

---

[3] Kindleberger and Aliber, *Manias, Panics, and Crashes*, pp.16, 25–6, 65, 87, 194, 213, 227–34, 242–6, 276–8, 300–11.

[4] See Grossman, *Unsettled Account*.

[5] 'Banking Mergers and Participations', p.452; Padovan, 'New Influences in Merchant Banking', p.126; Capie, *Bank of England*, pp.329–31, 339.

changed in 1986 as a result of the deregulation of the London Stock Exchange, known as Big Bang, which allowed banks, whether retail or investment, to become members while also abolishing the separation between brokers and dealers, ending the scale of fixed commission charges and introducing a screen-based trading system. The effect of this was to allow British banks to expand in all directions, including combining retail and investment banking. A number of British deposit banks took this opportunity. Barclays, for example, combined its small investment banking operations with both a broker and dealer in securities, to create a wholly owned investment bank, BZW.[6] However, this attempt to create British universal banks through mergers was a failure. Neither Lloyds nor Midland tried, NatWest quickly abandoned the idea while Barclays closed down BZW after ten years. Even those British investment banks that tried to follow the pattern of the US investment banks, by acquiring brokers and dealers, failed to make it work, being acquired by German or Swiss universal banks, as was the case with Kleinworts, Morgan Grenfell, and Warburgs. What appeared to be the most successful British investment bank, Warburgs, was bought by the Swiss Bank Corporation in 1995 with its securities affiliate, Mercury Asset Management, being acquired by the Wall Street investment bank, Merrill Lynch, in 1997.[7] British joint-stock banks nevertheless did expand the range of activities they were engaged in after 1986, though only slowly, so that even by 1997 their style of operation continued to remain focused on the Lend and Hold Model rather than the Originate and Distribute Model long associated with investment banking.[8]

This diversification of the nature of the business done by the large joint-stock banks was a product of the growing competition they faced, and this dated from even before 1970, rather than 1986.[9] Faced with the growing inroads into their business made by the likes of the building societies and the finance houses these joint-stock banks responded by making long-term loans for the finance of property and also became involved in project finance, which had previously been left to the merchant banks.[10] In order to reduce the risks they were running, the joint-stock banks chose not to make direct investments in property or even to lend to the large construction companies that were putting up buildings. Instead, the route chosen was to lend to those finance houses that specialized in this type of funding and to an emerging

[6] See C. Bellringer and R.C. Michie, 'Big Bang in the City: An Intentional Revolution or an Accident', *Financial History Review*, v. 21 (2014), pp.1–27.

[7] P. Augur, *The Death of Gentlemanly Capitalism: The Rise and Fall of London's Investment Banks* (London: Penguin, 2000), pp.329–30; Ferguson, *High Financier*, pp.371–82, 413.

[8] Ackrill and Hannah, *Barclays*, pp.226–41.

[9] Capie, 'British Financial Crises' in Dimsdale and Hotson (eds), *British Financial Crises*, p.21.

[10] T. Gourvish, 'Project Finance', in Green, Pohle-Fraser, and Fraser (eds), *The Human Factor*, pp.45–6.

group of property companies whose business it was to finance, own, and manage large buildings such as office blocks. Underlying this strategy was the assumption that the specialist finance and property companies would be able to repay the loan once the building was completed and sold, leaving the bank with a much better return than the short-term loans they were largely engaged in. Loans on property had always generated higher returns but they also involved greater risks because the bank was locked in until the building was completed and sold. Only then could the bank recover its money. However, with loans to specialist financial intermediaries and property companies the assumption made was these could repay a short-term loan if requested by re-financing their borrowing elsewhere. This was a realistic assumption as it was not only British banks that were involved but also much of London's financial community, including the growing number of foreign banks that were opening branches and setting up subsidiaries there.[11]

Bank advances to the property sector rose from £362 million in February 1971 to £2,584 million in February 1974. However, in December 1972 there was a freeze on business rents, so undermining confidence in the future returns on office building. Combined with rising interest rates and tightening credit, caused by a deteriorating international situation, the specialist lenders, known as secondary banks faced a growing liquidity crisis. Problems first emerged in November 1973 when one of these secondary banks, London and County Securities, found it was unable to obtain fresh funds to replace those that had to be repaid. This even led to a run on London and County Securities in December 1973 when savers queued to withdraw their deposits, though this was little reported in the press.[12] A report drawn up by the staff of the Bank of England, and published in their *Quarterly Bulletin* in 1978, explained what had happened: 'Through brokers, fringe institutions found that they were able to attract wholesale deposits, in substantial volume but mainly at short-term, by offering only modestly higher rates than the banks. Because of the attractions of the property market... a large proportion of the funds flowing into the fringe institutions was employed in that market or in lending for employment in that market, the apparent ability to renew the deposits at maturity leading the institutions to disregard the risk of becoming locked-in. Accordingly, when renewal of deposits became difficult, liquidity problems rapidly arose.' Subsequently, most of these secondary banks were either closed or absorbed by one or other of the joint-stock banks, with which they had a close

---

[11] Collins, *Money and Banking*, pp.214, 365–77, 405–34, 503, 582; Thomas, *Finance of British Industry*, pp.147–55, 163–5, 173–8, 218, 310, 335–6, Kinross, *Fifty Years in the City*, pp.116–17, 151, 192; The Wilson Committee on the Functioning of Financial Institutions Evidence, vol 1: Treasury, pp.47–53, vol 3: Insurance Companies 72–82, vol 4: Pension Funds 187, Progress Report 1977, p.36, and Finance of Small Firms 1979, pp.1–9, vol 2: CBI, p.1.

[12] Capie, *Bank of England*, pp.525–85.

relationship.[13] Such was the degree of connection between these secondary banks and the large joint-stock banks that rumours even circulated in November 1974 that the NatWest Bank was in difficulty. However, these were given neither credence nor publicity, and so no run resulted.[14] Instead, the crisis was attributed to the reckless behaviour of those running these fringe banks, which bordered on criminality in the case of the largest among them, London and County Securities.[15] By operating through the secondary banks the large joint-stock banks had escaped being associated with the risks taken and their consequences, and so retained the confidence of both the public and their own peers when a crisis did occur.

The collapse of the secondary banks in the crisis of 1974 did reduce some of the competitive pressure on the large joint-stock banks, though the rise of the building societies was inexorable.[16] In addition, there were a growing number of foreign banks with branches and subsidiaries in London, rather than agents and correspondent links. The consequence of this change was that they no longer operated through the established British banks but on their own authority, and so responded to domestic opportunities when they arose. In the 1970s these foreign banks expanded their activities away from an exclusively international focus to providing British companies with finance. Their ability to grow this branch of their business was greatly boosted by the abolition of exchange controls in 1979. The number of directly represented banks in London had grown from 107 in 1967 to 285 in 1977. Another seventy-three were represented by consortium banks, which were wholly owned subsidiaries acting for a number of separate banks. Despite restricting themselves to a largely international business these foreign banks had built up a domestic business. Sterling advances to UK residents by foreign banks rose from 6 per cent of such advances in 1967 to 16 per cent in 1977.[17] Once exchange controls ended, these foreign banks could offer their services to UK customers and operate in sterling without restraint, and their numbers continued to grow. By December 1985 there were a total of 490 foreign banks with an office, branch, or subsidiary in London, either of their own or as part of a consortium. Between 1980 and 1991 the share of UK bank lending handled by these foreign banks rose from 26 per cent to 35 per cent.[18]

---

[13] Bank of England, 'The Secondary Banking Crisis', pp.232–3; D. Vander Weyer, 'The Threats and Opportunities Facing British Banks: A 10-Year View', *Journal of the Institute of Bankers*, 101 (1980), p.72; 'The Performance of Major British Banks', pp.508–15.
[14] Ackrill and Hannah, *Barclays*, p.207.   [15] Capie, *Bank of England*, pp.525–85.
[16] Collins, *Money and Banking*, pp.365–77, 405–34, 503, 582.
[17] Pringle, 'Foreign Banks in London', p.48.
[18] Bank of England, 'Foreign Banks in London', pp.368–9; Bank of England, 'Major International Banks' Performance, 1980–1991', *Bank of England Quarterly Bulletin*, 32 (1992), pp.290–2.

The presence and activities of these foreign banks meant growing competition for the British joint-stock and merchant banks. Whereas the building societies were eroding the joint stock-banks depositor base, these foreign banks targeted loans to business customers, of which they had great experience. Many of the major players were European universal banks able to offer large business customers imaginative solutions to their financing needs. Others were US banks who were able in London to bridge the commercial/investment banking divide they could not do at home. The ending of exchange controls in 1979 removed the remaining barrier to the integration of domestic and international banking in the UK. This left the UK-focused banks exposed to foreign competition as they had long enjoyed almost exclusive access to their home market. Another consequence was that the British government, through the Bank of England, could no longer rely on controls over UK banks as a tool of monetary policy, as these could be easily circumvented. Recognizing this reality, these controls were removed between 1980 and 1982. Banks were no longer subject to minimum lending rates, cash and reserve ratios, and restrictions on the provision of instalment finance. The result was that the UK banks were freed to respond to the competitive pressure coming from the foreign banks by offering more attractive interest rates on savings, more generous terms on loans, and expanding into allied financial services such as insurance, mortgage lending, and investment banking. Competition also encouraged these UK banks to cut costs by closing branches and introducing new technology.[19]

Relaxing the restrictions long imposed on the large joint-stock banks had serious implications for the building societies. In the 1970s these had overtaken banks in terms of their share of deposits, dominating the market in personal savings, and were in total command of the provision of mortgage finance for home ownership. But from the beginning of the 1980s, building societies faced growing competition from banks for savings. By 1986 a shortage of retail funds was forcing building societies to tap the wholesale market for funds in order to meet demand for mortgage finance. Banks were also entering mortgage finance for the first time which generated a new threat to the building societies since the Second World War because their model of funding house purchases through stable retail deposits was now under pressure. The building societies could not immediately respond to this pressure because the Building Societies Act of 1962 restricted both the type of business they could do and how they conducted it. The cartel the building societies had long operated was ended in 1983, removing an internal constraint on their

---

[19] Dimsdale and Hotson, 'Financial Crises and Economic Activity in the UK since 1825' in Dimsdale and Hotson (eds), *British Financial Crises*, pp.43–4; A. Offer, 'Narrow Banking, Real Estate, and Financial Stability in the UK, c. 1870–2010', in Dimsdale and Hotson (eds), *British Financial Crises*, p.167; Ackrill and Hannah, *Barclays*, pp.200–13, 354.

ability to compete with banks. Not until the Building Societies Act of 1986, however, were building societies freed from many of the restrictions under which they operated, and so were able to compete with banks to a much greater degree. Building societies were also permitted to convert into banks if they so wished but initially only Abbey National followed this route. However, during the 1990s, especially in 1997, there was a rush of conversions among building societies to convert into banks, including the largest at the time, the Halifax. The result was to add a group of large and established financial institutions to the UK domestic banking arena after 1986, making it highly competitive as a result.[20]

After 1979 there was also a more relaxed attitude from the government towards mergers between banks though this did not extend to any of the four largest banks merging with each other or acquisitions that threatened the independence of the Scottish banking system. In 1986, as a by-product of its privatization programme, the trustee savings banks had been sold to investors as a single joint-stock company, called TSB. As such, it possessed a nationwide branch network and an established customer base, though one focused almost solely on savings products. It then expanded into general banking but less than ten years later it was allowed to merge with Lloyds, one of the large joint-stock banks, so removing one of the emerging competitors in the field of banking. Previously in 1989 the National Australia Bank had been allowed to acquire the Yorkshire Bank, one of the few remaining English regional banks. Of more significance was the Hong Kong and Shanghai Bank (HSBC) takeover of the Midland Bank in 1992. The Midland Bank was one of Britain's largest banks but had faded somewhat in the post-war years, especially as its extensive international business, based on a vast correspondent network, was undermined by the growth of large banks that could support direct representation in London. To remedy that loss it had acquired a US bank, the Crocker National Bank, but this turned out disastrously, leaving the Midland vulnerable to a takeover bid. As none of its UK rivals was permitted to mount such a bid HSBC appeared as its saviour. Though listed on the London Stock Exchange, and with long-standing UK connections, HSBC was managed from a head office in Hong Kong and was largely Asian focused with a very limited British banking operation. Nevertheless, it had been prevented from acquiring the Royal Bank of Scotland in 1982 on anti-competitive grounds though ten years on it was permitted to take over an even larger bank, on condition it moved its

---

[20] Williams, 'The Banks and their Competitors', p.143; 'The Development of the Building Societies Sector in the 1980s', *Bank of England Quarterly Bulletin*, 30 (1990), pp.502–10; B. Ritchie, *We're with the Woolwich*, pp.118, 137; Ackrill and Hannah, *Barclays*, p.200; A. Johnson, *Measuring the Economy: A Guide to Understanding the Statistics* (London: Penguin Books, 1988), pp.180–1.

head office to London, which it did, though continuing to operate out of Hong Kong.[21]

The effect of these changes after 1979 was to end the externally imposed compartmentalization of British banking, and to foster a much greater degree of competition for savings and loans. As early as 1982, the Governor of the Bank of England warned that banks were lending for longer periods using short-term deposits and that this was creating risks.[22] Such was also the verdict of a careful study of British banking since 1960 carried out by Grady under the supervision of Martin Weale, which was published in 1986. This warned of the growing risks involved in banking, in the face of increasing competition, and noted that 'A bank could never hope to call in its loans at the speed at which deposits can melt away, and has instead to rely on the fact that over the short-run, withdrawals and deposits will normally be roughly in balance.' They were concerned that the conditions that had led to the banking crisis of 1974 were beginning to re-emerge.[23] It was increasingly recognized that the risks being run by banks encompassed not only the traditional ones of borrower defaults and frauds and errors committed by staff but also those created by the more volatile environment within which banks were operating. Large fluctuations in exchange rates and interest rates, for example, could quickly lead to losses in the value of assets provided as collateral for loans while competitive pressures meant that the depositor base was no longer stable.[24] A minor and short-lived banking crisis did take place in the early 1990s, which was attributed by the Governor of the Bank of England to increased competition. The solution he proposed was adherence to the culture of sound banking through careful monitoring of the business being done and the incentives offered to staff. If bankers paid 'close attention to the control and pricing of risk' then British banking would be free of crises.[25] What this reflected was an ingrained belief that after a century of stability British banking was fundamentally sound and would remain so because of the training and good sense of British bankers, irrespective of the competitive pressures they faced and the environment they operated in. Supporting that belief was the continuing adherence to the Lend and hold Model among British banks, and building societies throughout the 1980s and into the 1990s, in spite of the growing securitization and re-sale of mortgage debt, for example. After 1970

---

[21] Turner, *Banking in Crisis*, pp.48–9; Ackrill and Hannah, *Barclays*, pp. 215–17, 257.

[22] C.W. McMahon, 'The Current Financial Scene', *Journal of the Institute of Bankers*, 102 (1982), p.7.

[23] J. Grady and M. Weale, *British Banking, 1960–85* (London: Macmillan, 1986), pp.22, 25, 28, 35, 198, 201–2.

[24] 'Risk Measurement and Capital Requirements for Banks', *Bank of England Quarterly Bulletin*, 35 (1995), p.177.

[25] Bank of England, 'Recent Banking Difficulties', *Bank of England Quarterly Bulletin*, 33 (1993), pp.103–5.

the joint-stock banks continued to lose market share in the collection of savings to the building societies. Building societies also continued to dominate the provision of finance for house purchase despite banks entering the field in the 1980s. In contrast, banks did increasingly lend to UK property companies despite the problems encountered in the mid 1970s. It was not only British banks that followed this route but foreign banks did so using the Lend and Hold Model with only 6 per cent of mortgages securitized in 1988, but the trend was developing.[26]

THE BANK OF ENGLAND

One reason for such a belief was the role that the Bank of England played as both lender of last resort and crisis manager of the banking system. One consequence of that role after 1945 had been to foster overly conservative behaviour among the largest banks that served neither savers nor borrowers particularly well but contributed to stability through inertia. However, by 1970 the Bank of England had become aware that one consequence of the controls imposed on the largest banks had been to encourage the growth of smaller rivals, as well as encouraging London branches of foreign banks to expand their UK business. The expansion of these rivals undermined the degree of control that the Bank of England could exercise. The Bank of England's eventual response was to encourage the large joint-stock banks to become more competitive and thus regain market share. This happened in 1971 with the policy termed Competition and Credit Control. Unfortunately, combined with a volatile international situation and expansionary monetary policy the result was a credit bubble that exploded in 1973/4.[27]

This was the first real test for the Bank of England after 1945. Its problem was that, coming after a long period of stability, it lacked both the experience and knowledge of how to react to a banking crisis, having few staff in this area. Though it had no direct responsibility for the unregulated shadow banking system, the Bank of England did take decisive action because of concerns that a crisis in one branch of banking could have consequences for those banks for which it did accept responsibility. As well as their links to the secondary banks, the large joint-stock banks were exposed through lending to the property companies, and these were in danger of collapsing if the supply of funds from the fringe banks dried up. It was for that reason that in 1973 the Bank persuaded the large deposit banks to provide financial assistance to these secondary banks, and so prevent them collapsing. It also forced foreign

---

[26] Collins, *Money and Banking*, pp.365–77, 405–34, 503, 582.
[27] F. Hirsch, 'The Bagehot Problem', in Goodhart and Illing (eds), *Financial Crises*, pp.188–9.

banks to provide support to their UK subsidiaries, as they too were involved, having also lent to the property companies. As the crisis worsened in 1974, when both the secondary banks and the property companies faced a solvency crisis because of falling property prices, the joint-stock banks pulled back their support because of concerns about their own liquidity. This forced the Bank to complete the rescue on its own.[28]

Successful as was the intervention in averting a systemic banking collapse in 1973/4, that crisis made the Bank of England fully aware of the limitations in its supervision of the banking system. What the crisis exposed was that excessive regulation of only one part of the banking system drove financial activity into areas that were unregulated. Problems in the unregulated part of the banking system had the potential to destabilize the regulated component. In the Banking Act of 1979 the Bank of England's coverage of the banking system was extended to all institutions that accepted deposits. This did not however prevent subsequent bank failures, as with the Johnson Matthey Bank in 1984/5. In the case of that bank the Bank of England intervened to save it because of the role it played in the gold market. Another Banking Act was introduced in 1987, which further extended the powers of the Bank of England, but further failures followed, namely the Bank of Credit and Commerce International (BCCI) in 1991 and Barings in 1995. As neither of these possessed any strategic value they were allowed to collapse.[29] What their failure did illustrate was the problem the Bank of England faced in supervising a banking system that was steadily becoming more international. BCCI was a foreign bank operating out of London, where it borrowed and lent indiscriminately, whereas Barings was a long-established British merchant bank destabilized by its Asian operations. The problem was that without exchange controls it was impossible to isolate the British banking system from the wider banking community, particularly as the City of London was re-emerging as a global financial centre and a magnet for banks from around the world. Supervision of the banking system had been further complicated in 1986 with the ending of the division between deposit banking and investment banking once the London Stock Exchange accepted banks as members. Another difficulty for the Bank of England was the internationalization of British banking that came about not only from the numerous branches of foreign banks in London but also HSBC's acquisition of the Midland Bank. This meant the Bank was faced with supervising a bank that now had major operations in three continents. As the City of London prospered as a global financial centre after 1979 the internationalization and diversification of

---

[28] L.S. Dyer, 'The Secondary Banking Crisis', *Journal of the Institute of Bankers*, 104 (1983), pp.46-8.

[29] Capie, *Bank of England*, pp.542-7, 583, 635-8; Turner, 'Holding Shareholders to Account', in Dimsdale and Hotson (eds), *British Financial Crises*, p.152.

the banking community posed increasing problems of supervision for the Bank. In the end, control over the British banking system was removed from the Bank of England by the Labour government elected in 1997. The Bank of England Act of June 1998 stripped the Bank of its responsibility for banking supervision, which was given to the newly created Financial Services Authority.[30]

The Bank of England had long been aware of its loss of power over the banking system beginning with the return of the UK to convertibility in 1959. Recognizing its own limitations, the Bank left responsibility for the supervision of the London branches of foreign banks to the bank of which they were part. Ultimately, this meant devolving the role of lender of last resort and crisis manager to another central banker.[31] That still left the Bank with responsibility for the British banking system and it had long guarded that role jealously, opposing, for example, a US-style regulatory authority. This opposition by the Bank was grounded not only in self-interest but also long practical experience of dealing with the problems of individual banks, each of which was too big to fail.

Once the episode of the Secondary Banking Crisis had passed and the lessons learnt, this system appeared to achieve the best of both worlds for banking, namely competition and stability, throughout the 1970 to 1997 period. The main lesson was that too rigid a control regime would stifle the largest banks, as these were the inevitable focus of attention, while allowing the smaller banks to take excessive risks because they escaped detection. Even though there was a banking crisis in the early 1990s, involving a number of newer and smaller banks, this did not pose the same risks to the entire banking system as had the Secondary Banking Crisis of 1973/4, suggesting that the Bank of England had learnt how to balance control and flexibility. The Bank of England was quick to provide emergency support, so avoiding a liquidity crisis, but did not prevent those banks that were insolvent from collapsing, beginning with the British and Commonwealth Bank and the Authority Bank in 1990.[32] With that experience behind it, the Bank of England was, naturally, unwilling to accept without resistance that it was to lose its role as banking supervisor. In 1997 Eddie George, then Governor of the Bank of England,

---

[30] Singleton, *Central Banking in the Twentieth Century*, pp.4–9, 18, 83, 127–32, 135–8, 146, 177, 216, 225–6, 229; Grady and Weale, *British Banking*, pp.36–9, 51–7, 60; Blunden, 'The Supervision of the UK Banking System', pp.213–18; Montgomery, 'The Clearing Banks', pp.89–91; Bank of England, 'The Secondary Banking Crisis and the Bank of England's Support Operations', *Bank of England Quarterly Bulletin*, 18 (1978), pp.230–6.

[31] Capie, *Bank of England*, pp.614–15, 625–8.

[32] A. Logan, 'The United Kingdom's Small Banks' Crisis of the Early 1990s: What Were the Leading Indicators of Failure?', *Bank of England Working Paper*, 139 (2001), pp.1–30; X. Freixas, B. M. Parigi, and J.-C. Rochet, 'Systemic Risk, Interbank Relations, and Liquidity Provision by the Central Bank', in Goodhart and Illing (eds), *Financial Crises*, p.408.

expressed serious doubts about the creation of a single regulator for the entire financial sector. 'The tighter the regulation the greater the costs—not just the direct costs of regulation itself, but more importantly the effects of the constraints imposed on the ability of intermediaries to compete by offering cheaper and more innovative and varied products and services—which would ultimately be to the detriment of the consumers of those products and services generally.'[33] He then followed that up in 1997 with another speech in which he argued strongly that whatever happened with financial regulation generally, banking supervision should be left with the Bank of England because he believed that the central bank needed to be fully aware of what was happening in each bank if it was to prevent it taking excessive risks and judging whether to provide liquidity support or not in a crisis.[34] A speech the same year by the Deputy Governor of the Bank of England followed the same line in claiming that 'banks are a unique type of financial institution' and so required their own regulator. This uniqueness required a careful balance to be struck between ensuring that the failure of any single bank did not lead to a systemic crisis while preventing banks operating in the belief that they possessed a guarantee that they would be rescued if problems arose. Intervention was limited to providing liquidity only to solvent banks and doing so in secret so as to avoid destabilizing other banks and thus the whole system. If a bank failure posed no systemic risk it would be allowed to fail, as had been past practice.[35]

Despite these protestations, the game was up for the Bank of England as the supervisor of the banking system because the incoming Labour government was committed to introducing a British version of the US regulatory regime. In doing so it disregarded those who expressed reservations about what a universal regulator could achieve compared to one more in tune with banking and its specific requirements, especially regarding liquidity.[36] Over the 1970-97 period the Bank of England had developed a tried-and-tested formula for supervising the British banking system. This recognized the need to be both flexible and responsive when dealing with individual banks because each was different. It also recognized that it was both impossible to supervise the whole system but necessary to do so. The impossibility related to the fact that only the individual bank knew, in detail, the business it was conducting and the nature of the risks it was exposed to and so the provision it needed to make. However, it was necessary to extend supervision to the entire system for, otherwise, those parts that were over-regulated would be stifled while the

[33] E. George, 'Some Thoughts on Financial Regulation', *Bank of England Quarterly Bulletin*, 36 (1996), pp.213-15.
[34] E. George, 'Are Banks Still Special? *Bank of England Quarterly Bulletin*, 37 (1997), p.114.
[35] H. Davies, 'Financial Regulation: Why, How and By Whom', *Bank of England Quarterly Bulletin*, 37 (1997), pp.107-10.
[36] Goodhart, Hartmann, Llewellyn, Rojas-Suarez, and Weisbrod, *Financial Regulation*, pp.39-59, 144-76.

non-regulated would be left without either restraint or support. That had been the case before 1970 but, in the wake of the Secondary Banking Crisis, a balance had been struck between these two extremes. In achieving that balance the Bank of England recognized its own limitations, and so left the supervision of the UK operations of foreign banks to their own regulators, and also the need to tailor what it did to meet individual circumstances whether related to particular banks or specific events. It was this experience and familiarity that was lost in 1998 when the newly formed Financial Services Authority replaced the Bank of England as supervisor of the British banking system.

MONEY MARKET

The one key role that the Bank of England retained after 1997 was that of lender of last resort to the British banking system. Over the 1970–97 period this role was becoming an increasingly difficult one to perform not only because of the growing complexity of the British banking system but also the scale, variety, and connections of the London money market. What emerged as early as the Secondary Banking Crisis of 1973/4 was the extensive use being made of parallel money markets over which the Bank of England had no control and for which it did not act as lender of last resort, unlike the position in the long-established but declining discount market. The large joint-stock banks participated in these parallel markets and so were at risk from a potential default by the secondary banks, as they were often counter-parties to the borrowing and lending that took place. In the discount market Treasury Bills were used as collateral, discount houses acted as intermediaries and the Bank of England was ready to act as lender of last resort. In the parallel markets banks either dealt directly with each other or through brokers, and the only collateral in most cases was the reputation of the counterparties that guaranteed repayment. The Bank of England had no relationship to the brokers and so there was no mechanism through which it could act as lender of last resort.[37]

But the discount market was in terminal decline after 1970, whereas the alternative money markets grew rapidly and inexorably. By 1974 the British overseas and the foreign banks located in London had largely abandoned the discount market with a ratio of 96 per cent /4 per cent in favour of the

---

[37] O'Brien, 'Euro-Currency Market'; Montgomery, 'The Clearing Banks', pp.89–91; Bank of England, 'The Role of the Bank of England in the Money Market', *Bank of England Quarterly Bulletin*, 22 (1982), p.89–94; Bank of England, 'The Role of Brokers in the London Money Markets', *Bank of England Quarterly Bulletin*, 30 (1990); Capie, *Bank of England*, pp.66, 102, 295–6, 304–5, 479–81.

inter-bank market. In that year the total value of lending involving overseas and foreign banks with head offices or branches in London was £16,057 million and it then doubled to £32,175 million by 1979.[38] This reflected the increasing appeal of London as a location for inter-bank borrowing and lending through a combination of restrictions in other centres and the facilities available in the City, especially the presence of so many other banks and the operations of the interdealer brokers.[39] The decline in the use of the discount market by British banks was more gradual. Whereas in 1971 UK banks had balances with other banks of £519 million (26 per cent of the total) and £1,441 million in the discount market (74 per cent of total) the position by 1979 was the reverse with £10,962 million lent to other banks (84 per cent) and £2,052 million (16 per cent) in the discount market.[40] That decline had begun on the 29th of December 1958 when the UK£ was made fully convertible into other major currencies, including the US$. As a result it became much easier for banks in London to switch to the US$ for their inter-bank operations. The UK£ still remained an important currency as it was extensively used throughout the sterling area and for international trade. This ended in the 1970s when sterling ceased to be an internationally important currency. On the 23rd June 1972, the UK£ was floated and the sterling area ceased to exist. From then on banks in London increasingly operated on the basis of the US$ when they borrowed from and lent to each other. Eventually, on the 23rd of October 1979 the UK government abandoned exchange controls, so removing the last impediment to London emerging as the centre for the global money market, by which time the US$ had become totally dominant.[41]

The Bank of England was well aware of the changes taking place in the London money market and the implications it had for its role as lender of last resort. A report by the Inter-Bank Research Organization in 1973 had concluded that London 'attracts business because of the range of markets and services that it offers and develops new markets and services because of the

---

[38] Source: *Bank of England Quarterly Bulletin Statistical Supplement, 1960-1980*. The data used is for the 31st of December of each year and excludes UK domestic banks. It only includes British overseas banks and those foreign banks with branches in London. These banks were permitted to accept deposits in London whereas those banks with only representative offices in London were not. Included are the balances these banks had with other banks and their lending to the London money market. In 1975 lending to the money market ceased to be separately reported having become a very small proportion of the total.

[39] A.A. Weismuller, 'London Consortium Banks', *Journal of the Institute of Bankers*, 95 (1974), p.186; B. Mitchell, 'An American Banker's View of the City', p.186; R. Pringle, 'The Foreign Banks in London', *Journal of the Institute of Bankers*, 99 (1978), p.48; Capie, *Bank of England*, p.481.

[40] Source: *Bank of England Quarterly Bulletin Statistical Supplement, 1972-1980*. The data used is for the 31st of December for each year. For the period 1971 to 1979 the data was compiled from the separate entries for each type of bank. The data includes both balances with other banks and lending to the money market.

[41] Capie, *Bank of England*, pp.610, 711, 730, 770.

scale of business it can attract'.[42] The arrival of numerous foreign banks with branches of their own meant they no longer operated through correspondent links to British banks, which looked to the Bank of England for support through the discount houses. Instead, these banks dealt directly with each other. By 1989 the number of foreign banks with a physical presence in the City of London, through a representative, office, affiliate, or branch, had reached 521.[43] The Bank was also well aware of the growth of the alternative money markets through which these banks borrowed and lent among each other as these increasingly encompassed the large UK deposit banks in these operations during the course of the 1970s and onwards. Not only was the Bank of England collecting the relevant data but its staff also produced regular reports on what was happening.[44] An unintended consequence of London remaining the centre of the international money market rather than it relocating to New York was that the central bank it looked to in an emergency was not the Federal Reserve but the Bank of England and that institution was no longer able to fulfil that role for a number of reasons. Firstly, the Bank of England's involvement in the London money market was driven by the needs of UK monetary policy and not the needs of the market, as had been the case in the past. Secondly, the London money market had grown in both scale and reach becoming the central money market for the world's banks.[45] Thirdly, the Bank of England was not in touch with this market because it was now 'out of the loop' as transactions took place directly between banks or via money market brokers whose role it was to arrange inter-bank business. It was noted in 1982 that: 'For the Bank to have a reasonable chance of balancing the market, it is important that the system's overall daily surplus of cash should be channelled through to the discount houses before the Bank's final operating decisions are taken. Whether this happens is greatly dependent upon the ability of the major banks to estimate accurately and in good time their daily cash position; to do this, they need to know about expected large

[42] *The Future of London as an International Financial Centre: Report by the Inter-Bank Research Organisation* (London: Cabinet Office, 1973), v.1, p.8.

[43] Bank of England, 'London as an International Financial Centre', *Bank of England Quarterly Review*, 29 (1989).

[44] Bank of England, 'The Overseas and Foreign Banks in London', *Bank of England Quarterly Bulletin*, 1 (1960–1), pp.18–20.

[45] Bank of England, 'The Eurocurrency Business of Banks in London', *Bank of England Quarterly Bulletin*, 10 (1970), pp.31–7; Bank of England, 'Reserve Ratios: Further Definitions', *Bank of England Quarterly Bulletin*, 11 (1971), p.483; Bank of England, 'The London Dollar Certificate of Deposit', *Bank of England Quarterly Bulletin*, 13 (1973), pp.446–9; Bank of England, 'Eurobanks and the Inter-Bank Market', *Bank of England Quarterly Bulletin*, 21 (1981), pp.351–9; Bank of England, 'Foreign Banks in London', *Bank of England Quarterly Bulletin*, 26 (1986), pp.368–73; Bank of England, 'Japanese Banks in London', *Bank of England Quarterly Bulletin*, 27 (1987), pp.518–21; Bank of England, 'The Role of Brokers', pp.221–5; Bank of England, 'The International Bond Market', *Bank of England Quarterly Bulletin*, 31 (1991).

movements of funds by their customers.' The discount market itself largely disappeared in 1986 when the London Inter-Bank Offered Rate (LIBOR) was introduced as the benchmark for short-term interest rates, to replace the rate generated in the discount market. The calculation of LIBOR was delegated to the British Bankers' Association and was based on the quotes received from a selection of banks located in London.[46]

There was always a counterparty risk as banks borrowed from and lent to each other. That risk had been traditionally minimized in two ways. The first was the use of collateral in the shape of bills of exchange, whether commercial or Treasury. The second was the existence of a lender of last resort that provided a reservoir of liquidity to the money market, and so balanced supply and demand. As the discount market declined in importance as the location of this inter-bank borrowing and lending, the Bank of England was less able to act as lender of last resort. As the London money market grew in size it dwarfed the resources that the Bank of England had available. Between 1977, when it stood at US$116 billion, and 1997, when it was US$1,155 billion, London inter-bank lending grew tenfold.[47] As the denomination in US$ indicates, the currency in use in this market was not the UK£ but the US$, and the Bank of England lacked the ability to create US$s.[48] The inter-bank borrowing and lending was not the only market in London through which banks built up commitments to each other and so were at risk of a counterparty default. It was through their London operations that banks from all over the world conducted their inter-bank activities, whether it involved foreign exchange, employing idle balances, borrowing to supplement a temporary shortfall, or the routine tasks of making and receiving payments on behalf of customers. London, for example, possessed the dominant foreign exchange market, with around one-third of global turnover. In the 1970s a revitalized foreign exchange market developed, with daily turnover rising from $4–5 billion a day in 1973 to $25 billion a day in 1979. By 1998 that turnover had reached $2.1 trillion a day. London was also the location for other inter-bank activity such as interest rates swaps, with over a third of global turnover of $0.3 trillion a day in 1998.[49]

---

[46] Bank of England, 'Role of the Bank', pp.318–20.
[47] Source: Bank for International Settlement: Locational Banking Statistics, 2011. The interbank data was calculated by subtracting bank lending to the non-bank sector from total bank lending. Cf. Bank for International Settlement, *Guidelines to the International Locational Banking Statistics*.
[48] Schenk, *Decline of Sterling*, pp.88–9, 99, 110, 114, 117, 125, 133–4, 212, 216–23, 225–9, 320; O'Brien, 'Euro-Currency Market', pp.245–9; Montgomery, 'The Clearing Banks', pp.89–91; Bank of England, 'Role of the Bank', p.89–94; Bank of England, 'The Role of Brokers', pp.221–5.
[49] Bank for International Settlement, *Triennial Central Bank Survey: Foreign Exchange and Derivatives Market Activity* (B.I.S., September 2010), Tables 5 and 9. (National total attributed to national financial centre); Atkin, *Foreign Exchange Market*, p.162.

Between 1970 and 1997 London's money market was transformed. The discount market disappeared and was replaced by a series of new markets. In these markets the currency in use was the US$ not the UK£. Foreign banks participated not through correspondent links with UK banks but directly using their London branches and/or UK subsidiaries. Discount houses no longer provided the intermediation as that was done either through direct bank-to-bank negotiation or via a new breed of inter-dealer broker. Finally, the scale of turnover reached previously unimaginable levels made possible by the revolution in global information technology. Under these circumstances the Bank of England was no longer able to act as lender of last resort to the London money market as it had once done. Instead, its focus was now domestic because it continued to fulfil that role for the British banking system, and was recognized as doing so in the new regulatory structure that emerged in 1997/8. That left the foreign banks that increasingly dominated activity in the London money market to look to their home central banks for lender-of last-resort support. No longer could the Bank of England act alone when providing lender-of-last-resort support for it now had to act in concert with other central banks if a crisis should occur.[50]

CONCLUSION

Before 1970 the British banking system was stable but that was only achieved through the Bank of England fostering a culture of conservatism among the large joint-stock banks and the established merchant banks. Even then that culture was increasingly challenged by those smaller and newer banks that saw opportunities to develop a profitable business, and by the likes of the building societies. Once the controls began to be relaxed after 1970 the result was a banking crisis in 1973/4. In the wake of that crisis many of the secondary banks disappeared but the result was not a return to the pre-1970 conditions. The Bank of England had gained from the post-war experience and the Secondary Banking Crisis and so framed a supervisory regime that was more flexible and more in tune with the needs of the banking system as a whole. The result was that, though banks continued to fail and crises happened, none had the same damaging consequences as that of 1973/4. The Bank of England was able to anticipate difficulties and so deal with them in such a way as to prevent a liquidity crisis while avoiding giving banks the impression that whatever risks they took they would be rescued if they faced collapse. Achieving such a

---

[50] Grady and Weale, *British Banking*, pp.28–31, 43, 64–5, 85–6, 92, 98, 110, 119, 121, 130, 139; Singleton, *Central Banking in the Twentieth Century*, pp.236–7; Grossman, *Unsettled Account*, pp.96, 168, 285, 286–9.

balance was only possible because the Bank was in close and constant touch with what was happening in British banking.

There was one area in which the Bank of England was not able to maintain its previous position and that was lender of last resort to the London money market. Over the years between 1970 and 1997 the London money market expanded exponentially in scale, variety, and complexity. The result was to place it beyond the ability of any central bank to act as lender of last resort placing the obligation on all to respond if a liquidity crisis did take place. No longer could the Bank act independently to provide lender of last resort to the global banking system, through the worldwide correspondent network maintained by the British banking system. Instead, it became the lender of last resort just to the British banking system and replaced the indirect relationship operated through the discount houses with direct links. Integral to that relationship was the insight into individual bank behaviour provided to the Bank of England's role as supervisor of the British banking system and its central position within the payments system. Though it retained the obligation to act as lender of last resort after 1997, the Bank of England lost its responsibility for banking supervision while it also made changes to its role in the payments system. Both changes were detrimental to its ability to anticipate emerging problems in banking, formulate a speedy and targeted response, and then execute that strategy before a liquidity crisis affecting a single bank became one infecting the entire system which then metamorphosed into a solvency crisis.

8

Competition and Complacency, 1997–2007

Before the collapse of the Northern Rock Bank in 2007 and the subsequent banking crisis, the British banking system was widely regarded as one of the most stable in the world. Explanations abound for the crisis experienced by British banking in 2007/8 with popular opinion favouring placing the blame on those in charge of the banks at the time. Such a verdict absolves the media from its contribution in creating a climate of distrust in which the stability of all banks was widely questioned. It also frees politicians from the responsibility they bore in fostering excessive growth in bank lending due to the economic policies followed. The Bank of England also escapes blame as changes in the regulatory system had removed its responsibility for supervising the banking system. That leaves the Financial Services Authority (FSA) to take the brunt of the criticism that is not directed at the banks themselves, and that organization no longer exists. When the debate is widened beyond the actions of individual bankers and the FSA, it moves onto the realm of anti-capitalism rhetoric in which the entire global banking system is seen to be deeply flawed, especially the combination of risky investment banking with safe retail banking. Unless subject to strict regulation and monitoring, bankers would inevitably gravitate towards highly speculative activities, or casino banking, as it was these that generated large short-term profits and the bonuses that followed but with disastrous long-term consequences. As such this attitude is reminiscent of US public opinion that followed the Wall Street Crash of 1929 and the subsequent collapse of the banking system, and led to the passage of the Glass-Steagall Act and the formation of the Securities and Exchange Commission. What is important is to move beyond both the immediate reaction to the banking crisis of 2007/8 and the anti-capitalism protests and focus on why the British banking system, once famed for its stability, had to be rescued by government intervention in 2007/8.

Regardless of whether this global crisis was primarily responsible for the near collapse and then government rescue of the British banking system, the question of resilience arises. In previous financial crises the British banking system had been able to withstand the pressures without government intervention. What this suggests is that changes had taken place within British banking since 1997 that made it more vulnerable to a financial crisis than it had been in the past. What many have identified is that a process of consolidation within British banking had the effect of concentrating all financial activity into a small number of business units. What was also novel about these banking businesses was the way they combined high-risk operations such as investment banking with low-risk retail banking. It was losses in the former that impacted the latter, destabilizing the bank and forcing the government to intervene before the entire system collapsed. Evidence that such a process was taking place has been found in the USA, which was the acknowledged epicentre of the global financial crisis. Conversely, there is the argument that what banking suffered from in the years before the crisis was excessive competition. This forced bankers to take greater and greater risks in the pursuit of profit as they were forced to pay more for the funds they borrowed and charge less for those they lent. Another possibility is that it was a decline of control exercised by the Bank of England, which was the undoing of the British banking system. The power of the Bank of England to supervise the banking system was ended in 1998, so removing the influence of the one body that had an intimate knowledge of the British banking system and so could intervene to modify behaviour. In place of the Bank of England there was the Financial Services Authority whose remit extended to the entire financial sector and so lacked an awareness of the unique risks posed by banks, especially their exposure to a liquidity crisis. In the event of such a crisis responsibility to take immediate action as lender of last resort was now shared between the Bank of England, the Financial Services Authority, and the UK Treasury, which was a new and untested arrangement. Finally, there is the possibility that the growth and success of the City of London as an international centre had located in Britain a banking system that was so large, diverse, and active that it was impossible for any authority to monitor and supervise adequately, and in the event of a crisis was beyond the ability of the Bank of England to act as lender of last resort. Hosting an international financial centre generated economic growth and prosperity for Britain as was evident in the twenty years before the crisis. However, it also made the British banking system highly vulnerable to a crisis imported from other countries around the world. It was not individual banks that had become too large to be allowed to fail but the entire British banking system.

Before the Global Financial Crisis it was recognized in the UK that banking crises were become more frequent around the world, but these were associated with emerging economies, not a country like Britain with sophisticated financial systems.[1] It was even recognized as early as 2005/6 that there were some

---

[1] G. Hoggarth, R. Reis, and V. Saporta, 'Costs of Banking System Instability: Some Empirical Evidence', *Bank of England Working Paper*, 144 (2001), pp.1–32.

signs that a major crisis could occur internationally because the successful monetary policies being pursued around the world were creating an asset-price bubble. There were, nevertheless, no real concerns that such a crisis was either imminent or likely to produce serious problems for British banking. Such opinions remained firmly entrenched until the crisis actually began in Britain during the course of 2007.[2] It was at that stage that responsibility for the UK banking crisis was blamed on external events, as with the Governor of the Bank of England's speech in October 2007: 'Three weeks ago, thousands of depositors queued on the streets outside branches of Northern Rock to take their money out. Those scenes, broadcast around the world, were shocking. How did they come about and how can we prevent them in future?' His explanation was that a glut of savings from countries such as China, Saudi Arabia, and Norway had found its way to the USA where it created a credit bubble. This eventually burst as borrowers defaulted, leaving banks with large losses, causing a collapse of confidence in the entire US banking system. In turn, that loss of confidence spread to the UK via France, and such was its severity that the authorities had no alternative but to intervene or face the collapse of those British banks that were exposed to the US crisis.[3] Such a verdict remained the orthodoxy among senior staff at the Bank of England for the next few years, though the media preferred to focus on the reckless behaviour of individual bankers.[4] This explanation for the crisis, that emphasized events external to Britain, was given added credence with the collapse of the Wall Street investment bank, Lehman Brothers, on 15th September 2008, because of the shockwaves its failure created among the world's banks. In the wake of the Lehman Brothers collapse, the British banking crisis was increasingly dated from September 2008 rather than the events surrounding

[2] C. Fisher and P. Gai, 'Financial Stability, Monetary Stability and Public Policy', *Bank of England Quarterly Bulletin*, 45 (2005), pp.441–7; Bank of England, 'The Governor's Speech in Edinburgh', *Bank of England Quarterly Bulletin*, 46 (2006), p.329; Sir John Gieve, 'Practical Issues in Preparing for Cross-Border Financial Crises', *Bank of England Quarterly Bulletin*, 46 (2006), p.452; Sir John Gieve, 'Pricing for Perfection', *Bank of England Quarterly Bulletin*, 47 (2007), pp.112–17; P. Tucker, 'Macro, Asset Price, and Financial System Uncertainties', *Bank of England Quarterly Bulletin*, 47 (2007), pp.122–30.
[3] M. King, 'The Governor's Speech in Northern Ireland', *Bank of England Quarterly Bulletin*, 47 (2007), pp.566–9.
[4] R. Lomax, 'Current Monetary Policy Issues', *Bank of England Quarterly Bulletin*, 47 (2007), pp.570–3 22 November 2007; M. King, 'The Governor's Speech in Bristol', *Bank of England Quarterly Bulletin*, 48 (2008), pp.82–4; Sir John Gieve, 'The Impact of the Financial Market Disruption on the UK Economy', *Bank of England Quarterly Bulletin*, 48 (2008), pp.85–90; Sir John Gieve, 'The Return of the Credit Cycle: Old Lessons in New Markets', *Bank of England Quarterly Bulletin*, 48 (2008), pp.91–5; Sir John Gieve, 'Sovereign Wealth Funds and Global Imbalances', *Bank of England Quarterly Bulletin*, 48 (2008), pp.196–202; Sir John Gieve, 'Learning from the Financial Crisis', *Bank of England Quarterly Bulletin*, 48 (2008), pp.1–13; Sir John Gieve, 'Rebuilding Confidence in the Financial System', *Bank of England Quarterly Bulletin*, 48 (2008), pp.1–9; M. Astley, J. Giese, M. Hume, and C. Kubelec, 'Global Imbalances and the Financial Crisis', *Bank of England Quarterly Bulletin*, 49 (2009), pp.179–88.

Northern Rock a year earlier.[5] However, even in those early years there were those who pointed out that it was developments within British banking that had made it so vulnerable to an international financial crisis.[6]

As time passed, a more reflective view emerged that took up the popular rhetoric that British banking had contributed to its own downfall. This view was voiced by Charles Bean, Deputy Governor for Monetary Policy at the Bank of England, in August 2009: 'To the public at large our present troubles are the fault of: whiz-kid financiers, who created financial instruments that even they didn't properly understand; greedy bankers, who pursued profit and personal reward without regard to risk or common sense; somnolent supervisors, who failed to adequately regulate and restrain those bankers; and negligent central bankers, who allowed an explosion in liquidity, credit, and asset prices that supported the whole rotten edifice. And all the while, the culprits were cheered on by an economics profession that was over-enamoured of theoretical models, blind to the lessons of history and subject to a severe case of "group think". Wasn't it blindingly obvious that the whole house of cards would come crashing down at some point?'[7] Increasingly the fragility of the British banking system came to the fore as an explanation of why this financial crisis had such catastrophic consequences compared to those of the past, though the Governor of the Bank of England, Mervyn King, continued to cling to the view that it was events in the global economy that had to take prime responsibility.[8] By 2012 it had become generally accepted that important as the Global Financial Crisis had been as a contributory cause of Britain's banking crisis, the fundamental problem lay with British banking itself. This view was even articulated within the Bank of England by those who had an intimate knowledge of the banking system and had now risen to positions of seniority once the previous management had departed One of these was Chris Salmon. 'With the benefit of hindsight, it all too easy to see that banks, as well as "shadow banks" had become over-leveraged, significant funding vulnerabilities had developed, and the system had become too-interconnected and opaque so that the distribution of risks

---

[5] M. King, Speech: *Bank of England Quarterly Bulletin*, 48 (2008), pp.1-9; M. King, Speech: *Bank of England Quarterly Bulletin*, 49 (2009), pp.1-13; A. Haldane, 'Rethinking the Financial Network', *Bank of England Quarterly Bulletin*, 49 (2009), pp.1-41.

[6] N. Jenkinson, 'Strengthening Regimes for Controlling Liquidity Risk: Some Lessons from the Recent Turmoil', *Bank of England Quarterly Bulletin*, 48 (2008), pp.223-7.

[7] C. Bean, 'The Great Moderation, the Great Panic and the Great Contraction', *Bank of England Quarterly Bulletin*, 49 (2009), pp.1-32.

[8] D. Miles, 'Monetary Policy and Financial Stability', *Bank of England Quarterly Bulletin*, 49 (2009), pp.1-19; 'Financial Crisis and G20 Financial and Regulatory Reform: An Overview', Paul Tucker, Speech of 3 September 2010, pp.1-7; M. King, Speech of 15th September 2010, *Bank of England Quarterly Bulletin*, 50 (2010), pp.1-7; M. King, 'Global Imbalances: The Perspective of the Bank of England', *Bank of England Quarterly Bulletin*, 51 (2011), pp.43-7; M. King, Speech: of 18 October 2011, *Bank of England Quarterly Bulletin*, 51 (2011), pp.2-3.

was unclear. Moreover, the public authorities did not have the ability to resolve banks in an orderly manner when they failed. In summary, the system was extremely fragile to shocks and the authorities lacked a comprehensive toolkit to deal with the consequences. To fix those flaws we need to make institutions individually safer, by making sure they hold sufficient loss-absorbing capital and liquid assets to guard against cash squeezes. We need to reduce the scope for shocks to be transmitted unexpectedly around the financial system ... by promoting clearing through central counterparties.'[9]

No longer was it possible to attribute the downfall of the British banking system to a Global Financial Crisis because it was now recognized that the problems were much closer to home and had developed during the course of the previous ten years. That is not to say that the Global Crisis was not a significant factor but it has to be put in the context of its interaction with a fragile British banking system to provide a creditable explanation. It acted as the trigger not the cause. This has turned the search for causes away from the global financial environment and the collapse of Lehman Brothers on the 15th of September 2008 and back to the 13th of September 2007 when Northern Rock was forced to seek emergency funding to avoid an imminent collapse.[10] For an explanation of why the British banking system succumbed to a Global Financial Crisis in 2007/8 after almost 150 years of resilience, a search must be made within the banking system itself, especially in what happened from 1997 onwards, as those ten years did involve major changes both domestically and internationally and at all levels and relationships.[11] In that period a number of British banks embraced the universal banking model, expanding away from a long-term focus on retail banking as they rapidly expanded their business at home and abroad. Domestically, the banking environment also became much more competitive with the conversion of building societies into banks and the invasion of England by the two Scottish banks. Again, domestically, the regulation of banking was also transformed with the creation of the Financial Services Authority in 1997, replacing the control over banking exercised by the Bank of England with a single agency responsible for financial services in their entirety. Internationally, the period also experienced the flourishing of the City of London as a global financial centre, building on the position established

---

[9] C. Salmon, 'Three Principles for Successful Financial Sector Reform', *Bank of England Quarterly Bulletin*, 52 (2012), pp.1-7. See also C. Bean, 'Central Banking in Boom and Slump', *Bank of England Quarterly Bulletin*, 52 (2012), pp.1-18.

[10] S. Chowla, L. Quaglietti, and L. Rachel, 'How Have World Shocks Affected the UK Economy?', *Bank of England Quarterly Bulletin*, 54 (2014), pp.167-76; D. Rule (Executive Director, Prudential Policy, Bank of England), Speech: 'Regulatory Reform, its Possible Market Consequences and the Case of Securities Financing', 6 November 2014, pp.1-11; A.G. Haldane, Speech: 'Central Bank Psychology', 17 November 2014, pp.1-28; M. Carney, Speech: 'Fortune Favours the Bold', 28 January 2015, pp.1-16.

[11] Singleton, *Central Banking in the Twentieth Century*, p.216.

after Big Bang in 1986 and the liberalization of global financial flows. It was the interaction between these elements that made the British banking system so vulnerable when a crisis did occur. It was not what happened in 2008, with the collapse of Lehman Brothers, that caused the crisis in British banking as that had already materialized a year earlier with the collapse of Northern Rock. Only by writing that earlier crisis out of history is it possible to attribute the problems that assailed British banking from 2008 onwards to circumstances beyond its own control and the domestic environment within which it operated.

CHANGE

There is ample evidence to support the view that there was marked change in UK banking between 1997 and 2007 involving the embrace of investment banking practices by the UK's retail banks. As late as 1997, over ten years after Big Bang, the long-standing separation of retail and investment banking practices remained in place within British banking. Though the major British banks had, by then, diversified the products and services they offered, and expanded into investment banking and related trading activities, this was not sufficient to change their overall character. They continued to depend on the Lend and Hold Model whereby short-term retail deposits were lent out on a largely short-term basis. This made them acutely conscious of the risks they ran because their survival could be instantly threatened by the sudden withdrawal of deposits caused by rumours. Eddie George, the Governor of the Bank of England, had an informed view of British banking and his verdict in 1997 was that, 'while there certainly have been important changes affecting the banks, and the environment in which they operate, they have not yet, at least, been such as to affect fundamentally their relevant key functions or the importance of those functions to the economy; nor have they altered fundamentally the distinctive characteristics of either the banks' liabilities or their assets.' What there had been was a gradual blurring of the boundaries between different types of banks.[12]

That position was to change radically from 1997 onwards through the increased adoption of investment banking techniques among UK retail banks, especially after 2002. This embrace of investment banking techniques was not seen as involving greater risks because it was underpinned by the sophisticated risk modelling that the banks carried out. No longer did higher returns imply higher risks. This belief can be seen in a speech delivered at the

[12] George, 'Are Banks Still Special?' pp.114–18.

end of June 2007 by Nigel Jenkinson, Executive Director for Financial Stability, and Mark Manning, Senior Manager at the Financial Resilience Division, both at the Bank of England: 'Financial innovation has delivered considerable benefits. New products have improved the ability to hedge and share risks and to tailor financial products more precisely to user demand. That has enabled financial intermediaries and users of financial services to manage financial risks more effectively, and has lowered the costs of financial intermediation. And innovation and capital market integration have facilitated the wider dispersal of risks, which may have increased the resilience of the financial system to weather small to medium-sized shocks. Innovation has also delivered new challenges and vulnerabilities. Dependence on capital markets and on sustained market liquidity has increased, as banks and other intermediaries place greater reliance on their ability to "originate and distribute" loans and other financial products, and to manage their risk positions dynamically as economic and financial conditions alter. In turn that places additional pressure on the robustness of financial market infrastructure to handle large changes in trading volumes and to cope with periods of strain. And the greater integration of capital markets means that if a major problem does arise it is more likely to spread quickly across borders... the flip side to increased resilience of the financial system to small and medium-sized shocks may be greater vulnerability to less frequent but potentially larger financial crises.'[13]

Even on the eve of the financial crisis there was still a prevailing belief that the new practices embraced by the UK's retail banks had, on balance, made them more not less resilient. Only with hindsight did a contrary view emerge as another expert at the Bank of England acknowledged in January 2011. According to Andrew Bailey, Executive Director of Banking and Chief Cashier at the Bank of England at the time, 'Sound banking is about having a strong capital base and a funding profile in terms of maturity that can withstand the sort of shocks in the world that will happen from time to time. It is not about expanding your bank rapidly and funding the growth in the overnight money market.' What the new practices, embraced by British retail bankers between 1997 and 2007, did not represent was 'sound banking' in the eyes of an expert who had experienced its eventual outcome. What hindsight revealed was the failure of greatly increased lending by banks to be matched by a growth in capital and reserves.[14]

Until the financial crisis of 2007 there was a growing belief that the new practices embraced by the retail banks meant a lower level of risk not a higher one. In the 'Lend and Hold Model long used by British retail banks the funds

[13] N. Jenkinson and M. Manning, 'Promoting Financial System Resilience in Modern Global Capital Markets: Some Issues', *Bank of England Quarterly Bulletin*, 47 (2007), pp.453–60.

[14] A. Bailey (Executive Director, Banking and Chief Cashier, Bank of England): Speech: The Outlook for Financial Regulation in the UK, 10 January 2011, pp.1–5.

deposited by savers were re-lent to individual and business customers on a short-term basis. This exposed the bank to a liquidity crisis because of the mismatch between the funds it was employing to make loans, which could be withdrawn instantly, and the loans it made as these were not due for repayment until some time in the future. Balancing this position required careful management, which was why banks constantly monitored the behaviour of all their customers to ensure that they had advance warning of any sudden withdrawals or defaults. Hence also the need to maintain adequate capital and reserves, plus a layer of liquid assets, as these could be called upon to meet a sudden surge of withdrawals or cover unexpected defaults among borrowers. Building societies and savings banks followed much the same model though they had to keep a higher level of liquidity because they lent longer-term. By no means was retail banking a risk-free activity for only by rigid adherence to basic banking principles was it undertaken safely.[15]

In contrast, investment banks used a Originate and Distribute Model. What this meant was that they issued stocks and bonds on behalf of borrowers and then sold these to investors. In the interval between the issue and sale of these securities investment banks could use the stocks and bonds they held as collateral for short-term loans from retail banks, and so meet the immediate need of borrowers. Once the securities had been sold the funds borrowed from the banks could be repaid.[16] In practice these clear distinctions between retail and investment banks did not exist. Retail banks raised funds not only by accepting deposits but also by issuing stocks and bonds and by borrowing in wholesale markets. The loans they made also varied in length covering not only short-term needs but also longer-term requirements as with business investment and property purchases. Short-term loans were often rolled over when they became due if the borrower was considered to be in a position to repay when asked. Finally, retail banks engaged with investors both through handling the issue of new securities and the buying or selling of existing securities. Conversely, investment banks accepted temporary deposits at the wholesale level and used borrowed funds to finance holdings of newly issued securities awaiting final disposal. Though appearing novel at the time this embrace of the Originate and Distribute Model by British retail banks was a reversion to older practice. Through the use of bills of exchange banks had lent money to a business via a securitized asset, which could be re-sold many times before maturity. It meant that banks could expand their lending far beyond their own resources, limited by the capital they raised and the deposits they

[15] M. Farag, D. Harland, and D. Nixon, 'Bank Capital and Liquidity', *Bank of England Quarterly Bulletin*, 53 (2013), pp.202-14.

[16] Dame Clara Furse, 'Taking the Long View: How Market-Based Finance Can Support Stability', *Bank of England Quarterly Bulletin*, 54 (2014), pp.1-8; K. Balluck, 'Investment Banking: Linkages to the Real Economy and the Financial System', *Bank of England Quarterly Bulletin*, 55 (2015), pp.1-19.

attracted, as long as these bills could be sold to others. Over time there was less need for the Originate and Distribute Model with the growth of large banks capable of recycling deposits internally and so balance supply and demand. The issue of Treasury Bills by the government, which expanded enormously from the First World War onwards, also reduced the demand for these short-term financial instruments among investors. Nevertheless, the Originate and Distribute Model never died away within retail banking, being revived time and again, especially during periods of credit restraint. It suited the position of banks as they experienced alternating conditions in which they were either short of funds to lend or found themselves with an excess supply. By tapping into the excess that existed in the system as a whole a bank could remedy any deficit. It was always tempting to extend these operations because it allowed an individual bank to expand its business through using the excess funds present in the system on a regular basis. Securitization appeared to provide a means of doing this on a safe basis.

The problem with the way that the Originate and Distribute Model was applied in British retail banking after 1997 lay not only with the extent to which it replaced the Lend and Hold Model but also the way in which it was done. When it involved bills of exchange the bank was in the position of being both a creditor and a debtor as long as they remained in circulation, and they did possess an active secondary market. The ultimate responsibility for payment lay with the borrower as the bill of exchange represented the loan they had received from the bank. If the bank sold the bill, it still retained responsibility for ensuring that it was paid when due, recovering that money from those who had borrowed from it in the first place. Hence the reason why the duration of bills of exchange was capped at ninety days, as this shortened the gap between the deposits of savers, which could be instantly withdrawn and the maturity of the loans made using them. The short-term nature of the bills and the existence of an active secondary market provided some security for a bank that it would be able to meet depositor withdrawals as bills were always becoming due for repayment or could be sold. In contrast, a different position existed in the case of securities because the investment bank had no responsibility to redeem them once purchased by investors. Securities either did not have a redemption date, as with corporate stocks, or had one far in the future, as with government and corporate bonds, and the investment bank acted only as the agent of the original issuer. What securities did have was an active secondary market, obtained by a quotation on a recognized stock exchange, through which the holder could sell them to another, at the prevailing price, and so recover the money invested when required. Though the investment bank played an active role in both issuing stocks and bonds and their subsequent trading they had no responsibility to buy back these securities and so had no problems with liquidity other than in that period when they were held using funds borrowed from retail banks. As practised, however, by retail banks, after 1997 the securities created were both longer-term, covering a duration of years, and were often sold to either in-house Special Purpose Vehicles or to other banks who financed their purchases using the short-term deposits of savers. The market that existed for these securities was also not obtained through a quotation on a recognized stock exchange but depended upon the willingness of the bank to buy them back if requested to do so. This meant the ultimate liability still remained with the bank.

The way the new model worked can be seen in the case of Northern Rock, which had been a mutually owned building society before it converted into a joint-stock bank in 1997. Northern Rock fully embraced the Originate and Distribute Model as that allowed it to expand its lending far above its rather limited retail base. The ratio of assets to capital, its leverage ratio, more than doubled from 22.8 per cent in June 1998 to 58.2 per cent in June 2007. As a bank, Northern Rock ran two parallel operations. One was internal to the bank and was a Lend and Hold operation with retail deposits being invested in mortgages. The other was external and was called Granite. Granite raised money by selling re-packaged mortgage loans in the real estate mortgage-backed securities market. The money it raised was placed with Northern Rock so that it could make new loans, which were then re-packaged and sold. Anticipating the success of this process Northern Rock borrowed extensively in the wholesale market, using the funds it obtained there to lend to mortgage customers. In turn these loans would be re-packaged and sold on, allowing the wholesale funds to be repaid. But there was the temptation to continue or even extend such borrowing because of the profits to be made using short-term funds paying a low rate of interest to finance longer-term lending generating a higher rate of interest, and this is what happened. By June 2007, to fund its lending, Northern Rock had issued £54 billion in notes and bonds and borrowed £27 billion from the wholesale market, with only £24 billion coming from retail customers. All this worked perfectly until the market for re-packaged loans froze on the 9th of August 2007, as that meant that Granite could not re-finance the lending using short-term funds by the issue of notes and bonds. As Granite was an integral part of the Northern Rock Bank, though operated separately, the problems it faced were also that of its parent. The immediate problem was not the maturity of the existing notes and bonds, though that would soon become one. By December 2007 notes and bonds had only fallen by £2 billion. Instead, it was the withdrawal of wholesale funds that created difficulties for Northern Rock as all banks pulled away from the inter-bank market to ensure that they retained a cushion of liquidity in the face of an emerging crisis. By December 2007 wholesale funding had shrunk by £16 billion. That was then followed by withdrawals by retail customers, down by £14 billion by December 2007. The result was a classic liquidity crisis as Northern Rock was unable to meet the outflow of short-term funds as these had been lent out on mortgage and the anticipated re-financing could not be accomplished. In the end the Bank of England stepped in to cover the deficit, providing £28 billion by December 2007, or almost exactly the amount lost through withdrawals by wholesale and retail customers. Northern Rock had become a very highly leveraged institution, which made it vulnerable to any reduction in its ability to borrow.[17]

What had taken place at Northern Rock was but an extreme example of the situation across the entire UK banking sector by 2007. The substitution of the Originate and Distribute Model, for the Lend and Hold one, had appeared to provide British retail banks with secure investment opportunities in property, and thus access to the potentially high yields this generated. This covered not only the finance of house purchase, which had long been the preserve of the building societies, but also the field of commercial property. Increasingly banks replaced long-term investors such as insurance companies and pension funds in lending to commercial property developers. Between 1997 and 2006, UK banks' lending to the commercial property sector increased fourfold. By the end of 2007, commercial real estate lending accounted for more than a third of the stock of lending to UK private non-financial companies by UK-resident banks. With commercial property prices rising 60 per cent between 2000 and 2006, and defaults a rarity, banks expanded the amount that they lent while the loan to valuation fell to 95 per cent. Homeowners were also using property as collateral for increased borrowing from banks as access to such funds became both cheaper and readily available because of the switch to the Originate and Distribute Model. The issue of mortgage-backed securities by major UK banks peaked at £111.5 billion in 2006 before falling back sharply to £71.7 billion in 2007 and then collapsing to £3.6 billion in 2008.[18] It was not only property to

---

[17] P. Tucker, 'Shadow Banking, Financing Markets and Financial Stability', *Bank of England Quarterly Bulletin*, 50 (2010),pp.1–13; G.S. Shin, 'Reflections on Northern Rock: The Bank Run that Heralded the Global Financial Crisis', *Journal of Economic Perspectives*, 23 (2009), pp.101–20.

[18] N. Jenkinson, 'Risks to the Commercial Property Market and Financial Stability', *Bank of England Quarterly Bulletin*, 47 (2007), pp.118–21; Tucker, 'Macro, Asset Price', pp.122–30; P. Tucker, 'A Perspective on Recent Monetary and Financial System Developments', *Bank of England Quarterly Bulletin*, 47 (2007), pp.310–16; Gieve, 'Return of the Credit Cycle', pp.91–5; Jenkinson, 'Strengthening Regimes', pp.223–7; Gieve, 'Learning from the Financial Crisis', pp.1–13; King, Speech: *Bank of England Quarterly Bulletin* (2008), pp.1–9; Astley, Giese, Hume, and Kubelec, 'Global Imbalances'; Bean, 'The Great Moderation', pp.1–32; D. Miles, 'Money, Banks and Quantitative Easing', *Bank of England Quarterly Bulletin*, 49 (2009), p.1–18; P. Alessandri and A.G. Haldane, Speech: 'Banking on the State' (2009), pp.1–30; K. Reinold, 'Housing Equity Withdrawal since the Financial Crisis', *Bank of England Quarterly Bulletin*, 51 (2011), p.132; D. Miles, 'Mortgages and Housing in the Near and Long Term', *Bank of England Quarterly Bulletin*, 51 (2011), pp.1–12; A. Bailey, Speech: *Bank of England Quarterly Bulletin*, 51 (2011), pp.1–17; D. Miles, 'Mortgages, Housing and Monetary Policy: What Lies Ahead', *Bank of England Quarterly Bulletin*, 51 (2011), pp.1–18; P. Tucker, 'Banking in a Market Economy: the International Agenda', *Bank of England Quarterly Bulletin*, 52 (2012), pp.15–32; P. Tucker, 'Competition, the Pressure for Returns, and Stability', *Bank of England Quarterly Bulletin*, 52 (2012), pp.1–11; A.G. Haldane, 'On Being the Right Size, 25 October 2012', *Bank of England*

which the Originate and Distribute Model was applied. Banks also made highly leveraged loans to finance management buy-outs of the companies they ran and then sold on these collateralized loan obligations.[19]

As banks expanded their lending between 1997 and 2007 it was based more and more on the expectation of the resale of securitized assets, and short-term borrowing in the wholesale markets, and less and less on capital, reserves, and retail deposits. The degree and pace at which this took place varied between individual banks but all followed the same route. As a result the entire sector was left dependent upon continued access to the wholesale money market and on the ability to re-sell securitized assets. In turn that position was dependent upon rising asset prices as that generated confidence among investors that the value of the bonds they were purchasing was justified and that the stream of interest payments would continue. When doubts began to emerge that this was not the case, beginning in the USA during the course of 2007, investors became increasingly reluctant to purchase new securitized assets. In turn, those providing funds to the money market became wary of lending to those banks that were dependent upon selling such securities in order to repay their loans. This left banks in this position in the perilous situation of being unable to re-sell the securitized assets on which they had already made loans and so re-pay the short-term funds they had borrowed, and even meet their commitments to those holding bonds that were due to mature. That was when their lack of capital and reserves, combined with a shortage of assets that they could sell, led to a liquidity crisis which spread from the wholesale to the retail market. In turn, that liquidity crisis became a solvency one as asset prices fell and borrowers defaulted on either interest payments or repayment, or both. In 2008 the aggregate trading losses suffered by the UK banking system were over £40 billion. This forced them to scale back not only their lending but also re-assess the risks they were running, leading them to withdraw from certain types of business, such as market making. This pattern of behaviour was observable across all UK banks regardless of size or type though there was a degree of variation between individual banks. Such behaviour had intensified after 2002. The leverage ratio of assets to capital, which had been steady at around 20-25 per cent between 1997 and 2002, (23.9 per cent in 1997, 21.3 per cent in 2002) had risen to 35.6 per cent in 2007, after which it fell back to 23.7 per cent by June 2011. Those banks and building societies that had lower leverage ratios, inefficient management, weaker earnings, and higher levels of arrears

---

Quarterly Bulletin, 52 (2012), p.1-18; J. Benford and O. Burrows, 'Commercial Property and Financial Stability', *Bank of England Quarterly Bulletin*, 53 (2013), pp.48-56; R. Meeks, B.D. Nelson, and P. Alessandri, 'Shadow Banks and Macroeconomic Instability', *Bank of England Working Paper*, 487 (2014), pp.1-66.

[19] D. Gregory, 'Private Equity and Financial Stability', *Bank of England Quarterly Bulletin*, 53 (2013), pp.40-2.

were the ones most affected by the financial crisis and so were forced to take drastic action as a consequence.[20]

CONCENTRATION

When the focus switches away from global events as an explanation for Britain's financial crisis of 2008/9 the question of why UK banking proved so vulnerable becomes the central question. For many that question is easily answered by reference to the fact that British banking had become dominated by a small number of very large banks that were 'too big to fail'. This trend towards concentration was not confined to the UK but was also observable around the world, being especially pronounced in the USA where the legislative barriers to bank mergers were removed during the 1990s. In keeping with the view that the financial crisis of 2007-9 was a global event, and accompanied by government intervention to rescue failing banks, the increased concentration of banking systems was thus seen as an important contributory factor to what took place. Andrew Haldane at the Bank of England, for example, has made the claim that, prior to the crisis, 'There has been a spectacular rise in the size and concentration of the financial system over the last two decades, with the rapid emergence of "super-spreader institutions" too big, connected, or important to fail.'[21] The argument is that those employed by these banks were in a position to indulge in highly risky behaviour because they could escape responsibility for any losses they made, as these fell on the shareholders, while benefitting from any profits through bonus payments and share options. Even if the losses threatened to bankrupt the bank, their careers were secure because the UK government would have no option but to intervene and save it from collapse due to its systemic importance. If this was the case, though, then the largest banks should have exhibited a greater propensity for risk-taking than the smaller. This is the reverse of the accusation usually levelled against British banking, especially the retail banks. The judgement has been that a small

---

[20] P. Tucker, 'Money and Credit: Banking and the Macroeconomy', *Bank of England Quarterly Bulletin*, 47 (2007), pp.96-106; P. Gai, S. Kapadia, S. Millard, and A. Perez, 'Financial Innovation, Macroeconomic Stability and Systemic Crises', *Bank of England Working Paper*, 340 (2008), pp.1-40; Miles, 'Monetary Policy and Financial Stability', pp.1-19; D. Miles, 'Leverage and Monetary Policy', *Bank of England Quarterly Bulletin*, 50 (2010), pp.1-22; Bailey, Speech: 'The Outlook for Financial Regulation', pp.1-5; W.B. Francis, 'UK Deposit-Taker Responses to the Financial Crisis: What Are the Lessons', *Bank of England Quarterly Bulletin*, 54 (2014), pp.1- 46; Dame Clara Furse, Speech: 'Liquidity Matters', 11 February 2015, pp.1-10.

[21] A.G. Haldane and R.M. May, 'Systemic Risk in Banking Ecosystems', *Nature*, 20 January 2011, pp.353-4. See also A.G. Haldane, 'The $100 Billion Question', *Bank of England Quarterly Bulletin*, 50 (2010), pp.1-27; Haldane, 'On Being the Right Size', pp.1-18; A. Haldane, Speech: 'A Leaf Being Turned', 29 October 2012, pp.1-11.

number of banks had gained a dominant position by the beginning of the twentieth century and with this relative immunity from competition they increasingly adopted a highly conservative culture, leaving risk-taking to the smaller and newer banks. What has to be shown is that in the decade before the financial crisis of 2007 there was a pronounced tendency towards consolidation, and thus an even greater dominance of a small number of banks, and this encouraged a risk-taking culture to prevail.[22]

Evidence has been put forward to support the view that a process of concentration did take place in the UK. Between 1990 and 2004 there was a decline in the number of UK-owned banks from 139 to 48. As a result the eight largest banks in 2004 accounted for 95 per cent of total system assets compared to the 91 per cent of the ten largest in 1990. Though this increase was mainly due to the failure of many small and specialized banks at the beginning of the period, it also included mergers between banks that were already large. In 2000 one of the largest of the English banks, NatWest, was acquired by the Royal Bank of Scotland, while in the following year the other major Scottish bank, the Bank of Scotland, merged with the largest ex-building society, the Halifax.[23] The problem with such an approach when applied to Britain is that it takes a very narrow view of the British banking system. The UK's resident banking sector comprised not only the domestically incorporated units of UK-owned banks but also the subsidiaries and branches of banks headquartered elsewhere in the world. The UK contained the world's largest banking sector by asset size, even compared to that of the USA. At the time of the Global Financial Crisis there were 611 banks operating in the UK of which over 300 conducted significant operations there, being split equally between UK-owned (49.5 per cent) and foreign-owned (50.5 per cent). These foreign-owned banks were not present in the UK solely to access the facilities of the City of London as an international financial centre. They also played a major role within the UK banking system competing with UK banks for customers, co-operating with them in business deals, and acting as counterparties in money market activities. If only UK-owned banks are studied then the level of concentration does appear very high but it becomes much more modest when foreign-controlled banks are included.[24]

---

[22] V. Acharya and T. Yorulmazer, 'Too Many to Fail: An Analysis of Time-Inconsistency in Bank Closure Policies, *Bank of England Working Paper*, 319 (2007), pp.1-53; A.K. Rose and T. Wieladek, 'Too Big to Fail: Some Empirical Evidence on the Causes and Consequences of Public Banking Interventions in the United Kingdom', *Bank of England Working Papers*, 460 (2012), pp.1-25; Nigel Jenkinson (Adviser to the Governor), Speech: 'Containing System-Wide Liquidity Risks: Some Issues and Challenges', 15 May 2009, pp.1-23.

[23] Davies, Richardson, Katinaite, and Manning, 'Evolution of the UK Banking System', pp.322-5; N. Mora and A. Logan, 'Shocks to Bank Capital: Evidence from UK Banks at Home and Away, *Bank of England Working Paper*, 387 (2010), pp.1-31.

[24] Mora and Logan, 'Shocks to Bank Capital', pp.1-31; Kristin Forbes (MPC), Speech: 'Financial "Deglobalization"?: Capital Flows, Banks, and the Beatles', 18 November 2014, pp.1-27; Rose and Wieladek, 'Too Big to Fail', pp.1-25.

Evidence to indicate that the UK-owned banking sector was becoming more concentrated is also lacking. By 2007 it was estimated that the ten largest UK banks accounted for 90 per cent of all UK-owned bank assets, which was the position at the beginning of the 1990s. The composition of these top ten banks was also subject to considerable change posing a significant challenge to the once dominant banks. Until the twenty-first century, English and Scottish banks occupied separate geographical spheres with each sovereign in their own parts of the UK. That changed in 2000 when the Royal Bank of Scotland (RBS) made a successful takeover bid for NatWest, one of England's largest banks. That was followed in 2001 when the Bank of Scotland merged with England's largest building society, the Halifax, which had recently converted into a bank. A close examination of the ten largest UK-owned banks in 2007 reveals how diverse they were and the degree of change compared to ten years before. Among the ten were four ex-building societies, namely Abbey National, Alliance and Leicester, Bradford and Bingley, and Northern Rock, indicating the challenge they now posed to the long-established banking giants. Also included were the two Scottish banks, Bank of Scotland and the RBS, greatly boosted by their English acquisitions. In addition there were two externally focused banks, HSBC and Standard Chartered, with only the former having a major UK presence since its takeover of the Midland Bank. Of the once dominant retail banks Lloyds now incorporated the savings bank movement since its merger with the Trustee Savings Bank. That left only Barclays in its original form as the sole survivor of the five banks that had dominated British retail banking since the First World War. If the search for concentration and dominance is extended to other types of banks, the case becomes even weaker. In the wake of Big Bang, Britain's once powerful investment banks had been swept aside, being either acquired by US and European banks or reduced to niche operations. The revival of British-owned investment banks only took place either immediately prior to the crisis or afterwards. RBS did attempt to cap its successful acquisition of NatWest by taking over part of the Dutch Bank, ABN-Amro, including its substantial London-based investment banking activities. However, that was quickly to unravel in the wake of the crisis. Only Barclays developed a major investment banking business and did so in 2008 through the opportunistic acquisition of the US operations of the failed Lehman Brothers. Internationally, when judged by the share of the assets of all commercial banks held by the three largest banks, the level of concentration in the UK in 2007 was in line with that of Canada, France, and Germany, though much higher than in the USA. As the epicentre of the Global Financial Crisis was the USA while Canada escaped largely unscathed, and France and Germany occupied a middling position, the causal connection between concentration and crisis within banking appears to be a false one.[25]

Evidence also indicates that banks should not expect to be bailed out by the government. The research conducted and published before the crisis all warned against taking that course of action. Prior to the crisis theoretical-level discussion did take place about how to respond to bank failure. What all of these made clear was that banks should not rely upon external assistance. Assistance would be confined to liquidity support and only provided to solvent banks. Though it was recognized that it could be difficult to distinguish between a bank that was illiquid and insolvent and one that was solvent but illiquid, such an attempt had to be made so as to ward against moral hazard. Moral hazard was when those running a bank behaved in a reckless manner because of the potential profits, relying on government support if the result brought the bank to the brink of ruin. There is no evidence that those running the largest British banks before the crisis of 2007 believed that the government would inevitably intervene to save their bank if it was on the verge of collapse. Ample warnings had been sounded about how such assistance would be conditional on solvency. Those running these banks simply did not contemplate failure as a possibility and neither did the public and the regulators.[26]

COMPETITION

Driving the adoption of investment banking practices among retail banks and building societies was the increasingly competitive environment within which they operated. In a competitive banking environment individual banks were always tempted to lend for longer to less secure borrowers and accept less liquid collateral. Otherwise business would be lost to rivals. The same

[25] Davies, Richardson, Katinaite, and Manning, 'Evolution of the UK Banking System', pp.322–5; Capie, *Bank of England*, pp.327–9; Logan, 'The United Kingdom's Small Banks' Crisis', pp.1–30; M. Stringa and A. Monks, 'Inter-Industry Contagion between UK Life Insurers and UK Banks: An Event Study', *Bank of England Working Paper*, 325 (2007), pp.1–31; C. Gondat-Laralde and E. Nier, 'The Economics of Retail Banking: An Empirical Analysis of the UK Market for Personal Current Accounts, *Bank of England Quarterly Bulletin*, 44 (2004); A.S. Posen (member of MOC), Speech: 'Deepen and Diversify UK Financial Infrastructure to Enable Small Business Growth', 2 February 2012, pp.1–15.

[26] Hoggarth, Reidhill, and Sinclair, 'On the Resolution of Banking Crises'; G. Irwin and D. Vines, 'The Efficient Resolution of Capital-Account Crises: How to Avoid Moral Hazard', *Bank of England Quarterly Bulletin*, 44 (2004); Acharya and Yorulmazer, 'Too Many to Fail', pp.1–53; Stringa and Monks, 'Inter-Industry Contagion', pp.1–31; V. Acharya and T. Yorulmazer, 'Cash-in-the-Market Pricing and Optimal Resolution of Bank Failures', *Bank of England Working Paper*, 328 (2007), pp.1–31. See Goodhart, Hartmann, Llewellyn, Rojas-Suarez, and Weisbrod, *Financial Regulation*; Goodhart and Illing (eds), *Financial Crises*.

environment also forced banks to pay higher interest on deposits and introduce more flexible withdrawals. This behaviour increased the risks that banks took as the chance of default was higher, the ability to recover losses was lower, and the liquidity mismatch between assets and liabilities was greater.[27] Competition had gradually built up after the abolition of exchange controls in 1979 followed by the Big Bang reforms of 1986. These had all contributed to a breakdown of the barriers that had compartmentalized the British banking system, leaving each segment of the market to be dominated by a few financial service providers whether it was in retail banking, investment banking, or the building society movement. However, it was after 1997 that competition intensified greatly with the conversion of a series of well-established building societies into banks and again after 2000/1 with the entry of the two largest Scottish banks into the crowded arena of English banking. The available evidence points to it being the fear of losing business and suffering declining profits that drove financial innovation before the crisis of 2007, not the security that came from market dominance and confidence in a government bailout in the event of a disaster. It was under these conditions that retail bankers searched for new ways to reduce their costs and expand their business. Embracing the practices of investment banking appeared to provide the solution. On the cost side there were tax advantages when lending was financed through the issue of bonds rather than raising capital and accepting deposits. Whereas the interest paid by a business on loans was tax deductible, that paid on dividends was not. This differential tax treatment was designed to allow businesses to offset the interest they paid on their borrowings against the revenue they generated, only paying tax on the profits that they made. When applied to banks it encouraged them to finance their lending not through increasing their capital from investors or collecting deposits, but by issuing bonds, as the interest they paid on these was tax deductible.[28]

In turn, the bonds that one bank issued could be bought by another with surplus funds or financed through short-term borrowing in the inter-bank money market. The result was to provide banks with access to an inexhaustible supply of low-cost finance, as long as the bonds could be sold and the inter-bank market remained accommodating, as was the case until the summer of 2007. Between 2000 and 2007 UK banks' trading books rose six times as fast as their banking books. These funds could then be lent out to eager borrowers who put them to increasingly imaginative use ranging from speculative property developments to leveraged buyouts. In essence, anything that could

---

[27] Hoggarth, Reis, and Saporta, 'Costs of Banking System Instability'.
[28] A.G. Haldane, S. Brennan, and V. Madouros, 'The Contribution of the Financial Sector: Miracle or Mirage?', *Bank of England Quarterly Bulletin*, 50 (2010), pp.1–12; R. Jenkins, 'The Capital Conundrum', *Bank of England Quarterly Bulletin*, 51 (2011), pp.1–4; Furse, 'Taking the Long View', pp.1–8.

generate an income stream became eligible for bank funding under the Originate and Distribute Model. In the process, banks became increasingly efficient at raising money through the issue of bonds and wholesale borrowing and re-lending that to borrowers. In 1997 the margin between the interest paid and that charged by UK banks was 3.7 per cent but it had fallen to 1.5 per cent by 2004. Over the same period the capital buffer maintained by UK banks to cover losses on loans and meet unexpected withdrawals fell from 21.5 per cent to 16.8 per cent. Under the Originate and Distribute Model, banks needed to hold less capital and reserves compared to the Lend and Hold one because the risks were perceived to be lower. No longer were loans held to maturity because they were now re-packaged and sold on, shifting the risks to others, or so it was believed until the crisis of 2007. Similarly, dependency upon wholesale funding was deemed to be more secure than the use of retail deposits, as these were now more mobile because of the increasing competition for savings. In the belief that wholesale funding was more permanent than retail deposits, banks could reduce the amount of capital and reserves they needed to maintain in order to meet withdrawals and redemptions. As capital and reserves generated little or no return, being kept as cash or highly liquid assets such as government debt, a reduction in its level compared to loans would greatly benefit the profits that a bank could generate. Judged from the performance of their share price British banks traditionally produced modest though steady returns but were transformed into growth businesses during of the 1990s. These gains were then lost between July 2007 and March 2009 when the equity prices of UK banks fell by over 80 per cent. Similarly, whereas the returns to shareholders in British retail banks were normally below 10 per cent when they stuck to the Lend and Hold Model they doubled or even trebled after the adoption of the Originate and Distribute Model became commonplace. Employees of banks were rewarded for the increased profits being generated through generous salaries, large bonuses, and options linked to the share price.[29]

---

[29] Gai, Kapadia, Millard, and Perez, 'Financial Innovation', pp.1–40; D. Clementi, 'Maintaining Financial Stability in a Rapidly Changing World: Some Threats and Opportunities', *Bank of England Quarterly Bulletin*, 41 (2001), pp.477; A. Clark, 'Prudential Regulation, Risk Management and Systemic Stability', *Bank of England Quarterly Bulletin*, 46 (2006), pp.464–7; Jenkinson, 'Risks to the Commercial Property Market', pp.118–21; Tucker, 'Macro, Asset Price', pp.122–30; Tucker, 'A Perspective', pp.310–16; Gieve, 'Return of the Credit Cycle', pp.91–5; Jenkinson, 'Strengthening Regimes', pp.223–7; Gieve, 'Learning from the Financial Crisis', pp.1–13; M. King, Speech: *Bank of England Quarterly Bulletin*, 48 (2008), pp.1–9; Astley, Giese, Hume, and Kubelec, 'Global Imbalances'; A.G. Haldane, 'Small Lessons from a Big Crisis', *Bank of England Quarterly Bulletin*, 49 (2009), pp.1–16; Bean, 'The Great Moderation', pp.1–32; Miles, 'Money, Banks and Quantitative Easing', pp.1–18; Alessandri and Haldane, 'Banking on the State', pp.1–30; A.G. Haldane, 'The Debt Hangover', *Bank of England Quarterly Bulletin*, 50 (2010), pp.1–19; Mora and Logan, 'Shocks to Bank Capital', pp.1–31; Haldane, Brennan, and Madouros, 'Contribution of the Financial Sector', pp.1–12; S. Aiyar, C.W. Calomiris, J. Hooley, Y. Korniyenko, and T. Wieladek, 'The International Transmission of Bank Capital Requirements: Evidence from the United Kingdom', *Bank of England Working Paper*, 497 (2014), pp.1–35.

There are those who contend that there was limited competition in British banking from 1997 to 2007, basing that judgement on the lack of new banks being formed. But such a perspective ignores the changing nature of banking in the UK in this period with the conversion of building societies into banks and the invasion of England by the two largest Scottish banks. These presented the established English banks with real competition, as these were not small challenger banks that would take years, if not decades, to build up to a scale that would allow them to actively compete for business. The ex-building societies already possessed a very extensive customer base having provided their numerous customers with both savings products and mortgage finance over many generations. It was relatively easy for them to add other banking services to what they already provided. In a similar fashion the Bank of Scotland could fuse its Scottish banking experience with the established retail network of the Halifax Bank to quickly become a major force within UK banking. The mission of RBS was simply to make the NatWest a much more profitable bank by introducing a more aggressive strategy and so justify the expectations of those investors who had financed its takeover bid.[30]

There is also abundant evidence to support the view that the UK banking system did become increasingly competitive after 1997 and that peaked in 2007. Even a narrow view of the UK financial system in 2007 identified seventeen domestic and 240 overseas banks actively competing for business, while a wider interpretation could push the number up to 611. There were also numerous non-bank lenders that occupied specific niches within the market, and they were, collectively, of an equal size to the banking sector. The switch from a Lend and Hold Model to the Originate and Distribute one meant that it was no longer necessary to have an extensive branch network to access savings as these could be tapped either in the wholesale market or via the Internet. This switch undermined the economies of scale that banks with extensive branch networks possessed as that placed them in direct contact with both savers and borrowers. Such banks were in a position to monitor and anticipate the actions of their customers which was of major importance when operating on the basis of retail deposits subject to immediate withdrawal and making short-term loans to business and individual customers on a regular basis, and always subject to default. When that responsibility to either the provider or borrower of funds was removed, it became possible for many different financial service firms to provide banking services.[31] As David Miles concluded,

---

[30] Haldane, 'On Being the Right Size', pp.1–18; Haldane, Speech: 'A Leaf Being Turned', pp.1–11.

[31] M. King, 'Prospects for the City: In or Out of EMU', *Bank of England Quarterly Bulletin*, 37 (1997), p.431; S. Senior and R. Westwood, 'The External Balance Sheet of the United Kingdom: Implications for Financial Stability?', *Bank of England Quarterly Bulletin*, 40 (2000), p.361; Tucker, 'Money and Credit', pp.96–106; Jenkinson, 'Strengthening Regimes', pp.223–7; Haldane,

'Banks specialize in assessing and monitoring the credit-worthiness of potential borrowers and there are substantial economies of scale to that.'[32]

As early as 2000, growing competition was being reported by those who studied the UK banking environment, with its consequences being clearly explained. P.J.N. Sinclair wrote, 'More banks imply more competition but also... greater risks of financial fragility. The... more banks there are, the harder it is for them to reach an understanding to limit competition... a troubled bank, desperate to survive if it possibly can, will be tempted to take great risks. Failure is an awful prospect, but it really makes no difference how large the bank's debts are in the event of failure... A large gamble, if successful, could pull the bank off the rocks towards which it may be heading.' But a large failure will have much greater social consequences.... The key point here is not just that more banks and greater competition raise the chance that one or more banks might slip into insolvency, but, still more important, that the risk of this is increased because of the greater incentive to take a gamble in this region. Free bet incentives also qualify the case for deposit insurance: fully insured depositors need no longer worry about where they lodge their funds, so riskier banks prosper at the expense of the taxpayers or shareholders of safer banks, and each bank is itself encouraged to take on more risk too.' Despite warning of the risks that competition created there was also a reluctance to intervene to limit it. 'A banking system with fewer banks may be a safer one. Yet safety is not everything. Competition brings undoubted benefits. Barriers to entry, official or natural, can act as a screen behind which collusion, inefficiency, and unhealthy lending practices flourish.... Fewer well-padded banks make for a safer, but growth-stifling financial environment. The faster growth that comes from keener competition among banks makes for a bumpier ride.'[33]

The degree of competition continued to intensify driven by the aggressive behaviour of the demutualized building societies and the attempts by the two Scottish banks to build on their English operations acquired through the

---

'Credit Is Trust', pp.1–21; S. Aiyar, 'How Did the Crisis in International Funding Markets Affect Bank Lending: Balance Sheet Evidence from the United Kingdom', *Bank of England Working Paper*, 424 (2011), pp.1–34; K. Anand, P. Gai, S. Kapadia, S. Brennan, and M. Willison, 'A Network Model of Financial System Resilience', *Bank of England Working Paper*, 458 (2012), pp.1–40; Rose and Wieladek, 'Too Big to Fail', pp.1–25; P. Danisewicz, D. Rheinhart, and R. Sowerbutts, 'On a Tight Leash: Does Organisational Structure Matter for Macroprudential Spillovers?', *Bank of England Working Paper*, 524 (2015), pp.1–30; P. Tucker, 'The Repertoire of Official Sector Interventions in the Financial System: Last Resort Lending, Market Making, and Capital', *Bank of England Quarterly Bulletin*, 49 (2009), pp.1–4; Sir Jon Cunliffe (member of the MPC, the FPC and the PRA), Speech: 'The Role of the Leverage Ratio and the Need to Monitor Risks outside the Regulated Banking Sector', 17 July 2014, pp.1–10; Forbes (MPC), Speech: 'Financial "Deglobalization"', pp.1–27.

[32] D. Miles, 'The Future Financial Landscape', *Bank of England Quarterly Bulletin*, 49 (2009), pp.1–17 (p.9). For a contrary view see Haldane, 'The $100 Billion Question', pp.1–27 and Haldane, Brennan, and Madouros, 'Contribution of the Financial Sector', pp.1–12.

[33] P.J.N. Sinclair, 'Central Banks and Financial Stability', *Bank of England Quarterly Bulletin*, 40 (2000), pp.385–6.

takeover of NatWest and Halifax. As banks grew in confidence that their strategies were both safe and profitable they competed with each other for customers by offering ever more generous terms. In the immediate wake of the crisis it was the competitive behaviour of one bank, Northern Rock, that was regarded as having destabilized the entire banking system. However, as time passed and the full picture emerged, it became obvious that the entire financial sector had responded to the same competitive pressures in the same way, and that meant a growing reliance upon the Originate and Distribute Model to finance lending on ever more generous terms to customers lacking adequate collateral.[34] According to Andrew Bailey of the Bank of England, the level of competition that developed between 1997 and 2007 was both 'reckless' and 'suicidal'.[35] By October 2012, Paul Tucker, Deputy Governor of the Bank of England, was able to sum up what had been taking place between 1997 and 2007: 'That excesses occurred in the run-up to the current crisis is not remotely in doubt. As leverage increased, asset prices rose, increasing net worth and so inducing more balance sheet expansion. The buoyancy in markets gave intermediaries the confidence to lend secured on wider classes of securities—temporarily enhancing day-to-day liquidity. Facing depressed returns from their core business of providing liquidity to customers, banks sought to sustain high headline returns by resorting to ever more leverage and maturity transformation. In other words, leverage fed upon itself.'[36]

A particular area of note was the increasingly competitive nature of the market for mortgages as ex-building societies, the remaining building societies, established banks, and new entrants all fought for market share. A total of 15 million households shared windfalls worth £37 billion when the likes of the Halifax, Northern Rock, and Bradford and Bingley were demutualized in 1997. The shares they received were then sold on to investors who pressured management to deliver higher returns by expanding the business done by these newly emerging banks. They achieved that by encouraging their existing customers to re-mortgage their homes, to capture the gains generated by rising property values, and use the proceeds to finance home improvements and general consumption. The result was a large rise in the UK household debt-to-income ratios as families borrowed to finance consumption in response

---

[34] Gondat-Laralde and Nier, 'The Economics of Retail Banking', p.154; Gieve, 'Pricing for Perfection', pp.112-17; Sir John Gieve, 'Economic Prospects and Policy Challenge', *Bank of England Quarterly Bulletin*, 49 (2009), pp.1-11; C. Bean, 'The UK Economy after the Crisis: Monetary Policy when It Is not so NICE', *Bank of England Quarterly Bulletin*, 50 (2010), pp.1-13; Haldane, Brennan, and Madouros, 'Contribution of the Financial Sector', pp.1-12; D. Miles, 'Central Bank Asset Purchases and Financial Markets', *Bank of England Quarterly Bulletin*, 54 (2014), pp.1-12.

[35] A. Bailey (Director of UK Banks and Building Societies), Speech: 'Promoting a Prudent and Stable Financial System', 24 November 2011, pp.1-7.

[36] Tucker, 'Competition, the Pressure for Returns', pp.1-11.

to the increasing ability to do so, using their homes as collateral. This was a major change from the past. In the era when housing finance was dominated by mutual building societies, which had a strong savings ethos, it was made difficult for homeowners to access the equity in their house. That position changed with the conversion of building societies from mutual organizations, owned by their members, to profit-orientated banks responsive to the demands of shareholders. With the traditional twenty-five-year mortgage the increasing equity that a homeowner possessed as the house price rose was locked up in the property until the loan was repaid. In contrast, under the new arrangements involving short-term renewable mortgages, homeowners could regularly capitalize on the increasing value of the property and even anticipate future gains if the loan-to-value ratio was greater than 100 per cent. This had the effect of bringing forward consumption as it could be financed through borrowing based on rising property values, creating a credit bubble in the process. Between 1997 and 2007 withdrawals of equity increased faster than additions. Homeowners were using property as collateral for increased borrowing either through taking on greater debt burdens when purchasing a house or using an existing property as collateral for further borrowing. Society as a whole was becoming increasingly leveraged prior to the financial crisis. By 2003 nearly 50 per cent of mortgage advances involved re-mortgaging. In 2007 an estimated 50 per cent of those who took out mortgages in the UK had little or no proof of their income though loans of 90–95 per cent of the value of the property, and even higher, had become common. As a result the amount of business being generated by a bank through the loans it made could be greatly expanded. Even though house prices continued to rise strongly, the low interest rates being charged by the banks and the generous loan-to-value ratios applied, underpinned a substantial increase in borrowing. The difference between the cost of funds to a lender and the interest they charged a mortgage borrower declined fairly steadily between 2000 and the onset of the crisis in 2007, from around 2/2.5 per cent at the end of the 1990s to 1.5 per cent. What this situation reflected was the intensity of the competition between banks and the belief that the switch from Lend and Hold to Originate and Distribute reduced risk. It was not only owner-occupiers who were in receipt of the increased lending made available by banks because there was also an explosion in the buy-to-rent market. Those buying houses for rent could offset the interest they paid on their mortgages against the revenue generated from the rents and the costs of maintaining the property giving them an advantage over owner-occupiers when it came to bidding for property in areas with a high rental demand. Between 2000 and 2007 the stock of mortgage debt relative to GDP rose by 27 per cent.[37]

---

[37] M. Davey, 'Mortgage Equity Withdrawal and Consumption', *Bank of England Quarterly Bulletin*, 41 (2001), pp.101–3; K. Aoki, J. Proudman, and G. Vlieghe, 'Why House Prices Matter', *Bank of England Quarterly Bulletin*, 41 (2001), pp.460–4; P. Tucker, 'Credit Conditions and

A similar situation developed with companies as banks competed to provide them with additional finance. Confidence about future profitability encouraged companies to borrow the funds that banks were eager to lend them. From about 1996 onwards companies increased the amount they were borrowing from banks in response to the abundant supply, either supplementing internal sources of finance or replacing more expensive capital in the form of shares. It was being reported that companies of all sizes and types were receiving approaches from banks offering them finance and they were in the position of being able to shop around for the best deal. Not just large companies but small and medium-sized ones found they could access finance much more readily than in the past, whether through the willingness of banks to continually rollover short-term loans or by re-packing corporate debt as securities. Between 2002 and 2007 the securitization market in the UK trebled, with banks and near-banks acting as both issuers and purchasers.[38]

BEFORE THE CRISIS

Having identified excessive competition as the prime cause for the British financial crisis of 2007/8 the next question that arises is why the regulatory authorities did not intervene to prevent it reaching a stage that endangered the banking system. Before the crisis there were signs that banks were taking excessive risks and this could endanger their survival. However, those

Monetary Policy', *Bank of England Quarterly Bulletin*, 44 (2004), p.371; K. Barker (member of MPC), 'The Housing Market and the Wider Economy', *Bank of England Quarterly Bulletin*, 45 (2005), p.111; T. Besley (member of MPC), 'Financial Markets and Household Consumption', *Bank of England Quarterly Bulletin*, 48 (2008), pp.107-11; Miles, 'Money, Banks and Quantitative Easing', pp.1-18; V. Bell and C. Young, 'Understanding the Weakness of Bank Lending', *Bank of England Quarterly Bulletin*, 50 (2010), pp.314-17; Reinold, 'Housing Equity Withdrawal', pp.129-32; Miles, 'Mortgages and Housing', pp.1-12; Miles, 'Mortgages, Housing and Monetary Policy', pp.1-18; D. Miles (member of MPC), Speech: 'Housing, Leverage and Stability in the Wider Economy', 14 November 2013, pp.1-20; A. Haldane, Speech: 'The Commercial Property Forum Twenty Years On', 18 December 2013, pp.1-7.

[38] S. Hall, 'Financial Effects on Corporate Investment in UK Business Cycles', *Bank of England Quarterly Bulletin*, 41 (2001), pp.452-8; A. Kearns and J. Young, 'Provision of Finance to Smaller Quoted Companies: Some Evidence from Survey Responses and Liaison Meetings', *Bank of England Quarterly Bulletin*, 42 (2002), pp.26-32; P. Brierley and M. Young, 'The Financing of Smaller Quoted Companies: A Survey', *Bank of England Quarterly Bulletin*, 44 (2004), pp.160-8; Tucker, 'Macro, Asset Price', pp.122-30; Jenkinson and Manning, 'Promoting Financial System Resilience', pp.453-60; Lomax, 'Current Monetary Policy Issues', pp.570-3; Haldane, 'Debt Hangover', pp.1-19; A.G. Haldane, 'Haircuts', *Bank of England Quarterly Bulletin*, 51 (2011), pp.1-6; A.S. Pose (member of MOC), Speech: 'Deepen and Diversify UK Financial Infrastructure to Enable Small Business Growth', February 2012, pp.1-15; B. Broadbent (member of MPC), Speech: 'Costly Capital and the Risk of Rare Disasters', 28 May 2012, pp.1-13.

expressing such concerns stopped short of advocating intervention, other than as a long-term objective.[39] Only in the wake of the crisis was there an acceptance that the risks within the banking system had been building up for some time and that the consequences should have been foreseen.[40] Some did claim to be wise after the event, such as Sir John Gieve, Deputy Governor for Bank Stability at the Bank of England, and who therefore blamed those who failed to heed his warnings. However, a careful reading of his statements made before the crisis suggests that, despite expressing concern, no immediate intervention was recommended. As he noted in December 2006, 'Our view remains that near-term risks to UK financial stability are low.'[41] Such a view was entirely understandable because of the general economic climate. In the decade leading up to the crisis of 2007 the British economy had prospered. Both inflation and unemployment remained relatively low while a sustained rate of economic growth was maintained, for which the Labour government took credit, particularly Gordon Brown as Chancellor of the Exchequer and then Prime Minister.[42] Economists took a less political stance pointing to the benign economic conditions worldwide and the introduction of inflation targeting by the previous Conservative government in 1992. 'By historical standards, the performance of the UK economy under inflation targeting has been unique. The size of business-cycle frequency fluctuations has been to date the lowest in recorded history: the unemployment-inflation trade-off displays the greatest stability ever: and the high-inflation persistence typical of the period between 1972 and 1992 has entirely vanished.'[43] Even the collapse of the speculative 'dotcom' boom had been overcome without any associated bank failures. Against this background of economic, monetary, and financial stability combined with rising prosperity, any immediate action to curb the excesses of the banking system appeared unjustified though some kind of correction in the longer-term was deemed necessary. One effect of intervention would be to reduce bank lending and so lower the rate of economic growth and even reverse it, which was an outcome few desired.[44] This thinking

---

[39] D. Alkman and G. Vlieghe, 'How Much Does Bank Capital Matter?', *Bank of England Quarterly Bulletin*, 44 (2004), p.56; Jenkinson, 'Risks to the Commercial Property Market', pp.118–21; Tucker, 'Macro, Asset Price', pp.122–30; R. Lomax, 'The MPC Comes of Age', *Bank of England Quarterly Bulletin*, 46 (2006), pp.106–11; Tucker, 'A Perspective', pp.310–16; Jenkinson and Manning, 'Promoting Financial System Resilience, pp.453–60.
[40] Jenkinson, 'Strengthening Regimes', pp.223–7.
[41] Gieve, 'Pricing for Perfection', pp.112–17; Gieve, 'Impact of the Financial Market Disruption', pp.85–90; Gieve, 'Rebuilding Confidence', pp.1–9.
[42] See the successive Budget speeches as archived on the UK Treasury website.
[43] L. Benati, 'Inflation-targeting Framework from an Historical Perspective', *Bank of England Quarterly Bulletin*, 45 (2005), pp.160–7. See Bank of England, 'The Monetary Policy Committee of the Bank of England: Ten Years On', *Bank of England Quarterly Bulletin*, 47 (2007), pp.24–36.
[44] L. Benati, 'Evolving Post-World War II UK Economic Performance', *Bank of England Working Paper*, 232 (2004); E. George, 'Britain and the Euro', *Bank of England Quarterly Bulletin*, 40 (2000); Fisher and Gai, 'Financial Stability', pp.444–7.

can be seen in a reflective piece by Sir John Gieve in a speech delivered on 17th January 2008: 'Over the past fifteen years the UK economy has experienced the most stable macroeconomic conditions on record with steady economic growth, low inflation and a declining trend in unemployment. For the most part the underlying balance sheet position of households and firms is robust and most indicators of financial fragility such as mortgage arrears, repossessions, and corporate insolvencies are at low levels.'[45]

Supporting this non-interventionist stance was a widely held belief that the sophisticated financial models that were now applied to bank lending had eliminated most risks. In the past, banks relied on bankers with practical training, considerable experience, and embedded in the community when deciding whether to make loans or refuse them, 'One of the key functions of banks is the assessment of credit risk based on a good knowledge of borrowers.'[46] When making loans these bank employees were however being increasingly replaced by graduates trained in economics who employed the latest mathematical models run on ever more powerful computers to estimate the probability of default. Instead of judging each loan on a case-by-case basis, the collective risk was scientifically measured, entered into a model, and a decision quickly taken. In this new regime the practical banker was relegated to a sales role or dispensed with, especially as electronic systems replaced the need for face-to-face contact. Unfortunately, the training these economists had received was very theoretical and involved little understanding of the role played by a bank within a financial system. The models being applied at both the level of the individual bank and in the Treasury, Bank of England, and the Financial Services Authority were based on the assumption of equilibrium and so discounted the probability of extreme events, such as financial crises. It is extremely difficult to model accurately the likelihood of infrequent high-impact events for which there are few precedents. Instead, it was simpler to leave them out of the model so creating a false impression of stability. However, it was on these models that banks increasingly relied when making their business decisions as well as those regulating their behaviour.[47] As

---

[45] Gieve, 'Impact of the Financial Market Disruption', pp.85-90.
[46] Clark, 'Prudential Regulation', pp.464-7.
[47] M. King, 'No Money, No Inflation: The Role of Money in the Economy', *Bank of England Quarterly Bulletin*, 42 (2002); Sir John Gieve, 'Hedge Funds and Financial Stability', *Bank of England Quarterly Bulletin*, 46 (2006); Jenkinson and Manning, 'Promoting Financial System Resilience', pp.453-60; Sir John Gieve, Speech: 'Seven Lessons From the Last Three Years', pp.1-22; Bean, 'The Great Moderation', pp.1-32; D. Aikman, P. Barrett, S. Kapadia, M. King, J. Proudman, T. Taylor, I. de Weymarn, and T. Tates, Paper: 'Uncertainty in Macroeconomic Policy Making: Art or Science?', 22 March 2010, pp.1-24; C. Bean, M. Paustian, A. Penalver, and T. Taylor (all Bank of England Staff): Paper: 'Monetary Policy after the Fall', 28 August 2010, pp.1-65; Tucker, 'Banking in a Market Economy', pp.15-32; Bean, 'Central Banking', pp.1-18.

Andrew Haldane observed, after the crisis, 'The model was wrong.'[48] It was not just one model that was wrong but all of them as none could cope with the unexpected. That was what the practical banker was capable of doing, using training and experience.

Nevertheless, even if there had been a willingness to intervene so as to pre-empt the build-up of excessive risk within the banking system there was a difficulty in knowing where the initiative would come from and where the responsibility would lie. The cause of this doubt was the new regulatory structure established by the incoming Labour government in 1997/8. This new structure was a response to the blurring of the distinctions between those providing financial services that had taken place since 1986. Instead of having a regulator for each type of financial services provider the idea was to combine them into one single authority. This was a policy recommendation from the Labour party, and they won the 1997 General Election. Anticipating their victory, Eddie George, Governor of the Bank of England, and his Deputy, Howard Davies, had mounted a pre-emptive strike that focused on the unique status of banks compared to all other businesses within the financial sector. This was not simply based on special pleading by the Bank of England, which was responsible for banking supervision, but reflected his intimate knowledge of the liquidity risks run by banks. Specifically he stressed that banks could fail even when solvent and this could have devastating consequences for the economy because of their central role in the payments system.[49] However, there was a general belief that the failure of a major British bank was highly unlikely, and certainly not one whose collapse would endanger the payments system.[50] As a result, these warnings were ignored and a complete re-structuring of banking supervision in the UK took place over the course of 1997/8.

Providing an insight into the thinking behind the new regulatory regime are the comments in a book produced by Ed Balls and Gus O' Donnell in 2002, under the auspices of Gordon Brown and the Treasury. This was a celebratory account though a careful reading produces a number of serious reservations about what, as yet, remained an unproven regime. The reasons for the need to change the regulatory regime were made clear. They were to do with the increasing complexity of financial products, the systemic risks posed by banks because of their pivotal role in the payments system, and the role played by deposit insurance in reducing systemic risk but creating a moral hazard as individuals would ignore the safety of individual institutions. To cope with the

---

[48] A.G. Haldane, Speech: 'Why Banks Failed the Stress Test', 13 February 2009, pp.1-23.
[49] George, 'Some Thoughts on Financial Regulation', pp.213-16; Davies, 'Financial Regulation', pp.107-10; E. George, 'Are Banks Still Special?', pp.114-18, E. George, 'International Regulatory Structure: A UK Perspective', 37 (1997), pp.214-20.
[50] Logan, 'The United Kingdom's Small Banks' Crisis', pp.1-30; Hoggarth, Reidhill, and Sinclair, 'On the Resolution of Banking Crises', pp.1-30.

blurring of the distinctions between the various participants in the financial system a single regulator was created. This left the FSA with responsibility for 600 separate banks along with seventy building societies, 270 friendly societies, 650 credit unions and 850 insurance companies. If that was not sufficient, it was also expected to oversee around 6,000 investment businesses. It was recognized that this was a daunting task for a single regulator, and could cause it problems, but these warnings were ignored. Also, in the four objectives set for the FSA, the explicit need to ensure the stability of the banking system was not included, though warnings were issued that a systemic crisis was always a possibility. Instead the FSA was given rather vague guidelines about maintaining market confidence in the UK financial system, promoting public awareness of the importance of UK financial services; protecting consumers and reducing financial crime. Rather than prioritizing the stability of the banking system, the agenda that the FSA was to follow was increasingly driven by the investigation into UK banking conducted in 1999 that focused on the need to promote competition. However, the FSA was concerned that 'in relation to the soundness of banks, a conflict could arise between promoting market confidence and promoting competition.' There was an inherent conflict of interest in the new regulatory structure between intervening in the banking system to promote either stability or competition. By 2002 the focus on competition had won. In contrast to the FSA, under the new regulatory structure the Bank of England was given a direct mandate to focus on monetary policy, providing the government with whatever assistance it required. A central bank was defined as 'The institution responsible for the conduct of monetary policy such as the Bank of England.'[51]

Once passed by Parliament, the Act setting up the FSA came into force on 1st June 1998. Central to the Act was a Memorandum of Understanding between HM Treasury, the Bank of England, and the FSA. This provided a framework for co-operation between all three in the field of financial stability. Other than that each had its own sphere. The UK Treasury was responsible for setting monetary and economic policy and so created the framework within which the entire financial sector operated. The FSA was given responsibility for supervising the activities of those who operated within the UK financial sector ranging from the largest UK banks, building societies, and insurance companies to the numerous independent financial advisors scattered across the country. The Bank of England, which had been given operational independence in May 1997, was allowed to retain control over the functioning of the payments system but its main responsibility was operational control over monetary policy. At the time, the new regulatory system was regarded as an

---

[51] E. Balls and G. O'Donnell (eds), *Reforming Britain's Economic and Financial Policy: Towards Greater Economic Stability* (London: Palgrave, 2002): see chapters 6, 7, and 17 in particular.

experiment being 'an extraordinarily bold and radical step, not attempted on anything like this scale in any other developed financial centre.'[52]

Although bank supervision had been transferred to the FSA, the 1998 Act gave the Bank of England a second Deputy Governor whose responsibility was maintaining financial stability. Unlike the responsibility the Bank of England possessed for monetary policy, which was accompanied by the authority to set interest rates, for maintaining financial stability it was given no equivalent powers. What this new regulatory structure meant for banking was to divide supervision between the Bank of England and the FSA and to give a role for the UK Treasury. What the change meant in practice for the banking system was that the experience of banking supervision, accumulated by the Bank of England over many years through trial and error, was lost. The staff that remained at the Bank of England lost direct contact with the banking system while those who joined the Financial Services Authority engaged in the general supervision of financial services. It was only a matter of time before the Bank of England and the FSA followed different paths as once close colleagues pursued separate careers, and new members of staff were recruited, leaving each organization to develop its own agenda. Making financial stability a tripartite responsibility meant that none took ownership of it because for each the priority lay elsewhere. This can be seen in terms of the important question of liquidity. The FSA was given responsibility for ensuring that the banking system possessed adequate liquidity on a day-to-day basis. The Bank of England was left with its role of lender of last resort as only it could create new money in the form of UK£s. Finally, the Treasury was responsible for authorizing the use of public money in any liquidity support operation. The split had the effect of depriving the Bank of England of the ability to constantly monitor banks, and thus spot emerging liquidity problems, without relocating it anywhere else. What was omitted when setting up the new supervisory structure for financial services in the UK was the importance of liquidity. The focus was all on solvency and ignored the unique features of banks. What appeared to have been important to the government in designing the new regulatory structure was not the stability of the banking system but devolving the execution of monetary policy to an independent agency and so removing it from the political arena, especially with a Labour government that was not trusted by the City.[53]

---

[52] P. Rogers, 'Changes at the Bank of England', *Bank of England Quarterly Bulletin*, 37 (1997), pp.240–2; Bank of England, 'Reforms to the UK Monetary Policy Framework and Financial Services Regulation', *Bank of England Quarterly Bulletin*, 37 (1997), p.316; Bank of England, 'The Bank of England Act', *Bank of England Quarterly Bulletin*, 38 (1998), pp.93–9; E. George, 'The New Lady of Threadneedle Street', *Bank of England Quarterly Bulletin*, 38 (1998), pp.173–7; E. George, 'Central Bank Independence', *Bank of England Quarterly Bulletin*, 48 (1998), pp.405–7.

[53] Sinclair, 'Central Banks', pp.383–9; Clementi, 'Maintaining Financial Stability', pp.475–8; A. Bailey (Executive Director for Banking Services and Chief Cashier), Speech: 'The Financial

For the UK Treasury, the priority was the public finances, the maintenance of a healthy economy and pleasing their political masters, and so they left the detail of how financial stability was achieved and maintained to the FSA and the Bank of England. Under the Memorandum of Understanding formulated in 1997/8 the UK Treasury only had a role to play in the event of a crisis and then only as part of a tripartite grouping including the Bank of England and the FSA. Though the Treasury was responsible, along with the other branches of government, for creating the environment that fuelled the credit boom preceding the crisis, it did not have any direct authority over the banking system, including powers of intervention in the face of emerging risks. That authority rested jointly with the Bank of England and the FSA. Under the arrangements established in 1997/8 the Bank of England was responsible for the overall stability of the financial system, including the banks. In contrast, the FSA had responsibility for the individual businesses within the financial sector. As it was recognized that a crisis within the financial sector could be caused through the difficulties of a single unit, if it was large enough, or a group of smaller units, the Bank of England and the FSA were expected to work closely together. For that reason, Howard Davies, Deputy Governor at the Bank of England, was appointed the first head of the FSA. For those reasons the failure to intervene must focus on why neither the Bank of England nor the FSA took the initiative either alone or together.[54]

For the FSA, the explanation is not difficult to discover. Under the new arrangements the FSA had been given an impossible task. Its remit covered the entire UK financial sector whether it was an individual providing financial advice or selling insurance in provincial towns to the largest City banks with thousands of employees and global operations. The FSA was expected to supervise all these in the same way with the result that the unique predicament of banks, with their constant concern about liquidity, were not in position to receive specialist attention. In the case of banks, the FSA had only partial responsibility as their wholesale operations came under the jurisdiction of the Bank of England. The preservation of the payments system was considered to be of such key importance that the Bank of England was left with its management and supervision. In addition, the Bank of England was also left with responsibility for the City of London as a financial centre with its core markets for money, foreign exchange, and derivatives. What this reflected was a deeper divide in responsibility between the Bank of England and the FSA. The former

Crisis Reform Agenda', 13 July 2010, pp.1–9; Sir David Lees and J. Footman, 'The Court of the Bank of England', *Bank of England Quarterly Bulletin*, 54 (2014), pp.30–1.

[54] Sir John Gieve, 'Financial System Risks in the United Kingdom: Issues and Challenges', *Bank of England Quarterly Bulletin*, 46 (2006), pp.337–41; Gieve, 'Practical Issues', pp.452–4; Jenkinson, 'Risks to the Commercial Property Market', pp.118–21; R. Sharp (member of FPC), Speech: 'The Financial Policy Committee of the Bank of England: An Experiment in Macroprudential Management—the View of an External Member', 4 June 2014, pp.1–12.

was in charge of wholesale activity, within which banks dealt with each other at home and abroad, while the FSA was put in control of the retail side of the business undertaken in the financial sector, which was predominantly domestic. Even for the largest UK banks, most of their UK-based business was of a domestic nature. What this did was to make the FSA very consumer-orientated. Its role was to protect the retail purchaser of financial products whether it was those being sold insurance, pensions, mortgages, or provided with personal and business loans. This remit covered over 25,000 separate providers of financial services, making the small number of banks the least of the FSA's concerns as consumers appeared to be relatively content with the services with which they were provided at the retail level, as the banks were long-established and well-run businesses with mechanisms for handling complaints and the resources to provide compensation in the event of losses that were their responsibility. It was not that the FSA lacked both trained staff and the ability to supervise the banking system, rather that its focus was the interests of the consumer of financial services not the stability of the provider.[55]

The central failing of the FSA was that it did not ensure that banks were adequately prepared for a liquidity crisis rather than a solvency one, even though it was aware that it was the former that usually led to the latter. However, at the time the FSA was only following current orthodoxy. Operating under the assumption that a run on a British bank, and certainly one of any size, was highly unlikely, the need to maintain high levels of liquidity was not considered necessary. There was a widely held belief that the management of British banks could be relied on to ensure that they not only remained solvent at all times, but also possessed adequate levels of liquidity. If this was not the case, other banks would soon be aware, which would alert the FSA, leading it to quickly intervene. No such signals were received even in the case of the Northern Rock Bank, the first one to fail in the crisis of 2007. A major reason for the absence of such signals was the use of international standards setting the level of assets that a bank was expected to maintain against liabilities. Only in retrospect did it emerge how inadequate these capital ratios were, especially when it came to liquidity rather than solvency. What this reflected was the treatment of banks as simply another form of business, with little regard for their unique vulnerability to a liquidity crisis. What the FSA was not in a position to cope with, because of its consumer-orientated focus, was the degree to which market pressures were encouraging banks to interpret

---

[55] M. Burnett and M. Manning, 'Financial Stability and the United Kingdom's External Balance Sheet', *Bank of England Quarterly Bulletin*, 43 (2003), pp.463-74; Clark, 'Prudential Regulation', pp.464-7; A. Bailey (Executive Director), Speech: 'The Supervisory Approach of the Prudential Regulation Authority', 19 May 2011, pp.1-8; H. Sands (Chief Executive, PRA), Speech, 19 May 2011, pp.1-4; A.G. Haldane and V. Madouros, Speech: 'The Dog and the Frisbee', 31 August 2012, pp.1-36; Sharp, Speech: 'The Financial Policy Committee', pp.1-12.

the rules governing capital ratios in such a way that they maintained the lowest level of liquidity possible as that meant that they had more funds to lend to borrowers and so could generate higher profits and increase pay and bonus levels.[56]

The FSA also faced the problem that the UK branches of banks headquartered abroad were not subject to its prudential regulation unlike domestically headquartered banks and resident foreign subsidiaries, but were regulated by their home-country regulatory authorities. There was also the added difficulty that, as the FSA was focused on the UK consumer it was hardly in a position to supervise the operations of banks that were both international and heavily engaged in complex wholesale markets. Cross-border lending accounted for a substantial 26 per cent of the total lending of UK-owned banks and foreign subsidiaries resident in the UK in 2006 and the average bank had cross-border credit outstanding in sixty-five countries. As a result, the FSA could do little more than concentrate on systems, processes, and structures rather than the business risks that each bank was running, such as that relating to the growth of lending or the quality of loans being made. For that reason the FSA was unaware of the growing vulnerabilities within the banking system especially at the bank-specific level, as with Northern Rock.[57]

With the FSA focusing on consumer protection only, the Bank of England remained as the one authority that could have intervened to reduce the risks being run by the banking system. The maintenance of financial stability was one of its core responsibilities. Though deprived of banking supervision it did retain a watching brief, receiving regular confidential updates from all the banks detailing their capital position. Every UK-resident bank had to file confidential quarterly returns with the Bank of England, containing detailed balance sheet data. In addition the Bank of England collected data for the Bank for International Settlements on the aggregate external liabilities of all UK-resident banks. The resulting data set provided the staff at the Bank of England with a complete balance sheet for every institution in the British banking sector. This information was used in aggregate by the Bank of

---

[56] P. Jackson, 'Bank Capital Standards: The New Basel Accord', *Bank of England Quarterly Bulletin*, 40 (2000), pp.55–62; Jenkinson, Speech: 'Containing System-Wide Liquidity Risks', pp.1–23; M. King, Speech: 20 October 2009, pp.1–10; Bailey, Speech: 'The Financial Crisis Reform Agenda', pp.1–9; M. King, Speech: 'Banking: from Bagehot to Basel and Back Again', 25 October 2010, pp.1–25; A. Bailey, Speech: 'Capital Discipline', 9 January 2011, pp.1–22; H. Sands, Speech: 19 May 2011, pp.1–4; M. Cohrs (member of MPC), Speech: 'Crisis and Crash: Lessons for Regulation', 23 March 2012, pp.1–11; P. Tucker, S. Hall, and A. Pattani, 'Macroprudential Policy at the Bank of England', *Bank of England Quarterly Bulletin*, 53 (2013), p.200; P. Tucker, Speech: 'The Reform of International Banking: Some Remaining Challenges', pp.1–7; A.G. Haldane, Speech: 'Managing Global Finance as a System', 29 October 2014, pp.1–27.

[57] S. Aiyar, C.W. Calomiris, and T. Wieladek, 'Does Macropru Leak? Evidence from a UK Policy Experiment', *Bank of England Working Paper*, 445 (2012), pp.1–44; Aiyar, Calomiris, Hooley, Korniyenko, and Wieladek, 'International Transmission', pp.1–35.

England to inform those taking decisions regarding the setting of interest rates as part of its monetary policy role. The Bank of England had sufficient information to inform itself about what was happening in the UK. Thus, it was not a lack of information that made intervention impossible but more a failure to either fully recognize the implications of what was taking place or accept that the Bank had a responsibility to intervene, given the changes that had taken place with the creation of the Financial Services Authority. It shared this information with the Financial Services Authority for the purposes of bank regulation, having used it in the past to set bank-specific capital ratios. In 2001 that task was handed over to the FSA.[58]

What this transfer of responsibility reflected was the low priority given by the Bank of England to its banking role, including the maintenance of financial stability, in contrast to its monetary policy role. This balance towards monetary policy and away from banking became increasingly pronounced after 2003, when Mervyn King, a monetary economist, replaced Eddie George, a practical banker, as Governor. The Bank of England became something akin to a monetary policy institute staffed by economists rather than the banker's bank or even the government's bank that it had long been. There appeared to be an ingrained belief that if prices could be stabilized through the setting of interest rates then financial stability would be the result, with the stability of individual firms being left to a separate regulatory authority. The crisis showed that this was not the case. There is also the possibility that the policies followed may have fostered over-confidence leading to a speculative bubble while the economic models employed ignored the risks inherent in financial institutions. Such a view did appear to be borne out by results that came from the policy of inflation targeting begun in 1992. With the independence given to the Bank of England in 1997, combined with the loss of banking supervision, operational control over monetary policy increasingly became the main focus of the Bank of England. Compared to the dull but essential routine of maintaining the payments system, the setting of interest rates by the Monetary Policy Committee attracted widespread public attention, putting the Bank and its Governor in the media spotlight. Though doubts crept in that control over interest rates was not sufficient to insulate the economy from financial turbulence the implementation of monetary policy remained central to the agenda pursued by the Bank right up to the financial crisis of 2007. Even after the crisis Mervyn King, as the Governor of the Bank, was unwilling for it to return to the field of banking supervision, believing that this responsibility should remain with the FSA. This suggests that the Bank, as he had shaped it, was exclusively focused on the implementation of monetary policy on behalf of the

---

[58] Aiyar, 'How Did the Crisis', pp.1–34; Rose and Wieladek, 'Too Big to Fail', pp.1–25; J. Bridges, D. Gregory, M. Nielsen, S. Pezzinia, A. Radia, and M. Spaltro, 'The Impact of Capital Requirements on Bank Lending', *Bank of England Working Paper*, 486 (2014), pp.1–35.

UK government, and should leave banking supervision to others, as it would distract it from this central purpose. This was despite the fact that evidence was emerging, dating from even before the crisis, that such a single-minded approach might even have contributed to the property asset bubble that lay at the centre of the banking industry's problems, through fostering an environment of low interest rates and low inflation.[59] Such was the conclusion that Donald Kohn, an external member of the newly formed Financial Policy Committee at the Bank of England, reached in November 2013. Before the crisis there was no 'entity with both the responsibility and the authority to do something about systemic risks'. The absence of such a body meant that a serious void existed in the UK's regime for regulating the financial system. The success achieved through the Bank of England's stewardship of monetary policy resulted in a damping of inflation and the suppression of business cycles prior to the crisis, which encouraged a complacency regarding financial stability. His verdict was that, 'When the downturn came, the lack of preparation, including the build-up of leverage and the greater reliance on short-term wholesale funding to finance long-term assets meant that the financial sector was greatly exposed to unexpected developments and its problems made the economic cycle much worse.'[60]

It was only as the Mervyn King regime ended that those located in the Bank of England's banking division came to the fore. What this represented was the deep division that had existed within the Bank between those who saw it as a bank and those who saw it as the agency implementing the government's monetary policy. This had long existed but the latter triumphed over the former with the creation of the FSA in 1997, and their triumph was reflected in the appointment of Mervyn King as Deputy Governor and then to succeed Eddie George, as Governor. As Andrew Bailey, Executive Director for Banking Services and Chief Cashier, observed in July 2010, 'The part of the 1997 reforms that worked well is the framework for monetary policy. It was very clearly defined. Institutions and their design do matter in terms of successful

---

[59] L. Benati, 'Long-Run Evidence on Money Growth and Inflation', *Bank of England Quarterly Bulletin*, 45 (2005), p.349; Fisher and Gai, 'Financial Stability', pp.444–7; Bank of England, 'The Governor's Speech in Edinburgh'; Sir John Gieve, 'Stability and Change', *Bank of England Quarterly Bulletin*, 46 (2006), p.333; Lomax, 'The MPC Comes of Age', pp.106–11; Tucker, 'Macro, Asset Price', pp.122–30; Bank of England, 'The Monetary Policy Committee', pp.272–84; Tucker, 'A Perspective', pp.310–16; P. Tucker, 'Central Banking and Political Economy: The Example of the United Kingdom's Monetary Policy Committee', *Bank of England Quarterly Bulletin*, 47 (2007), pp.445–52; M. King, 'Banking and the Bank of England', *Bank of England Quarterly Bulletin*, 48 (2008), pp.310–13; Gieve, 'Seven Lessons', pp.1–22; Bean, 'The UK Economy', pp.1–13; C. Beam, Speech: 'Central Banking Then and Now', 12 July 2011, pp.1–20.

[60] D. Kohn (member of FPC), Speech: 'The Interactions of Macroprudential and Monetary Policies: A View from the Bank of England's Financial Policy Committee', 6 November 2013, pp.1–10. See D. Kohn, Speech: 'The Financial Policy Committee at the Bank of England', 2 December 2011, pp.1–8.

policy-making.' Similarly, in a paper jointly authored by Charles Bean, Matthias Paustian, Adrian Penalver, and Tim Taylor, all at the Bank of England, and published in August 2010, 'It is now pretty clear that price stability is not a sufficient condition for financial stability.' By then it was accepted that a focus on controlling inflation to the exclusion of other policy aims led to a situation in which financial stability was taken for granted, either because the economic models that lay behind bank behaviour were sufficiently robust to eliminate the risks that they were taking or a blind faith that banking crises did not happen in a country such as the UK with a sophisticated financial system. Whichever it was, the result was disastrous.

With the appointment of Mark Carney, an ex-banker, as Governor of the Bank of England, the institution he now headed no longer prioritized the implementation of government monetary policy over its responsibility for maintaining the stability of the banking system. This was something of a reversion to the era that had existed before 1997.[61]

CONCLUSION

What had been allowed to happen during the ten years before the crisis was the development of a financial system that was unstable at many levels. It was unstable at the regulatory level through the creation of the tripartite system, as this left no single agency with overall authority to act immediately and decisively in a crisis. The result was delay and indecision when the crisis appeared. It was unstable at the market level as the Bank of England's role as lender of last resort had been eroded both through the enormous growth of the London money market but also through the switch to the use of the US$ as a basis for inter-bank lending and borrowing. The Bank of England could only directly support UK banks and their £sterling operations, not the money market as a whole, as it was reliant on the co-operation of other central banks for the supply of additional currencies, especially the US$. As with the internal tripartite system the external arrangements between central banks did not lend itself to immediate and decisive action in face of a crisis. Finally, at the level of individual institutions the financial system had also become unstable as a result of two separate developments. The first was that banking had become

---

[61] Bailey, Speech: 'The Financial Crisis Reform Agenda', pp.1–9; Bean, Paustian, Penalver, and Taylor, Paper: 'Monetary Policy after the Fall', pp.1–65; Bailey, Speech: 'The Outlook for Financial Regulation', pp.1–5; A. Bailey, Speech: 'Why Prudential Regulation Matters', 11 October 2011, pp.1–4; P. Fisher, Speech: 'Policy Making at the Bank of England: The Financial Policy Committee', 12 March 2012, pp.1–11; S. Manning, 'The Bank of England as a Bank', *Bank of England Quarterly Bulletin*, 54 (2014), pp.129–35; Carney, Speech: 'Fortune Favours the Bold', pp.1–16.

increasingly competitive. This process had begun with the ending of exchange controls in 1979 as that ended the external compartmentalization of the British banking system into a £sterling-based system and US$-based system. Now all banks could target a single market on the same basis, exposing the UK-based institutions to greatly increased foreign competition, especially in wholesale lending and corporate business. That competition was then intensified in 1986. Not only was the division between investment and retail banking ended with the Big Bang reform of the London Stock Exchange but also the division between banks and building societies in the domestic market for savings and loans. It was that latter development that most intensified competition as building societies converted from mutually owned financial institutions specializing in providing mortgages to home owners using retail deposits, into profit-maximizing companies seeking business across a wide spectrum of financial activities ranging from funding through wholesale markets to the re-packaging and re-sale of home loans. Finally, the aggressive expansion of the two Scottish banks into England, by acquiring their larger rivals, introduced a new competitive element into the British financial system. Before 2000 there had been an informal separation between banking in Scotland and in England, which left the Scottish banks supreme in their own locality, and so not fully integrated into the management structure of the British banking system. Attempts had been made by English banks to acquire the smaller Scottish banks but that had been prevented through political opposition. However, the converse did not apply and so RBS was permitted to acquire NatWest, which was one of the largest English banks at the time, and one that was very conservatively managed. Under the management of RBS, NatWest was very aggressively managed, unbalancing the stability of the British banking system. The action of the RBS was then followed by the Bank of Scotland, which was desperate not to be outdone by its younger Scottish rival. Its move was to acquire the Halifax Bank, which had been the largest building society in the UK even before merging with one of its closest rivals, the Leeds Permanent, and then converting itself into a bank. Thus one of England's largest banks, NatWest, and its largest ex-building society, the Halifax, both fell under the control of two Edinburgh-based financial institutions and the culture that had ensured their stability over the previous century was lost. Instead, they were run by those with no understanding of the difference between a bank and any other business. Andy Hornby at the Bank of Scotland was a brilliant retailer while Fred Goodwin was an accountant by training, not a banker. Lost in the process was the warning that Eddie George had iterated in 1997 that banks were different. Thus, change had taken place at all three levels that had contributed to the stability of the British banking system over the course of the twentieth century. Change in any one would have been serious enough but the combination was lethal, as was to be shown in 2007/8.

9

Catastrophe and Convalescence, 2007–2015

Reviewing what happened to British banking after 1997, and putting it in a global context, suggests that a crisis of some kind was likely to occur at some time. The increasingly competitive nature of banking encouraged a climate of risk-taking which was evident in numerous countries around the world but especially in the USA and the UK. If the view is taken that the crisis, which happened between 2007 and 2009, was so severe that no banking system could withstand its effects, then events in Britain were nothing more than an example of the damage that such a financial tsunami could inflict. Support for such a stance comes from those who regard the financial crisis of 2007–9 as equivalent to that of 1929–32. Such a perspective resonates well in the USA where the Wall Street Crash signalled the onset of a catastrophic banking collapse followed by a deep and prolonged economic depression. In contrast, the British banking system did not experience a crisis in the 1930s leading to a British perspective that regards the financial crisis of 2007–9 as unprecedented or without parallel.[1] That British perspective is important because it suggests that, even in the face of a severe financial crisis, banking systems can prove to be resilient. Allied to that is the fact that not all banking systems experienced a crisis in 2007/9, even among countries closely integrated into the world economy, such as Canada and Australia.[2] The absence of a financial crisis in those countries also undermines those who claim that the inter-connectedness of banking systems spread the problems of one country to all others, placing responsibility for what happened in the UK on events in the USA. Probably no

---

[1] Dimsdale and Hotson, 'Financial Crises and Economic Activity in the UK since 1825' in Dimsdale and Hotson (eds), *British Financial Crises*, p.57; Turner, *Banking in Crisis*, p.7.

[2] Reinhart and Rogoff, *This Time is Different*, pp.4–13, 60, 155, 205, 210, 243–4, 273, 292, 387: Kindleberger and Aliber, *Manias, Panics, and Crashes*, pp.16, 25–6, 65, 87, 194, 213, 227–34, 242–6, 276–8, 300–11; Cassis, *Crises and Opportunities*, pp.4, 49, 51, 57, 59, 64, 88, 123–5, 158; P.T. Hoffman, G. Postel-Vinay, and J.-L. Rosenthal, *Surviving Large Losses: Financial Crises, the Middle Class and the Development of Capital Markets* (Cambridge, Mass.: Belknap Press/ Harvard UP, 2007), pp.2, 63, 104, 128, 136–4, 154, 196.

major banking system was so inter-connected both internally and externally over the century before the crisis of 2007–9 than that of Britain and it was the one famed for stability.[3] What was different about the nature of interconnectedness in 2007–9 was the presence of global banks with branches and operations spread around the globe.[4] The result was the creation of banks that were not only so big that they could evade the ability of regulators to supervise them but also so big that only governments could rescue them when they got into difficulties.[5] Hence the pressure from regulators for the introduction of simpler banking structures containing smaller banks and a lower degree of interconnectedness.

In many ways this appears to be a plea to a return to an earlier era of British banking, characterized by domestic compartmentalization and international barriers. However, the regulatory regime in place after the Second World War was a deeply flawed one as it stifled innovation, encouraged evasion, and led to the financial crisis of 1973/4. Only the underlying economic growth and financial stability of that period, which is unlikely ever to be repeated, masked its failings. In contrast, Lord Neuberger, in a speech in 2014, briefly and accurately pinpointed what was required from financial regulation, but then he was not only President of the Supreme Court of the UK but had also worked for a bank, N.M. Rothschild and Sons, in 1970-3. To him 'regulation is necessary and important, but it must be kept to a minimum, it must be targeted, and it must be effective. Regulation in the financial world failed to stop the rather obvious abuses of LIBOR fixing and PPI selling by UK banks, ... Where regulation fails, a standard response is that we need more of it, whereas the correct response is that we need different regulation not more regulation.'[6] What the regulatory changes of 1997/8 had correctly recognized was that banking had changed and so a new regime was required. What those responsible for the regulatory regime that was introduced were mistaken in assuming was that a banking system dominated by a small number of very large banks was inherently safe if the environment within which it operated was a stable one, irrespective of the individual strategy followed. What they had ignored when framing the new regulatory regime was Britain's own banking experience and the insights that provided into the solutions devised in the wake of past crises, including financial ones as severe of that 2007–9. By 2015 the failure to learn from that past experience was being recognized by some, though there remained an obsession with US rather than British practice, possibly because it appeared to offer quick legal remedies rather than slower practical solutions.[7]

---

[3] Liu, Quiet, and Roth, 'Banking Sector Interconnectedness', pp.2–7.
[4] Jones, *Multinationals and Global Capitalism*, p.288.
[5] Davies, Richardson, Katinaite, and Manning, 'Evolution of the UK Banking System', p.329.
[6] Lord Neuberger, Speech: 'The Future of the Bar', Belfast 20 June 2014.
[7] Jakab and Kumhof, 'Banks are not Intermediaries', pp.1–57.

The events of 2007/8 in Britain were neither unparalleled nor unprecedented but bear remarkable similarities to an earlier banking era characterized by frequent financial crises and banking collapses. That era lasted until 1866. Out of that era came a response in the shape of the transformation of the Bank of England into a lender of last resort to the London money market and, through that, to the British, and even global, banking system. Such a role exceeded the Bank of England's capacity after 1970, because it required the concerted action of the world's major central banks to achieve the same end. However, the Bank of England did also acquire another role after 1866, which was crisis manager to the British banking system, including acting as lender of last resort to British banks and their British operations. This the Bank of England carried out successfully in such cases as Barings in 1890 and Williams Deacon's in 1930, as the failure of each of these had the capacity to destabilize the entire British banking system. The Bank of England acted as crisis manager on a discretionary basis, choosing not to assist the City of Glasgow Bank in 1878 or Farrow's Bank in 1920, which was the correct call as neither failure destabilized the banking system as a whole. In the absence of crises between 1945 and 1970 the Bank of England lost many of the skills that had made it a successful crisis manager, but it regained them sufficiently to provide an effective response to the Secondary Bank Crisis of 1973/4, which it had partly caused through the restrictions in place before 1970 and then the rapid liberalization. In subsequent crises involving either individual banks or even groups of banks, such as those of the small banks in 1990, the Bank of England however proved to be an effective crisis manager. It took pre-emptive action by providing liquidity, as in 1990, and helped to arrange solutions, as with the arranged merger between HSBC and the Midland Bank in 1992. That leads to the question many have asked and failed to have answered, as to why the Bank of England did not both anticipate the failure of the Northern Rock Bank in 2007 and then act to prevent its threatened collapse from destabilizing the entire British banking system.[8]

LENDER OF LAST RESORT/CRISIS MANAGER

Under the reorganization of 1997/8 the Bank of England had been left with the role of lender of last resort to the British banking system. It took this position seriously, undertaking research into when it should intervene and in what way. Before the crisis of 2007, the thinking at the Bank of England focused much more on the risks attached to being too willing to provide liquidity support

[8] Congdon, *Central Banking*, pp.13–16, 25–7, 111, 123–7.

than the consequences that would arise if one or more banks were allowed to fail in a liquidity crisis. It was made clear in 1998, by no less a person than the Governor, Eddie George, that in acting as lender of last resort, 'The central bank safety net is not there to protect individual institutions from failure. It is there to protect the stability of the financial system as a whole. In the absence of a serious systemic threat, the right course would normally be to allow the institution to fail. If any institution felt that it could rely on being bailed out if it ran into real difficulty, the result would be "moral hazard".' Safe in the knowledge that they would be rescued, banks would be encouraged to take excessive risks creating a fragile financial system as a result. For that reason it was made clear that there could be nothing automatic about lender-of-last resort assistance, and when it was provided it would always be on the most onerous terms that the borrower could bear. It was not provided to protect shareholders or the management.[9] That thinking was to colour the judgements made by the Bank of England regarding the provision of liquidity right up to the financial crisis of 2007/8 and beyond. What had not been factored into the thinking was the risk of contagion as fears about the stability of a single bank spread throughout the entire system. Such an occurrence was deemed unlikely in a UK context until after the crisis that befell Northern Rock in August 2007. It had long been recognized that the larger the bank the more it was able to self-insure against a liquidity crisis through its ability to move funds internally and to access different inter-bank markets. The airing that was given to the policy that any lender-of-last-resort support would be both unlikely and conditional further undermines the argument that bank behaviour was driven by confidence among banks, whether from their owners or their employees, that they would be rescued by the state if they got into difficulties because of reckless lending.[10]

This thinking found expression in a speech delivered by Sir John Gieve, whose responsibility at the Bank of England was financial stability, on the 13th of November 2006. To avoid 'moral hazard' authorities had to ensure that support was only forthcoming under the most exceptional of circumstances. That meant that the option of closing down a failing bank was a real one. 'In the end, banks fail because they run out of cash.' The reason for publicizing

[9] George, 'The New Lady', pp.174–7.
[10] Hoggarth, Reidhill, and Sinclair, 'On the Resolution of Banking Crises', pp.1–15; Irwin and Vines, 'Efficient Resolution of Capital-Account Crises'; Gieve, 'Financial System Risks', pp.338–40; Stringa and Monks, 'Inter-Industry Contagion', pp.1–31; Acharya and Yorulmazer, 'Cash-in-the-Market Pricing', pp.1–31; Nier, Yang, Yorulmazer, and Alentorn, 'Network Models', pp.1–28; Aiyar, Calomiris, Hooley, Korniyenko, and Wieladek, 'International Transmission', pp.1–35; D. Reinhart and S.J. Riddiough, 'The Two Faces of Cross-Border Banking Flows: An Investigation into the Links between Global Risk, Arms-length Funding and Internal Capital Markets', *Bank of England Working Paper*, 498 (2014), pp.1–47; S. Langfield, X. Liu, and T. Ota, 'Mapping the UK Interbank System', *Bank of England Working Paper*, 516 (2014), pp.1–38.

such a drastic course of action was because the existence of a lender of last resort could encourage banks to become less careful with their liquidity management specifically and their financial management generally as they could call on the central bank for support if and when required.[11]

It was not just that the Bank of England was pre-disposed not to intervene as lender of last resort if it could possibly be avoided. The Bank was also in an increasingly difficult position regarding its role as lender of last resort because it became more and more detached from both domestic banking and the London money market from the mid 1990s onwards. This can be traced in a number of important areas. One was the management of the payments system which was reduced to a rather mechanical operation rather than one providing insights into the relative standing of individual banks and the overall liquidity of the money market. The Bank of England had been left as both custodian of the payments system and lender of last resort to the banks after the reorganization of financial supervision in 1997/8. The two roles were closely connected as knowledge of what was happening with inter-bank debits and credits, through the payments system, kept the Bank of England in touch with the inter-bank money market. The Bank of England played a central role in the payments system co-operating closely with a small number of key banks responsible for settling payment transactions. The UK payments system was a tiered one in which a few banks acted on behalf of the whole system. Linked to each of these settlement banks were numerous other banks located not just in the UK but also from around the world because of the City of London's importance as a global financial centre. In 2014, the London inter-bank market comprised 490 separate banks of which 176 were direct participants and another 314 were indirect participants operating through one or more of the 176 banks. Beyond these there were around another 4,000 banks that were linked in to the payments system to a lesser or greater degree. Within this huge constituency of banks there existed an exclusive group, numbering fourteen in 2006, that played a central role within the payments system and it was these with which the Bank of England maintained a close and constant relationship. Each of these settlement banks was expected to hold a reserve of liquid assets, which was there not only to ensure it had the resilience to survive a crisis but also cover its payment needs. Even within this exclusive group there was an elite, consisting of no more than four banks that were responsible for approximately 80 per cent of the payment transactions. If any banks could be labelled 'too big to fail' it was these four banks. Despite the internationalization of the London money market, these four banks were all British, comprising Barclays, HSBC (through owning Midland), Lloyds and RBS (through owning NatWest). They were the key element in the CHAPS, the Clearing House Automated Payments

---

[11] Gieve, 'Practical Issues', pp.453–67.

Scheme, which handled high-value sterling transactions where payments averaged £250 billion a day.

This payments system had been changed in 1996 with profound consequences for the potential role that the Bank of England could play as lender of last resort. In 1996 the payments system was moved onto a real-time gross settlement (RTGS) basis. Prior to that year payments were settled at the end of each day on a net basis. This method of operation did involve the risk that a failure of a settlement bank to meet its net payments would leave other banks short of funds to meet their payments and so destabilize the entire payments network. Banks lent to and borrowed from each other throughout the day without collateral, which exposed them to losses if one bank defaulted. To deal with that risk, which grew as the volume of inter-bank activity expanded, a new method of operation was introduced whereby each bank made and received payments simultaneously. The result was to remove any risk from a default at the level of the settlement banks, which also eliminated the exposure of the Bank of England to any resulting losses. In 2001 the system operated by the Bank of England, that handled the delivery and payment of securities, (CREST) was also moved to a RTGS basis. This made both payment systems much more resilient and that was proved to be the case during the crisis of 2007/8 when they operated normally, but it did put a much greater strain on liquidity. As the settlement banks were not always in a position to make payments, and did not want to exceed the agreed limit set with the Bank of England, it encouraged them to internalize their operations using the network of banks for which they handled payments or borrow from the inter-bank money market. What this meant was that the Bank of England had pushed payments down to a level that it was not in a position to monitor. Instead of being aware of which banks were facing liquidity pressures, through having to make rather than receive payments, the Bank of England saw only the agreed limits and the processing of transactions. Beneath that there was unsecured lending and borrowing as each bank attempted to minimize the liquidity it needed to hold. This exposed the settlement bank to credit risk because it was ultimately responsible for the payments, whether or not the bank for which it was acting met its obligation to pay at the end of the day. Given the dependence of the payments system on a small number of settlement banks, the failure of one of these could have posed a serious problem for the entire system. This risk nearly materialized during the financial crisis of 2007, as Northern Rock used another bank through which to make and receive payments. The problem was that under the RTGS payments system the Bank of England was unaware of the issues facing Northern Rock until it was too late to intervene in a timely matter and so pre-empt a run. At the time of the crisis over half the payments were on behalf of non-settlement banks, indicating the degree of risk that existed lower down the system and away from the oversight of the Bank of England. It was only after the crisis that steps were taken to increase the Bank's oversight and to reduce the risks being run at the lower level by making liquidity more readily available.[12] With hindsight the switch from a net to a gross system in 1996 had reduced the ability of the Bank to act as lender of last resort in such a way as to forestall a crisis, considering that the bank that was the first to face liquidity difficulties in August 2007 was a relatively small domestically focused lender, namely Northern Rock.

Before the crisis of 2007/8 there was a continued rapid growth in the London money market. This market was being used not only by banks to borrow and lend among each other on a temporary basis but was also being relied upon as part of their funding operations by those banks using the Originate and Distribute Model. The problem of placing such a heavy reliance

---

[12] Bank of England, 'Risk, Cost and Liquidity in Alternative Payment Systems', *Bank of England Quarterly Bulletin*, 39 (1999), p.78; E. Nier, J. Yang, T. Yorulmazer, and A. Alentorn, 'Network Models and Financial Stability', *Bank of England Working Paper*, 346 (2008), pp.1–28; C. Becher, S. Millard, and K. Soramaki, 'The Network Topology of CHAPS Sterling', *Bank of England Working Paper*, 355 (2008), pp.1–26; P. Gai and S. Kapadia, 'Contagion in Financial Networks', *Bank of England Working Paper*, 383 (2010), pp.1–35; C. Kubelec and F. Sa, 'The Geographical Composition of National External Balance Sheets: 1980–2005', *Bank of England Working Paper*, 384 (2010), pp.1–52; A.V. Wetherilt, P. Zimmerman, and K. Soramaki, 'The Sterling Unsecured Loan Market during 2006–08: Insights from Network Theory', *Bank of England Working Paper*, 398 (2010), pp.1–39; M. Adams, M. Galbiati, and S. Giansante, 'Liquidity Costs and Tiering in Large-Value Payment Systems', *Bank of England Working Paper*, 399 (2010), pp.1–21; M. Galbiati and K. Soramakii, 'Liquidity-Saving Mechanisms and Bank Behaviour', *Bank of England Working Paper*, 400 (2010), pp.1–27; B. Norman, R. Shaw, and G. Speight, 'The History of Interbank Settlement Arrangements: Exploring Central Banks' Role in the Payment System', *Bank of England Working Papers*, 412 (2011), pp.1–32; R.J. Garratt, L. Mahadeva, and K. Svirydzenka, 'Mapping Systemic Risk in the International Banking Network', *Bank of England Working Paper*, 413 (2011), pp.1–40; Aiyar, 'How Did the Crisis', pp.1–34; M. Perlin and J. Schanz, 'System-wide Liquidity Risk in the United Kingdom's Large-Value Payment System: An Empirical Analysis', *Bank of England Working Paper*, 427 (2011), pp.1–35; C. Salmon, Speech: 'The Case for More CHAPS Settlement Banks', 5 July 2011, pp 1–9; E. Carter, 'Considering the Continuity of Payments for Customers in a Bank's Recovery or Resolution', *Bank of England Quarterly Bulletin*, 52 (2012), pp.147–53; A. Dent and W. Dison, 'The Bank of England's Real-Time Gross Settlement Infrastructure', *Bank of England Quarterly Bulletin*, 52 (2012), pp.234–41; C. Salmon, Speech: 'Towards a New Architecture for Payment Arrangements', 24 January 2012, pp.1–8; E. Benos, R. Garratt, and P. Zimmerman, 'Bank Behaviour and Risks in CHAPS Following the Collapse of Lehman Brothers', *Bank of England Working Paper*, 451 (2012), pp.1–34; N. Davey and D. Gray, 'How Has the Liquidity-Saving Mechanism Reduced Banks' Intraday Liquidity Costs in CHAPS?', *Bank of England Quarterly Bulletin*, 53 (2013), pp.180–3; K. Finan, A. Lacaosa, and J. Sunderland, 'Tiering in CHAPS', *Bank of England Quarterly Bulletin*, 53 (2013), pp.372–7; R. Ali, J. Barrdear, R. Clews, and J. Southgate, 'Innovations in Payment Technologies and the Emergence of Digital Currencies', *Bank of England Quarterly Bulletin*, 53 (2013), pp.262–70; E. Kelsey and S. Rickenbach, 'Enhancing the Resilience of the Bank of England's Real-Time Gross Settlement Infrastructure', *Bank of England Quarterly Bulletin*, 53 (2013), pp.316–17; C. Salmon, Speech: 24 January 2013, pp.1–9; C. Salmon, Speech: 'The UK Payments Landscape', 4 November 2013, pp.1–6; Langfield, Liu, and Ota, 'Mapping the UK Interbank System', pp.1–38; E. Denbee, R.J. Garratt, and P. Zimmerman, 'Variations in Liquidity Provision in Real-Time Payment Systems, *Bank of England Working Paper*, 513 (2014), pp.1–15; Liu, Quiet, and Roth, 'Banking Sector Interconnectedness', pp.1–7.

on money market funding was that it was a much more volatile source of funds than retail deposits, especially when expertly managed within integrated banking groups. Within an internal market, a bank had the power to shift liquidity from one corner of the group to another and collectively manage supply and demand based on detailed information about immediate requirements. In contrast, in an external market even rumours of possible payment difficulties could cause the supply of funds to either dry up or even be withdrawn, so creating a liquidity crisis for the bank concerned.[13]

The City of London was home to many different markets. These included the foreign exchange market, which continued to grow rapidly from the mid 1990s, and had London at its centre. Though involving the buying and selling of different currencies, banks used the huge liquidity present in the foreign exchange market, with daily turnover measured in trillions of US$, to not only match their foreign exchange exposure on the liabilities side with their assets but also to borrow and lend among themselves. By agreeing to sell a certain amount of a currency on the spot market, and buy it back on the forward market, a bank was able to borrow short-term at a cost that reflected the difference between the two prices. Such operations grew exponentially as banks realized that they could borrow in the currency of a country where interest rates were low and re-lend in the currency of a country where interest rates were high, profiting from the differential at minimal cost and risk because of the ease and cheapness of trading in the foreign exchange market. Experiencing even more dramatic expansion was the Over-The-Counter (OTC) derivatives market. Banks used the OTC market as an aid in matching their borrowing with their lending, and so reduce the risk that they were running. Long-dated loans could be swapped for short-dated ones and variable interest rate payments with fixed ones, for example. The growing volume and variety of the products on offer in the OTC market contributed to the growing popularity of the Originate and Distribute Model by, apparently, reducing the risks involved compared to the Lend and Hold one. However, in neither the foreign exchange nor the OTC market was there a single lender of last resort ready to intervene if a liquidity crisis arose because of a default. In both these markets the centre of activity was in London but the principal currency in use was the US$. In the foreign exchange market the switch from a net to a gross basis, as in the UK payments system, was meant to have eliminated default risk but all that had happened was that it had pushed the risks down to other levels, such as the exposure of settlement banks to their correspondents. In the OTC market the exposure was of a bilateral nature as these deals were negotiated between two banks, with inter-dealer brokers acting solely as intermediaries. Thus, if a crisis occurred in either of these

---

[13] Reinhart and Riddiough, 'The Two Faces of Cross-Border Banking Flows', pp.1–47.

markets, that were highly international and US$ based, the Bank of England was in no position to provide support unless it had negotiated access to other currencies, especially the US$.[14]

As the City of London increasingly occupied a central position of the interbank money market, the volume and variety of the activity that took place there grew exponentially. Not only did these markets largely operate on the basis of a currency other than the UK£ but also many of the banks involved were not supervised by the UK authorities. Between 1997 and 2007 the value of inter-bank lending taking place in London increased from $1.2 trillion to $3.7 trillion and then only fell back to $3.1 trillion in 2010.[15] The UK authorities had responsibility only for those banks domiciled in the UK, including subsidiaries of foreign banks. The London branches of foreign banks were the responsibility of the central bank of the country in which their parent was based, and did not even report their inter-bank exposures to the British authorities. This meant that the Bank of England had neither responsibility nor knowledge of their activities, despite them being major players in the various London money markets. Much of this activity did require the use of collateral as in the repro market. A repro market required a simultaneous sale and repurchase agreement, providing the vendor with immediate access to funds and the buyer with a use for otherwise idle funds. There was however also a substantial amount of activity that comprised unsecured lending among banks based on trust, with around twenty large banks being at the heart of these activities. These comprised the largest UK banks, because the markets were on their doorstep, and foreign banks with a global reach, because London provided them with international access. These core banks had the capacity to diversify counterparty risk since they were connected to so many different banks both within London and elsewhere in the world. The risk was that the

---

[14] Bank of England, 'The Foreign Exchange and Over-the-Counter Derivatives Markets in the United Kingdom', *Bank of England Quarterly Bulletin*, 38 (1998), pp.349–55; S. Wharmby, 'The Foreign Exchange and Over-The-Counter Derivatives Markets in the United Kingdom', *Bank of England Quarterly Bulletin*, 41 (2001); P. Williams, 'The Foreign Exchange and Over-The-Counter Derivatives Markets in the United Kingdom', *Bank of England Quarterly Bulletin*, 44 (2004); G. Christodoulou and P. O'Connor, 'The Foreign Exchange and Over-The-Counter Derivatives Markets in the United Kingdom', *Bank of England Quarterly Bulletin*, 46 (2006), pp.548–55; T. Broderick and C. Cox, 'The Foreign Exchange and Over-The-Counter Interest Rate Derivatives Markets in the United Kingdom', *Bank of England Quarterly Bulletin*, 50 (2010), pp.355–61; J. O'Connor, J. Wackett, and R. Zammit, 'The Use of Foreign Exchange Markets by Non-Banks', *Bank of England Quarterly Bulletin*, 51 (2011), pp.119–23; N. Smyth, 'Trading Models and Liquidity Provision in OTC Derivatives Markets', *Bank of England Quarterly Bulletin*, 51 (2011), pp.333–7; J. Lowes and T. Nenova, 'The Foreign Exchange and Over-The-Counter Interest-Rate Derivatives Market in the United Kingdom', *Bank of England Quarterly Bulletin*, 53 (2013), pp.395–9.

[15] Source: Bank for International Settlement: Locational Banking Statistics, 2011. The inter-bank data was calculated by subtracting bank lending to the non-bank sector from total bank lending. Cf. Bank for International Settlement, *Guidelines to the International Locational Banking Statistics*.

default of one of these core banks would endanger the whole system because of these connections, making the existence of a lender of last resort important. This was recognized at the time. In January 1998 the Bank of England introduced foreign exchange swaps as a way of providing liquidity in currencies other than the UK£. The Bank of England sold sterling for foreign currency on the spot market, matching that with forward purchases of sterling for foreign currency. There was no foreign exchange risk and it meant that the Bank of England could provide liquidity in foreign currencies but only to the extent that there were foreign buyers of sterling. Apart from that provision, the financial stability risks posed by the banking sector was dependent on the institutions themselves, which was a source of concern.[16]

The Bank of England nevertheless remained 'the marginal supplier of liquidity to the banking system', though this role was confined to British domestic banks and sterling money market.[17] However, as with the changes to the payments system, its connection was becoming steadily more tenuous. It was in 1996 that the repro market was introduced for UK government debt, which ended the need to have separately capitalized gilt-edged market makers with whom the Bank of England had maintained close relations. On 1 April 1998 the management of the UK government's sterling debt was transferred from the Bank of England to the UK Debt Management Office. Increasingly the Bank of England was separated from the day-to-day business of British banks and the London money market. Instead, banks were being driven to make use of the inter-bank market to meet their liquidity requirements rather than expect to tap the Bank of England for funds, even when these operations took place in sterling. Though the Bank of England was left with its role of lender of last resort to UK banks and the sterling money market the mechanisms that it had available to fulfil that role were lost to it. Instead, the Bank of England became steadily more focused on its role as guardian of the government's monetary policy and detached from its role of bankers' bank. The Bank of England no longer held large deposits from banks, from which it could lend to meet day-to-day liquidity needs. What the Bank of England wanted was to discourage banks from relying upon it to meet both their day-to-day liquidity needs and emergency funds if they faced a temporary crisis. Instead, the aim was to force banks to make their own liquidity provision either through internal prudence or using the inter-bank money markets to top up when required. Forgotten in this new policy was the role that the Bank of England

[16] Bank of England, 'The First Year of the Gilt Repo Market', *Bank of England Quarterly Bulletin*, 37 (1997), p.187; Bank of England, 'Sterling Wholesale Markets: Developments in 1998', *Bank of England Quarterly Bulletin*, 39 (1999), p.34–7; Senior and Westwood, 'External Balance Sheet', pp.351–63; Burnett and Manning, 'Financial Stability', pp.463–74; Langfield, Liu, and Ota, 'Mapping the UK Interbank System', pp.1–38.

[17] Bank of England, 'The Bank of England's Operations in the Sterling Money Markets', *Bank of England Quarterly Bulletin*, 37 (1997), pp.204–5. See George, 'The New Lady', pp.174–7.

had traditionally played as lender of last resort not only to individual banks in crisis but also to the sterling money markets. As with many other areas of the Bank of England's banking responsibilities, the burden had been shifted onto others including the banks themselves.[18]

It was only in the light of the financial crisis that the Bank of England rediscovered its role as lender of last resort, as was made clear in 2010. 'The experience of the financial crisis has influenced the Bank's thinking about the design of its operating framework. As a result, the Bank has adopted an operating framework that more clearly separates monetary policy implementation and the provision of liquidity insurance, that allows it to supply reserves through a variety of channels and that, through its operations, provides the Bank with information about the liquidity needs of the banking system.' Until then the Bank of England appeared much more concerned with the question of moral hazard than acting as lender of last resort. If liquidity was to be made freely available to banks the Bank of England's task of implementing the government's monetary policy would be made more difficult. The Bank of England's focus on implementing monetary policy clashed with its role as lender of last resort to the domestic banking system.[19] As Paul Fisher, Executive Director for Markets, explained in 2010, 'In normal times, we ask the banks to choose their own targets for reserve accounts and then lend just enough cash to the system as a whole so that the banks can collectively meet the aggregate of their targets. The commercial banks will then lend to, or borrow from each other in the inter-bank market, to distribute the total amount of cash around the system so that each individual institution can meet its target. Each bank is incentivized to meet its reserves target by the application of penalty rates to those who are—on average over a monthly maintenance period—either excessively short or long. If an institution cannot meet its target through the inter-bank market, it can use the bank's standing deposit and lending facilities. Under these facilities, reserve account holders can deposit with, or borrow from the Bank overnight for unlimited amounts at a fixed penalty to Bank Rate. So, in practice, these facilities impose a narrow corridor on either side of the Bank Rate.' Under this system the Bank of England set a ceiling to the amount of liquidity in the system leaving the banks

---

[18] Bank of England, 'The First Year of the Gilt Repo Market', p.187; Bank of England, 'Sterling Wholesale Markets', p.34–7; Bank of England, 'The Bank of England's Operations in the Sterling Money Markets', *Bank of England Quarterly Bulletin*, 42 (2002), pp.153–6; A.V. Wetherilt, 'Money Market Operations and Volatility in UK Money Market Rates', *Bank of England Quarterly Bulletin*, 42 (2002), pp.420–3; Bank of England, 'Reform of the Bank of England's Operations in the Sterling Money Markets: A Consultative Paper', *Bank of England Quarterly Bulletin*, 44 (2004), pp.217–22; S. Breeden and R. Whisker, 'Collateral Risk Management at the Bank of England', *Bank of England Quarterly Bulletin*, 50 (2010), pp.94–102; R. Clews, C. Salmon, and O. Weeken, 'The Bank's Money Market Framework', *Bank of England Quarterly Bulletin*, 50 (2010), pp.292–300.

[19] Clews, Salmon, and Weeken, 'The Bank's Money Market Framework', pp.292–300.

to redistribute the total among themselves depending on need, as some banks had excess liquidity while others were in deficit. This model was designed to fulfil the Bank's role in implementing domestic monetary policy but it lacked the flexibility required by an active money market in which supply and demand continually ebbed and flowed. The result was that even the sterling-based inter-bank market lacked an adequate lender of last resort both on a daily basis and when faced with a crisis.[20]

CRISIS AND AFTER

The changes that had taken place in British banking from the mid 1990s onwards had, collectively and accumulatively, transformed it from a highly resilient system into one that was now vulnerable in a crisis. That crisis eventually materialized during 2007. By July of 2007 it had become evident that there was a developing financial crisis in the USA, caused by excessive lending to those with poor credit ratings, especially for house purchases. It was not yet clear what the implications were for the UK.[21] The previous month those at the Bank of England in operational charge of ensuring financial stability, Nigel Jenkinson and Mark Manning, had expressed confidence that 'financial institutions are in a strong financial position', but did add the caveat that 'risk-taking has increased and the vulnerability of the financial system as a whole to a sharp change in conditions has risen'.[22] Those last words were prophetic as a financial crisis then developed rapidly in Britain which none of the members of the tripartite group were prepared for. No provision had been made in the new arrangements for dealing with a failing bank in such a way as to avoid its problems destroying public confidence in both that particular bank and the system as a whole. In the past, the Bank of England would have taken a decision either to provide liquidity support, so averting a crisis while a solution was worked out, or to let the bank fail calculating that its collapse would not destabilize the entire system. Now such a decision was shared between the UK Treasury, the FSA, and the Bank of England, which both created delays and increased the possibility of news leaking out that a particular bank was in difficulties.

Northern Rock Bank was experiencing funding difficulties during the course of August 2007, which is why it approached the Bank of England for

[20] P. Fisher, Speech: 'Managing Liquidity in the System', 30 September 2010, pp.1–12.
[21] Sir John Gieve, 'Uncertainty, Policy and Financial Markets', *Bank of England Quarterly Bulletin*, 47 (2007), pp.437–44; Astley, Giese, Hume, and Kubelec, 'Global Imbalances', pp.183–8.
[22] Jenkinson and Manning, 'Promoting Financial System Resilience', pp.453–60.

emergency assistance. Before anything could be agreed, the story broke on the 13th of September 2007 that the Northern Rock and the Bank of England were in discussion regarding emergency support, because it was in financial difficulties. The balance between which decision to take was a fine one: Northern Rock was both relatively small and highly specialized, being an ex-building society based in Newcastle with a limited branch network. It was also not a direct member of the payments system so its disappearance would not be an immediate threat to the stability of that system. Nevertheless, it had been expanding rapidly through embracing the Originate and Distribute Model to an extreme degree. Judging from the previous research carried out by the staff of the Bank of England on the question of moral hazard, there did exist the definite possibility that Northern Rock would be denied assistance by the tripartite group as a warning to other banks, especially those that were direct participants in the payments system, so as to restrain their lending and encourage them to bolster their capital and reserves. As it was, the hands of the tripartite group were forced by the public reaction to the news that the Northern Rock Bank was in difficulties. Once the news broke on the BBC, accompanied by alarmist reporting, retail depositors rushed to close their accounts and withdraw all their savings. This is what had been happening unobtrusively at the wholesale level since at least the beginning of June, as the ripples from the crisis in the USA made those lending to banks and buying the re-packaged loans increasingly nervous about the risks that now appeared to exist in once safe processes and products. As result there was a liquidity squeeze, which meant that those banks reliant on the inter-bank market for temporary funds could not obtain it. It was for that reason that Northern Rock had been forced to seek outside assistance, as it was no longer able to finance its lending commitments through accessing the inter-bank market for short-term funds and then sell on the loans it had made once they were re-packaged as bonds. Instead, it was facing having to repay loans and maturing bonds without the means of doing either. Faced with the problems at Northern Rock being exposed, and the public's extreme action, the decision was taken to guarantee depositors' savings at Northern Rock and provide extra liquidity to banks in general, so averting the wider banking crisis that was threatening. Rather than lend money to each other, and so earn interest, banks chose to hold more reserves with the Bank of England, and so ensure that it was available when required. By acting as an intermediary in the sterling inter-bank market, the Bank of England removed that counterparty risk and so restored liquidity. In response to the crisis the Bank of England suspended its cautious attitude towards the amount of credit it would provide and the collateral it demanded. An additional £9 billion of liquidity was injected into the money market in September 2007, or an increase of over 50 per cent compared to the position in July. Further support was provided in December 2007. As so much of the lending and borrowing had been conducted in US$s, the Bank of England arranged with the New York Federal Reserve Bank to swap pounds for dollars so as to meet the demand for liquidity regardless of the currency. Once these actions had been taken there was a belief that the incident had been dealt with, and a complete banking crisis avoided.[23]

Whether the decision to intervene and save Northern Rock would have been taken without the media hysteria and the panic withdrawals by the public has to be doubted, considering the concerns at the Bank of England over the question of moral hazard. For Northern Rock, what began as a liquidity crisis became a solvency one, as it became impossible to price the value of the assets that it held, forcing the government to take it into public ownership in February 2008, in order to guarantee its immediate future as doubts circulated regarding its viability. The fate of Northern Rock exposed the complications that arose when a bank experienced difficulties and the authorities intervened to prevent its collapse. On the 10th of June 2008 the Governor of the Bank of England, Mervyn King, hinted at why the government had been forced to intervene to save Northern Rock, but not its shareholders, from being allowed to become bankrupt, as would have been the case with another business. 'the failure of a bank can have an impact that goes well beyond the importance of that bank alone—so-called systemic risk. That is why central banks have sometimes acted as "lender of last resort".' What he then revealed was the extreme reluctance with which such a decision had been taken. 'It can then be difficult for the authorities to make a credible commitment that in future banks will be allowed to fail. And that can in turn encourage banks to take greater risks—both in maturity transformation and lending—enabling them to earn higher profits. Because the authorities will face an incentive to

---

[23] Bank of England, 'Markets and Operations', *Bank of England Quarterly Bulletin*, 47 (2007), pp.590-10; King, 'The Governor's Speech in Northern Ireland', pp.566-9; Lomax, 'Current Monetary Policy Issues', pp.570-3; A. Sentance, 'A Tale of Two Shocks: Global Challenges for UK Monetary Policy', *Bank of England Quarterly Bulletin*, 47 (2007), pp.613-20; Jenkinson, 'Strengthening Regimes', pp.223-7; N. Jenkinson, A. Penalver, and N. Vause, 'Financial Innovation: What Have We Learnt?' *Bank of England Quarterly Bulletin*, 48 (2008), pp.330-8; Astley, Giese, Hume, and Kubelec, 'Global Imbalances', pp.183-8; Gieve, 'Seven Lessons', pp.1-22; Jenkinson, Speech: 'Containing System-Wide Liquidity Risks', pp.1-23; A. Bailey, Speech: 'Recovery and Resolution Plans', 17 November 2009, pp.1-6; P. Fisher, Speech: 'The Bank of England's Balance Sheet: Monetary Policy and Liquidity Provision during the Financial Crisis', 19 November 2009, pp.1-21; M. Cross, P. Fisher, and O. Weeken, 'The Bank's Balance Sheet during the Crisis', *Bank of England Quarterly Bulletin*, 50 (2010), pp.37-41; Breeden and Whisker, 'Collateral Risk Management', pp.94-102; Clews, Salmon, and Weeken, 'The Bank's Money Market Framework', pp.292-300; Fisher, Speech: 'Managing Liquidity in the System', pp.1-12; Miles, 'Mortgages and Housing', pp.1-12; S. John, M. Roberts, and O. Weeken, 'The Bank of England's Special Liquidity Scheme', *Bank of England Quarterly Bulletin*, 52 (2012), pp.57-63; C. Jackson and M. Sim, 'Recent Developments in the Sterling Overnight Money Market', *Bank of England Quarterly Bulletin*, 53 (2013), pp.224-30; A. Alphandary, 'Risk Managing Loan Collateral at the Bank of England', *Bank of England Quarterly Bulletin*, 54 (2014), p.191.

step in to rescue banks tomorrow, there is an incentive for banks to take more risk today.'[24] This reluctance to intervene to save a failing bank remained a consistent view of Mervyn King, as revealed in a retrospective comment made in October 2010. 'In September 2007, everyone thought that the crisis was one of liquidity and as a result there was an expectation central banks could provide the solution. But it quickly became clear that it was in fact a crisis of solvency. If a crisis is in fact one of insolvency, brought on by excessive leverage and risk, then central bank liquidity provision cannot provide the answer. Central banks can offer liquidity insurance only to solvent institutions or as a bridge to a more permanent solution. It is this structure, in which risky long-term assets are funded by short-term deposits, that makes banks so hazardous.'[25]

As it was, the seriousness of the crisis engulfing British banking had left no alternative to intervention if a catastrophic collapse was to be avoided. Increasingly it was recognized that the problems did not lie with one rogue bank, namely Northern Rock, but were common to the whole sector, though to varying degrees, ranging from the largest to the smallest and irrespective of whether they were mutual organizations or shareholder-owned companies. In response to this situation, what had been emergency measures and regarded as truly exceptional, became accepted procedures and even enshrined in law. The Banking Special Provisions Act was passed in February 2008. It provided a legal framework to deal with a failing bank so as to maintain financial stability, ensure confidence in the banking sector, safeguard depositors in banks and to protect public funds. This was then used to resolve the problems of Bradford and Bingley over a weekend by transferring its deposit-taking activities to Santander while leaving the rest in public ownership. It was also used to resolve the difficulties of the Dunfermline Building Society in March 2009, again over a weekend, by transferring the depositors, branches, and head office as well as the prime mortgages to the Nationwide. That left the more difficult assets outside the scheme. The non-intervention stance maintained by Mervyn King, as Governor of the Bank of England, had been superseded by events as their seriousness and consequences became evident.[26]

What this reflected was a return to recognizing that banks were a unique kind of business because of their exposure to a liquidity crisis long before a solvency crisis became an issue. This was the warning that Eddie George had tried to get across in 1997 but was then forgotten in the ten years that followed as the UK Treasury used banks as its spearhead for driving growth in the

---

[24] King, 'Banking and the Bank of England', pp.310–13. See also M. King, Speech: 'Finance: A Return from Risk', 17 March 2009, pp.1–16; P. Tucker, Speech: 'The Crisis Management Menu', 16 November 2009, pp.1–16.

[25] King, Speech: 'Banking: from Bagehot to Basel and Back Again', pp.1–25.

[26] A. Bailey, Speech: 'The UK Bank Resolution Regime', 26th November 2009, pp.1–9.

economy, the FSA concentrated on protecting the interests of savers and borrowers, and the Bank of England became obsessed with its monetary policy mission to the exclusion of all else. Only in the wake of the twin crises of 2007/8 did the question of bank liquidity rear its head again, and those who had long warned of the risks it posed were given their voice back.[27] As Andrew Haldane observed in 2011 and Paul Tucker in 2013, 'Banks are special.'[28] Lessons had been learnt from the crises.

By the middle of 2008 the optimism that the crisis of 2007 had been dealt with had evaporated as it was recognized that the financial problems facing the entire British banking system were both deeper and broader than originally believed. What had begun as a liquidity crisis soon became a solvency one as asset prices fell, leaving exposed those banks that had become over-reliant on financing their investments by borrowing, often from other banks. By December 2007 access to liquid funds had become even more constrained forcing the major central banks to provide co-ordinated support. There was then a noticeable deterioration in the ability of banks to obtain external funding after the collapse of the US investment bank Bear Stearns in March 2008. This effectively closed the mortgage-backed securities market. In response, the Bank of England introduced the Special Liquidity Scheme in April 2008 through which banks could swap temporarily illiquid securities for UK Treasury Bills. These Treasury Bills could then be used as collateral to borrow cash. It was a one-off temporary measure designed to give banks time to strengthen their balance sheet and diversify their sources of funding. However, the crisis was much bigger than originally envisaged and so could not be solved by a one-off measure taken in isolation. The lack of liquidity persisted throughout 2008 making it difficult for banks to fund themselves using the money markets. Across the world there was a lack of confidence in assets created from packages of bank loans, most notably mortgage-backed securities. That lack of confidence was prompted by the downturn in the US housing market and, in particular, the problems associated with sub-prime mortgages there. The markets in which those assets normally traded had, in effect, closed, so it had become very difficult for banks to exchange those assets for cash—the assets had become 'illiquid'. As a result, many banks had an 'overhang' of assets on their balance sheets, which they could not readily sell or use to secure borrowing. This overhang created uncertainty about the financial position of banks, including whether, given the size of their balance sheets, they had sufficient capital to cover a decline in the value of their assets. This made it more difficult for banks to attract funding, including from other

---

[27] A. Bailey, 'Financial Stability: Objective and Resolution', 17 March 2011, pp.1–5.
[28] A.G. Haldane, Speech: 'Control Rights (and Wrongs)', 24 October 2011, pp.1–29; P. Tucker, Speech: 'Banking Reform and Macroprudential Regulation: Implications for Banks' Capital Structure and Credit Conditions', 13 June 2013, pp.1–12.

banks, and, in turn, affected their ability and willingness to lend money to individuals and businesses.

The need for further intervention was accentuated following the collapse of Lehman Brothers in September 2008. Despite being a Wall Street investment bank, Lehman Brothers was a major player in the London money and securities markets, acting as counterparty in numerous deals. With its demise it became almost impossible to sell or even value for collateral purposes the mortgage-backed securities that banks had used to obtain funding. In response, the Bank of England, operating on behalf of the UK government, had no alternative but to continue with and even expand its Special Lending Scheme. At its peak on the 30th of January 2009 the scheme had lent Treasury Bills with a face value of £185 billion against securities with a nominal value of £287 billion. Prior to these financial crises, the Bank of England had primarily focused on the implementation of monetary policy to the neglect of its banking responsibilities, including its role as lender of last resort. During the evolving financial crisis of 2007/8 the Bank was forced to resume its banking responsibilities. What had happened in 1997 was that the incoming Labour government had hijacked the Bank for its own purpose, devolving responsibility for banking supervision to the FSA and leaving in limbo the role to be played as lender of last resort in a crisis. The Bank had to re-learn this role as the crisis developed, which explains the slow and inadequate response. It was not until October 2008 that it was in a position to provide banks and the money market with the emergency liquidity required in a crisis. The purpose of the measures put in place was to provide banks with the liquidity they had previously obtained from the money market. There was also an added international dimension to the liquidity crisis in London as borrowing and lending was largely based on the use of the US$ rather than the UK£ but the Bank of England could only provide sterling from its own resources. The solution arrived at was a swap facility between central banks with the Federal Reserve providing the $s but it took the crisis associated with the collapse of Lehman Brothers to fully develop these arrangements. In contrast, the Bank of England could take pride in the fact that the payments system had withstood the shock of both financial crises and continued to operate normally, though under enormous pressure.[29]

---

[29] King, 'Governor's Speech in Bristol', pp.82–4; Gieve, 'Return of the Credit Cycle', pp.91–5; Tucker, 'Money and Credit', pp.96–106; T. Besley, 'Financial Markets', pp.107–11; Bank of England, 'Markets and Operations', *Bank of England Quarterly Bulletin*, 48 (2008), pp.126–45; Fisher, Speech: 'The Bank of England's Balance Sheet', pp.1–21; Miles, 'Monetary Policy and Financial Stability', pp.1–19; P. Fisher, Speech: 'An Unconventional Journey: The Bank of England's Asset Purchase Programme', 11 October 2010, pp.1–10; John, Roberts, and Weeken, 'The Bank of England's Special Liquidity Scheme', pp.57–63; Dent and Dison, 'The Bank of England's Real-Time Gross Settlement Infrastructure', pp.236–41; Jackson and Sim, 'Recent Developments', pp.224–30; M. Joyce, A. Lasosa, I. Stevens, and M. Tong, 'The Financial Market Impact of Quantitative Easing', *Bank of England Working Paper*, 393 (2010), pp.1–43.

What the Northern Rock crisis had done was to alert the tripartite group to how vulnerable the British banking system had become in the event of a financial crisis, compared to the unstated confidence in its resilience that had long underpinned all policy decisions and planning agendas. Many had thought the worst was over once the problems of Northern Rock and the other ex-building societies had been dealt with. These problems revolved around the Originate and Distribute Model and could be handled by the provision of continuing liquidity support and depositor guarantees while the loans were gradually repaid or re-financed. However, a completely new dimension to the difficulties faced by British banks arose after the collapse of the Wall Street investment bank, Lehman Brothers on the 15th of September 2008. In the light of that later crisis, that of August 2007 was described as the 'Little Panic', and was increasingly forgotten, whereas the one of September/October 2008 became the 'Great Panic', and so central to the debate on what needed to be done to avoid it happening again. However, it was the experience gained in dealing with the little crisis, beginning with Northern Rock on August 2007 and rumbling on through 2008, that had allowed the tripartite group to put together a set of policies and procedures that stood them in good stead when the post-Lehman Brothers crisis took place. Instead of involving relatively small and specialized financial institutions, such as the ex-building societies, the Lehman Brothers collapse moved the two Scottish-owned banks to the centre stage, as these were both direct participants in the payments system. The lesser problem was HBOS, which was exposed not so much through its banking operation, as that was largely confined to Scotland where it operated as the Bank of Scotland. Instead, it was its large ex-building society, the Halifax, which was the problem as it had embraced the Originate and Distribute Model though to a much lesser degree than its smaller rivals like Northern Rock. That failure to fully embrace the model to the same degree as its smaller rivals, had cost the Halifax market share. Even before its merger with the Leeds Permanent and then its conversion into a bank in 1997, the Halifax had been the market leader. In ignorance of the underlying problems of HBOS, an industry-based solution to its problems appeared possible through an arranged merger with Lloyds TSB. The government actively supported such a move despite the fact that it would create a banking behemoth that was certainly too big to fail. The real problem, though, was not HBOS but RBS. This had taken over the NatWest Bank, giving it control of one of the UK's largest banks, ranking alongside Barclays, HSBC, and Lloyds in dominating the provision of business credit within the UK and being central to both the payments system and inter-bank borrowing and lending. For those reasons the collapse of RBS would have been catastrophic for the UK banking system, being one of the four banks that were 'too big to fail'. Unfortunately, the aggressive lending policies pursued after the takeover of NatWest by RBS, as it strove to become one of the largest banks in the world, had brought it to the edge of collapse. A high dependency on the Originate and Distribute Model involving risky commercial loans and interbank borrowing left it the most exposed of the four major UK banks and the Lehman Brothers collapse proved to be the tipping point. On the 13th of October 2008 the UK government was forced to inject nearly £40 billion of public funds to stabilize RBS and HBOS as their survival was threatened because they lacked the capital required to cover their losses on highly leveraged loans and could no longer re-finance themselves through short-term wholesale funding.[30]

As Mervyn King said on the 21st of October 2008, 'Not since the beginning of the First World War has our banking system been so close to collapse.'[31] Though the origins of that later crisis also lay in the USA, which acted out its own scenario leading to the collapse of Lehman Brothers in September 2008, the events that had taken place in the UK a year earlier, and were then repeated on a grander scale in the wake of the collapse of Lehman Brothers, provided ample evidence that what took place in the UK was not simply the accidental by-product of a global crisis but had deep domestic origins. In many ways the Northern Rock crisis meant that the UK authorities were better prepared for the Global Crisis when it took place than they would otherwise have been. Over the course of 2008, procedures were put in place to provide rapid and effective intervention in the face of a banking crisis that were absent in August 2007. Northern Rock was the first casualty of the catastrophic state into which British banking had entered by 2007 but what emerged was a plan of how to deal with a financial crisis that centred on banks, not money or the stock market. The events of September and October 2008 required decisive action by governments and central banks around the world, including those of the UK, to prevent a complete collapse of the international banking system. Subsequent government intervention was also required to prevent a financial crisis becoming an economic crisis. One element of that was the programme of Quantitative Easing introduced in January 2009. This involved the large-scale purchase from the banking sector of now illiquid assets, so freeing up funds for lending out to customers. As banks were forced to revert to the Lend and Hold Model, requiring a much higher leverage ratio, they lacked the funds to meet

---

[30] Gieve, 'Learning from the Financial Crisis', pp.1-13; Gieve, 'Rebuilding Confidence', pp.1-9; Haldane, 'Rethinking the Financial Network', pp.1-41; Bean, 'The Great Moderation', pp.1-32; M. Joyce, M. Tong, and R. Woods, 'The United Kingdom's Quantitative Easing Policy: Design, Operation and Impact', *Bank of England Quarterly Bulletin*, 51 (2011); M. Dive, R. Hodge, C. Jones, and J. Purchase, 'Developments in the Global Securities Lending Market', *Bank of England Quarterly Bulletin*, 51 (2011), pp.224-32; P. Fisher, Speech: 'Central Bank Policy on Collateral', 14 April 2011, pp.1-10; D. Miles, Speech: 'Monetary Policy and Banking Fragility', 27 July 2011, pp.1-18; Sir Jon Cunliffe, Speech: 'Regulatory Reform and Returns in Banking', 20 October 2014, pp.1-10.

[31] King, Speech: *Bank of England Quarterly Bulletin* (2008), pp.1-9.

the needs of their customers, so greatly restricting the supply of credit and capital for the economy. Quantitative Easing was designed to cover this shortage on a temporary basis.[32]

In the aftermath of these two crises, but especially the later one in September 2008, consideration was given as to how to avoid a repetition of what had happened. One solution was to ensure that banks were no longer able to combine the Lend and Hold Model with the Originate and Distribute one as that was seen to have been the prime cause, as it left the banking system highly vulnerable in a crisis. One powerful convert to this view was the Governor of the Bank of England, supported by the political elite, as it placed the blame for the catastrophe that had overwhelmed British banking on the banks and bankers themselves, which resonated well with the public and the media. 'It is not sensible to allow large banks to combine high street retail banking with risky investment banking or funding strategies, and then provide an implicit guarantee against failure. Something must give. Either those guarantees to retail depositors should be limited to banks that make a narrower range of investments, or banks which pose greater risks to taxpayers and the economy in the event of failure should face higher capital requirements, or we must develop resolution powers such that large and complex financial institutions can be wound down in an orderly manner. Or, perhaps, an element of all three. Privately owned and managed institutions that are too big to fail sit oddly with a market economy.'[33] The flaw in this analysis is that the first bank to fail was Northern Rock. It was neither too big nor too connected to be allowed to fail. It was saved because the authorities were unaware of what was happening in British banking and so could not head off a crisis. That position was then compounded by the delay before lender-of-last-resort support was provided, allowing a panic to develop. In the wake of these twin errors, change in British banking and the way it was regulated became inevitable. By the end of October 2009, Paul Tucker, who was now Deputy Governor at the Bank of England with responsibility for Financial Stability, observed that 'we face a choice between an overhaul of the regulatory regime and directly altering the structure of the banking system.'[34] What this reflected was a recognition that the changes introduced in 1997/8 had failed and a complete re-think was required. This was no simple matter. Along with the question of moral hazard went the issue of how to maintain essential financial services without

---

[32] J. Benford, S. Berry, K. Nikolov, C. Young, and M. Robson, 'Quantitative Easing', *Bank of England Quarterly Bulletin*, 49 (2009), pp.91–2; M. King, Speech: 20 January 2009, pp.1–13; C. Bean, Speech: 'Quantitative Easing, An Interim Report', 13 October 2009, pp.1–14; Bell and Young, 'Understanding the Weakness of Bank Lending', pp.311–19.

[33] M. King, Speech: 17 June 2009, pp.1–9. See also P. Tucker, Speech: 'Regimes for Handling Bank Failures: Redrawing the Banking Social Contract', 30 June 2009, pp.1–14.

[34] P. Tucker, Speech: 'The Debate on Financial System Resilience: Macroprudential Instrument', 22 October 2009, pp.1–18.

providing banks with a guarantee against failure. If the regulations introduced were too restrictive, a shadow banking system would develop beyond the perimeter of bank regulation by offering better terms to both savers and borrowers.[35]

There was also an urgent need to develop a formal mechanism through which a failing bank could be rescued in such a way that both penalized its owners and managers, as they were held responsible for the difficulties that it was in, but did not endanger the payments system or destroy confidence in banks. This required quick and decisive action carried out in secret, as had been the practice before the changes made in 1997/8. What came to the fore after the twin crises of 2007 and 2008 was that a failing bank could not be treated as any other business but had to be placed in special measures, including preserving the trust of other banks and the public and keeping it operational because of its role within the payments system. As had long been the case in the UK, only if a bank was small and marginal could it be closed down without serious implications for either the integrity of the payments system or the stability of the banking system. This continued to be the case even after the events of 2007 and 2008. The Southsea Mortgage and Investment Company, which was small, was wound up with little fuss in June 2011. Before that, in March 2009, the Dunfermline Building Society was also closed without causing widespread problems, after its funding difficulties were exposed. In its case, the Nationwide Building Society took over the business, which was a well-tried procedure used in the case of a failing bank or building society. The problems that beset Lloyds Bank after its takeover of HBOS, made larger banks or building societies wary of taking over a smaller rival because that would make them responsible for all the losses in the event that the problems that had led to the near-death experience turned out to be of a very serious nature. The risks were especially large if the acquiring bank was only marginally larger than the one being taken over, rather than considerably smaller. The Lloyds/HBOS experience made it highly unlikely that the solution for a failing bank was its merger with a larger rival because the combined entity could then be brought to the brink of collapse if the problems were of sufficient magnitude. This made the need for a government-backed special resolution vehicle to deal with a large failing bank all the more imperative, and that was one of the positive responses put in place after the twin crises of 2007/8.

The difficulty arose when the bank in question was sufficiently large so that its failure would have widespread ramifications, or was sufficiently well known to spread fears about the safety of other banks. Under these circumstances intervention was required to insulate it from the rest of the sector and provide reassurance about overall stability. The dilemma revolved around how to

---

[35] P. Tucker, Speech: 'The Crisis Management Menu', 16 November 2009, pp.1–16.

achieve that while penalizing those who had benefitted in the past from the bank's success, particularly the employees through salaries and bonuses and the owners through the profits they received. If that could not be done then there was no restraint on risk-taking as the owners and employees of conservatively run banks would go unrewarded while the risk-takers would be saved in the event of a collapse. However, the choice was not as clear-cut as that because the shareholders in banks had lost out either to the extent of the total value of their holding as in the case of Northern Rock, or through a serious depreciation in the share price and dividend stream. In the emergency legislation of 2008, government was given permission to take a bank into public ownership. This was replaced by the Banking Act 2009, which named the Bank of England as the resolution authority for all UK-incorporated firms that were authorized to accept deposits. Omitted were both investment banks and UK branches of foreign banks, so restricting the scope for potential intervention and exposing the difficulty of dealing with a foreign-owned failing bank with extensive operations in London.

Only the government possessed the funds required to support a large failing bank. Though the business of the Bradford and Bingley Bank was transferred to the Abbey National Bank, part of the Spanish-owned Santander Bank in September 2008, without compensation for the shareholders, financial support from the government was necessary, which received in return the outstanding mortgages and other financial assets. Similarly, in October 2008 the businesses of both the Heritable Bank, a subsidiary of Landsbanki of Iceland, and Kaupthing Singer and Friedlander, owned by the Kaupthing Bank of Iceland, were transferred to the ING Direct Bank but, again, only with government support. In the following year, in March 2009, the business of the Dunfermline Building Society was transferred to the Nationwide Building Society with the government providing financial support. What was happening was that the business of these failing banks and building societies was transferred to existing banks while the government provided financial support, receiving in return such assets as the loan book and the mortgages.[36]

What also emerged after the crises is the degree to which the intense competition that had preceded it had fostered a climate in which all that mattered was the generating of increased business by whatever means

---

[36] A. Bailey, Speech: 'The UK Bank Resolution Regime', 26 November 2009, pp.1-9; M. King, Speech: 16 June 2010, pp.1-8 ; Bailey, Speech: 'The Financial Crisis Reform Agenda', pp.1-9; P. Tucker, Speech: 'Developing an EU Cross-Border Crisis Management Framework', 30 September 2010, pp.1-7; G. Davies and M. Dobler, 'Bank Resolution and Safeguarding the Creditors Left Behind', *Bank of England Quarterly Bulletin*, 51 (2011), pp.213; Carter, 'Considering the Continuity of Payments', pp.147-53; A. Gracie, Speech: 'Total Loss-Absorbing Capacity: The Thinking Behind the FSB Term Sheet', 4 December 2014, pp.1-8; A. Gracie, Speech: 'Resolution in Context: The Policy Drivers of the New Paradigm', 8 December 2014, pp.1-10.

possible. The same circumstances that intensified risk-taking among banks and their employees also condoned market manipulation and the mis-selling of financial products that not only bordered on fraud but crossed that boundary. Such a situation was made possible because banks were left largely free to regulate themselves as it was believed they could be trusted to do so compared to the thousands of independent financial advisors. In the same way as the role of exchanges as bodies that regulated markets were seen to be redundant so the need to supervise the relationship between banks and their customers was not deemed necessary.[37]

The financial crisis demonstrated the need for a new approach to financial regulation, but that had to wait the fall of the Labour government, whose child the previous system had been. In 2010 a Conservative/Liberal-Democrat coalition took power, introducing a new regulatory structure with the Financial Services Act of 2012. This was much more focused on ensuring the stability of the banking system through preventing another crisis developing and then dealing with it quickly if it did threaten. In many ways this was a return to the situation prevailing before 1997, with the Bank of England responsible for the banking system, but possessed of much more formal authority. A single body, the Prudential Regulation Authority (PRA) was allocated responsibility for monitoring the safety and soundness of individual businesses within the UK financial sector, working closely with the market and auditors. Complementing the PRA was a separate body, the Financial Conduct Authority (FCA), which was tasked with protecting the consumer of financial services and products. In this way there would be no confusion between maintaining business stability and ensuring a fair deal for consumers. Whereas the PRA and the FCA could be seen as the inheritors of the FSA's role, as they were responsible for the activities of individual businesses, a new body was created with specific responsibility for financial stability. This was the Financial Policy Committee (FPC) and its role was to bridge the gap between regulating banks as businesses and controlling banks as monetary agents which had been exposed in the twin crises of 2007/8. What the creation of the FPC recognized was the uniqueness of banks because of their exposure to liquidity risks. The Bank of England and the UK Treasury were given the power to deal jointly with failing institutions through the Special Resolution Regime set up in 2009. Finally, the Monetary Policy Committee remained with its monetary policy responsibilities.[38] What was also put in place as a result of

---

[37] M. Shaffik, Speech: 'Making Markets Fair and Effective', 27 October 2014, pp.1–8; A. Hauser, 'Realigning Private and Public Interests in Wholesale Financial Markets: The Fair and Effective Markets Review', 29 January 2015, pp.1–9; A. Hauser, Speech: 'From Darkness Cometh Light? Some Early Messages from the Fair and Effective Markets Review Consultation Responses' 25 February 2015, pp.1–10.
[38] A. Bailey, Speech: 'The Supervisory Approach of the Prudential Regulation Authority', 19 May 2011, pp.1–8; H. Sands, Speech: 19 May 2011, pp.1–4; P. Tucker, Speech: 'Macro and

the crises was a much greater degree of international co-operation between central banks because only they, collectively, could supply the limitless amount of liquidity in the appropriate currencies when and where it was required. During the crisis bilateral foreign currency swap lines had been agreed between the central banks of the UK, USA, Canada, Switzerland, Japan, and the Eurozone.[39]

Though radical changes in financial regulation were made in the wake of the crisis, which recognized the importance of stability at the individual and collective level, those agencies tasked with achieving this stability were also given secondary objectives in line with broader government policy. Those broader objectives focused on promoting economic growth and achieving that through maintaining and enhancing competition. In the wake of the crisis the priority was stability, but these added objectives indicate the residual power of the government to intervene in banking so as to achieve their own end. From a regulator's perspective the less complicated banks were, the easier they would be to supervise. In this preference there was nostalgia for the compartmentalization of the banking system as had existed in the quarter century after the Second World War. Forgotten in that nostalgia was how compartmentalization had fostered the growth of a shadow banking system that nearly brought the entire banking system down in the Secondary Banking Crisis of 1974. Shadow banking had grown because the needs of both savers and borrowers were not being met by the existing providers, leading to a search for alternatives. Also forgotten was the degree to which global integration had removed national boundaries leaving banks to expand internationally rather than remain rooted to their domestic markets. An important cause of the drive

---

Microprudential Supervision', 29 June 201, pp.1-8; D. Kohn, Speech: 'The Financial Policy Committee at the Bank of England', 2 December 2011, pp.1-8; A. Bailey, S. Breeden, and G. Stevens, 'The Prudential Regulation Authority', *Bank of England Quarterly Bulletin*, 52 (2012), pp.354-62; P. Fisher, Speech: 'Policy Making at the Bank of England: The Financial Policy Committee, 12 March 2012, pp.1-11; A. Clark, Speech: 'What Is the FPC for?', 24 May 2012, pp.1-10; A. Bailey, Speech: 'Prudential Regulation: Challenges for the Future', 4 October 2012, pp.1-7; A. Bailey, Speech: 'The Future of Banking Regulation in the UK', 17 October 2012, pp.1-7; P. Tucker, 'Competition, the Pressure for Returns and Stability', 17 October 2012, pp.1-11; C. Bean, 'Central Banking in Boom and Slump', 31 October 2012, pp.1-18; A. Bailey, Speech: 'The Challenges in Assessing Capital Requirements for Banks', 6 November 2012, pp.1-6; E. Murphy and S. Senior, 'Changes to the Bank of England', *Bank of England Quarterly Bulletin*, 53 (2013), pp.20-6; Tucker, Hall, and Pattani, 'Macroprudential Policy', pp.192-200; Farag, Harland, and Nixon, 'Bank Capital and Liquidity', pp.202-7; Lees and Footman, 'The Court of the Bank of England', pp.30-3; P. Fisher, Speech: 'Microprudential, Macroprudential and Monetary Policy: Conflict, Compromise or Co-ordination?', 1 October 2014, pp.1-11; Sir Jon Cunliffe, Speech: 'Regulatory Reform and Returns in Banking', 20 October 2014, pp.1-10; M. Stewart (Director, Banks, Building Societies and Credit Unions, PRA), Speech: 'Two Years on from the March 2013 Publication of "A Review of Requirements for Firms Entering into or Expanding in the Banking Sector"', 11 March 2015, pp.1-6.

[39] M. Carney, Speech: 'The UK at the Heart of a Renewed Globalisation', 24 October 2013, pp.1-10; A.G. Haldane, 'Managing Global Finance as a System', 29 October 2014, pp.1-27.

behind the new regulatory structure introduced in 1997/8 was this process of convergence and globalization and it was still there after the financial crises of 2007/8. Rather than lessons from Britain's own banking history, those planning the new regulatory structure looked across the Atlantic to the USA and sought to adapt practice there to a UK context, despite the fundamental differences that existed.[40] There was also the question of the European Union which had a major influence on the design of the new regulatory structure to be adopted. As Sir Jon Cunliffe, Deputy Governor Financial Stability, pointed out at the beginning of 2015, 'The UK is the home to financial firms and infrastructure that are truly global in their reach and activity.... If EU regulation and internationally agreed standards diverge materially, it will both create barriers to that activity and opportunities for regulatory arbitrage making it more difficult ensure UK financial stability.'[41]

CONCLUSION

There were two banking crises in the space of a year, beginning in September 2007 and ending in October 2008. It is important to understand both because they were linked, though there has been a tendency to ignore the first and concentrate on the second.[42] If the first is ignored so are the reasons why the British banking system was so fragile in 2007 and so much better prepared in 2008. Each of these crises was different or, as a paper produced at the Bank of England expressed it, 'No banking crisis is alike.'[43] Nevertheless each crisis could trace its origins to events in the USA as the sequence of events reveals. However, of equal importance is the speed and degree to which the British banking system succumbed:

- July 2007: First real signs of a crisis emerge in the USA
- 9 August 2007: Start of the crisis in Europe and the USA
- 20 August 2007: Stigma attached to those banks using central bank borrowing facilities

---

[40] P. Tucker, Speech: 'The Reform of International Banking: Some Remaining Challenges', 1 October 2013, pp.1–7; Sir Jon Cunliffe, Speech: 'Ending Too Big to Fail—Progress to Date and Remaining Issues', 13 May 2014, pp.1–8; Furse, 'Taking the Long View: How Market-Based Finance Can Support Stability', 28 March 2014, pp.1–8; Garratt, Mahadeva, and Svirydzenka, 'Mapping Systemic Risk', pp.1–40; N. Arinaminpathy, S. Kapadia, and R. May, 'Size and Complexity in Model Financial Systems', *Bank of England Working Paper*, 465 (2012), pp.1–36.

[41] Sir Jon Cunliffe, Speech: 'Financial Stability, the Single Market and Capital Markets Union', 20 January 2015, pp.1–9.

[42] Liu, Quiet, and Roth, 'Banking Sector Interconnectedness', pp.1–7.

[43] N. Oulton and M. Sebastia-Barriel, 'Long- and Short-Term Effects of the Financial Crisis on Labour Productivity, Capital, and Output', *Bank of England Working Paper*, 470 (2013), pp.1–54.

- 13 September 2007: Bank of England makes access to credit easier
- 14 September 2007: Northern Rock granted liquidity support by Bank of England
- 17 March 2008: J.P. Morgan to buy Bear Stearns
- 21 April 2008: Bank of England launches Special Liquidity Scheme
- 15 September 2008: The collapse of Lehman Brothers
- 17 September 2008: Disclosure of merger talks between HBOS and Lloyds TSB
- 29 September 2008: Bradford and Bingley part nationalized
- 8 October 2008: Announcement of bank recapitalization plan.

The crisis in the UK began around August 2007 but it then escalated between the collapse of Bear Stearns in March 2008 and the collapse of Lehman Brothers in September 2008, reaching a peak after that latter event. As perceptions of counterparty risk increased, banks hoarded liquidity for precautionary motives, further restricting the liquidity available to other banks. Runs also occurred in other funding markets, such as asset-backed commercial paper and structured vehicles. From this perspective, stress spread from banks with direct exposure to US subprime loans to other banks. These banks responded to this stress on the liabilities side of their balance sheet by retrenching on the assets side through reduced lending to the financial markets. This transmitted the stress to those banks that were borrowing from the financial markets. Finally, this financial contagion was transmitted to the rest of the economy through the reduced lending on domestic assets.[44]

The banking crisis that took place in Britain in 2007 was neither unprecedented nor unparalleled. However, the search has to be extended back to 1866 and beyond to discover similar crises of equal magnitude and significance in the UK. In the years between 1866 and 1997 practices and procedures were learnt through trial and error that helped prevent similar crises achieving the same magnitude and significance as those of 1866 and before. What was then lost after 1997 was the appreciation of why these practices and procedures were important and how they had worked in the past. What was put in their place was an untried regime, which appeared to work until tested and was then found seriously wanting. However, it can never be known whether prompt intervention as practiced in the past would have prevented a banking crisis in 2007. The collapse of one or more banks was likely by then given the switch from the Lend and Hold Model to the Originate and Distribute one, and the risks that posed if liquidity dried up, as it would do at some time. Though contemporaries believed they had discovered a new way of conducting

[44] Wetherilt, Zimmerman, and Soramaki, 'Sterling Unsecured Loan Market', pp.1–39; Aiyar, 'How Did the Crisis', pp.1- 34; Aiyar, Calomiris, and Wieladek, 'Does Macropru Leak?'; Benos, Garratt, and Zimmerman, 'Bank Behaviour', pp.1-34.

banking, in reality they had only re-discovered an old one, and were unaware of the risks attached to it. What the crisis of 2007 did do was alert the authorities to the dangers now present in the British banking system rather than the rogue activities of a single bank. In responding to these intrinsic dangers the Bank of England, in particular, developed valuable tools that could then be employed when a bigger crisis took place, which it did in September 2008. Even then the scale of the crisis was not fully understood as the initial response was to persuade Lloyds TSB to rescue HBOS. This reflected a belief that the crisis could be contained. In the following month the Government intervened to save both RBS and Lloyds TSB/HBOS. The crisis of 2008 would have been much worse, however, had not that of 2007 taken place, because dealing with the latter taught the Bank of England valuable lessons which were then applied over the coming year. If RBS, owner of NatWest, had been the bank in the spotlight in 2007, rather than Northern Rock, and the same scenario had played out, then the payments system could have collapsed with dire consequences for the entire financial system and the economy. For that alone the British public should be grateful to Northern Rock and particularly its shareholders whose loss was total.[45]

---

[45] I was one of those shareholders, owning 1,500 shares along with my wife. We still hold these shares!

10

Comments and Conclusion

Britain possesses an especially long and rich banking history. As a result it contains numerous examples and episodes which contribute to an understanding of how banks have developed and why, the way that banks cope with crises, the relationship between banks and governments, and the role played by banks within the financial system According to the American economist, Raymond Goldsmith, who was an expert on global financial systems, England was 'the first country to develop a modern financial system, and the originator of many, if not most, of the financial institutions, which still dominate the financial scene in most of the world'.[1] For that reason alone the history of banking in Britain is of global interest. At the very least the ability of the British banking system to survive both local and global financial crises, without requiring government intervention, for almost 150 years should make it the subject of investigation and analysis. Recently, however, the focus has been on why the British banking system succumbed to the financial crisis of 2007/8, and continues to suffer its consequences. An equally valid approach is to ask why and how that same banking system avoided such a fate in the past when others did not. Discovering why an event did not take place can be as instructive as finding out why one did.

Another reason why the history of British banking should be studied is because of its enduring success. In the City of London, Britain hosts an international banking centre that acts as the global hub for the banking industry, linking together banks from around the world. This hub not only provides banks with access to a worldwide payments system but also a means through which they can lend and borrow among themselves and match assets and liabilities across time, space, amount, and currency. The City of London became the leading international banking centre during the nineteenth century and has retained that position ever since.[2] Catherine Shenk has referred to

---

[1] R.W. Goldsmith, *Comparative National Balance Sheets: A Study of Twenty Countries, 1688-1978* (Chicago: University of Chicago Press, 1985), p.227.

[2] Committee on the Global Financial System, *Long Term Issues in International Banking* (Basel: Bank for International Settlements, 2010), p.12; Cassis, *Capitals of Capital*; L. Allen,

the 'remarkable consistency in the attractions of the City of London for international banking despite repeated global financial crisis and ongoing financial innovation'.[3] A wide ranging survey conducted by Von Peter, for the Bank for International Settlement, in 2007, concluded that London ranked first as an international banking centre by whatever measure was used, including the number of bank offices, inter-bank market activity or the degree of connectivity. In particular, that survey calculated that London was connected to more banking centres around the world than any other city and that those connections were more direct.[4]

However, Britain's own banking history has been rather neglected in favour of that of the USA in looking at historical examples as guides to future development. This is true not only of banking but generally, as the USA is taken as representative of the position in all developed economies. As Robert Johnson, President, Institute for New Economic Thinking, observed in 2014, 'The examples that we use in textbooks are often based on US data and institutions and don't produce much excitement elsewhere, particularly in the emerging economies.'[5] No greater example of this reliance on US evidence exists than in the study of the Global Financial Crisis. Not only is there a high degree of dependence on the timing and pattern of the crisis in the USA as representative of the general picture, but the proposed solutions emanating from the media and governments are based on the banking system as operating in the USA. Overlooked is an alternative explanation of what took place based on the UK experience and the possibility of a UK solution arising out of that country's rich banking history.

The problem of learning from past experience is that the lessons it provides are neither straightforward nor unambiguous but mixed and contradictory. There is no objective truth that can be used to guide future action so as to achieve a definite outcome. That does not mean that history is of no value, for the past contains the only experience that is available. Once that is recognized it becomes possible to use history in a nuanced way and so provide useful lessons. The first step in achieving that is to note that the past is a battlefield

---

The Global Financial System, 1750–2000 (London: Reaktion, 2001), cf. ch. 8, 'The Evolution of International Banking'.

[3] Schenk, *Decline of Sterling*, p.240. See also M. Fratianni, 'The Evolutionary Chain of International Financial Centers', in P. Alessandrini, M. Fratianni, and A. Zazzoro (eds), *The Changing Geography of Banking and Finance* (Dordrecht: Springer, 2009), ch. 12, pp.251–76.

[4] G. Von Peter, 'International Banking Centres: A Network Perspective', *BIS Quarterly Review* (2007), pp.33–5, 37–8, 40 + Tables. Cf. IFSL Research, *International Financial Markets in the UK* (London: IFSL, 2009); HM Treasury, *UK International Financial Services, The Future: A Report from UK-based Financial Services Leaders to the Government* (London: HM Treasury, 2009). For a less comprehensive study which also indicates London's continuing importance as an international banking centre, see S.R. Choi, D. Park, and A.E. Tschoegel, 'Banks and the World's Major Banking Centers', October 2014.

[5] *Financial Times* 23 September 2014.

continuously fought over by those searching for evidence to support their views. To that end they select from all the available information that which seems relevant to the questions they are asking. In turn those questions are driven by current considerations and perceptions with the result that much of the information found in the past is either ignored or set aside as being marginal or irrelevant. Hindsight is a two-edged weapon. On the one hand it can provide perspective, so revealing to later generations that which is hidden from contemporaries. On the other hand it can cloud judgement by imposing on the past the priorities of the present. Once it is recognized that hindsight can simultaneously aid understanding and distort the conclusions reached, it becomes possible to use the lessons of history as an analytical tool of value to policy makers.

In searching for both explanation and solution in Britain's financial history, when beginning with the Global Financial Crisis, care must be taken to avoid falling into the trap of determinism, as identified by Nassim Taleb, 'When you look at the past, the past will always be deterministic, since only one single observation took place. Our mind will interpret most events not with the preceding ones in mind, but the following ones.'[6] Conversely, it is also important not to fall into the alternative trap in treating the Global Financial Crisis as an event driven only by its own inner momentum. According to Gladwell, 'The name given to that one dramatic moment in an epidemic when everything can change all at once is the tipping point.'[7] Instead, the argument presented in this book is that context is of critical importance in explaining why Britain experienced a serious banking crisis in 2007/8. That crisis was neither inevitable, despite its global nature, nor driven by its own momentum but was produced by an interaction between the banking system that had developed in Britain over the previous 150 years and the changes that took place especially in the ten years before 2007. Britain's banking crisis of 2007/8 cannot be studied in a vacuum but only in the context of its relationship to what had happened before and what took place at the time, while its significance can only be tested when the detail of what took place is fully understood.

Though the financial crisis of 2008 was global, much of what took place in Britain can be traced to local conditions, especially if due attention is paid to the chronology of what took place at that time. As early as the middle of 2007 problems had begun to emerge at those British banks that had converted from operating as building societies, beginning with the Newcastle-based Northern Rock Bank in 2007. These banks had attempted to grow quickly by adopting the Originate and Distribute business model rather than stick to the Lend and

---

[6] N.T. Taleb, *Fooled by Randomness: The Hidden Role of Chance in Life and in the Markets* (New York: Random House 2005), pp.55–6.
[7] M. Gladwell, *The Tipping Point: How Little Things Can Make a Big Difference* (London: Little Brown, 2000), p.9.

Hold one that had served them well in the past. This made them dependent upon the re-packaging and re-sale of the loans made to customers and borrowing extensively in the wholesale money markets. The use of this model was not confined to the de-mutualized building societies but was extensively adopted by any bank that sought to expand its business rapidly. These included a number of the remaining building societies, the mutually owned Co-operative Bank and, especially, the two Scottish banks, RBS and HBOS, as they also attempted to expand rapidly through extending their operations into England, and even abroad. Since the Global Financial Crisis there have been a series of damming revelations about the behaviour of British bankers over the previous ten years, as they abandoned caution in the pursuit of corporate profits and personal bonuses. What the crisis also exposed was the inadequacy of the financial regulatory system in place as that should have identified and then curbed the risks that banks were taking and prevented both the mis-selling and manipulation. In particular, the Bank of England was found wanting as it failed to intervene to prevent the problems of one small bank, Northern Rock, destabilizing the entire British banking system.

The cumulative effect of the crisis of 2007/8, and the revelations, was to transform the reputation of British banking that had been built up over the previous 150 years. No longer were British banks seen as trusted guardians of the nation's savings. No longer was the standard of behaviour maintained by British bankers regarded as being the highest in the world. No longer was the British system of financial regulation held up as the model to be copied by others. No longer was the Bank of England believed to symbolize central banking competence. But the legitimate questions that should have arisen from what took place in British banking, beginning with the problems at Northern Rock in mid-2007, were swept aside when the crisis became a global one a year later. Rather than seeing a return to the past as a solution to the current predicament of British banking, the desire became one to fashion an entirely new banking system, learning lessons not from UK but US experience. The new banking system would be one involving legally enforceable rules and regulations, dictating to banks what they could and could not do. Such a response was driven by politicians and the media, who believed that legislation was the only way to prevent a repetition of both the crisis and the abuses. The alternative approach of leaving banks and the banking system to devise and implement their own solutions was not even considered. Forgotten is Britain's own financial history in which banking achieved its reputation for stability without the need for legislation.

The Bank of England was set up as a company in 1694 and only slowly acquired the role of a central bank by responding to the challenges and opportunities it faced in the following centuries. It was not taken into state ownership and control until 1946, long after the British banking system had established its reputation for stability. Similarly, British banks were, for long, neither stable nor trusted. Failure was commonplace and bankers were prosecuted, and even faced the death penalty, for stealing from their customers. What led to the reputation for stability was the formation of ever larger banks, pursuing a diversified business through a nationwide network of branches, and closely managed and monitored from a single head office, usually in London. These were not the only banks in Britain but it was their stability and the trust placed in them that gained the British banking system the reputation that was eventually lost in the Global Financial Crisis. These banks based their operations on the Lend and Hold Model and it was their success that transformed the British banking system, including forcing the Bank of England into playing the role of lender of last resort.

What are the lessons of history for British banking from a post-Global-Financial-Crisis perspective. The first is that the stability inherent in the British banking system, as demonstrated between the wars, needs to be restored. The reasons for that stability lay not in legislation but in the existence of a small number of large banks with a diversified business model and strictly enforced code of banking behaviour. Underpinning that stability were actions taken by the Bank of England as a selective lender of last resort to these banks. The second is to recognize that the increasingly competitive nature of British banking after 1997 undermined the conservative code of conduct and replaced it with one in which risk-taking and market manipulation were richly rewarded. The third is to acknowledge that hosting a global financial centre generates both large rewards and creates large risks, and that ways have to be devised at an international level to retain the former and minimize the latter. The fourth is that both governments and regulators need to accept that banking is not like any other business, to be conducted in the same way. Instead, the peculiar nature of the risks run in banking, and what a banking collapse could mean for the economy, needs to be acknowledged, and so banking should be treated differently from other areas of business. The fifth is that in planning the future shape and direction of British banking, lessons are learnt from banking systems that were similar in structure to that in Britain, and share a common inherited culture, but proved to be resilient in the face of the Global Financial Crisis. Such banking systems are to be found in Australia and Canada but not the United States or even Continental Europe.

Unfortunately what examination there has been has tended to focus on the structure and behaviour of the largest banks rather than the environment within which they operated, both nationally and internationally. Over the last thirty years British banking was transformed. In 1979 it had become a cosy cartel closely monitored by the Bank of England and operating largely free from foreign competition because of exchange controls. Those banks could, in turn, rely on the Bank of England to act as lender of last resort to the London money market in the event of a crisis, and so prevent a collapse. At that time the criticism of banks was that their conservative lending practices were responsible for the sluggish growth of the UK economy. By 2007 British banks operated in a global economy largely free from exchange controls and had to compete for business against a number of long established rivals, especially the ex-building societies, while the long-standing division between English and Scottish banks had broken down. These banks had also changed the model under which they operated since the late nineteenth century. Increasingly the Lend and Hold Model was supplanted by the Originate and Distribute one which greatly increased the risks that were being run. Though attributed to the changes that were introduced in 1986, at the time of Big Bang, this switch in the model was much more a result of the intensification of competition at the retail level from the mid-1990s onwards. This switch in the model also coincided with a change in the regulatory framework through which bank behaviour was monitored and lender-of-last-resort support was provided. In particular, the Bank of England lost many of its banking functions and became, increasingly, little more than a manager of the payments system and a monetary policy institute acting on behalf of the government. In turn the government saw only the benefits that arose from the expansion and risk-taking of the banks and was unaware of the potential consequences.

Resulting from this focus on banks has emerged the widely held belief that the cause of the crisis was because British banks had become too big to fail. Secure in the knowledge that they could rely on government support in the event of a crisis, British banks had indulged in a frenzy of lending that generated large profits for their shareholders and huge bonuses for their staff. New financial products, investment vehicles, and trading systems had been invented that appeared to provide depositors and investors with high and safe returns while simultaneously providing borrowers with abundant loans at low interest rates regardless of their credit rating or business model. When the crisis did eventually occur it was the government that was forced to intervene to prevent a systemic collapse so saving the banks, their shareholders, and their employees from the consequences of their risk-taking. Hence the desire after the Global Financial Crisis to restructure British banking in such a way as would reduce these risks. The main solutions proposed involved separating retail and investment banking, increasing the level of capital and reserves that the largest banks must maintain, forcing the largest domestic banks to down-size, and making British banking more competitive at the retail level. Each of these has implications for British banks that could increase their costs and reduce their ability to meet the needs of their customers, so leading them to lose business to rivals not operating under the same restrictions. The question is whether what happened to British banking in 2007/8 requires such a solution. The evidence from Britain's own banking history suggests not. A transformation took place in the British banking system over the course of the nineteenth century that made it both resilient and competitive. It was not until 1997 that the structure and operation of the British banking system that had emerged by the twentieth century was radically altered. In 2007 there was a banking crisis that was strangely reminiscent of those that had occurred regularly in the century prior to 1866, with the last one taking place in that year. The lessons learnt over the space of almost 150 years had been undone in ten.

APPENDIX 1

Number of British Banks, 1700–2008

Year	Number Started	Number Ended	Total Number
1700	1	0	49
1701	1	0	50
1702	0	0	50
1703	0	0	50
1704	0	0	50
1705	0	0	50
1706	3	0	53
1707	0	1	52
1708	0	0	52
1709	0	1	52
1710	0	0	51
1711	0	0	51
1712	6	1	57
1713	3	1	59
1714	2	1	60
1715	2	1	61
1716	5	0	65
1717	0	0	65
1718	1	1	66
1719	0	1	65
1720	2	3	66
1721	1	2	64
1722	1	3	63
1723	1	1	61
1724	0	1	60
1725	0	0	59
1726	0	0	59
1727	3	2	62
1728	1	1	61
1729	7	0	67
1730	6	1	73
1731	0	1	72
1732	1	0	72
1733	1	2	73
1734	0	0	74
1735	2	4	73
1736	3	0	72
1737	10	2	82
1738	8	3	88
1739	1	2	86
1740	1	1	85

(*Continued*)

Appendix 1

Year	Number Started	Number Ended	Total Number
1741	1	1	85
1742	1	5	85
1743	0	2	80
1744	7	1	85
1745	0	1	84
1746	1	0	84
1747	1	1	85
1748	5	1	89
1749	3	1	91
1750	10	1	100
1751	4	2	103
1752	0	1	101
1753	6	3	106
1754	7	5	110
1755	6	1	111
1756	2	0	112
1757	4	2	116
1758	16	1	130
1759	4	1	133
1760	20	3	152
1761	3	3	152
1762	8	4	157
1763	5	3	158
1764	12	5	167
1765	10	1	172
1766	8	2	179
1767	4	1	181
1768	10	6	190
1769	7	5	191
1770	24	4	210
1771	25	2	231
1772	12	9	241
1773	19	7	251
1774	17	9	261
1775	7	6	260
1776	5	2	259
1777	10	4	267
1778	18	9	281
1779	7	6	279
1780	31	1	304
1781	8	7	311
1782	47	5	351
1783	35	2	381
1784	19	11	398
1785	20	4	407
1786	11	3	414
1787	25	4	436
1788	27	5	459
1789	19	5	473
1790	113	7	581
1791	36	6	610

Appendix 1

Year	Number Started	Number Ended	Total Number
1792	43	9	647
1793	57	13	695
1794	11	7	693
1795	12	5	698
1796	16	11	709
1797	40	9	738
1798	8	14	737
1799	10	6	733
1800	100	29	827
1801	47	13	845
1802	24	9	856
1803	18	13	865
1804	41	23	893
1805	29	13	899
1806	53	22	939
1807	59	17	976
1808	65	14	1024
1809	72	15	1082
1810	55	25	1123
1811	25	32	1124
1812	30	30	1123
1813	22	27	1115
1814	12	29	1100
1815	21	47	1092
1816	21	77	1066
1817	11	10	1000
1818	29	14	1019
1819	20	22	1025
1820	11	32	1014
1821	20	26	1002
1822	8	21	984
1823	12	21	975
1824	18	29	972
1825	22	75	965
1826	11	61	901
1827	15	13	855
1828	8	6	850
1829	18	18	862
1830	16	22	860
1831	15	19	853
1832	19	26	853
1833	24	19	852
1834	20	22	853
1835	27	20	858
1836	75	61	913
1837	17	38	869
1838	16	16	847
1839	14	21	845
1840	13	27	838
1841	10	36	821

(*Continued*)

Appendix 1

Year	Number Started	Number Ended	Total Number
1842	5	27	790
1843	6	20	769
1844	6	20	755
1845	6	11	741
1846	4	11	734
1847	5	21	728
1848	5	12	712
1849	2	10	702
1850	2	8	694
1851	8	14	694
1852	5	8	685
1853	9	13	686
1854	3	5	676
1855	9	17	680
1856	8	12	671
1857	7	16	666
1858	8	12	658
1859	8	11	654
1860	10	10	653
1861	9	17	652
1862	29	6	664
1863	29	21	687
1864	32	27	698
1865	17	25	688
1866	17	43	680
1867	8	14	645
1868	4	13	635
1869	5	5	626
1870	9	11	630
1871	5	12	624
1872	19	8	631
1873	10	12	633
1874	5	10	626
1875	10	12	626
1876	4	4	618
1877	8	13	622
1878	10	20	619
1879	15	19	614
1880	20	24	615
1881	9	9	600
1882	7	12	598
1883	3	18	589
1884	7	21	578
1885	8	5	565
1886	4	11	565
1887	2	11	556
1888	10	18	555
1889	15	19	552
1890	8	19	541
1891	14	39	536
1892	13	28	510

Appendix 1

Year	Number Started	Number Ended	Total Number
1893	11	26	494
1894	8	21	476
1895	3	8	458
1896	1	41	451
1897	1	15	411
1898	4	16	400
1899	12	17	396
1900	2	27	382
1901	6	18	361
1902	2	18	345
1903	3	12	330
1904	2	11	320
1905	3	15	312
1906	4	12	301
1907	9	11	298
1908	6	7	294
1909	7	8	294
1910	4	8	290
1911	9	12	291
1912	8	11	287
1913	9	10	285
1914	2	15	277
1915	3	1	265
1916	2	8	266
1917	6	7	264
1918	5	15	262
1919	20	24	267
1920	13	22	256
1921	12	16	246
1922	12	14	242
1923	10	19	238
1924	8	14	227
1925	9	10	222
1926	6	5	218
1927	5	5	218
1928	7	8	220
1929	5	13	217
1930	5	12	209
1931	1	7	198
1932	7	5	198
1933	2	8	195
1934	9	8	196
1935	7	9	195
1936	7	10	195
1937	2	1	187
1938	2	3	188
1939	1	7	186
1940	0	3	179
1941	1	4	177
1942	0	2	173

(Continued)

Appendix 1

Year	Number Started	Number Ended	Total Number
1943	6	5	177
1944	1	3	173
1945	2	3	172
1946	4	5	173
1947	8	4	176
1948	3	6	175
1949	2	5	171
1950	4	6	170
1951	4	7	168
1952	2	4	163
1953	1	2	160
1954	3	4	161
1955	8	6	165
1956	1	3	160
1957	5	7	162
1958	6	4	161
1959	3	8	160
1960	6	5	158
1961	3	5	156
1962	9	10	160
1963	4	2	154
1964	8	3	160
1965	5	4	162
1966	7	8	165
1967	4	0	161
1968	9	8	170
1969	12	22	174
1970	9	18	161
1971	16	11	159
1972	15	8	163
1973	20	10	175
1974	11	10	176
1975	5	7	171
1976	3	4	167
1977	10	10	173
1978	6	4	169
1979	2	0	167
1980	31	24	198
1981	16	13	190
1982	14	13	191
1983	13	15	191
1984	6	9	182
1985	16	20	189
1986	25	25	194
1987	30	35	199
1988	31	35	195
1989	13	21	173
1990	14	15	166
1991	5	7	156
1992	5	12	154
1993	7	20	149

Appendix 1

Year	Number Started	Number Ended	Total Number
1994	2	5	131
1995	5	8	131
1996	5	6	128
1997	9	10	131
1998	4	8	125
1999	6	15	123
2000	6	7	114
2001	8	9	115
2002	7	6	113
2003	4	7	111
2004	3	4	107
2005	4	6	107
2006	3	2	104
2007	1	6	103
2008	1	0	98

APPENDIX 2
Number of Registered Building Societies, 1876–2010

Year	Total	Difference
1876	701	–
1877	863	+162
1878	969	+106
1879	1101	+132
1880	1224	+123
1881	1333	+109
1882	1581	+248
1883	1787	+206
1884	1994	+207
1885	2190	+196
1886	2251	+61
1887	2273	+22
1888	2388	+115
1889	2520	+132
1890	2648	+128
1891	2809	+161
1892	2632	−177
1893	2328	−304
1894	2158	−170
1895	2469	+311
1896	2486	+17
1897	2527	+41
1898	2493	−34
1899	2402	−91
1900	2286	−116
1901	2191	−95
1902	2122	−69
1903	1956	−166
1904	2006	+50
1905	1927	−69
1906	1851	−76
1907	1791	−61
1908	1749	−42
1909	1706	−43
1910	1723	+17
1911	1608	−115
1912	1583	−25
1913	1550	−33
1914	1581	+31
1915	1451	−130
1916	1402	−49

Appendix 2

Year	Total	Difference
1917	1336	−66
1918	1336	0
1919	1311	−25
1920	1271	−40
1921	1184	−87
1922	1150	−34
1923	1112	−38
1924	1112	0
1925	1092	−20
1926	1064	−28
1927	1054	−10
1928	1035	−19
1929	1026	−9
1930	1026	0
1931	1013	−13
1932	1014	+1
1933	1013	−1
1934	1007	−6
1935	999	−8
1936	985	−14
1937	977	−8
1938	974	−3
1939	960	−14
1940	952	−8
1941	947	−5
1942	931	−16
1943	924	−7
1944	905	−19
1945	890	−15
1946	874	−16
1947	858	−16
1948	847	−11
1949	835	−12
1950	819	−16
1951	807	−12
1952	796	−11
1953	782	−14
1954	777	−5
1955	783	+6
1956	773	−10
1957	755	−18
1958	744	−11
1959	732	−12
1960	726	−6
1961	706	−20
1962	681	−25
1963	662	−19
1964	635	−17
1965	605	−30

(Continued)

Appendix 2

Year	Total	Difference
1966	576	−29
1967	554	−22
1968	525	−29
1969	504	−21
1970	481	−23
1971	467	−14
1972	456	−11
1973	447	−9
1974	416	−31
1975	382	−32
1976	364	−18
1977	339	−25
1978	316	−23
1979	287	−29
1980	273	−14
1981	253	−20
1982	227	−27
1983	206	−21
1984	190	−16
1985	167	−23
1986	151	−16
1987	138	−13
1988	131	−7
1989	110	−21
1990	101	−9
1991	94	−7
1992	88	−6
1993	84	−4
1994	82	−2
1995	80	−2
1996	77	−3
1997	71	−6
1998	71	0
1999	69	−2
2000	67	−2
2001	65	−2
2002	65	0
2003	63	−2
2004	63	0
2005	63	0
2006	60	−3
2007	59	−1
2008	55	−4
2009	52	−3
2010	49	−3

APPENDIX 3

Number of Trustee Savings Banks, 1829–1967

Year	Total	Difference
1829	476	–
1830	480	4
1831	474	–6
1832	478	4
1833	482	4
1834	482	–
1835	483	1
1836	491	8
1837	513	22
1838	522	9
1839	541	19
1840	546	5
1841	553	7
1842	563	10
1843	567	4
1844	571	4
1845	579	8
1846	591	12
1847	595	4
1848	583	–12
1849	577	–6
1850	573	–4
1851	577	4
1852	576	–1
1853	582	6
1854	585	3
1855	591	6
1856	599	8
1857	603	4
1858	607	4
1859	624	17
1860	638	14
1861	645	7
1862	621	–24
1863	603	–18
1864	577	–26
1865	561	–16
1866	551	–10
1867	539	–12
1868	513	–26

(*Continued*)

Appendix 3

Year	Total	Difference
1669	507	−6
1870	496	−11
1871	489	−7
1872	483	−6
1873	481	−2
1874	474	−7
1875	470	−4
1876	463	−7
1877	458	−5
1878	454	−4
1879	449	−5
1880	442	−7
1881	437	−5
1882	430	−7
1883	421	−9
1884	411	−10
1885	409	−2
1886	405	−4
1887	400	−5
1888	382	−18
1889	346	−36
1890	324	−22
1891	303	−21
1892	281	−22
1893	267	−14
1894	257	−10
1895	245	−12
1896	239	−6
1897	232	−7
1898	231	−1
1899	231	−
1900	230	−1
1901	229	−1
1902	228	−1
1903	224	−4
1904	224	−
1905	224	−
1906	224	−
1907	222	−2
1908	222	−
1909	222	−
1910	219	−3
1911	215	−4
1912	211	−4
1913	202	−9
1914	196	−6
1915	191	−5
1916	189	−2
1917	179	−10
1918	171	−8
1919	163	−8

Appendix 3

Year	Total	Difference
1920	163	–
1921	152	−11
1922	148	−4
1923	147	−1
1924	146	−1
1925	140	−6
1926	131	−9
1927	123	−8
1928	119	−4
1929	113	−6
1930	107	−6
1931	106	−1
1932	102	−4
1933	100	−2
1934	102	2
1935	104	2
1936	105	1
1937	102	−3
1938	101	−1
1939	99	−2
1940	99	–
1941	93	−6
1942	91	−2
1943	89	−2
1944	88	−1
1945	87	−1
1946	87	–
1947	87	–
1948	86	−1
1949	85	−1
1950	84	−1
1951	85	+1
1952	85	–
1953	85	–
1954	84	−1
1955	84	–
1956	84	–
1957	84	–
1958	84	–
1959	84	–
1960	83	−1
1961	80	−3
1962	80	–
1963	80	–
1964	80	–
1965	79	−1
1966	78	−1
1967	77	−1

APPENDIX 4

Number of US Banks, 1782–2013[1]

Year	Total	Difference
1782	1	1
1783	1	–
1784	2	1
1785	2	–
1786	1	–1
1787	2	1
1788	2	–
1789	2	–
1790	3	1
1791	5	2
1792	12	7
1793	15	3
1794	15	–
1795	20	5
1796	22	2
1797	22	–
1798	22	–
1799	25	3
1800	28	3
1801	32	4
1802	35	3
1803	53	18
1804	64	9
1805	71	7
1806	78	7
1807	83	5
1808	86	3
1809	92	6
1810	102	10
1811	117	15
1812	143	26
1813	147	4
1814	202	55
1815	212	10
1816	232	20
1817	262	30

[1] There are breaks in the series between 1833 and 1834, 1895 and 1896, and 1933 and 1934. These will change the overall trend in the number of banks but these breaks should not be treated as significant.

Appendix 4

Year	Total	Difference
1818	338	76
1819	341	3
1820	327	−14
1821	273	−54
1822	267	−6
1823	274	7
1824	300	24
1825	330	30
1826	331	1
1827	333	2
1828	355	22
1829	369	14
1830	381	12
1831	424	43
1832	464	40
1833	517	53
1834	506	−11
1835	704	198
1836	713	9
1837	788	75
1838	829	41
1839	840	11
1840	901	61
1841	784	−117
1842	692	−92
1843	691	−1
1844	696	5
1845	707	11
1846	707	–
1847	715	8
1848	751	36
1849	782	31
1850	824	42
1851	879	55
1852	913	34
1853	750	−163
1854	1208	458
1855	1307	99
1856	1398	91
1857	1416	18
1858	1422	6
1859	1476	54
1860	1562	86
1861	1601	39
1862	1492	−109
1863	1532	40
1864	1556	34
1865	1643	87
1866	1931	88

(*Continued*)

Appendix 4

Year	Total	Difference
1867	1908	−23
1868	1887	−21
1669	1878	−9
1870	1937	59
1871	2175	238
1872	2419	244
1873	3298	879
1874	3552	254
1875	3336	−216
1876	3448	112
1877	3384	−64
1878	3229	−155
1879	3335	106
1880	3555	220
1881	3427	−128
1882	3572	145
1883	3835	263
1884	4113	278
1885	4350	237
1886	4338	−12
1887	6170	1832
1888	6647	477
1889	7244	597
1890	8201	957
1891	8641	440
1892	9336	695
1893	9492	156
1894	9508	16
1895	9818	310
1896	11474	1656
1897	11438	−36
1898	11530	92
1899	11835	305
1900	12427	592
1901	13424	997
1902	14488	1064
1903	15814	1326
1904	17037	1223
1905	18152	1115
1906	19786	1634
1907	21361	1575
1908	22531	1170
1909	23098	567
1910	24514	1416
1911	25183	669
1912	25844	661
1913	26664	820
1914	27236	572
1915	27390	154
1916	27739	349
1917	28298	559

Appendix 4

Year	Total	Difference
1918	28856	558
1919	29147	291
1920	30291	1144
1921	30456	165
1922	30120	−336
1923	29829	−291
1924	28988	−841
1925	28442	−546
1926	27742	−700
1927	26650	−1092
1928	25798	−852
1929	24970	−828
1930	23679	−1291
1931	21654	−2025
1932	18734	−2920
1933	14207	−4527
1934	14146	−61
1935	14125	−21
1936	13973	−52
1937	13797	−176
1938	13661	−136
1939	13538	−123
1940	13442	−96
1941	13430	−12
1942	13347	−83
1943	13274	−73
1944	13268	−6
1945	13302	34
1946	13359	57
1947	13403	44
1948	13419	16
1949	13436	27
1950	13446	10
1951	13455	9
1952	13439	−16
1953	13432	−7
1954	13323	−109
1955	13237	−86
1956	13218	−19
1957	13165	−53
1958	13124	−41
1959	13114	−10
1960	13126	12
1961	13115	−11
1962	13124	9
1963	13291	167
1964	13493	202
1965	13544	51
1966	13538	−6
1967	13514	−24

(*Continued*)

Appendix 4

Year	Total	Difference
1968	13487	−27
1969	13473	−14
1970	13511	38
1971	13612	101
1972	13733	121
1973	13976	243
1974	14230	254
1975	14384	154
1976	14410	26
1977	14411	1
1978	14391	−20
1979	14364	−27
1980	14434	70
1981	14414	−20
1982	14451	37
1983	14469	18
1984	14496	27
1985	14417	79
1986	14210	−207
1987	13723	−487
1988	13137	−586
1989	12715	−422
1990	12347	−368
1991	11927	−420
1992	11467	−460
1993	10961	−506
1994	10453	−508
1995	9943	−510
1996	9530	−413
1997	9144	−386
1998	8777	−367
1999	8582	−195
2000	8315	−267
2001	8082	−233
2002	7888	−194
2003	7770	−118
2004	7631	−139
2005	7526	−105
2006	7401	−125
2007	7284	−117
2008	7088	−196
2009	6840	−248
2010	6530	−310
2011	6291	−239
2012	6096	−195
2013	5876	−220

APPENDIX 5

Timeline: UK Banking

1694 Bank of England: Charter granted.
1708 Bank of England: Granted monopoly of joint-stock banking in England.
1770 Bankers' Clearing House formed in London.
1797 Suspension of the convertibility of bank notes into gold.
1821 Restoration of the convertibility of bank notes into gold.
1826 Banking Act: Joint-stock banks permitted but not within sixty-five miles of London.
1833 Banking Act: Joint-stock banks permitted throughout England.
1844 Bank Charter Act/Joint Stock Banks Act: No new banks could issue bank notes; note issue of existing banks capped; banks lost the right to issue notes on closure or takeover.
1854 Bankers' Clearing House admits joint-stock banks as members.
1857 Restrictions on joint-stock bank formation repealed.
1864 Bank of England becomes a member of the Bankers' Clearing House.
1879 Joint-stock banks granted limited liability if accounts were externally audited.
1914 Suspension of the convertibility of bank notes into gold.
1946 Bank of England nationalized.
1979 Bank of England is given the statutory authority to regulate UK banking.
1986 Financial Services Act: Statutory regulation of the UK financial sector.
1986 Building Societies Act: Building societies could become banks.
1987 Bank of England is given additional authority over UK banking.
1997 Building Societies are given more freedom to operate as banks.
1998 Bank of England loses responsibility for regulating banks.
1998 Financial Services Authority is given responsibility for regulating banks.
2000 Financial Services and Markets Act: unified system of statutory regulation.
2012 Financial Services Authority abolished. Replaced by
   The Financial Policy Committee (within the Bank of England)
   The Prudential Regulation Authority (within the Bank of England)
   The Financial Conduct Authority.

APPENDIX 6

Timeline: US Banking

1781 Bank of North America.
1791 First Bank of the United States: Charter granted.
1811 First Bank of the United States: Charter not renewed.
1816 Second Bank of the United States: Charter granted.
1836 Second Bank of the United States: Charter not renewed.
1863/4 National Banking Acts.
1913 Federal Reserve Act.
1932 Federal Home Loan Bank Act.
1933 Banking Act (Glass-Steagall Act).
1933 Federal Deposit Insurance Corporation.
1933 The Home Owners Loan Act.
1934 Federal Savings and Loan Insurance Corporation.
1934 Federal Credit Union Act.
1935 Banking Act.
1980 Depository Institutions Deregulation and Monetary Control Act.
1982 Garn-St.Germain Act.
1989 Financial Institutions Reform, Recovery, and Enforcement Act.
1994 Riegle-Neal Interstate Banking and Branching Act.
1995 Federal Deposit Insurance Corporation merges with the Resolution Trust Corporation.
1999 Bliley Act (repeal of the Glass-Steagall Act).
2010 Dodd-Frank Act.

Bibliography

Acharya, V. and Yorulmazer, T., 'Cash-in-the-Market Pricing and Optimal Resolution of Bank Failures', *Bank of England Working Paper*, 328 (2007)

Acharya, V. and Yorulmazer, T., 'Too Many to Fail: An Analysis of Time-Inconsistency in Bank Closure Policies', *Bank of England Working Paper*, 319 (2007)

Ackrill, M. and Hannah, L., *Barclays: The Business of Banking, 1690–1996* (Cambridge: CUP, 2001)

Adams, M., Galbiati, M., and Giansante, S., 'Liquidity Costs and Tiering in Large-Value Payment Systems', *Bank of England Working Paper*, 399 (2010)

Aitchison, W.J., 'On the Ratio a Banker's Cash Reserve Should Bear to his Liability on Current and Deposit Accounts, as Exemplified by the London Clearing Joint-Stock Banks', *Journal of the Institute of Bankers*, 6 (1885)

Aiyar, S., 'How Did the Crisis in International Funding Markets Affect Bank Lending: Balance Sheet Evidence from the United Kingdom', *Bank of England Working Paper*, 424 (2011)

Aiyar, S., Calomiris, C.W., Hooley. J., Korniyenko, Y., and Wieladek, T., 'The International Transmission of Bank Capital Requirements: Evidence from the United Kingdom', *Bank of England Working Paper*, 497 (2014)

Aiyar, S., Calomiris, C.W., and Wieladek, T., 'Does Macropru Leak? Evidence from a UK Policy Experiment', *Bank of England Working Paper*, 445 (2012)

Alborn, T.L., *Conceiving Companies: Joint-Stock Politics in Victorian England* (London: Routledge, 1998)

Alessandri, P. and Haldane, A.G., Speech: 'Banking on the State' (2009)

Alexander, J., 'The Economic Structure of the City of London at the End of the Seventeenth Century', *Urban History Yearbook* (1989)

Alford, W.E., *British Economic Performance, 1945–1975* (London: Macmillan, 1988)

Ali, R., Barrdear, J., Clews, R., and Southgate, R., 'Innovations in Payment Technologies and the Emergence of Digital Currencies', *Bank of England Quarterly Bulletin*, 53 (2013)

Alkman, D. and Vlieghe, G., 'How Much Does Bank Capital Matter?', *Bank of England Quarterly Bulletin*, 44 (2004)

Allen, F. and Gale, D., *Understanding Financial Crises* (Oxford: OUP, 2007)

Allen, L., *The Global Financial System, 1750–2000* (London: Reaktion, 2001)

Alphandary, A., 'Risk Managing Loan Collateral at the Bank of England', *Bank of England Quarterly Bulletin*, 54 (2014)

Anand, K., Gai, P., Kapadia, S., Brennan, S., and Willison, M., 'A Network Model of Financial System Resilience', *Bank of England Working Paper*, 458 (2012)

Anderson, M., Edwards, J.R., and Matthews, D., 'A Study of the Quoted Company Audit Market in 1886', *Accounting, Business and Financial History*, 6 (1996)

Anson, M. and Gourvish, T., *Leopold Joseph: A History, 1919–2000* (London: [n.p.], 2002)

Bibliography

Aoki, K., Proudman, J., and Vlieghe, G., 'Why House Prices Matter', *Bank of England Quarterly Bulletin*, 41 (2001)

Arinaminpathy, N., Kapadia, S., and May, R., 'Size and Complexity in Model Financial Systems', *Bank of England Working Paper*, 465 (2012)

Armstrong, J., 'Hooley and the Bovril Company', *Business History*, 28 (1986)

Arnold, P., *The Bankers of London* (London: Hogarth Press, 1938)

Ashworth, H., *The Building Society Story* (London: Franey, 1980)

Astley, M., Giese, J., Hume, M., and Kubelec, C., 'Global Imbalances and the Financial Crisis', *Bank of England Quarterly Bulletin*, 49 (2009)

Atack, J., 'Financial Innovations and Crises: The View Backwards', in J. Atack and L. Neal (eds), *The Origin and Development of Financial Markets and Institutions: from the Seventeenth Century to the Present* (Cambridge: CUP, 2009)

Atkin, J., *The Foreign Exchange Market in London: Development since 1900* (London: Taylor & Francis, 2005)

Atkin, J.M., *British Overseas Investment, 1918-31* (New York: Arno, 1977)

Attfield, J.B., 'The Advantages, or Otherwise, of the Establishment of Branches by Bankers, from the Point of View (a) of the Bankers and (b) of the General Interests of the Community', *Journal of the Institute of Bankers*, 13 (1892)

Augur, P., *The Death of Gentlemanly Capitalism: The Rise and Fall of London's Investment Banks* (London: Penguin, 2000)

Bagchi, A.K., *The Evolution of the State Bank of India, v.2, The Era of the Presidency Banks, 1876-1920* (Delhi: State Bank of India, 1997)

Bagehot, W., *Lombard Street: A Description of the Money Market* (London: H.S. King, 1873)

Bailey, A., Speech, *Bank of England Quarterly Bulletin*, 51 (2011)

Bailey, A., Speeches, see also <http://www.bankofengland.co.uk/publications/pages/speeches/default.aspx>

Bailey, A., Breeden, S., and Stevens, G., 'The Prudential Regulation Authority', *Bank of England Quarterly Bulletin*, 52 (2012)

Ball, M. and Sunderland, D., *An Economic History of London, 1800-1914* (London: Routledge, 2001)

Balls, E. and O'Donnell, G. (eds), *Reforming Britain's Economic and Financial Policy: Towards Greater Economic Stability* (London: Palgrave, 2002)

Balluck, K., 'Investment Banking: Linkages to the Real Economy and the Financial System', *Bank of England Quarterly Bulletin*, 55 (2015)

Balogh, T., *Studies in Financial Organization* (London: CUP, 1947)

Bank for International Settlement, *Triennial Central Bank Survey: Foreign Exchange and Derivatives Market Activity* (September 2010)

Bank for International Settlement, *Guidelines to the International Locational Banking Statistics* (2011)

Bank for International Settlement, *Locational Banking Statistics* (2011)

Bank of England, 'Commercial Bills', *Bank of England Quarterly Bulletin*, 1 (1960-1)

Bank of England, 'The Overseas and Foreign Banks in London', *Bank of England Quarterly Bulletin*, 1 (1960-1)

Bank of England, 'Bank Liquidity in the United Kingdom', *Bank of England Quarterly Bulletin*, 2 (1962)

Bank of England, 'Inflows and Outflows of Foreign Funds', *Bank of England Quarterly Bulletin*, 2 (1962)

Bank of England, 'UK Banks' External Liabilities and Claims in Foreign Currencies', *Bank of England Quarterly Bulletin*, 4 (1964)

Bank of England, 'The UK and US Treasury Bill Market', *Bank of England Quarterly Bulletin*, 5 (1965)

Bank of England, 'The London Discount Market: Some Historical Notes', *Bank of England Quarterly Bulletin*, 7 (1967)

Bank of England, 'Overseas and Foreign Banks in London', *Bank of England Quarterly Bulletin*, 8 (1968)

Bank of England, 'The Eurocurrency Business of Banks in London', *Bank of England Quarterly Bulletin*, 10 (1970)

Bank of England, 'Reserve Ratios: Further Definitions', *Bank of England Quarterly Bulletin*, 11 (1971)

Bank of England, 'Banking Mergers and Participations', *Bank of England Quarterly Bulletin*, 12 (1972)

Bank of England, 'The London Dollar Certificate of Deposit', *Bank of England Quarterly Bulletin*, 13 (1973)

Bank of England, 'New Banking Statistics', *Bank of England Quarterly Bulletin*, 15 (1975)

Bank of England, 'The Secondary Banking Crisis and the Bank of England's Support Operations', *Bank of England Quarterly Bulletin*, 18 (1978)

Bank of England, 'Eurobanks and the Inter-Bank Market', *Bank of England Quarterly Bulletin*, 21 (1981)

Bank of England, 'The Role of the Bank of England in the Money Market', *Bank of England Quarterly Bulletin*, 22 (1982)

Bank of England, 'Developments in UK Banking and Monetary Statistics since the Radcliffe Report', *Bank of England Quarterly Bulletin*, 25 (1985)

Bank of England, 'Foreign Banks in London', *Bank of England Quarterly Bulletin'*, 26 (1986)

Bank of England, 'Japanese Banks in London', *Bank of England Quarterly Bulletin*, 27 (1987)

Bank of England, 'London as an International Financial Centre', *Bank of England Quarterly Review*, 29 (1989)

Bank of England, 'The Development of the Building Societies Sector in the 1980s', *Bank of England Quarterly Bulletin*, 30 (1990)

Bank of England, 'The Role of Brokers in the London Money Markets', *Bank of England Quarterly Bulletin*, 30 (1990)

Bank of England, 'The International Bond Market', *Bank of England Quarterly Bulletin*, 31 (1991)

Bank of England, 'The Performance of Major British Banks, 1970–90', *Bank of England Quarterly Bulletin*, 31 (1991)

Bank of England, 'Banking Statistics Review', *Bank of England Quarterly Bulletin*, 32 (1992)

Bank of England, 'Major International Banks' Performance, 1980–91', *Bank of England Quarterly Bulletin*, 32 (1992)

Bank of England, 'Recent Banking Difficulties', *Bank of England Quarterly Bulletin*, 33 (1993)

Bank of England, 'Risk Measurement and Capital Requirements for Banks', *Bank of England Quarterly Bulletin*, 35 (1995)

Bank of England, 'The Bank of England's Operations in the Sterling Money Markets', *Bank of England Quarterly Bulletin*, 37 (1997)

Bank of England, 'The First Year of the Gilt Repo Market', *Bank of England Quarterly Bulletin*, 37 (1997)

Bank of England, 'Reforms to the UK Monetary Policy Framework and Financial Services Regulation', *Bank of England Quarterly Bulletin*, 37 (1997)

Bank of England, 'The Bank of England Act', *Bank of England Quarterly Bulletin*, 38 (1998)

Bank of England, 'The Foreign Exchange and Over-the-Counter Derivatives Markets in the United Kingdom', *Bank of England Quarterly Bulletin*, 38 (1998)

Bank of England, 'Risk, Cost and Liquidity in Alternative Payment Systems', *Bank of England Quarterly Bulletin*, 39 (1999)

Bank of England, 'Sterling Wholesale Markets: Developments in 1998', *Bank of England Quarterly Bulletin*, 39 (1999)

Bank of England, 'The Bank of England's Operations in the Sterling Money Markets', *Bank of England Quarterly Bulletin*, 42 (2002)

Bank of England, 'Reform of the Bank of England's Operations in the Sterling Money Markets: A Consultative Paper', *Bank of England Quarterly Bulletin*, 44 (2004)

Bank of England, 'The Governor's Speech in Edinburgh, Scotland', *Bank of England Quarterly Bulletin*, 46 (2006)

Bank of England, 'Markets and Operations', *Bank of England Quarterly Bulletin*, 47 (2007)

Bank of England, 'The Monetary Policy Committee of the Bank of England: Ten Years On', *Bank of England Quarterly Bulletin*, 47 (2007)

Bank of England, 'Markets and Operations', *Bank of England Quarterly Bulletin*, 48 (2008)

Bank of England Speeches <http://www.bankofengland.co.uk/publications/pages/speeches/default.aspx>

The Banker, 'The City at War', *The Banker* (August 1941)

The Banker, 'The Changing Discount Market', *The Banker* (March 1947)

Bankers' Almanac, *Register of Bank Name Changes and Liquidations* (East Grinstead: Reed Information Services, 1992)

Bankers Magazine, 'The Changing Character of the London Foreign Exchange Market', *Bankers Magazine* (July 1938)

Banner, S., *Anglo-American Securities Regulation: Cultural and Political Roots, 1690-1860* (Cambridge: CUP, 1998)

Barclays Bank Archive: Balance Sheets of Bassett, Son and Harris 29 June 1889, 30 June 1891, 30 June 1893

Bareau, P., 'Eclipse of the Merchant Banker', *The Banker* (August 1942)

Barker, K., 'The Housing Market and the Wider Economy', *Bank of England Quarterly Bulletin*, 45 (2005)

Barnett, D., *London, Hub of the Industrial Revolution: A Revisionary History, 1775-1825* (London: Tauris, 1998)

Barnett, R.W., 'The History of the Progress and Development of Banking in the United Kingdom from the Year 1800 to the Present Time, *Journal of the Institute of Bankers*, 1 (1880)

Barnett, R.W., 'The Effect of the Development of Banking Facilities upon the Circulation of the Country', *Journal of the Institute of Bankers*, 2 (1881)

Barnett, R.W., 'The Reign of Queen Victoria: A Survey of Fifty Years of Progress', *Journal of the Institute of Bankers*, 6 (1887)

Barrett Whale, P., 'English and Continental Banking', *Journal of the Institute of Bankers*, 52 (1931)

Barron, C.M., *London in the Later Middle Ages: Government and People, 1200–1500* (Oxford: OUP, 2004)

Baster, A.S.J., *The Imperial Banks* (London: P.S. King, 1929)

Baster, A.S.J., *The International Banks* (London: P.S. King, 1935)

Batiz-Laso, B. and Boyns, T., 'The Business and Financial History of Mechanization and Technological Change in Twentieth-Century Banking', *Accounting, Business and Financial History*, 14 (2004)

Battilossi, S., '"Ephors" from Growth to Governance: How Modern Theories Are Re-shaping Historians' View of the Economic Functions of Bankers', in E. Green, M. Pohle-Fraser, and I.L. Fraser (eds), *The Human Factor in Banking History: Entrepreneurship, Organization, Management and Personnel* (Alpha Bank: Athens), 2008

Battilosssi, S. and Cassis, Y. (eds), *European Banks and the American Challenge: European Banking under Bretton Woods* (Oxford: OUP, 2002)

Bean, C., 'The Great Moderation, the Great Panic and the Great Contraction', *Bank of England Quarterly Bulletin*, 49 (2009)

Bean, C., 'The UK Economy after the Crisis: Monetary Policy when It Is not so NICE', *Bank of England Quarterly Bulletin*, 50 (2010)

Bean, C., 'Central Banking in Boom and Slump', *Bank of England Quarterly Bulletin*, 52 (2012)

Bean, C., Speeches, see <http://www.bankofengland.co.uk/publications/pages/speeches/default.aspx>

Becher, C., Millard, S., and Soramaki, K., 'The Network Topology of CHAPS Sterling', *Bank of England Working Paper*, 355 (2008)

Bell, S. and Kettell, B., *Foreign Exchange Handbook* (London: Graham and Trotman, 1983)

Bell, V. and Young, C., 'Understanding the Weakness of Bank Lending', *Bank of England Quarterly Bulletin*, 50 (2010)

Bellringer, C. and Michie, R.C., 'Big Bang in the City: An Intentional Revolution or an Accident', *Financial History Review*, v. 21 (2014)

Benati, L., 'Evolving Post-World War II UK Economic Performance', *Bank of England Working Paper*, 232 (2004)

Benati, L., 'Inflation-targeting Framework from an Historical Perspective', *Bank of England Quarterly Bulletin*, 45 (2005)

Benati, L., 'Long-Run Evidence on Money Growth and Inflation', *Bank of England Quarterly Bulletin*, 45 (2005)

Benford, J., Berry, S., Nikolov, K., Young, C., and Robson, M., 'Quantitative Easing', *Bank of England Quarterly Bulletin*, 49 (2009)

Benford, J. and Burrows, O., 'Commercial Property and Financial Stability', *Bank of England Quarterly Bulletin*, 53 (2013)

Benos, E., Garratt, R., and Zimmerman, P., 'Bank Behaviour and Risks in CHAPS Following the Collapse of Lehman Brothers', *Bank of England Working Paper*, 451 (2012)

Besant, W. and Rice, J., *Ready-Money Mortiboy: A Matter-of-Fact Story* (London: Chatto & Windus, 1872)

Besley, T., 'Financial Markets and Household Consumption', *Bank of England Quarterly Bulletin*, 48 (2008)

Billings, M. and Capie, F., 'Financial Crisis, Contagion and the British Banking System between the World Wars', *Business History*, 53 (2011)

Black, I.S., 'Geography, Political Economy and the Circulation of Finance Capital in Early Industrial England', *Journal of Historical Geography*, 15 (1989)

Black, I.S., 'Money, Information and Space: Banking in Early Nineteenth-Century England and Wales', *Journal of Historical Geography*, 21 (1995)

Black, I.S., 'The London Agency System in English Banking, 1780-1825', *The London Journal*, 21 (1996)

Blainey, G. and Hutton, G., *Gold and Paper, 1858-1982: A History of the National Bank of Australasia* (Melbourne: Macmillan Australia, 1983)

Bloomfield, A.I., *Short-Term Capital Movements under the Pre-1914 Gold Standard* (Princeton: Princeton UP, 1963)

Blunden, Sir George, 'The Supervision of the UK Banking System', *Bank of England Quarterly Bulletin*, 15 (1975)

Bogue, A.G., *Money at Interest: The Farm Mortgage on the Middle Border* (Lincoln, NE: University of Nebraska Press, 1955)

Bordo, M.D., 'The Lender of Last Resort: Alternative Views and Historical Experience', in C. Goodhart and G. Illing (eds), *Financial Crises, Contagion, and the Lender of Last Resort: A Reader* (Oxford: OUP, 2002)

Bordo, M.D. (ed.), *Financial Market and Institutions in Historical Statistics of the United States: Earliest Times to the Present*, Millenial Ed. (New York: CUP, 2006)

Boreham, B.B., 'The London Information Market', *The Banker* (August 1945)

Borer, M.C., *The City of London: Its History, Institutions and Commercial Activities* (London: Museum Press, 1962)

Born, K.E., *International Banking in the 19th and 20th Centuries* (Leamington Spa: Berg, c.1983)

Bostock, F., 'The British Overseas Banks and Development Finance in Africa after 1945', in G. Jones (ed.), *Banks and Money: International and Comparative Finance in History* (London: Frank Cass, 1991)

Bowden, S., 'Competition and Collusion in the Finance Sector in the Post War Period', *Financial History Review*, 4 (1997)

Breeden, S. and Whisker, R., 'Collateral Risk Management at the Bank of England', *Bank of England Quarterly Bulletin*, 50 (2010)

Brett, E., 'The History and Development of Banking in Australasia', *Journal of the Institute of Bankers*, 3 (1882)

Brewer, J., *The Sinews of Power: War, Money and the English State, 1688-1783* (London: Unwin Hyman, 1989)

Bridges, J., Gregory, D., Nielsen, M., Pezzinia, S., Radia, A., and Spaltro, M., 'The Impact of Capital Requirements on Bank Lending', *Bank of England Working Paper*, 486 (2014)

Brierley, P. and Young, M., 'The Financing of Smaller Quoted Companies: A Survey', *Bank of England Quarterly Bulletin*, 44 (2004)

Broadbent, B., Speeches, see <http://www.bankofengland.co.uk/publications/pages/speeches/default.aspx>

Broadberry, S.N., *Market Services and the Productivity Race, 1850-2000* (Cambridge: CUP, 2006)

Broadberry, S. and Howlett, P., 'The United Kingdom: "Victory at all Costs"', in M. Harrison (ed.), *The Economics of World War II: Six Great Powers in International Competition* (Cambridge: CUP, 1998)

Broadberry, S. and Howlett, P., 'The United Kingdom during World War I: Business as Usual?' in S. Broadberry and M. Harrison (eds), *The Economics of World War I* (Cambridge: CUP, 2005)

Broderick, T. and Cox, C., 'The Foreign Exchange and Over-The-Counter Interest Rate Derivatives Markets in the United Kingdom', *Bank of England Quarterly Bulletin*, 50 (2010)

Brown, H.G., 'The Position of Foreign Companies in England', *Journal of the Institute of Bankers*, 27 (1906)

Bill to Amend the Law Relating to Trade Unions, Friendly Societies, Building Societies and Certain Other Societies for Purposes Connected with the Present Emergency, and to Make Further Provision with Respect to the Amalgamation and Transfer of Engagements of Trade Unions and Building Societies (London: HMSO, 1940)

Burn, G., 'The State, the City and the Euromarkets', *Review of International Political Economy*, v. 6 (1999)

Burn, G., *The Re-emergence of Global Finance* (Basingstoke: Palgrave Macmillan, 2006)

Burnett, M. and Manning, M., 'Financial Stability and the United Kingdom's External Balance Sheet', *Bank of England Quarterly Bulletin*, 43 (2003)

Burrell, H.V., 'The Opening of Foreign Branches by English Banks', *Journal of the Institute of Bankers*, 35 (1914)

Butlin, S.J., *Australia and New Zealand Bank: The Bank of Australasia and the Union Bank of Australia Limited, 1828-1951* (London: Longmans, 1961)

Butson, H.E., 'The Banking System of the United Kingdom', in H.P. Willis and B.H. Beckhart (eds), *Foreign Banking Systems* (London: Pitman and Sons, 1929)

Cain, P.J. and Hopkins, A.G., *British Imperialism*, 2 vols. (London: Longman, 1993)

Cairncross, A., *The British Economy since 1945: Economic Policy and Performance, 1945-1990* (Oxford: Blackwell, 1992)

Calomiris, C.W. and Haber, S.H., *Fragile by Design: The Political Origins of Banking Crises and Scarce Credit* (Princeton: Princeton UP, 2014)

Cameron, R., 'Banking and Industrialisation in Britain in the Nineteenth Century', in A. Slaven and D.H. Aldcroft (eds), *Business, Banking and Urban History* (Edinburgh: John Donald, 1982)

Capie, F., *The Bank of England, 1950s-1979* (Cambridge: CUP, 2010)

Capie, F., 'British Financial Crises in the Nineteenth and Twentieth Centuries', in N. Dimsdale and A. Hotson (eds), *British Financial Crises since 1825* (Oxford: OUP, 2014)

Capie, F. and Collins, M., *Have the Banks Failed British Industry? An Historical Survey of Bank/Industry Relations in Britain, 1870-1990* (London: Frank Cass, 1992)

Capie, F. and Rodrik-Bali, G., 'Concentration in British Banking, 1870-1920', *Business History*, 24 (1982)

Capie, F. and Webber, A., *A Monetary History of the United Kingdom, 1870-1982* (London: Allen & Unwin, 1985)

Capie, F. and Woods, G., *Money over Two Centuries: Selected Topics in British Monetary History* (Oxford: OUP, 2012)

Carlos, A.M. and Neal, L., 'The Micro-foundations of the Early London Capital Market: Bank of England Shareholders during and after the South Sea Bubble, 1720-25', *Economic History Review*, lix (2006)

Carnevali, F., *Europe's Advantage: Banks and Small Firms in Britain, France, Germany, and Italy since 1918* (Oxford: OUP, 2005)

Carney, M., Speeches, see <http://www.bankofengland.co.uk/publications/pages/speeches/default.aspx>

Carosso, V.P., *Investment Banking in America* (Cambridge, Mass.: Harvard UP, 1970)

Carosso, V.P., *The Morgans: Private International Bankers, 1854-1913* (Cambridge: Mass: Harvard UP, 1987)

Carruthers, B.G., *City of Capital: Politics and Markets in the English Financial Revolution* (Princeton: Princeton UP, 1999)

Carswell, J., *The South Sea Bubble*, rev. ed. (Stroud: Alan Sutton, 1993)

Carter, E., 'Considering the Continuity of Payments for Customers in a Bank's Recovery or Resolution', *Bank of England Quarterly Bulletin*, 52 (2012)

Cassis, Y., 'Management and Strategy in the English Joint Stock Banks, 1890-1914', *Business History*, 27 (1985)

Cassis, Y., *Capitals of Capital: A History of International Financial Centres, 1780-2005* (Cambridge: CUP, 2006)

Cassis, Y., 'Private Banks and the Onset of the Corporate Economy', in Y. Cassis and P.L. Cottrell (eds), *The World of Private Banking* (Farnham: Ashgate, 2009)

Cassis, Y., *Crises and Opportunities: The Shaping of Modern Finance* (Oxford: OUP, 2011)

Cassis, Y., 'Do Financial Crises Lead to Policy Change?', in N. Dimsdale and A. Hotson (eds), *British Financial Crises since 1825* (Oxford: OUP, 2014)

Center for Medieval and Renaissance Studies (eds), *The Dawn of Modern Banking* (Los Angeles: Yale UP, 1979)

Channon, D.F., *The Service Industries: Strategy, Structure and Financial Performance* (London: Macmillan, 1978)

Chapman, S.D., 'Fixed Capital Formation in the British Cotton Manufacturing Industry', in J.P.P. Higgins and S. Pollard (eds), *Aspects of Capital Investment in Great Britain, 1750-1850: A Preliminary Survey* (London: Methuen, 1971)

Chapman, S.D., *The Rise of Merchant Banking* (London: Allen & Unwin, 1984)

Chapman, S.D., *Merchant Enterprise in Britain: From the Industrial Revolution to World War I* (Cambridge: CUP, 1992)

Chappell, N.M., *New Zealand's Banker's Hundred: A History of the Bank of New Zealand, 1861-1961* (Wellington: Bank of New Zealand, 1961)

Checkland, O., Nishimura, S., and Tamaki, N. (eds), *Pacific Banking, 1859-1959: East Meets West* (Basingstoke: Macmillan, 1994)

Choi, S.R., Park, D., and Tschoegel, A.E., 'Banks and the World's Major Banking Centers', October 2014. Available online <fic.wharton.upenn/fic/papers/14/14–16.pdf>

Chowla, S., Quaglietti, L., and Lomax, R., 'How Have World Shocks Affected the UK Economy?' *Bank of England Quarterly Bulletin*, 54 (2014)

Christodoulou, G. and O'Connor, P., 'The Foreign Exchange and Over-The-Counter Derivatives Markets in the United Kingdom', *Bank of England Quarterly Bulletin*, 46 (2006)

Church, R.A., *The Great Victorian Boom, 1850–1873* (London: Macmillan, 1975)

Citizen, A., *The City Today* (London: New Fabian Research, 1938)

Clapham, Sir John, *The Bank of England: A History*, 2 vols. (Cambridge: CUP, 1944)

Clare, G., *A Money-Market Primer and Key to the Exchanges* (London: Effingham Wilson, 1893)

Clark, A., 'Prudential Regulation, Risk Management and Systemic Stability', *Bank of England Quarterly Bulletin*, 46 (2006)

Clark, G., *The Wealth of England from 1496 to 1760* (Oxford: OUP, 1946)

Clark, R.J., 'British Banking: Changes and Challenges', *Journal of the Institute of Bankers* 89 (1968)

Clarke, W.M., *The City and the World Economy* (London: Institute of Economic Affairs, 1965)

Clay, H., 'Finance and the International Market', *The Banker*, xx (October 1931)

Cleary, E.J., *The Building Society Movement* (London: Elek Books, 1965)

Cleaver, G. and P., *The Union Discount: A Centenary Album* (London: Union Discount, 1985)

Clementi, D., 'Maintaining Financial Stability in a Rapidly Changing World: Some Threats and Opportunities', *Bank of England Quarterly Bulletin*, 41 (2001)

Clendenning, E.W., *The Euro-Dollar Market* (Oxford: OUP, 1970)

Cleveland, H. van B. and Huertas, T.F., *Citibank, 1812–1970* (Cambridge: Mass.: Harvard UP, 1985)

Clews, R., Salmon, C., and Weeken, O., 'The Bank's Money Market Framework', *Bank of England Quarterly Bulletin*, 50 (2010)

Cochrane, S., *Assessing the Impact of World War I on the City of London*, University of Oxford Department of Economics Discussion Paper Series 456 (Oxford: University of Oxford, 2009)

Cockerell, H.A.L. and Green, E., *The British Insurance Business, 1547–1970* (London: Heineman, 1976)

Cohrs, M., Speeches, see <http://www.bankofengland.co.uk/publications/pages/speeches/default.aspx>

Cole, A.C., 'Notes on the London Money Market', *Journal of the Institute of Bankers*, 25 (1904)

Cole, W.A., 'The Relations between Banks and Stock Exchanges', *Journal of the Institute of Bankers*, 20 (1899)

Coleman, D.C., 'London Scriveners and the Estate Market in the late 17th Century', *Economic History Review*, 4 (1951/2)

Collins, M., *Money and Banking in the UK: A History* (London: Routledge, 1988)

Collins, M., 'English Bank Lending and the Financial Crisis of the 1870s', *Business History*, 32 (1990)

Collins, M. and Baker, M., 'Bank of England Autonomy: A Retrospective', in C-L. Holtfrerich, J. Reis, and G. Toniolo (eds), *The Emergence of Modern Central Banking from 1918 to the Present* (Aldershot: Ashgate, 1999)

Collins, M. and Baker, M., 'Financial Crises and Structural Change in English Commercial Bank Assets, 1860-1914', *Explorations in Economic History*, 36 (1999)

Collins, M. and Baker, M., 'English Commercial Bank Stability, 1860-1914', *Journal of European Economic History*, 31 (2000)

Collins, M. and Baker, M., *Commercial Banking and Industrial Finance in England and Wales, 1860-1913* (Oxford: OUP, 2003)

Collins, W., 'The Biter Bit', in R.C. Bull (ed.), *Great Tales of Mystery* (London: Weidenfeld & Nicolson, 1960)

Colville, J.R., 'London, Europe's Financial Centre', *The Banker*, 1966

Colville, J.R., 'Foreign Banks in London', *The Banker*, 1967

Committee on Finance and Industry, *Report: Cmd* 3897 (London, HMSO, 1931)

Committee on Industry and Trade, *Final Report: Cmd* 3282 (London: HMSO, 1929)

Committee on the Global Financial System, *Long Term Issues in International Banking* (Basel: Bank for International Settlements, 2010)

Committee on the Working of the Monetary System, *Report of the Radcliffe Committee on the Working of the Monetary System* (London: HMSO, 1959)

Committee to Review the Functioning of Financial Institutions, *Report of the Wilson Committee to Review the Functioning of Financial Institutions* (London: HMSO, 1980)

Congdon, T., *Central Banking in a Free Society* (London: IEA, 2009)

Conrad, J., *Chance* (London: Methuen, 1914)

Conway, L.T., *The International Position of the London Money Market, 1931-1937* (Philadelphia: [n.p.], 1946)

Cope, S.R., 'The Goldsmids and the Development of the London Money Market during the Napoleonic Wars', *Economica*, ns 9 (1942)

Corfield, P.J., *The Impact of English Towns, 1700-1800* (Oxford: OUP, 1982)

Cork, N., 'The Late Australian Banking Crisis', *Journal of the Institute of Bankers*, 15 (1894)

Cottrell, P.L., 'Commercial Enterprise', in R. Church (ed.), *The Dynamics of Victorian Business: Problems and Perspectives to the 1870s* (London: Allen and Unwin, 1980)

Cottrell, P.L., 'London's First "Big Bang"? Institutional Change in the City, 1855-83', in Y. Cassis and P.L. Cottrell (eds), *The World of Private Banking* (Farnham: Ashgate, 2009)

Crafts, N.F.R., *British Economic Growth during the Industrial Revolution* (Oxford: Clarendon Press, 1985)

Crick, W.F. and Wadsworth, J.E., *A Hundred Years of Joint Stock Banking* (London: Hodder & Stoughton, 1936)

Cross, M., Fisher, P., and Weeken, O., 'The Bank's Balance Sheet during the Crisis', *Bank of England Quarterly Bulletin*, 50 (2010)

Crump, A., *The Key to the London Money Market*, 6th edn. (London: Longmans Green, 1877)

Crump, N., 'The London and New York Markets in the Autumn of 1925', *Journal of the Institute of Bankers*, 47 (1926)

Crump, N., 'Finance and the Crisis', *Journal of the Institute of Bankers*, 59 (1938)

Crump, N., 'The Evolution of the Money Market', *Journal of the Institute of Bankers*, 59 (1938)

Cunliffe, Sir Jon, Speeches, *see* <http://www.bankofengland.co.uk/publications/pages/speeches/default.aspx>

Danisewicz, P., Rheinhart, D., and Sowerbutts, R., 'On a Tight Leash: Does Organisational Structure Matter for Macroprudential Spillovers?' *Bank of England Working Paper*, 524 (2015)

Davey, M., 'Mortgage Equity Withdrawal and Consumption', *Bank of England Quarterly Bulletin*, 41 (2001)

Davey, N. and Gray, D., 'How Has the Liquidity-Saving Mechanism Reduced Banks' Intraday Liquidity Costs in CHAPS?', *Bank of England Quarterly Bulletin*, 53 (2013)

Davies, G. and Dobler, M., 'Bank Resolution and Safeguarding the Creditors Left Behind', *Bank of England Quarterly Bulletin*, 51 (2011)

Davies, H., 'Financial Regulation: Why, How and By Whom', *Bank of England Quarterly Bulletin*, 37 (1997)

Davies, K.G., 'Joint-Stock Investment in the Later 17th Century', *Economic History Review*, 4 (1951/2)

Davies, M., *The Origins and Development of Cartelisation in British Banking* (Bangor: Institute of European Finance, 1993)

Davies, R., Richardson, P., Katinaite, V., and Manning, M., 'Evolution of the UK Banking System', *Bank of England Quarterly Bulletin*, 50 (2010)

Dawes, M. and Ward Perkins, C.N., *Country Banks of England and Wales: Private Provincial Banks and Bankers, 1688–1953* (Canterbury: Chartered Institute of Bankers, 2001)

de Vries, J. and Van der Woude, A., *The First Modern Economy: Success, Failure and Perseverance, 1500–1815* (Cambridge: CUP, 1997)

Denbee, E., Garratt, R.J. and Zimmerman, P., 'Variations in Liquidity Provision in Real-Time Payment Systems, *Bank of England Working Paper*, 513 (2014)

Dennett, L., *A Sense of Security: 150 Years of Prudential* (Cambridge: Granta Editions, 1998)

Dent, A. and Dison, W., 'The Bank of England's Real-Time Gross Settlement Infrastructure', *Bank of England Quarterly Bulletin*, 52 (2012)

Diaper, S., 'Merchant Banking in the Inter-War Period: The Case of Kleinwort, Sons & Co.', *Business History*, 28 (1986)

Dick, J., 'Banking Statistics: A Record of Nine Years' Progress, 1874–1883', *Journal of the Institute of Bankers*, 5 (1884)

Dick, J., 'Banks and Banking in the UK in 1891', *Journal of the Institute of Bankers*, 13 (1892)

Dick, J., 'Banking Statistics of the United Kingdom in 1896, Compared with Former Times', *Journal of the Institute of Bankers*, 18 (1897)

Dickson, P.G.M., *The Financial Revolution in England: A Study in the Development of Public Credit, 1688–1756* (London: Macmillan, 1967)

Dimsdale, N. and Horsewood, N., 'The Financial Crisis of 1931 and the Impact of the Great Depression on the British Economy', in N. Dimsdale and A. Hotson, *British Financial Crises since 1825* (Oxford: OUP 2014)

Dimsdale, N. and Hotson, A. (eds), *British Financial Crises since 1825* (Oxford: OUP, 2014)

Dimsdale, N. and Hotson, A., 'Financial Crises and Economic Activity in the UK since 1825', in N. Dimsdale and A. Hotson (eds), *British Financial Crises since 1825* (Oxford: OUP 2014)

District Bank: Foreign Dept Minute Book, 8 June 1918

Dive, M., Hodge, R., Jones, C., and Purchase, J., 'Developments in the Global Securities Lending Market', *Bank of England Quarterly Bulletin*, 51 (2011)

Dixon, K.F., *The Development of the London Money Market, 1780–1830*, London University Ph.D (1962)

Dowling, S.W., *The Exchanges of London* (London: Butterworth, 1929)

Drummond Fraser, Sir D., 'British Home Banking since 1911', *Journal of the Institute of Bankers*, 46 (1925)

Drury, A.C., *Finance Houses: Their Development and Role in the Modern Financial Sector* (London: Waterlow Publishers, 1982)

Duffy, I.P.H., *Bankruptcy and Insolvency in London during the Industrial Revolution* (New York & London: Garland Publishing, 1985)

Duke, W.K., *Bills, Bullion and the London Money Market* (London: Pitman, 1937)

Dunn, J.F., 'Banking in 1837 and in 1897 in the United Kingdom, India and the Colonies: A Comparison and a Contrast', *Journal of the Institute of Bankers*, 18 (1898)

Dyer, L.S., 'The Secondary Banking Crisis', *Journal of the Institute of Bankers*, 104 (1983)

Dyos, H.J. and Aldcroft, D.H., *Century to the 20th* (Harmondsworth: Penguin, 1974)

Easton, H.T., *Money, Exchange and Banking* (London: Pitman, 1908)

Edwards, D., Edwards, M. and Matthews, D., 'Accountability in a Free-Market Economy: The British Company Audit, 1886', *Abacus*, 33 (1997)

Einzig, P., 'The Future of the London Foreign Exchange Market', *The Banker*, xx (Nov 1931)

Einzig, P., 'London as the World's Banking Centre', *The Banker*, xxvii (September 1933)

Einzig, P., 'Dollar Deposits in London', *The Banker*, cx (Jan 1960)

Einzig, P., *A Dynamic Theory of Forward Exchange* (London: Macmillan, 1961, 2nd ed. 1967)

Einzig, P., *The History of Foreign Exchange* (London: Macmillan, 1962)

Einzig, P., *A Textbook on Foreign Exchange* (London: Macmillan, 1966)

Einzig, P., *The Euro-Bond Market* (London: Macmillan, 1969)

Ellinger, B., *The City: The London Financial Markets* (London: P.S. King & Son, 1940)

Elliot, G., *The Mystery of Overend Gurney: A Financial Scandal in Victorian London* (London: Methuen, 2006)

Ellis, A., *Heir to Adventure: The Story of Brown, Shipley and Company* (London: Brown, Shipley, 1960)

Erskine, Sir George, 'Finance for Industry', *Journal of the Institute of Bankers*, 76 (1955)

Escher, M., *Foreign Exchange Explained* (New York: Macmillan, 1917)

Evitt, H.E., 'Exchange Dealings under Current Conditions', *Journal of the Institute of Bankers*, 52 (1931)

Fairman, W., *The Stocks Examined and Compared*, 3rd ed. (London: [n.p.], 1798)

Farag, M., Harland, D., and Nixon, D., 'Bank Capital and Liquidity', *Bank of England Quarterly Bulletin*, 53 (2013)

Federal Deposit Insurance Corporation, *Historic Banking Database* <https://www.fdic.gov/>

Feiertag, O. and Minoglou, I.P., 'European Banking Historiography at a Turning Point', in O. Feiertag and I.P. Minoglou (eds), *European Banking Historiography: Past and Present* (Athens: Alpha Bank, 2009)

Ferguson, N., *The World's Banker: The History of the House of Rothschild* (London: Weidenfeld & Nicolson, 1998)

Ferguson, N., 'The Rise of the Rothschilds: The Family Firm as Multinational', in Y. Cassis and P.L. Cottrell (eds), *The World of Private Banking* (Farnham, Ashgate, 2009)

Ferguson, N., *High Financier: The Lives and Time of Siegmund Warburg* (London: Penguin Books, 2010)

Fforde, J., *The Bank of England and Public Policy, 1941-1958* (Cambridge: CUP, 1992)

Finan, K., Lacaosa, A. and Sunderland, J., 'Tiering in CHAPS', *Bank of England Quarterly Bulletin*, 53 (2013)

Financial News, *The Stock Exchange: An Investors' Guide* (London: Financial News, 1933)

Financial News, *The City, 1884-1934* (London: Financial News, 1934)

Fisher, C. and Gai, P., 'Financial Stability, Monetary Stability and Public Policy', *Bank of England Quarterly Bulletin*, 45 (2005)

Fisher, P., Speeches, *see* <http://www.bankofengland.co.uk/publications/pages/speeches/default.aspx>

Flandreau, M., Galinard, C., Obst, C., and Nogues, P., 'The Bell Jar: Commercial Interest Rates between Two Revolutions, 1688-1789', in J. Atack and L. Neal (eds), *The Origin and Development of Financial Markets and Institutions: From the Seventeenth Century to the Present* (Cambridge: CUP, 2009)

Flandreau, M. and Ugolini, S., 'The Crisis of 1866', in N. Dimsdale and A. Hotson (eds), *British Financial Crises since 1825* (Oxford: OUP, 2014)

Fletcher, G.A., *The Discount Houses in London: Principles, Operations and Change* (London: Macmillan, 1976)

Fletcher, J.S., *The Middle Temple Murder* (London: Ward Lock, 1920)

Fletcher, J.S., *The Mystery of the London Banker: Being Entry Number Seven in the Case-Book of Ronald Camberwell* (London: George Harrap, 1933)

Floud, R. and Johnson, P. (eds), *The Cambridge Economic History of Modern Britain* (Cambridge: CUP, 2004)

Fohlin, C., 'Bank Securities Holdings and Industrial Finance before World War I: Britain and Germany Compared', *Business and Economic History*, 26 (1997)

Forbes, K., Speeches, *see* <http://www.bankofengland.co.uk/publications/pages/speeches/default.aspx>

Forester, C.S., *Payment Deferred* (London: Bodley Head, 1926) [reprinted London: Penguin, 2011]

Foster, E.F., *Seasonal Movements of Exchange Rates and Interest Rates under the Pre-World War I Gold Standard* (New York: Garland Publishing, 1994)

Fowler, W., 'Banking Reserves', *Journal of the Institute of Bankers*, 21 (1900)
Francis, W.B., 'UK Deposit-Taker Responses to the Financial Crisis: What Are the Lessons', *Bank of England Quarterly Bulletin*, 54 (2014)
Fraser, D.D., 'A Decade of Bank Amalgamations, 1897–1906', *Journal of the Institute of Bankers*, 29 (1907)
Fraser, D.D., 'Some Modern Phases of British Banking, 1896–1911', *Journal of the Institute of Bankers*, 34 (1913)
Fraser, R., *Financial Times* (London: Jonathan Cape, 1942)
Fraser, W.L., *All to the Good* (London: New English Library, 1963)
Fratianni, M., 'The Evolutionary Chain of International Financial Centers', in P. Alessandrini, M. Fratianni, and A. Zazzoro (eds), *The Changing Geography of Banking and Finance* (Dordrecht: Springer, 2009)
Freixas, X., Parigi, B.M., and Rochet, J.-C., 'Systemic Risk, Interbank Relations, and Liquidity Provision by the Central Bank', in C. Goodhart and G. Illing (eds), *Financial Crises, Contagion, and the Lender of Last Resort: A Reader* (Oxford: OUP, 2002)
Frowen, S.F. (ed.), *A Framework of International Banking* (Guildford: Guildford Education Press, 1979)
Fry, F. (ed.), *A Banker's World: the Revival of the City, 1957–1970* (London: Hutchinson, 1970)
Fuller, F.J. and Rowan, H.D., 'Foreign Competition in its Relation to Banking', *Journal of the Institute of Bankers*, 22 (1901)
Furniss, E.S., *Foreign Exchange: The Financing Mechanism of International Commerce* (New York: Houghton Mifflin, 1922)
Furse, Dame Clara, Speeches, *see* <http://www.bankofengland.co.uk/publications/pages/speeches/default.aspx>
Furse, Dame Clara, 'Taking the Long View: How Market-Based Finance Can Support Stability', *Bank of England Quarterly Bulletin*, 54 (2014)
Gai, P. and Kapadia, S., 'Contagion in Financial Networks', *Bank of England Working Paper*, 383 (2010)
Gai, P., Kapadia, S., Millard, S., and Perez, A., 'Financial Innovation, Macroeconomic Stability and Systemic Crises', *Bank of England Working Paper*, 340 (2008)
Galbiati, M. and Soramakii, K., 'Liquidity-Saving Mechanisms and Bank Behaviour', *Bank of England Working Paper*, 400 (2010)
Gall L. et al., *The Deutsche Bank, 1870–1995* (London: Weidenfeld & Nicolson, 1995)
Garratt, R.J., Mahadeva, L., and Svirydzenka, K., 'Mapping Systemic Risk in the International Banking Network', *Bank of England Working Paper*, 413 (2011)
Gauci, P., *Emporium of the World: The Merchants of London, 1660–1800* (London: Hambledon Press, 2007)
Gellender, E.E., 'The Relations between Banks and Stock Exchanges', *Journal of the Institute of Bankers*, 20 (1899)
George, E., 'Some Thoughts on Financial Regulation', *Bank of England Quarterly Bulletin*, 36 (1996)
George, E., 'Are Banks Still Special? *Bank of England Quarterly Bulletin*, 37 (1997)
George, E., 'International Regulatory Structure: A UK Perspective', *Bank of England Quarterly Bulletin*, 37 (1997)
George, E., 'Central Bank Independence', *Bank of England Quarterly Bulletin*, 48 (1998)

George, E., 'The New Lady of Threadneedle Street', *Bank of England Quarterly Bulletin*, 38 (1998)
George, E., 'Britain and the Euro', *Bank of England Quarterly Bulletin*, 40 (2000)
Gibson, E.C., 'A Critical and Historical Account of the Working of the American Federal Reserve Banking System', *Journal of the Institute of Bankers*, 48 (1927)
Gibson, N.J., 'Money, Banking and Finance', in A.R. Prest (ed.), *The UK Economy: A Manual of Applied Economics* (London: Weidenfeld & Nicolson, 1966)
Gieve, Sir John, 'Financial System Risks in the United Kingdom: Issues and Challenges', *Bank of England Quarterly Bulletin*, 46 (2006)
Gieve, Sir John, 'Hedge Funds and Financial Stability', *Bank of England Quarterly Bulletin*, 46 (2006)
Gieve, Sir John, 'Practical Issues in Preparing for Cross-Border Financial Crises', *Bank of England Quarterly Bulletin*, 46 (2006)
Gieve, Sir John, 'Stability and Change', *Bank of England Quarterly Bulletin*, 46 (2006)
Gieve, Sir John, 'Pricing for Perfection', *Bank of England Quarterly Bulletin*, 47 (2007)
Gieve, Sir John, 'Uncertainty, Policy and Financial Markets', *Bank of England Quarterly Bulletin*, 47 (2007)
Gieve, Sir John, 'The Impact of the Financial Market Disruption on the UK Economy', *Bank of England Quarterly Bulletin*, 48 (2008)
Gieve, Sir John, 'Learning from the Financial Crisis', *Bank of England Quarterly Bulletin*, 48 (2008)
Gieve, Sir John, 'Rebuilding Confidence in the Financial System', *Bank of England Quarterly Bulletin*, 48 (2008)
Gieve, Sir John, 'The Return of the Credit Cycle: Old Lessons in New Markets', *Bank of England Quarterly Bulletin*, 48 (2008)
Gieve, Sir John, 'Sovereign Wealth Funds and Global Imbalances', *Bank of England Quarterly Bulletin*, 48 (2008)
Gieve, Sir John, 'Economic Prospects and Policy Challenge', *Bank of England Quarterly Bulletin*, 49 (2009)
Gieve, Sir John, Speeches, see <http://www.bankofengland.co.uk/publications/pages/speeches/default.aspx>
Gissing, G., *The Whirlpool* (London: Lawrence and Bullen, 1897)
Gladwell, M., *The Tipping Point: How Little Things Can Make a Big Difference* (London: Little Brown, 2000)
Goetzmann, W.N. and Geert Rouwenhorst, K. (eds), *The Origins of Value: The Financial Innovations that Created Modern Capital Markets* (Oxford: OUP, 2005)
Goldsmith, R.W., *Comparative National Balance Sheets: A Study of Twenty Countries, 1688–1978* (Chicago: University of Chicago Press, 1985)
Gondat-Laralde, C. and Nier, E., 'The Economics of Retail Banking: An Empirical Analysis of the UK Market for Personal Current Accounts', *Bank of England Quarterly Bulletin*, 44 (2004)
Goodhart, C., *The Business of Banking, 1891–1914* (London: Weidenfeld & Nicolson, 1972)
Goodhart, C., 'Monetary Policy and Debt Management in the United Kingdom: Some Historical Viewpoints', in K.A. Chrystal (ed.), *Government Debt Structure and Monetary Conditions* (London: Bank of England, 1999)

Goodhart, C., 'Myths about the Lender of Last Resort', in C. Goodhart and G. Illing (eds), *Financial Crises, Contagion, and the Lender of Last Resort: A Reader* (Oxford: OUP, 2002)

Goodhart, C., Hartmann, P., Llewellyn, D., Rojas-Suarez, L,. and Weisbrod, S., *Financial Regulation: Why, How and Where Now?* (London: Routledge, 1998)

Goodhart, C. and Illing, G. (eds), *Financial Crises, Contagion, and the Lender of Last Resort: A Reader* (Oxford: OUP, 2002)

Gore, Mrs, *The Man of Business or Stokeshill Place* (London: J. and C. Brown, 1837)

Gore, Mrs, *The Money Lender* (London: [n.p.], 1854)

Gourvish, T., 'Project Finance and the Archives of Entrepreneurship: The Channel Tunnel, 1957-1975', in E. Green, M. Pohle-Fraser, and I.L. Fraser (eds), *The Human Factor in Banking History: Entrepreneurship, Organization, Management and Personnel* (Athens, Alpha Bank, 2008)

Gracie, A., Speeches, see <http://www.bankofengland.co.uk/publications/pages/speeches/default.aspx>

Grady, J. and Weale, M., *British Banking, 1960-85* (London: Macmillan, 1986)

Grant, A.T.K., *A Study of the Capital Market in Post-War Britain* (London: Macmillan, 1937)

Gray, F.W., 'Impressions of New York Banking', *Journal of the Institute of Bankers*, 50 (1929)

Greengrass, H.W., *The Discount Market in London: Its Organization and Recent Development* (London: Pitman, 1930)

Gregory, D., 'The Production of Regions in England's Industrial Revolution', *Journal of Historical Geography*, 14 (1988)

Gregory, D., 'Private Equity and Financial Stability', *Bank of England Quarterly Bulletin*, 53 (2013)

Gregory, T.E., 'The Practical Working of the Federal Reserve Banking System of the United States', *Journal of the Institute of Bankers*, 50 (1929)

Griffiths, B., 'The Development of Restrictive Practices in the UK Monetary System', *Economic and Social Studies*, 41 (1973)

Grossman, R.S., *Unsettled Account: The Evolution of Banking in the Industrialized World Since 1800* (Princeton: Princeton UP, 2010)

HM Treasury, *UK International Financial Services, The Future: A Report from UK-based Financial Services Leaders to the Government* (London: HM Treasury, 2009)

Haldane, A.G., 'Credit Is Trust', *Bank of England Quarterly Bulletin*, 49 (2009)

Haldane, A.G., 'Rethinking the Financial Network', *Bank of England Quarterly Bulletin*, 49 (2009)

Haldane, A.G., 'Small Lessons from a Big Crisis', *Bank of England Quarterly Bulletin*, 49 (2009)

Haldane, A.G., 'The $100 Billion Question', *Bank of England Quarterly Bulletin*, 50 (2010)

Haldane, A.G., 'The Debt Hangover', *Bank of England Quarterly Bulletin*, 50 (2010)

Haldane, A.G., 'Haircuts', *Bank of England Quarterly Bulletin*, 51 (2011)

Haldane, A.G., 'On Being the Right Size, 25 October 2012', *Bank of England Quarterly Bulletin*, 52 (2012)

Haldane, A.G., Speeches, see <http://www.bankofengland.co.uk/publications/pages/speeches/default.aspx>

Haldane, A.G., Brennan, S., and Madouros, V., 'The Contribution of the Financial Sector: Miracle or Mirage?' *Bank of England Quarterly Bulletin*, 50 (2010)

Haldane, A.G. and May R.M., 'Systemic Risk in Banking Ecosystems', *Nature*, 20 January 2011

Hall, N.F., 'The Control of Credit in the London Money Market', *Journal of the Institute of Bankers*, 59 (1938)

Hall, S., 'Financial Effects on Corporate Investment in UK Business Cycles', *Bank of England Quarterly Bulletin*, 41 (2001)

Hall, Sir Peter, *Cities in Civilization: Culture, Innovation, and Urban Order* (London: Phoenix Giant, 1998)

Hancock, D., *Citizens of the World: London Merchants and the Integration of the British Atlantic Community, 1735–1785* (Cambridge: CUP, 1995)

Hannah, L., *The Rise of the Corporate Economy* (London: Methuen, 1976)

Hannah, L., 'The Twentieth Century Transformation of Banking and its Effect on Management Training for Bankers', in E. Green, M. Pohle-Fraser, and I.L. Fraser (eds), *The Human Factor in Banking History: Entrepreneurship, Organization, Management and Personnel* (Athens: Alpha Bank, 2008)

Hart, M., Jonker, J., and Van Zanden, J.L., *A Financial History of the Netherlands* (Cambridge: CUP, 1997)

Hartwell, R.M., *The Industrial Revolution and Economic Growth* (London: Methuen, 1971)

Hawtrey, R.G., *The Art of Central Banking* (London: Longmans, 1932)

Heller, M., *London Clerical Workers, 1880–1914: Development of the Labour Market* (London: Pickering and Chatto, 2011)

Henderson, J.M., 'The Joint-Stock Companies Acts, 1862–1900, in Relation to Banking', *Journal of the Institute of Bankers*, 27 (1906)

Henry, J.A. and Stepmann, H.A., *The First Hundred Years of the Standard Bank* (London: OUP, 1963)

Hills, S., Thomas, R., and Dimsdale, N., 'The UK Recession in Context: What Do Three Centuries of Data Tell Us?' *Bank of England Quarterly Bulletin*, 50 (2010)

Hilton, B., *Corn, Cash, Commerce: The Economic Policies of the Tory Governments, 1815–1830* (Oxford: OUP, 1977)

Hilton Price, F.G., *A Handbook of London Bankers* (London: [n.p.], 1876 and 1890/1)

Hirsch, F., 'The Bagehot Problem', in C. Goodhart and G. Illing (eds), *Financial Crises, Contagion, and the Lender of Last Resort: A Reader* (Oxford: OUP, 2002)

Hobson, O.R., *How the City Works* (London: News Chronicle, 1940)

Hobson, O.R., 'Financial Control after the War', *Journal of the Institute of Bankers*, 63 (1942)

Hobson, O.R., 'Future of the City', *Journal of the Institute of Bankers*, 57 (1946)

Hoffman, P.T., Postel-Vinay, G., and Rosenthal, J-L., *Surviving Large Losses: Financial Crises, the Middle Class and the Development of Capital Markets* (Cambridge, Mass.: Belknap Press/Harvard UP, 2007)

Hoggarth, G., Reidhill, J., and Sinclair, P., 'On the Resolution of Banking Crises: Theory and Evidence', *Bank of England Working Paper*, 209 (2004)

Hoggarth, G., Reis, R., and Saporta, V., 'Costs of Banking System Instability: Some Empirical Evidence', *Bank of England Working Paper*, 144 (2001)

Holder, R.F., *Bank of New South Wales: A History* (Sydney: Angus & Robertson, 1970)

Holderness, B.A., *Pre-Industrial England: Economy and Society, 1500–1750* (London: J.M. Dent, 1976)

Hollow, M., *Rogue Banking: A History of Financial Fraud in the Inter-War Britain* (Basingstoke: Palgrave Macmillan, 2015)

Hollow, M., Akinbami, F., and Michie, R.C. (eds), *Complexity and Crisis in the Financial System: Critical Perspectives on the Evolution of American and British Banking* (Cheltenham: Edward Elgar, 2016)

Holmes, A.R. and Green, E., *Midland: 150 Years of Banking Business* (London: Batsford, 1986)

Horne, H.O., *A History of Savings Banks* (London: OUP, 1947)

Howarth, W., *The Banks in the Clearing House* (London: Effingham Wilson, 1905)

Howson, S., *Domestic Monetary Management in Britain, 1919–38* (Cambridge: CUP, 1975)

Howson, S. and Winch, D., *The Economic Advisory Council, 1930–1939: A Study in Economic Advice during Depression and Recovery* (Cambridge: CUP, 1977)

Hughes, J., *The Vital Few: American Economic Progress and its Protagonists* (New York: Houghton Mifflin, 1966)

IFSL Research, *International Financial Markets in the UK* (London: IFSL, 2009)

Ikle, M., *Switzerland: An International Banking and Finance Center* (Stroudsburg: Dowden, Hutchinson & Ross, 1972)

Ingham, G., *Capitalism Divided? The City and Industry in British Social Development* (London: Macmillan, 1984)

Inouye, J., *Problems of the Japanese Exchange, 1914–1926* (Glasgow: Macmillan, 1931)

Institute of Bankers, *The London Discount Market Today* (London: Institute of Bankers, 1962)

Institute of Bankers, *The Bank of England Today* (London: Institute of Bankers, 1964)

Institute of International Finance, 'Effects of the War on British Banking' (New York, IIF), 124 (1943)

Inter-Bank Research Organisation, *Future of London as an International Financial Centre* (London: Cabinet Office, 1973)

Irwin, G. and Vines, D., 'The Efficient Resolution of Capital-Account Crises: How to Avoid Moral Hazard', *Bank of England Quarterly Bulletin*, 44 (2004)

Jackson, C. and Sim, M., 'Recent Developments in the Sterling Overnight Money Market', *Bank of England Quarterly Bulletin*, 53 (2013)

Jackson, P., 'Bank Capital Standards: The New Basel Accord', *Bank of England Quarterly Bulletin*, 40 (2000)

Jakab, Z. and Kumhof, M., 'Banks Are not Intermediaries of Loanable Funds: And Why It Matters', *Bank of England Working Paper*, 529 (2015)

James, J.A., 'Panics, Payments Disruptions and the Bank of England before 1826', *Financial History Review*, 19 (2012)

Jenkins, R., 'The Capital Conundrum', *Bank of England Quarterly Bulletin*, 51 (2011)

Jenkinson, N., 'Risks to the Commercial Property Market and Financial Stability', *Bank of England Quarterly Bulletin,* 47 (2007)

Jenkinson, N., 'Strengthening Regimes for Controlling Liquidity Risk: Some Lessons from the Recent Turmoil', *Bank of England Quarterly Bulletin,* 48 (2008)

Jenkinson, N., Speeches, *see* <http://www.bankofengland.co.uk/publications/pages/speeches/default.aspx>

Jenkinson, N. and Manning, M., 'Promoting Financial System Resilience in Modern Global Capital Markets: Some Issues', *Bank of England Quarterly Bulletin,* 47 (2007)

Jenkinson, N., Penalver, A., and Vause, N., 'Financial Innovation: What Have We Learnt?' *Bank of England Quarterly Bulletin,* 48 (2008)

Jerome, J.K., *Three Men in a Boat* (London: Arrowsmith, 1889)

John, A.H., 'Insurance Investment and the London Money Market of the 18th Century', *Economica,* ns 20 (1953)

John, S., Roberts, M., and Weeken, O., 'The Bank of England's Special Liquidity Scheme', *Bank of England Quarterly Bulletin,* 52 (2012)

Johnson, A., *Measuring the Economy: A Guide to Understanding the Statistics* (London: Penguin Books, 1988)

Johnston, T., *The Financiers and the Nation* (London: Methuen, 1931)

Jones, G., *The History of the British Bank of the Middle East* (Cambridge: CUP, 1986)

Jones, G., *British Multinational Banking, 1830–1990* (Oxford: OUP, 1993)

Jones, G., *Multinationals and Global Capitalism from the Nineteenth to the Twenty-First Century* (Oxford: OUP, 2005)

Jones, R.W., 'Statutory Requirements Relating to the Balance Sheets of Limited Companies', *Journal of the Institute of Bankers,* 51 (1930)

Joseph Travers & Sons, *Chronicles of Cannon Street: A Few Records of an Old Firm* (London: Joseph Travers and Sons, 1958)

Joslin, D., *A Century of Banking in Latin America* (London: OUP, 1963)

Journal of the Institute of Bankers, 'The Financial Crisis of November 1890', *Journal of the Institute of Bankers,* 12 (1891)

Journal of the Institute of Bankers, 'Memorandum by the Committee of London Clearing Bankers to the Company Law Amendment Committee', *Journal of the Institute of Bankers,* 65 (1944)

Joyce, M., Lasosa, A., Stevens, I., and Tong, M., 'The Financial Market Impact of Quantitative Easing', *Bank of England Working Paper,* 393 (2010)

Joyce, M., Tong, M., and Woods, R., 'The United Kingdom's Quantitative Easing Policy: Design, Operation and Impact', *Bank of England Quarterly Bulletin,* 51 (2011)

Keane, D., 'The Setting of the Royal Exchange: Continuity and Change in the Financial District of the City of London, 1300–1871', in A. Saunders (ed.), *The Royal Exchange* (London: Guardian Royal Exchange, 1991)

Kearns, A. and Young, J. 'Provision of Finance to Smaller Quoted Companies: Some Evidence from Survey Responses and Liaison Meetings', *Bank of England Quarterly Bulletin,* 42 (2002)

Keene, D., 'Medieval London and its Region', *London Journal,* 14 (1989)

Kelsey, E. and Rickenbach, S., 'Enhancing the Resilience of the Bank of England's Real-Time Gross Settlement Infrastructure', *Bank of England Quarterly Bulletin,* 53 (2013)

Kennedy, W.P., *Industrial Structure, Capital Markets and the Origins of British Economic Decline* (Cambridge: CUP, 1987)

Kenwood, A.G. and Lougheed, A.L., *Technological Diffusion and Industrialisation before 1914* (London: Croom Helm, 1982)

Kerridge, E., *Trade and Banking in Early Modern England* (Manchester: Manchester UP, 1988)

Keynes, J.M., 'The Prospects of Money, November 1914', *Economic Journal*, 24 (1914)

Kindleberger, C.P. and Aliber, R.Z., *Manias, Panics, and Crashes: A History of Financial Crises* (Basingstoke: Palgrave Macmillan, 2005)

King, F.H.H., *The Hongkong Bank in Late Imperial China 1864–1902* (Cambridge: CUP, 1987)

King, F.H.H., *The History of the Hongkong and Shanghai Banking Corporation* (Oxford: OUP, 1988)

King, F.H.H., *The Hongkong Bank in the Period of Imperialism and War, 1895–1918* (Cambridge: CUP, 1988)

King, M., 'Prospects for the City: In or Out of EMU', *Bank of England Quarterly Bulletin*, 37 (1997)

King, M., 'No Money, No Inflation: The Role of Money in the Economy', *Bank of England Quarterly Bulletin*, 42 (2002)

King, M., 'The Governor's Speech in Northern Ireland', *Bank of England Quarterly Bulletin*, 47 (2007)

King, M., 'The MPC Ten Years On', *Bank of England Quarterly Bulletin*, 47 (2007)

King, M., 'Banking and the Bank of England', *Bank of England Quarterly Bulletin*, 48 (2008)

King, M., 'The Governor's Speech in Bristol', *Bank of England Quarterly Bulletin*, 48 (2008)

King, M., Speech, *Bank of England Quarterly Bulletin*, 48 (2008)

King, M., Speech, *Bank of England Quarterly Bulletin*, 49 (2009)

King, M., 'Global Imbalances: The Perspective of the Bank of England', *Bank of England Quarterly Bulletin*, 51 (2011)

King, M., Speeches, *see also* <http://www.bankofengland.co.uk/publications/pages/speeches/default.aspx>

King, W.T.C., *History of the London Discount Market* (London: Routledge, 1936)

King, W.T.C., 'War and the Money Market', *Journal of the Institute of Bankers*, 58 (1947)

King, W.T.C., 'The London Discount Market', in *Current Financial Problems and the City of London* (London: Institute of Bankers, 1949)

Kinross, J., *Fifty Years in the City: Financing Small Business* (London: Murray, 1982)

Kinsey, S. and Newton, L., *International Banking in an Age of Transition: Globalisation, Automation, Banks and their Archives* (Aldershot: Ashgate, 1998)

Kleinwort, C., 'The City in Britain's Invisible Earnings', *The Banker*, 121 (1971)

Kohn, D., Speeches, *see* <http://www.bankofengland.co.uk/publications/pages/speeches/default.aspx>

Krugman, P. (ed.), *Currency Crises* (Chicago: University of Chicago Press, c.2000)

Kubelec, C. and Sa, F., 'The Geographical Composition of National External Balance Sheets: 1980–2005', *Bank of England Working Paper*, 384 (2010)

Kurgan-Van Hentenryk, G., 'The Social Origins of Bank Managers', in E. Green, M. Pohle-Fraser, and I.L. Fraser (eds), *The Human Factor in Banking History: Entrepreneurship, Organization, Management and Personnel* (Athens: Alpha Bank, 2008)

Laidler, D., 'Two Views of the Lender of Last Resort: Thornton and Bagehot', Paper Presented at a Conference in Paris (September 2002)

Lander, J.E., *Operations in the London Money Market, 1858–67* (Ph.D., University of London, 1972)

Langfield, S., Liu, X., and Ota, T., 'Mapping the UK Interbank System', *Bank of England Working Paper*, 516 (2014)

Langton, J., 'The Industrial Revolution and the Regional Geography of England', *Transactions: Institute of British Geographers*, 9 (1984)

Lavington, F., *The English Capital Market* ([n.p.]: Methuen, 1921)

Lee, T.A. and Parker, R.H. (ed.), *The Evolution of Corporate Financial Reporting* (Sunbury-on-Thames: Thomas Nelson, 1979)

Lees, Sir David and Footman, J., 'The Court of the Bank of England', *Bank of England Quarterly Bulletin*, 54 (2014)

Lever, C., *Davenport Dunn or the Man and the Day* (Leipzig: Tauchnitz, 1859) 2 vols.

Lever, C., *That Boy of Norcott's* (London: Smith, Elder, 1869)

Lever, E.H., *Foreign Exchange from the Investor's Point of View* (London: Institute of Actuaries, 1925)

Linton, C.W., 'The Commercial Banks and the London Discount Market', in *The London Discount Market Today* (London: Institute of Bankers, 1962)

Liu, Z., Quiet, S., and Roth, B., 'Banking Sector Interconnectedness: What It Is, How Can We Measure It and Why Does It Matter?' *Bank of England Quarterly Bulletin*, 55 (2015)

Lloyd, G.I.H., 'The London Money Market and the War Crisis', *Journal of the Canadian Bankers Association*, 22 (1914/15)

Lloyd George, D., *War Memoirs* (London: Odhams, 1933)

Lloyds Bank Colonial and Foreign Department, Correspondence

Lloyds Bank Ltd, Foreign Business Regulations, 1925

Logan, A., 'The United Kingdom's Small Banks' Crisis of the Early 1990s: What Were the Leading Indicators of Failure?' *Bank of England Working Paper*, 139 (2001)

Lomax, R., 'The MPC Comes of Age', *Bank of England Quarterly Bulletin*, 46 (2006)

Lomax, R., 'Current Monetary Policy Issues', *Bank of England Quarterly Bulletin*, 47 (2007)

Lord Neuberger, Speech: 'The Future of the Bar', Belfast 20 June 2014

Lowes, J. and Nenova, T., 'The Foreign Exchange and Over-The-Counter Interest-Rate Derivatives Market in the United Kingdom', *Bank of England Quarterly Bulletin*, 53 (2013)

Lubbock, J.W., *On the Clearing of the London Bankers* (London: [n.p.], 1860)

Macdonald, J.C., 'The Economic Effects, National and International of the Concentration of Capital in Few Controlling Hands', *Journal of the Institute of Bankers*, 21 (1900)

Mackenzie, Sir Compton, *Realms of Silver: One Hundred Years of Banking in the East* (London: Routledge & Kegan Paul, 1954)

Madden, J.T. and Nadler, M., 'The Paris Money Market', *Bulletin of the Institute of International Finance, New York* (1 June 1931)

Manning, S., 'The Bank of England as a Bank', *Bank of England Quarterly Bulletin*, 54 (2014)

Markham Lester, V., *Victorian Insolvency: Bankruptcy, Imprisonment for Debt, and Company Winding-Up in Nineteenth-Century England* (Oxford: Clarendon Press, 1995)

Marshall, D., *Industrial England, 1776–1851* (London: Routledge and Kegan Paul, 1973)

Martineau, H., *Berkeley the Banker* (London: Fox, 1832–4) 2 vols.

Mason, D.M., 'Our Money Market and American Banking and Currency Reform', *Journal of the Institute of Bankers*, 30 (1909)

Matthews, D., *A History of Auditing: The Changing Audit Process in Britain from the Nineteenth Century to the Present Day* (London: Routledge, 2006)

Matthews, P.W. and Tuke, A.W., *History of Barclays Bank Ltd* (London: Blades, East & Blades, 1926)

McMahon, C.W., 'The Current Financial Scene', *Journal of the Institute of Bankers*, 102 (1982)

Meeks, R., Nelson, B.D., and Alessandri, P., 'Shadow Banks and Macroeconomic Instability', *Bank of England Working Paper*, 487 (2014)

Merrett, D.T., *ANZ Bank: A History of the Australia and New Zealand Banking Group Limited and its Constituents* (London: Allen & Unwin, 1985)

Michie, R.C., 'The City of London and British Banking, 1900–1939', in C. Wrigley (ed.), *A Companion to Early Twentieth-Century Britain* (Oxford: OUP, 2003)

Michie, R.C., 'The City of London and the British Government: The Changing Relationship', in R.C. Michie and P.A. Williamson (eds), *The British Government and the City of London in the Twentieth Century* (Cambridge: CUP, 2004)

Michie, R.C., 'A Financial Phoenix: The City of London in the Twentieth Century', in Y. Cassis and É. Bussière (eds), *London and Paris as International Financial Centres* (Oxford: OUP, 2005)

Michie, R.C., 'The City of London and the British Regions: From Medieval to Modern', in W. Lancaster, D. Newton, and N. Vall (eds), *An Agenda for Regional History* (Newcastle-upon-Tyne: Northumbria UP, 2007)

Michie, R.C., 'The Emergence and Survival of a Financial Cluster in Britain', in *Learning from Some of Britain's Successful Sectors: An Historical Analysis of the Role of Government*, BIS Economics Paper 6 (2010)

Michie, R.C., 'The City of London and International Banking in the Nineteenth and Twentieth Centuries: The Asian Dimension', in S. Nishimura, T. Suzuki, and R. Michie (eds), *The Origins of International Banking in Asia: The Nineteenth and Twentieth Centuries* (Oxford: OUP, 2012)

Michie, R.C., 'Financial Capitalism', in L. Neal and J.G. Williamson (eds), *The Cambridge History of Capitalism, The Spread of Capitalism: From 1848 to the Present, v.2* (Cambridge: CUP, 2014)

Middleton, R., *Government versus the Market: The Growth of the Public Sector, Economic Management and British Economic Performance, c.1890–1979* (Cheltenham: Edward Elgar, 1996)

Midland Bank Overseas, *Description of Operations* (August 1930)

Miles, D., 'Monetary Policy and Financial Stability', *Bank of England Quarterly Bulletin*, 49 (2009)

Miles, D., 'Money, Banks and Quantitative Easing', *Bank of England Quarterly Bulletin*, 49 (2009)
Miles, D., 'The Future Financial Landscape', *Bank of England Quarterly Bulletin*, 49 (2009)
Miles, D., 'Leverage and Monetary Policy', *Bank of England Quarterly Bulletin*, 50 (2010)
Miles, D., 'Mortgages and Housing in the Near and Long Term', *Bank of England Quarterly Bulletin*, 51 (2011)
Miles, D., 'Mortgages, Housing and Monetary Policy: What Lies Ahead', *Bank of England Quarterly Bulletin*, 51 (2011)
Miles, D., 'Central Bank Asset Purchases and Financial Markets', *Bank of England Quarterly Bulletin*, 54 (2014)
Miles, D., Speeches, see <http://www.bankofengland.co.uk/publications/pages/speeches/default.aspx>
Miller, H.F.R., 'An Examination of the Bank Charter Act of 1844 with a View to Amendment', *Journal of the Institute of Bankers*, 40 (1919)
Miller, H.F.R., *The Foreign Exchange Market: A Practical Treatise on Post-War Foreign Exchange* (London: E. Arnold, 1925)
Mitchell, B., 'An American Banker's View of the City', *Journal of the Institute of Bankers*, 95 (1974)
Mitchell, B., *British Historical Statistics* (Cambridge: CUP, 1988)
Moffit, L., *England on the Eve of the Industrial Revolution* (London: P.S. King, 1925)
Moggridge, D.E., *British Monetary Policy, 1924–31* (Cambridge: CUP, 1972)
Montgomery, C.J., 'The Clearing Banks, 1952–77: An Age of Progress', *Journal of the Institute of Bankers*, 98 (1977)
Mora, N. and Logan, A., 'Shocks to Bank Capital: Evidence from UK Banks at Home and Away', *Bank of England Working Paper*, 387 (2010)
Morgan, E.V., *Studies in British Financial Policy 1914–25* (London: Macmillan, 1952)
Morrison, A.D. and Wilhelm, W.J., Jr, *Investment Banking: Institutions, Politics, and Law* (Oxford: OUP, 2007)
Moshenskyi, S., *History of the Weksel: Bill of Exchange and Promissory Note* ([n.p.], Xlibris Corporation, 2008)
Mottram, R.H., *Our Mr Dormer* (London: Chatto & Windus, 1927)
Mottram, R.H., *The Boroughmonger* (London: Chatto & Windus, 1929)
Mottram, R.H., *Castle Island* (London: Chatto & Windus, 1931)
Muirhead, S., *Crisis Banking in the East: The History of the Chartered Mercantile Bank of India, London and China, 1853–93* (Aldershot: Ashgate, 1996)
Munn, C.W., 'The Development of Joint-Stock Banking in Scotland, 1810–1845', in A. Slaven and D.H. Aldcroft (eds), *Business, Banking and Urban History* (Edinburgh: John Donald, 1982)
Munn, C.W., 'The Emergence of Central Banking in Ireland', *Irish Economic and Social History*, 10 (1983)
Munn, C.W., *Clydesdale Bank: The First One Hundred and Fifty Years* (London: Clydesdale Banking Company, 1988)
Munn, C.W., 'The Emergence of Joint-Stock Banking in the British Isles: A Comparative Approach', in R.P.T. Davenport-Hines and G. Jones (eds), *The End of Insularity: Essays in Comparative Business History* (London: Frank Cass, 1988)

Murphy, A.L., *The Origins of the English Financial Markets: Investment and Speculation before the South Sea Bubble* (Cambridge: CUP, 2009)

Murphy, E. and Senior, S., 'Changes to the Bank of England', *Bank of England Quarterly Bulletin*, 53 (2013)

Nevin, E. and Davies, E.W., *The London Clearing Banks* (London: Elek, 1970)

Newton, L., *Change and Continuity: the Development of Joint-stock Banking in the Early Nineteenth Century* (Reading: Henley Business School, 2007)

Newton, L., 'The Birth of Joint-Stock Banking: England and New England Compared', *Business History Review*, 84 (2010)

Newton, S., *Modernization Frustrated: The Politics of Industrial Decline in Britain since 1900* (London: Unwin Hyman, 1988)

Nier, E., Yang, J., Yorulmazer, T., and Alentorn, A., 'Network Models and Financial Stability', *Bank of England Working Paper*, 346 (2008)

Nishimura, S., *The Decline of Inland Bills of Exchange in the London Money Market 1855–1913* (Cambridge: CUP, 1971)

Norman, B., Shaw, R., and Speight, G., 'The History of Interbank Settlement Arrangements: Exploring Central Banks' Role in the Payment System', *Bank of England Working Papers*, 412 (2011)

Nwanko, G.O., 'British Overseas Banks in the Developing Countries', *Journal of the Institute of Bankers*, 93 (1972)

O'Brien, L.K., 'The Technique of the United Kingdom Exchange Control', in *The Pattern and Finance of Foreign Trade* (London: Institute of Bankers, 1949)

O'Brien, R.S., 'The Euro-Currency Market', *Journal of the Institute of Bankers*, 92 (1971)

O'Connor, J., Wackett, J., and Zammit, R., 'The Use of Foreign Exchange Markets by Non-Banks', *Bank of England Quarterly Bulletin*, 51 (2011)

Odate, G., *Japan's Financial Relations with the United States* (New York: Columbia University, 1922)

Offer, A., 'Narrow Banking, Real Estate, and Financial Stability in the UK, c.1870–2010', in N. Dimsdale and A. Hotson (eds), *British Financial Crises since 1825* (Oxford: OUP, 2014)

Oliphant, Mrs, *Hester: A Study in Contemporary Life* (London: Macmillan, 1883)

Oliphant, Mrs, *At His Gates* [serialized in *Good Words for 1872* (London: Strahan and Co)]

Ollerenshaw, P., *Banking in Nineteenth-Century Ireland: The Belfast Banks, 1825–1914* (Manchester: Manchester UP, 1987)

Orbell, J., *Baring Brothers and Co. Ltd: A History to 1939* (London: Baring Brothers, 1958)

Orbell, J., 'The Historical Structure and Functions of British Banking', in J. Orbell and A. Turton, *British Banking: A Guide to Historical Records* (Aldershot: Ashgate, 2001)

Orbell, J., 'Private Banks and International Finance in the Light of the Archives of Baring Brothers', in Y. Cassis and P.L. Cottrell (eds), *The World of Private Banking* (Farnham: Ashgate, 2009)

Orbell, J. and Turton, A., *British Banking: A Guide to Historical Records* (Aldershot: Ashgate, 2001)

Oulton, N. and Sebastia-Barriel, M., 'Long- and Short-Term Effects of the Financial Crisis on Labour Productivity, Capital and Output', *Bank of England Working Paper*, 470 (2013)

Padovan, J., 'New Influences in Merchant Banking', *Journal of the Institute of Bankers*, 98 (1977)

Parker, R.H., 'Regulating British Corporate Financial Reporting in the Late Nineteenth Century', *Accounting, Business and Financial History* 1 (1990)

Peake, E.G., *An Academic Study of Some Money Market and Other Statistics* (London: P.S. King, 1923)

Peel, G., *The Economic Impact of America* (London: Macmillan, 1928)

Perlin, M. and Schanz, J., 'System-wide Liquidity Risk in the United Kingdom's Large-Value Payment System: An Empirical Analysis', *Bank of England Working Paper*, 427 (2011)

Perry, S.E., 'The History of Companies' Legislation in England in its Practical Aspect, and its Effect upon our Industrial and Banking Development', *Journal of the Institute of Bankers*, 29 (1908)

Perry, S.E., 'English and American Banking Methods: A Comparison and Contrast', *Journal of the Institute of Bankers*, 30 (1909)

Peters, J., 'The British Government and the City/Industry Divide: The Case of the 1914 Financial Crisis', *Twentieth Century British History*, 4 (1993)

Phelps, C.W., *The Foreign Expansion of American Banks: American Branch Banking Abroad* (New York: Ronald Press, 1927)

Phillips, H.W., *Modern Foreign Exchange and Foreign Banking* (London: Macdonald & Evans, 1926)

Phillips Oppenheim, E., *The Bank Manager* (London: Hodder & Stoughton, 1934)

Plender, Sir William, *Enemy Banks (London Agencies): Report to the Chancellor of the Exchequer* (London: HMSO, 1917)

Pohl, M. and Burk, K., *Deutsche Bank in London, 1873–1914* (Munich: Piper, 1998)

Pollard, S. (ed.), *The Gold Standard and Employment Policies between the Wars* (London: Methuen, 1970)

Pollard, S., *The Development of the British Economy, 1914–1980*, 3rd edn. (London: Edward Arnold, 1983)

Pollard, S. and Crossley, D.W., *The Wealth of Britain* (London: Batsford, 1968)

Pose, A.S., Speeches, *see* <http://www.bankofengland.co.uk/publications/pages/speeches/default.aspx>

Pownall, G.W., 'The Proportional Use of Credit Documents and Metallic Money in English Banks', *Journal of the Institute of Bankers*, 2 (1881)

Pratt, E.A., *A History of Inland Transport and Communication* (London: Kegan Paul Trench Trubner, 1912)

Pressnell, L., *Country Banking in the Industrial Revolution* (Oxford: OUP, 1956)

Price, S.J., *Building Societies, Their Origin and History*, 2nd ed. (London: Franey, 1959)

Pringle, R., 'The Foreign Banks in London', *Journal of the Institute of Bankers*, 99 (1978)

Reade, C., *Hard Cash: A Matter of Fact Romance* (London: [n.p.], 1863)

Reade, C. and Boucicault, D., *Foul Play* (London: Bradbury, 1868)

Reed, R., *National Westminster Bank: A Short History* (London: National Westminster Bank, 1983)

Reinhart, C.M. and Rogoff, K.S., *This Time is Different: Eight Centuries of Financial Folly* (Princeton: Princeton UP, 2009)

Reinhart, D. and Riddiough, S.J., 'The Two Faces of Cross-Border Banking Flows: An Investigation into the Links between Global Risk, Arms-length Funding and Internal Capital Markets', *Bank of England Working Paper*, 498 (2014)

Reinold, K., 'Housing Equity Withdrawal since the Financial Crisis', *Bank of England Quarterly Bulletin*, 51 (2011)

Report and Proceedings of the Sub-Committee of the Committee of Imperial Defence or Trading with the Enemy, Cabinet Office, National Archives Kew, (1912)

Riddell, C. [writing as F.G. Trafford], *George Geith of Fen Court* (London: R. Bentley, 1866)

Riddell, C., *Joy after Sorrow* (London: Hutchinson, 1873)

Riley, J.C., *International Government Finance and the Amsterdam Capital Market, 1740–1815* (Cambridge: CUP, 1980)

Ritchie, B., *We're with the Woolwich: The Story of the Woolwich Building Society 1847–1997* (London: James & James, 1997)

Roberts, R., *Saving the City: The Great Financial Crisis of 1914* (Oxford: OUP, 2013)

Roberts, R., '"How We Saved the City": The Management of the Financial Crisis of 1914', in N. Dimsdale and A. Hotson (eds), *British Financial Crises since 1825* (Oxford: OUP, 2014)

Robinson, E., *The City Banker or Love and Money* (London: Skeet, 1856)

Robson, B., 'Coming Full Circle: London versus the Rest, 1890–1980', in G. Gordon (ed.), *Regional Cities in the UK, 1890–1980* (London: Harper & Row, 1986)

Rogers, P., 'Changes at the Bank of England', *Bank of England Quarterly Bulletin*, 37 (1997)

Root, H.l., *The Fountain of Privilege: Political Foundations of Markets in Old Regime France and England* (Berkeley: University of California Press, 1994)

Rose, A.K. and Wieladek, T., 'Too Big to Fail: Some Empirical Evidence on the Causes and Consequences of Public Banking Interventions in the United Kingdom', *Bank of England Working Papers*, 460 (2012)

Rosenberg, K. and Hopkins, R.T., *The Romance of the Bank of England* (London: Thornton Butterworth, 1933)

Ross, D.M., 'The Unsatisfied Fringe in Britain, 1930s–80s', *Business History*, 38 (1996)

Rozenraad, C., 'The International Money Market', *Journal of the Institute of Bankers*, 24 (1902)

Rozenraad, C., *The History of the Growth of London as the Financial Centre of the World and the Means of Maintaining that Position* (London: Effingham Wilson, 1903)

Rule, D., Speeches, *see* <http://www.bankofengland.co.uk/publications/pages/speeches/default.aspx>

Rybczynski, T.M., 'The Merchant Banks', *Economic and Social Studies*, 41 (1973)

Salmon, C., 'Three Principles for Successful Financial Sector Reform', *Bank of England Quarterly Bulletin*, 52 (2012)

Salmon, C., Speeches, *see* <http://www.bankofengland.co.uk/publications/pages/speeches/default.aspx>

Sands, H., Speeches, *see* <http://www.bankofengland.co.uk/publications/pages/speeches/default.aspx>

Sangway, J., *Clare's Money Market Primer and Key to the Exchanges* (London: Pitman, 1936)

Saville, R., *Bank of Scotland: A History, 1695-1995* (Edinburgh: Edinburgh UP, 1996)

Saw, R., *The Bank of England, 1694-1944* (London: Harrap, 1944)

Sayers, R.S., *Lloyds Bank in the History of English Banking* (Oxford: OUP, 1957)

Sayers, R.S., *Gilletts in the London Money Market, 1867-1967* (Oxford: OUP, 1968)

Sayers, R.S., *The Bank of England, 1891-1944* (Cambridge: CUP, 1976)

Scammell, W.M., *The London Discount Market* (London: St Martin's Press, 1968)

Scarborough Jackson, W., *Nine Points of the Law* (London: Lane, 1903)

Schearme, J.A., 'English and American Banking Methods: A Comparison and Contrast', *Journal of the Institute of Bankers*, 30 (1909)

Schenk, C.R., 'The Origins of the Euro-Dollar Market in London, 1955-1963', *Explorations in Economic History*, 35 (1998)

Schenk, C.R., *Hong Kong as an International Financial Centre: Emergence and Development 1945-65* (London: Routledge, 2001)

Schenk, C.R., *The Decline of Sterling: Managing the Retreat of an International Currency, 1945-1992* (Cambridge: CUP, 2010)

Schuster, F., 'Foreign Trade and the Money Market', *Journal of the Institute of Bankers*, 25 (1904)

Schwartz, L.D., *London in the Age of Industrialisation: Entrepreneurs, Labour Force and Living Conditions, 1700-1850* (Cambridge: CUP, 1992)

Schwarz, A.J., 'Earmarks of a Lender of Last Resort', in C. Goodhart and G. Illing (eds), *Financial Crises, Contagion, and the Lender of Last Resort: A Reader* (Oxford: OUP, 2002)

Scott, G.J., 'The Bill-Broker in the Bank Parlour', *Journal of the Institute of Bankers*, 42 (1921)

Scott, W.R., *The Constitution and Finance of English, Scottish and Irish Joint-Stock Companies to 1720* (Cambridge: CUP, 1912)

Seabourne, T., 'The Summer of 1914', in F. Capie and E. Wood (eds), *Financial Crises and the World Banking System* (London: Macmillan, 1986)

Select Committee on Building Societies (No. 2) Bill, 'Special Report and Reports, together with the Proceedings of the Committee, Minutes of Evidence, Appendix and Index' (London: HMSO, 1894)

Seligman, V., *Bank Holiday* (London: Longmans, Green, 1934)

Senior, S. and Westwood, R., 'The External Balance Sheet of the United Kingdom: Implications for Financial Stability?' *Bank of England Quarterly Bulletin*, 40 (2000)

Sentence, A., 'A Tale of Two Shocks: Global Challenges for UK Monetary Policy', *Bank of England Quarterly Bulletin*, 47 (2007)

Seton Merriman, H., *Roden's Corner* (London: Nelson, 1898)

Seyd, E., *The London Banking and Bankers' Clearing House System* (London: Cassell, Petter & Galpin, 1931)

Shaffik, M., Speeches, *see* <http://www.bankofengland.co.uk/publications/pages/speeches/default.aspx>

Shapiro, S., *Capital and the Cotton Industry in the Industrial Revolution* (Ithaca, N.Y.: Cornell UP, 1967)
Sharp, R., Speeches, see <http://www.bankofengland.co.uk/publications/pages/speeches/default.aspx>
Shaw, E.R., *The London Money Market* (London: Heinemann, 1975)
Shepherd, D.K., *The Growth and Role of UK Financial Institutions, 1880-1962* (London: Methuen, 1971)
Shewell Cooper, F., 'Company Law in Relation to Bankers', *Journal of the Institute of Bankers*, 42 (1921)
Shin, G.S., 'Reflections on Northern Rock: The Bank Run that Heralded the Global Financial Crisis', *Journal of Economic Perspectives*, 23 (2009)
Siegel, J., *For Peace and Money: French and British Finance in the Service of Tsars and Commissars* (Oxford: OUP, 2014)
Sinclair, P.J.N., 'Central Banks and Financial Stability', *Bank of England Quarterly Bulletin*, 40 (2000)
Singleton, J., *Central Banking in the Twentieth Century* (Cambridge: CUP, 2011)
Smith St. Aubyn, Business Diary 1891-1960. London Metropolitan Archives CLC/B/2002
Smyth, N., 'Trading Models and Liquidity Provision in OTC Derivatives Markets', *Bank of England Quarterly Bulletin*, 51 (2011)
Spalding, W.F., 'The Establishment and Growth of Foreign Branch Banks in London, and the Effect, Immediate and Ultimate, upon the Banking and Commercial Development of this Country', *Journal of the Institute of Bankers*, 32 (1911)
Spalding, W.F., 'The Foreign Exchanges and the War', *Journal of the Institute of Bankers*, 36 (1915)
Spalding, W.F., *Eastern Exchange Currency and Finance*, 4th edn. (London: Pitman, 1924)
Spalding, W.F., *Dictionary of the World's Currencies and Foreign Exchanges* (London: Pitman, 1928)
Spring-Rice, D., 'The Financial Machinery of the City of London', *Journal of the Institute of Bankers*, 50 (1929)
Stasavage, D., *Public Debt and the Birth of the Democratic State: France and Great Britain, 1688-1789* (Cambridge: CUP, 2003)
Steele, F.E., 'On Changes in the Bank Rate of Discount: First, their Causes and Secondly, their Effects on the Money Market, on the Commerce of the Country, and on the Value of all Interest-Bearing Securities', *Journal of the Institute of Bankers*, 12 (1891)
Steele, F.E., 'Bank Amalgamations', *Journal of the Institute of Bankers*, 18 (1897)
Stewart, M., Speeches, see <http://www.bankofengland.co.uk/publications/pages/speeches/default.aspx>
Stewart Patterson, E.L., *Domestic and Foreign Exchange* (New York: Alexander Hamilton Institute, 1917)
Straker, F., 'The Daily Money Article', *Journal of the Institute of Bankers*, 25 (1904)
Stringa, M. and Monks, A., 'Inter-Industry Contagion between UK Life Insurers and UK Banks: An Event Study', *Bank of England Working Paper*, 325 (2007)

Sunderland, D., *Financing the Raj: The City of London and Colonial India, 1858-1940* (Woodbridge: Boydell Press, 2013)

Sykes, E., 'The Growth of London as the Financial Centre of the World, and the Best Means of Maintaining that Position', *Journal of the Institute of Bankers*, 23 (1902)

Sykes, E., 'Some Effects of the War on the London Money Market', *Journal of the Institute of Bankers* 36 (1914)

Sykes, J., *The Amalgamation Movement in English Banking, 1825-1924* (London: King, 1926)

Sylla, R., 'Comparing the UK and US Financial Systems, 1790-1830', in J. Atack and L. Neal (eds) *The Origin and Development of Financial Markets and Institutions: From the Seventeenth Century to the Present* (Cambridge: CUP, 2009)

Taleb, N.T., *Fooled by Randomness: The Hidden Role of Chance in Life and in the Markets* (New York: Random House 2005)

Tamaki, N., *The Life Cycle of the Union Bank of Scotland, 1830-1954* (Aberdeen: Aberdeen UP, 1983)

Tamaki, N., *Japanese Banking: A History 1859-1959* (Cambridge: CUP, 1995)

Taylor, C.W., 'The Case against the Nationalisation of the Banks', *Journal of the Institute of Bankers*, 56 (1935)

Taylor, J., *Boardroom Scandal: The Criminalization of Company Fraud in Nineteenth-Century Britain* (Oxford: OUP, 2013)

Teichova, A., Kurgan-Van Hentenryk, G., and Ziegler, D. (eds), *Banking, Trade and Industry: Europe, America and Asia from the Thirteenth to the Twentieth Century* (Cambridge: CUP, 2011)

Temin, P. and Voth, H.-J., *Prometheus Shackled: Goldsmith Banks and England's Financial Revolution after 1700* (Oxford: OUP, 2013)

Thackstone, H.H., 'Work of the Foreign Branch of a Commercial Bank', in *Current Financial Problems and the City of London* (London: Institute of Bankers, 1949)

Thomas, S.E., *The Principles and Arithmetic of Foreign Exchange* (London: Macdonald & Evans, 1925)

Thomas, S.E., *Banking and Exchange* (London: Gregg Publishing, 1930)

Thomas, S.E., *British Banks and the Finance of Industry, 1897-1960* (London: P.S. King & Son, 1931)

Thomas, S.E., *The Rise and Growth of Joint-Stock Banking* (London: Pitman, 1934)

Thomas, W.A., *The Finance of British Industry, 1918-1976* (London: Methuen, 1978)

The Times Digital Archive, 1785-2008

The Times, *The City of London* (London: The Times, 1928)

Tolliday, S., *Business, Banking, and Politics* (Cambridge, Mass.: Harvard UP, 1987)

Toynbee, A., *Lectures on the Industrial Revolution of the Eighteenth Century in England* (London: Longmans, Green, 1884), new edn. (1908)

Trafford, F.G. *see* Riddell, C.

Trebilcock, C., *Phoenix Assurance and the Development of British Insurance, 1782-1870* (Cambridge: CUP, 1985)

Tritton, J.H., 'Bills of Exchange and their Functions', *Journal of the Institute of Bankers*, 23 (1902)

Tritton, J.H., 'The Short Loan Fund on the London Money Market', *Journal of the Institute of Bankers* 23 (1902)
Truptil, R.J., *British Banks and the London Money Market* (London: Jonathan Cape, 1936)
Tucker, P., 'Credit Conditions and Monetary Policy', *Bank of England Quarterly Bulletin*, 44 (2004)
Tucker, P., 'Central Banking and Political Economy: The Example of the United Kingdom's Monetary Policy Committee', *Bank of England Quarterly Bulletin*, 47 (2007)
Tucker, P., 'Macro, Asset Price, and Financial System Uncertainties', *Bank of England Quarterly Bulletin*, 47 (2007)
Tucker, P., 'Money and Credit: Banking and the Macroeconomy', *Bank of England Quarterly Bulletin*, 47 (2007)
Tucker, P., 'A Perspective on Recent Monetary and Financial System Developments', *Bank of England Quarterly Bulletin*, 47 (2007)
Tucker, P., 'The Repertoire of Official Sector Interventions in the Financial System: Last Resort Lending, Market Making, and Capital', *Bank of England Quarterly Bulletin*, 49 (2009)
Tucker, P., 'Shadow Banking, Financing Markets and Financial Stability', *Bank of England Quarterly Bulletin*, 50 (2010)
Tucker, P., 'Banking in a Market Economy: the International Agenda', *Bank of England Quarterly Bulletin*, 52 (2012)
Tucker, P., 'Competition, the Pressure for Returns, and Stability', *Bank of England Quarterly Bulletin*, 52 (2012)
Tucker, P., Speeches, *see* <http://www.bankofengland.co.uk/publications/pages/speeches/default.aspx>
Tucker, P., Hall, S., and Pattani, A., 'Macroprudential Policy at the Bank of England', *Bank of England Quarterly Bulletin*, 53 (2013)
Tuke, A.W. and Gillman, R.J.H., *Barclay's Bank Ltd, 1926-1969* (London: Barclays Bank, 1969)
Turner, J.D., *Banking in Crisis: The Rise and Fall of British Banking Stability, 1800 to the Present* (Cambridge: CUP, 2014)
Turner, J.D., 'Holding Shareholders to Account: British Banking Stability and Contingent Capital', in N. Dimsdale and A. Hotson (eds), *British Financial Crises since 1825* (Oxford: OUP, 2014)
Tyson, G., *100 Years of Banking in Asia and Africa* (London: National and Grindlays Bank, 1963)
Vallance, A., *The Centre of the World* (London: Hodder & Stoughton, 1935)
Vander Weyer, D., 'The Threats and Opportunities Facing British Banks: A 10-Year View', *Journal of the Institute of Bankers*, 101 (1980)
Von Peter, G., 'International Banking Centres: A Network Perspective', *BIS Quarterly Review* (2007)
Wadsworth, J., *Counter Defensive: The Story of a Bank in Battle* (London: Hodder & Stoughton, 1946)
Wardley, P., 'The Anatomy of Big Business: Aspects of Corporate Development in the Twentieth Century', *Business History*, 33 (1991)

Wardley, P., *Women, Mechanization, and Cost-Savings in Twentieth-Century British Banks and Other Financial Institutions* (Helsinki: WEHC, 2006)

Ward-Perkins, C.N., 'Banking Developments', in G.D.N. Worswick and P.H. Ady (eds), *The British Economy, 1945–1950* (Oxford: OUP, 1952)

Warren, H., *The Story of the Bank of England* (London: [n.p.], 1903)

Watson, K., 'Banks and Industrial Finance: The Experience of Brewers, 1880–1913', *Economic History Review*, 49 (1996)

Watts, R.L. and Zimmerman, J.L., 'Agency Problems, Auditing, and the Theory of the Firm: Some Evidence', *Journal of Law and Economics*, 36 (1983)

Webb, A.D., *The New Dictionary of Statistics* (London: Routledge, 1911)

Weismuller, A.A., 'London Consortium Banks', *Journal of the Institute of Bankers*, 95 (1974)

Westminster Bank, The, *The Financial Machinery of the Import and Export Trade* (London: Westminster Bank, 1925)

Wetherilt, A.V., 'Money Market Operations and Volatility in UK Money Market Rates', *Bank of England Quarterly Bulletin*, 42 (2002)

Wetherilt, A.V., Zimmerman, P., and Soramaki, K., 'The Sterling Unsecured Loan Market during 2006–08: Insights from Network Theory', *Bank of England Working Paper*, 398 (2010)

Weyman, S.J., *Ovington's Bank* (London: John Murray, 1922)

Wharmby, S., 'The Foreign Exchange and Over-The-Counter Derivatives Markets in the United Kingdom', *Bank of England Quarterly Bulletin*, 41 (2001)

Whitaker, A.C., *Foreign Exchange* (New York: Appleton, 1919)

Whitmore, F., *The Money Machine* (London: Pitman, 1930)

Wilcox, M.G., 'Capital in Banking: An Historical Survey', *Journal of the Institute of Bankers*, 100 (1979)

Wilgress, L.D., 'The London Money Market', *Journal of the Canadian Bankers' Association*, 20 (1912/13)

Wilkins, M., 'Disjunctive Sets? Business and Banking History', in E. Green, M. Pohle-Fraser, and I.L. Fraser (eds), *The Human Factor in Banking History: Entrepreneurship, Organization, Management and Personnel* (Athens: Alpha Bank, 2008)

Williams, D., 'Trading Links: Patterns of Information and Communication, the Steamship and the Modernization of East-West Commerce', in P.L. Cottrell, M. Pohle-Fraser, and I.L. Fraser (eds), *East Meets West: Banking, Commerce and Investment in the Ottoman Empire* (Aldershot: Ashgate, 2008)

Williams Deacon's Bank, *Williams Deacon's, 1771–1970* (Manchester: Williams Deacon's Bank, 1971

Williams, L., 'The Banks and their Competitors', *Journal of the Institute of Bankers*, 101 (1980)

Williams, P., 'The Foreign Exchange and Over-The-Counter Derivatives Markets in the United Kingdom', *Bank of England Quarterly Bulletin*, 44 (2004)

Wilson, C., *Anglo-Dutch Commerce and Finance in the 18th Century* (Cambridge: CUP, 1941)

Wilson, R., *Capital Imports and the Terms of Trade: Examined in the Light of 60 years of Australian Borrowing* (Melbourne: [n.p.], 1931)

Winter, E.M., 'London's Global Reach? Reuters News and Network, 1865, 1881, and 1914', *Journal of World History*, 21 (2010)
Winton, J.R., *Lloyds Bank, 1918-1969* (Oxford: OUP, 1982)
Withers, H., *The English Banking System* (Washington: Government Printing Office, 1910)
Wood, J.H., *A History of Central Banking in Great Britain and the United States* (Cambridge: CUP, 2005)
Wood, Mrs H., *The Shadow of Ashlydyat* (London: Richard Bentley and Sons, 1863)
Wood, R.J., *Commercial Bank of Australia* (Melbourne: Hargreen, 1990)
Wrigley, E.A., 'A Simple Model of London's Importance in Changing English Society and Economy, 1650-1750', *Past and Present* 37 (1967)
Wrigley, E.A., *Continuity, Chance and Change: The Character of the Industrial Revolution in England* (Cambridge: CUP, 1988)
Ziegler, D., *Central Bank, Peripheral Industry: The Bank of England in the Provinces, 1826-1913* (Leicester: Leicester UP, 1990)
Ziegler, P., *The Sixth Great Power: Barings 1762-1929* (London: Collins, 1988)

Index

Abbey National 190, 216, 258
ABN-Amro 216
Accepting Houses Association 128
Agra and Masterman's Bank 80
agricultural sector 98, 109
Alliance and Leicester 216
alternative money markets 175, 177, 181, 196, 198
Amsterdam 50, 56
Argentina 81
armaments industry, inter-war reorganization 156
Army savings bank 99
audits 85-8
Australia
  financial crises, exemption from between 1914 and 1945 125
  Global Financial Crisis 237, 268
  and London money market 100, 104-5, 107-8
  property bubble, bursting of (1893) 100
Authority Bank 194

Bailey, Andrew 208, 222, 234-5
Balfour, Jabez 99
bank, definition of 1, 2-3
  and number of banks 23-4, 27
Bank Charter Act (1844) 40, 42, 81, 116
Bankers' Almanac Register of Bank Name Changes and Liquidations 26-7
Bankers' Clearing House 57, 82, 119
Bankers' Industrial Development Company 156
Bank for International Settlement 1, 20, 232
Banking Acts
  1979 193
  1987 193
  2009 258
Banking Special Provisions Act (2008) 251
Bank of Credit and Commerce International (BCCI) 184, 193
Bank of England 267
  1694-1825 47, 48, 49, 50-5, 54, 56-7, 60-1, 66, 71
    establishment 48, 50
  1825-1914 76, 81-3, 113-23
    Barings rescue (1890) 32, 43, 116, 121-2, 123, 239
    charter renewal (1844) 81
    deposits (1870 and 1913) 117
  1914-1918 36, 43, 126, 127, 128, 129, 161
  1918-1939 149-50, 151-7, 268
    Williams Deacon's rescue (1930) 18, 32, 154, 155, 161, 239
  1939-1945 157, 158, 159
  1945-1970 163, 164, 172-81, 182, 183, 268
    domestic competition controls, removal of (1970) 19
    structure and operation of banking system 164, 165-6, 169, 170, 171
  1970-1997 19, 187, 189, 192-9, 200-1
    secondary banks rescue (1974) 32
  1997-2007 226, 228, 229, 230-1, 232-3
  2007-2015 252, 253, 259, 262
banking industry and government, relationship between 10, 11
bills of exchange 82-3
Competition and Credit Control policy 192
competition
  domestic competition controls, removal of (1970) 19
  with joint-stock banks 117-18
  with London banks 81-2
and consolidation of banks 76
deposits (1870 and 1913) 117
economies of scale 31, 34
establishment 48, 50
Exchange Equalization Account 153
Federal Reserve, compared with 130
financial crises
  1793 62
  1810 62-5, 66-8, 69
  1825 67
  2007/8 17, 202-5, 212, 228, 232-5, 248-59, 262, 263, 267, 268, 269
high finance, study of 47
inter-bank money market 41
Lend and Hold Model 35-7, 42, 61, 83, 123
lender of last resort, role 11-12, 18, 21, 42-3, 239
  1825-1914 115-18, 121-3
  1914-1918 127, 161
  1918-1939 151, 152, 153, 154, 155, 160-1, 268
  1945-1970 174, 175, 176, 178-9, 183
  1970-1997 192, 194, 196, 197, 199, 200, 201

Bank of England (cont.)
  1997-2007 203, 229, 235
  2007/8 financial crisis 253, 256, 268
  2007-2015 239-48
  limited liability 53, 91
  long-term perspective 45
  Memorandum of Understanding with HM Treasury and FSA 228, 230
  mergers, approval of 32
  Monetary Policy Committee 233, 259
  nationalization (1946) 36, 126, 172, 182
  note issue monopoly 41, 42
  number of UK banks 22
  Originate and Distribute Model 37-8, 40, 42, 68
  Payments Act (1819) 66
  risk-assessment models 226
  Special Liquidity Scheme 252, 253, 262
  stability of banking system 18-19
  supervisory role 11, 173
Bank of England Act (1998) 194
bank offices
  competition 97-8
  numbers (1911 and 1924) 142
  ratio to population (1911 and 1924) 142
Bank of France 153
Bank of London and South Africa (BOLSA) 165, 176
Bank of Scotland
  British Linen Bank acquisition 164
  entry into English banking 218, 220
  establishment 53
  financial crisis (2007/8) 254
  Halifax acquisition 215, 216, 220, 221-2, 236
  limited liability 91
  London money market 107
  size 216
  see also HBOS
bankruptcies
  of companies
    1780s-1825 64, 65
    1800-1861 76
    1870-1914 95
  in inter-bank money market 60
Barclays Bank
  1825-1914 86, 87
    audited balance sheet (1891) 87
    consolidation 78, 80
    formation 86
    number of branches 79
    share of deposits 78
  1918-1939 134, 137, 138, 155
  1945-1970 164, 165
  1970-1997 185, 186
  1997-2007 216

acquisitions 138, 164
  attempted merger with Lloyds Bank 164
  Union Bank of Manchester 137
business perspective 14
CHAPS 241
economies of scale 39
in fiction 144
international banking activities 155, 165
number of employees (1910 vs 1939) 39
Barings Bank
  acceptance business (1930-1939) 150
  failure (1995) 184, 193
  near failure (1890) 17, 18, 32, 39, 43, 70, 81, 86, 87, 116, 121-2, 123, 239
  Originate and Distribute Model 52
  structure and operation 185
Barned's Banking Company 80
Bassett, Son and Harris 86-7
Bean, Charles 205, 235
Bear Stearns 252, 262
Belfast Bank 138
Berkeley's Bank 71
Besant, W., *Ready-Money Mortiboy* (co-author J. Rice) 74
Big Bang reforms 19, 34, 40, 44, 186, 216, 218, 236, 269
bill brokers 42
  and Bank of England 120, 121, 152, 153
  emergence 37, 56-7
  and lender of last resort 114-15
  Union Bank of Scotland 106
bills of exchange 35-8, 40-3, 47
  1694-1825 51, 52, 54-5, 56, 57, 60-1
  1810 financial crisis 62, 64-5, 68
  1825-1914 82-3, 84, 104, 109-11, 114-15, 118-19
  1890 Barings crisis 121-2
  1914-1918 126, 127
  1945-1970 170, 179
  1970-1997 199
  1997-2007 209-10
  counterparty risk 179
  demise 82-3, 84
  discount houses 118-19
  international communications 104
  lender of last resort 114-15
  London money market 109-11
  see also Treasury Bills
Birkbeck Bank 43
Blunden, Sir George 173
Boldero, Edward 62
Bowles and Company 64
Bradford and Bingley 216, 222, 251, 258, 262
branch banking system 1825-1914

Index

average number of branches
   (1850–1913) 77
   competition 78, 79–80, 97–8
   foreign banks 104–5
   UK banks with exclusively overseas
      operations 102
   1918–1939 142, 150
   1945–1970 181
   1970–1997 189
   1997–2007 220, 232
   2007/8 financial crisis 232
   closure of branches 189
   competition 78, 79–80, 97–8, 220
   foreign banks 104–5, 150, 181, 232
   superiority to unitary banking system 130
   vulnerabilities 80
Brasenose College, Oxford 88
Brickwood and Company 64
British and Commonwealth Bank 194
British Bankers' Association 128, 199
British Linen Bank 138, 164
British Linen Company 53
British Mutual Banking Company 101
British Mutual Investment Loan and Discount
   Company 101
British Overseas Bank 154
Brown, Gordon 225, 227
building societies
   1914–1918 126
   1918–1939 139, 145
   1939–1945 159
   1945–1970 164, 168–9
   1970–1997 19, 184, 200
      structure and operation 188, 189–90,
         191–2
   1997–2007 209, 212, 213
      competition 217, 220
   competition 92, 99–100, 139, 168–9,
      217, 220
   consolidation 31
   conversion into banks 24, 190, 206, 216,
      218, 220, 222–3, 236
   deposits
      1880 vs 1913 100
      1919 vs 1938 138
   failures 81
   growth of 8
   number of 27–8, 30, 99, 278–80
Building Societies Acts
   1874 27
   1962 189
   1986 190
business role of banks 7–9,
   13–14
buy-to-rent market 223
BZW 186

calculating machines 141
Canada
   concentration of banking 216
   financial crises, exemption from between
      1914 and 1945 125
   Global Financial Crisis 216, 237, 260, 268
Canadian Bank of Commerce 107
Capital and Counties Bank 133
Carney, Mark 235
casino banking 202
centralized clearing system 4
certificates of deposit 176
Charing Cross Bank 80, 100
chartered accountants 85–8
Chartered Bank 165
Charterhouse Industrial Development
   Corporation 140
cheques 4
Chief Registrar of Friendly Societies 28
City and Westminster Bank 78, 134
City Bank 104
City of Glasgow Bank 43, 70, 79, 80, 85, 116,
   117, 122, 123, 239
City of London 264–5
   1694–1825 47–8, 49, 58, 61
   1825–1914 70, 92, 105–14
      domestic and overseas banks, relations
         between 102
   1914–1945 125, 126
      concentration of power within British
         banking 132–3
   1945–1970 175–81, 182
   1970–1997
      Bank of England 193
      Big Bang reforms 44
      inter-bank money market 196–200
   1997–2007 206–7
   2007/8 financial crisis 203, 241
   2007–2015 244–5
   as international financial centre 9–10, 92
Clearing House 57, 82, 119
Clearing House Automated Payments Scheme
   (CHAPS) 241–2
clearing system 4
Clydesdale Bank 138
Cocks, Biddulph and Co. 88
collateralized loan obligations 213
Collins, Wilkie, 'The Biter Bit' 71
Commercial Bank of Australia 100, 104
commercial banks 8
   1825–1914 78, 79, 88, 89, 91–4, 97–101
      deposits (1870 vs 1913) 117
   1914–1918 14, 126, 127
   1918–1939 133, 134
      competition 138
      deposits (1919 vs 1938) 138

commercial banks (*cont.*)
  1945–1970 158, 160
  1970–1997 185, 189
  1997–2007 216
  2007–2015 247
  consolidation 31, 78
  personal guarantees for loans 41
  see also joint-stock banks
Committee on Finance and Industry (Macmillan Committee) 6, 18, 131–2, 134
Committee on Industry and Trade 131
communications, advances in 78, 94
competition
  between banks and building societies
    1945–1970 168–9
    1970–1997 189–90
    1997–2007 217–18, 220
  between banks and companies 101
  between banks and other financial institutions 3
  between banks at international level 8, 100–1, 102–5
  between banks at national level 19, 20, 23, 29, 42
    1825–1914 93–100
    1918–1939 138–45
    1945–1970 163, 167, 169–70, 173
  between banks in London 54, 57
  between banks in the USA 25
  between financial centres 125
  British overseas banks 155
  financial crisis (2007/8) 236, 237, 258–9, 268, 269
  international 16
  promotion of 228
Competition and Credit Control policy 192
Conrad, Joseph, *Chance* 75
Conservative/Liberal-Democrat coalition 259
Conservative Party/government 225
Consolidated Debt (consols) 50
Co-operative Bank 267
Co-operative Credit Bank 80
Co-operative Wholesale Society 23
correspondent networks 55, 57, 69
  1825–1914 79–80, 82, 103, 104, 106, 107, 108, 110, 113
  1918–1939 155
  1945–1970 175, 177, 182
cotton textile industry 57–8
Coucicault, Dion, *Foul Play* (co-author Charles Reade) 73
counterparty risk 4, 179, 199, 245, 249, 262
country banks
  1694–1825 48, 55–6
    1810 crisis and its aftermath 63, 64, 67
    number of 46, 55

  and City of London, connections between 61, 105
Cox and Co. 137
CREST 242
Crocker National Bank 190
Cunliffe, Sir Jon 261
Cunliffe, Walter 128

Davies, Howard 227, 230
deposit insurance, USA 25
Deutsche Bank 108
Disconto-Gesellschaft 108
discount houses/market 42
  1810 crisis 62–5
  1825–1914 114–15, 118, 120–1, 123
  1914–1918 126, 128
  1918–1939 151, 152–3
  1939–1945 159–60
  1945–1970 174–5, 176–7, 178, 180, 182
  1970–1997 196, 197, 198, 199, 200
  joint-stock 40, 42
  lender of last resort 114–15
District Bank 164
dotcom boom 225
Dresdner Bank 108
Dunfermline Building Society 251, 257, 258

East India Company 50, 61
economic performance 19, 269
  1694–1825 60, 68
  1825–1914 90
  1945–1970 163
  1997–2007 225
  Germany 44
  vs stability of banking system 6, 7
economies of scale 31–4, 38–9, 220–1
England
  bank offices, number of
    1883–1911 98
    1911 and 1924 142
  banks, number of
    1883–1911 97
    1911 and 1924 134
  branches, average number of 77
  cash/near cash to total assets ratios 112–13
  concentration of banks in inter-war period 137–8
  ratio of bank offices to population (1883–1911) 98
English Bank of the River Plate 81
English Joint Stock Bank 80
entrants *see* new entrants into banking
Eurocurrency market 180
Eurodollar market 176, 178
European Economic Community 166, 185
European Union 261

Eurozone 260
exchange controls, abolition of (1979) 34, 188, 189, 197, 218, 236
exchange risks 147, 148
Exchequer Bills 66
exits from banking
 1810 crisis and its aftermath 63, 65, 66
 1825 onwards 67
 1918-1939 143
 trends 29-30

Farrow's Bank 143, 239
Federal Deposit Insurance Corporation (FDIC) 24
Federal Reserve
 1931 financial crisis 153
 comparisons with Bank of England 130
 founding 116
 Global Financial Crisis 250, 253
 liquidity provided directly to banks 152
Federal Reserve Act (1913) 116
Federal Savings and Loan Insurance Corporation 24
finance companies 40, 164, 168, 186, 187
 specialist 140, 141
Financial Conduct Authority (FCA) 259
financial crises 13, 17
 1793 47, 62
 1810 46, 61-9
 1825 47, 67
 1866 70
 1873 70
 1893 100, 107-8, 113
 1907 70
 1929-32 130, 131, 143, 237
  see also Wall Street Crash
 1931 140, 150, 153
 1973/4 (Secondary Banking Crisis) 18, 19, 32, 184, 187-8, 191, 192-3, 194, 196, 200, 238, 239, 260
 1990/1 184
 2007/8 (Global Financial Crisis) 25, 203-6, 216-17, 237, 238, 248, 249, 252, 255, 260-2, 265, 266, 267, 268, 269
 2007/8 (UK) 91, 202-6, 214, 224-35, 237-63, 266-70
  analyses 13
  banking stability as priority 20
  Bank of England 17, 202-5, 212, 228, 232-5, 248-59, 262, 263, 267, 268, 269
  business role of banks 9
  causes 34
  failure/near failure of US banks 25
  number of banks 23
  Originate and Distribute Model 34-5, 43-4
  service role of banks 7
  stability, neglect of 18
  banking-population life cycle 25
  causes 34
  global 113
  see also 2007/8 (Global Financial Crisis) *above*
financial innovation 208, 218
Financial Policy Committee (FPC) 259
financial revolution 47-61
Financial Services Authority (FSA) 194, 196
 establishment 20, 206, 228
 financial crisis (2007/8) 202, 203, 230-2, 233, 248, 252
 Memorandum of Understanding with HM Treasury and Bank of England 228, 230
 regulatory regime 34
 responsibilities 228, 229-33, 253
 risk-assessment models 226
First World War 123, 126-30
 Bank of England 36, 43, 126, 127, 128, 129, 161
 inter-bank money market 146-7
 resilience of British banking 14
 Treasury Bills 151
Fisher, Paul 247
Fletcher, J.S.
 The Middle Temple Murder 143
 The Mystery of the London Banker 143
foreign exchange market
 1918-1939 148-50, 151, 153-4
 1939-1945 159
 1945-1970 180
 1970-1997 199
 2007-2015 244
foreign exchange reserves 175
foreign exchange swaps 246
Forester, C.S., *Payment Deferred* 143-4
France
 concentration of banking 216
 Global Financial Crisis 216
 and London money market 109
 Revolutionary and Napoleonic wars (1793-1815) 50, 61-2, 64
Fraser, Ronald, *Financial Times* 144-5
friendly societies 98

George, Eddie 194-5, 207, 227, 233, 236, 240, 251
 bank, definition of 2, 3, 15
Germany
 comparisons with UK banking system 132, 133
 concentration of banking 216
 economic growth and banking model 44

Index

Germany (cont.)
　First World War 126, 129
　Global Financial Crisis 216
　and London money market 108-9
　universal banks 16, 165, 185, 186
Gieve, Sir John 225, 226, 240
Gilletts 120
Gissing, George, *The Whirlpool* 75
Glass-Steagall Act (USA) 185, 202
global banks 164-5, 238
Global Financial Crisis *see* financial crises: 2007/8 (Global Financial Crisis)
globalization 7
Glorious Revolution (1688) 68
Goldsmid, Abraham 64
Gold Standard 71
　1919 departure from 125, 147, 148
　1925 return to 147, 148
　1931 departure from 125, 149, 150, 153
　London money market 111
Golschmidt, Jacob 132
Goodwin, Fred 236
Gore, Mrs, *The Man of Business or Stokeshill Place* 71
Granite 211
Grays Building Society 185
Great Western Railways Savings Bank 99

Haldane, Andrew 31, 214, 227, 252
Halifax Bank
　2007/8 financial crisis 254
　conversion into bank 190, 222, 254
　merger with Bank of Scotland 215, 216, 220, 222, 236
Hatry, Clarence 141
HBOS 267
　financial crisis (2007/8) 254, 255
　Lloyds TSB acquisition 254, 257, 262, 263
Heritable Bank 258
high finance
　and low finance, connection between 61
　study of 47-8
hire purchase companies 167-8
Hitchens, A.K. 87
Hitchens, Harrison, and Company 87
Hoare, R.G. 87-8
Hong Kong and Shanghai Banking Corporation (HSBC) 190-1
　CHAPS 241
　London money market 108
　merger with Midland Bank 190, 193, 216, 239
　prevention from acquisition of Royal Bank of Scotland 190
　size 216
Hornby, Andy 236

income tax, introduction of 62
India 109
India Office 120
Industrial and Commercial Finance Corporation 19, 171
industrial reorganization, inter-war period 155-6
Industrial Revolution
　and financial revolution, comparative timing of 56
　financing of 48, 51, 57-8
ING Direct Bank 258
Institute of Bankers 22-3, 85
Institute of Chartered Accountants 88
institutional investors 4
insurance companies 53, 212
inter-bank call market 159-60
inter-bank money market 5-6, 93, 105-14
　1694-1825 56-7, 60
　1914-1918 146-7
　1918-1939 145-51, 153
　1945-1970 174, 176-9, 182
　1970-1997 196-200, 201
　exchange controls, UK's abandonment of 197
　1997-2007 213, 218
　2007/8 financial crisis 34-5, 211, 249
　2007-2015 241, 242, 243-4, 245, 246, 248
　trends 41
interest rate swaps 199
International Monetary Fund (IMF) 20
inter-war period 130-3, 160-1
　Bank of England 151-7
　competition 138-45
　concentration 133-8
　money market 145-51
investment banks
　1945-1970 166
　1970-1997 185, 186
　1997-2007 207, 209, 210, 216
　2007/8 financial crisis 203
　decline of UK ownership 8
　transition to 8
Ireland
　autonomy of inter-war banking system 138
　bank offices, number of
　　1883-1911 98
　　1911 and 1924 142
　banks, number of
　　1883-1911 97
　　1911 and 1924 134
　branches, average number of 77
　competition 94
　concentration of banks in inter-war period 137-8
　and London money market 106

note issuance 117
ratio of bank offices to population (1883–1911) 98

Jackson, W. Scarborough, *Nine Points of the Law* 75
Japan 260
Jenkinson, Nigel 208, 248
Jerome, Jerome K., *Three Men in a Boat* 74
Johnson Matthey Bank 184, 193
joint-stock banks
　1694–1825 46, 54
　1914–1918 127, 128
　1918–1939 134, 135, 136
　　competition 138, 139, 140, 141–2
　　money market 150
　1939–1945 157, 158
　1945–1970
　　Bank of England 172
　　competition 168–70
　　structure and operation of banking system 165–6, 167, 171
　1970–1997 184
　　Bank of England 192, 193
　　money market 196
　　structure and operation 185, 186–8, 189, 192
　assets and liabilities
　　1911/14 95–6, 135
　　1921/4 135, 136
　　1938 136
　and Bank of England 22, 37, 42, 50, 51, 116, 117–18, 122, 172, 192, 193
　competition 93, 97, 98, 100, 103, 104, 117–18, 138, 139, 140, 141–2, 168–70
　conservatism 91
　consolidation 75
　economies of scale 38–9
　emergence 46
　and hire purchase companies 168
　Lend and Hold Model 40–2, 82–3, 120
　lender of last resort 116
　limited liability 85
　London Clearing House 82, 119
　London money market 112
　in novels 71, 72, 74
　Originate and Distribute Model 42
　semi-permanence 29
　trends 33
　vulnerabilities 80
joint-stock companies 50, 119
joint-stock discount houses 40, 42
joint-stock finance companies 40
Joseph Travers and Sons 101
J.P. Morgan 262

Kaupthing Bank 258
Kaupthing Singer and Friedlander 258
Keynes, John Maynard 7, 130, 131
King, Mervyn 205, 233–4, 250–1, 255, 256
Kleinworts 185, 186
Knowles and Foster 162
Kohn, Donald 234

Labour Party/government
　2007/8 financial crisis 225
　Bank of England 194, 195, 253
　government intervention in British banking, proposals for 156
　nationalization programme 171
　regulatory structure 227, 229, 259
land mortgage companies 100
Landsbanki 258
Leeds Banking Company 80
Leeds Permanent 236, 254
Lehman Brothers
　Barclays' acquisition of US operations 216
　collapse (2008) 17, 204, 206, 207, 253, 254, 255, 262
Leicestershire Banking Company 83, 84
Lend and Hold Model 34, 35–7, 38–9, 40–2, 45, 266–7
　1694–1825 61
　1825–1914 83–4, 89, 123
　1918–1939 146
　1945–1970 171, 182
　1970–1997 186, 191, 192
　1997–2007 207, 208–9, 210, 212, 220, 223
　　Northern Rock 211
　2007/8 financial crisis 255–6, 268, 269
　Bank of England 35–7, 42, 61, 83, 116, 123
　competition 94, 97
　and domestic bills 170
　joint-stock banks 40–2, 82–3, 120
　liquidity requirements 93
　London money market 105, 106, 107, 113
　scale of banks 83–4, 89
　smooth operation of 171
　US banking 123
lender of last resort 6, 250
　Bank of England as 11–12, 18, 21, 42–3, 239
　　1825–1914 115–18, 121–3
　　1914–1918 127, 161
　　1918–1939 151, 152, 153, 154, 155, 160–1, 268
　　1945–1970 174, 175, 176, 178–9, 183
　　1970–1997 192, 194, 196, 197, 199, 200, 201
　　1997–2007 203, 229, 235
　　2007/8 financial crisis 253, 256, 268
　　2007–2015 239–48

330
Index

lender of last resort (*cont.*)
  financial crisis (2007/8) 203, 253,
    256, 268
  for foreign banks 200
  and inter-bank money market 35
  international 153
  lacking in the US 123
  need for 114
Lever, Charles, *Davenport Dunn or the Man and the Day* 71–2, 80
Liberator Building Society 28, 43, 99, 122, 123
  in fiction 75
limited liability 22
Lloyds Bank
  1825–1914 103
    growth (1865–1914) 39, 79
    nationwide expansion 78
    number of branches 79
    share of deposits 78
  1918–1939 134, 138, 155
  1945–1970 164
  1970–1997 185, 186
  2007–2015 241
  acquisitions 138
    attempted, with Barclays Bank 164
    attempted, with National Bank of India 155
    Bank of London and South Africa 165
    Capital and Counties Bank 133
    Cox and Co. 137
    HBOS 254, 257, 262, 263
    TSB 190, 216
  business perspective 14
  CHAPS 241
  economies of scale 39
  international banking activities 103, 155
London and County Bank 108
London and County Securities 187, 188
London and Westminster Bank 108
London City and Midland Bank 103, 134
London Clearing House 57, 82, 119
London County and Westminster Bank 85
London Inter-Bank Offered Rate (LIBOR) 199, 238
London Stock Exchange
  1914–1918 126
  1918–1939 136, 140, 152
  banks accepted as members 193
  Big Bang reforms 19, 186, 236
  brokers 111
  HSBC 190
  membership restrictions 166, 185
low finance
  and high finance, connection between 61
  study of 47–8
Lushington, Stephen 62

Macmillan Committee (Committee on Finance and Industry) 6, 18, 131–2, 134
Macmillan Gap 6, 132
management buy-outs 213
Manchester and Salford Bank 80
Manning, Mark 208, 248
manufacturing sector
  1914–1945 125, 131–2, 137, 140
  1945–1970 163, 171–2
  banks' contribution to finance of 12
  growth of businesses 78
  long-term finance, need for 16
market making 213
Martineau, Harriet, *Berkeley the Banker* 71
Martins Bank 164
media role in 2007/8 financial crisis 249, 250
merchant banks
  1825–1914 91, 103–4
  1914–1918 128
  1918–1939 140, 145
  1939–1945 157
  1945–1970 166
  1970–1997 185, 186, 189
  Accepting Houses Association 128
  British banking as international model 8
  criticisms of 16
  investment bank model, transition to 8
Mercury Asset Management 186
Merrill Lynch 186
Midland Bank
  1825–1914
    balance sheets 83–4
    employees, number of 85
    nationwide expansion 78
    number of branches 79
    overseas business 103
    share of deposits 78
  1918–1939 137, 138, 151
    foreign exchange market 149
    Treasury Bills 151
  1939–1945 157–8
  1945–1970 164
    stake in Montagu Trust 166
  1970–1997 185, 186
    international rivals, comparative scale of 8
  2007–2015 241
  business perspective 13
  CHAPS 241
  diversification 137
  mergers 138
    with HSBC 190, 193, 216, 239
  overseas business 103, 157–8
Miscellaneous Provisions Societies Bill 28
money market *see* inter-bank money market

Index

Montagu Trust 166
moral hazard 21, 88, 116, 217, 227, 240, 247, 249, 250, 256
Morgan Grenfell 185, 186
mortgage-backed securities 212
Mottram, R.H.
  The Boroughmonger 144
  Castle Island 144
  Our Mr Dormer 144
Mullins 152
Munster Bank 80, 117
mutual organizations 98

National and Provincial Bank 78, 134
National Australia Bank 190
National Bank of India 155
National Bank of Scotland 138
National Debt
  1691 50
  1694–1825 50, 58–9, 63
  1825–1914 96, 99, 106
  1914–1918 129
  1918–1939 157
  1939–1945 159
  1950 171
  1960 171
  1970 171
  Bank of England's role 43
  trustee savings banks 99
  Union Bank of Scotland 106
National Giro Bank 169
nationalization programme 171
National Penny Bank 43
National Provincial and Westminster Bank 164
National Provincial Bank 164
Nationwide Building Society 251, 257, 258
NatWest Bank 185, 186, 188
  acquisition by RBS 215, 216, 220, 222, 236, 254
  CHAPS 241
Naval savings bank 99
Netherlands 10–11, 49–50
Neuberger, Lord 238
New Cross Building Society 184
new entrants into banking
  1810 crisis 63
  1825–1914 67, 69, 98
  1918–1939 143
  1997–2007 220
  securities, use of 69
  trends 29–30
New York 125, 147, 159, 180
New Zealand 107–8
Nivisons 120
Norman, Montagu 43, 123, 156

Northern Rock
  2007/8 financial crisis 17, 204–7, 211–12, 222, 231–2, 239–40, 242–3, 248–51, 254–6, 262–3, 266–7
  conversion into bank 222
  Originate and Distribute Model 44, 211, 249
  shareholders 258
  size 216
North of England Joint Stock Banking Company 80
North of Scotland Bank 138
novels, banks in 71–5, 143–5
number of banks
  UK 21–8, 29–30, 31, 46–7, 271–7
  1810 crisis 63, 64, 66, 68
  1910–1920 133
  country banks 46, 55
  England and Wales vs Scotland vs Ireland 97
  with exclusively overseas operations 102
  Global Financial Crisis 215
  London (1754, 1774, 1799) 55
  USA 22, 24–6, 27, 32, 33, 284–8
number of building societies 27–8, 30, 99, 278–80
number of savings banks 27, 28, 30, 281–3

Oliphant, Mrs
  At His Gates 74
  Hester 74
Oriental Commercial Bank 80
Originate and Distribute Model 34–5, 37–8, 40, 42, 45
  1694–1825 52, 60
  1945–1970 168
  1970–1997 186
  1997–2007 209–10, 212–13, 219, 220, 222, 223
  Northern Rock 44, 211, 249
  2007/8 financial crisis 43–4, 254, 256, 262, 266–7, 269
  2007–2015 243, 244
  Royal Bank of Scotland 255
  Bank of England 37–8, 40, 42, 68
  London money market 113
  unitary banking system 83
Overend and Gurney 40, 42, 70, 115, 116, 118–19, 123
  in fiction 74
Over-The-Counter (OTC) derivatives market 244–5

parallel money markets
  1945–1970 175, 176, 180
  1970–1997 196

Index

partnerships
  1810 crisis 66
  audits 86–7
  limits on numbers of partners 53, 66, 68, 76
  note issuance 53
  Scotland 53–4
  unlimited liability 53, 54
Paustian, Matthias 235
Payments Act (1819) 66
payments system
  2007/8 financial crisis 241–3, 253, 254, 257
  as core function of banking 3–4
Penalver, Adrian 235
'penny' banks 127
pension funds 212
Peretz, David 20
Phillips Oppenheim, E., *The Bank Manager* 144
Phoenix Insurance Company 53
Pole, Thornton, and Company 67
postal service 56
Post Office Savings Bank 99, 117
Price Waterhouse 86–7
professionalism of banking 85
property companies 187, 192, 193
Prudential Insurance Company 101
Prudential Regulation Authority (PRA) 259

Quakers 80
Quantitative Easing programme 255–6

railways 78
Reade, Charles
  Foul Play (co-author Dion Coucicault) 73
  Hard Cash 73
real-time gross settlement (RTGS) basis, payments system 242–3
Rent and Mortgage Restriction Act (1915) 139
repro market 245–6
Resolution Trust Corporation 24
retail banks
  1918–1939 154
  1945–1970 164
  1970–1997 186
  1997–2007 202, 203, 206, 207–9, 210–11, 212, 213, 231, 236, 269
    competition 217–18, 219, 220
    concentration 214–15, 216
  2007/8 financial crisis 203, 249, 256, 269
  British banking as international model 8
  as cartel 8
  consolidation 30, 164
Rice, J., *Ready-Money Mortiboy* (co-author W. Besant) 74
Richardson, Thomas 57

Riddell, Charlotte, *George Geith of Fen Court* 74
risk–assessment models 226–7
risk–return strategies 5
Rothschilds 52, 185
Rowton and Marshall 64
Royal Bank of Scotland (RBS) 267
  1970–1997 9
  1997–2007 218, 220
  2007/8 financial crisis 254–5, 263
  acquisitions
    attempted, of ABN-Amro 216
    attempted, by HSBC 190
    NatWest 215, 216, 220, 221–2, 236, 254
    Williams Deacon's Bank 137, 154, 155
  charter 53
  size 216
Royal British Bank 80
Royal Exchange 58, 61

Santander 251, 258
Savings and Loan sector 24, 98
savings banks
  1825–1914 98–9
  1919 vs 1938 deposits 138
  1939–1945 159
  1945–1970 168
  1997–2007 209
  consolidation 31
  number of 27, 28, 30, 281–3
  see also trustee savings banks
scale
  consequences of 80–8
  economies of 31–4, 38–9, 220–1
Schroders 140, 185
Scotland
  bank offices, number of
    1883–1911 98
    1911 and 1924 142
  banks, number of
    1883–1911 97
    1911 and 1924 134
  branches, average number of 77
  cash/near cash to total assets ratios 112–13
  competition 94
  concentration of banks in inter-war period 137–8
  financial revolution 53–4
  independence of banking system 138, 190, 236
  joint-stock banks 46
  and London money market 106–7
  note issuance 117
  partnerships 53–4
  post-war period 164

Index

ratio of bank offices to population (1883–1911) 98
superiority of banking system 90–1
Scott, G.J. 145–6
Secondary Banking Crisis *see* financial crises: 1973/4
secondary banks
  1970–1997 200
    Bank of England 192–3
    money market 196
    structure and operation 187–8
  1997–2007 210
Second World War 157–60, 161
Securities and Exchange Commission 202
Securities Management Trust and National Shipbuilding Security 156
Select Committee on Building Societies 28
Seligman, Vincent, *Bank Holiday* 145
service role of banks 3–7
Seton Merriman, Henry, *Roden's Corner* 75
settlement banks 241–2
shadow banking system
  1945–1970 170, 260
  1970–1997 192
  2007/8 financial crisis 205, 257
  growth of 8
shareholders, numbers of 91
size of banks, inter-war period 154–5
Smith St. Aubyn 128, 150
South Africa 109
South Sea Company/bubble 50, 51
Southsea Mortgage and Investment Company 257
specialist finance houses 140, 141
Special Purpose Vehicles 211
Special Resolution Regime 259
Standard Bank of South Africa 165
Standard Chartered 216
start-up firms 140
Stead, W.T., *Two and Two Make Four* 75
steel industry, inter-war reorganization 156
sterling
  1945–1970 175–6, 177, 178, 180
  1970–1997 197
Strahan, Paul, and Bates 80
Swiss Bank Corporation 186
Switzerland 165, 185, 186, 260

taxation 62, 170, 171
Taylor, Tim 235
technological advances 8, 141, 189, 226–7
telegraph 78, 104
telegraphic transfers 104
Thomas Coles and Sons 64

timelines
  UK banking 289
  US banking 290
Tipperary Bank 80
Trafford, F.G. (pseudonym of Charlotte Riddell), *George Geith of Fen Court* 74
training of bank staff 84–5, 95, 137
transport, advances in 78, 94
Treasury (UK)
  2007/8 financial crisis 203, 227, 248, 251, 259
  bank merger proposals 133
  First World War 126, 127, 128, 129
  Memorandum of Understanding with Bank of England FSA 228, 230
  responsibilities 228, 229, 230
  risk-assessment models 226
Treasury Bills
  1914–1918 128–9, 146–7
  1918–1939 135, 136, 150–2, 156, 161
  1945–1970 174, 175
  1970–1997 196
  1997–2007 210
  Special Liquidity Scheme 252, 253
trustee savings banks
  competition 98–9
  deposits (1870 and 1913) 117
  number of 98–9, 281–3
  TSB 190, 216
  see also savings banks
TSB 190, 216
Tucker, Paul 222, 252, 256

UK Debt Management Office 246
Ulster Bank 138
unemployment 131
Union Bank of Manchester 137
Union Bank of Scotland 106, 145
unitary banking system 130
United States of America (USA)
  comparisons with UK banking system 2, 130
  concentration of banking 214, 216
  deposit insurance 25
  dynamism of banking system 44
  Glass-Steagall Act 185, 202
  global banks 165
  Global Financial Crisis 25, 203, 204, 213, 216, 237, 238, 248, 249, 252, 255, 260, 261, 265, 268
  government intervention in banking system 172
  instability of banking system 123
  interest rate ceiling on deposits 176, 178
  investment banks 186
  land mortgage companies in the UK 100
  London branches of US banks 178, 189

United States of America (USA) (cont.)
  New York 125, 147, 159, 180
  number of banks 22, 24–6, 27, 32, 33, 284–8
  railroad bonds 111
  regulatory regime 195
  Securities and Exchange Commission 202
  study of banking history 265
  timeline of banking 290
  unitary banking system 16, 79
  see also Federal Reserve; US dollar; Wall Street Crash
universal banks 8, 165, 206
  1945–1970 181
  1970–1997 185, 186, 189
  Germany 16, 165, 185, 186
US dollar
  1945–1970 175–6, 177, 178, 180
  1970–1997 197, 199, 200

Wales
  bank offices, number of
    1883–1911 98
    1911 and 1924 142
  banks, number of
    1883–1911 97
    1911 and 1924 134
  branches, average number of 77
  cash/near cash to total assets ratios 112–13

concentration of banks in inter-war period 137–8
ratio of bank offices to population (1883–1911) 98
Wall Street Crash (1929) 25, 116, 125
  comparison with Global Financial Crisis 237
  public opinion following 202
  US government intervention in banking 157
Warburgs 9, 186
Western Bank of Scotland 80
West of England and South Wales District Bank 80
Westminster Bank 138, 164
Weyman, Stanley J., *Ovington's Bank* 144
Whiteley's 101
Wilgress, L.D. 112
William of Orange 49
Williams Deacon's Bank
  acquisition by Manchester and Salford Bank (1836) 80
  rescue (1930) 18, 32, 137, 154, 155, 161, 239
Wood, Mrs Henry, *The Shadow of Ashlydyat* 72–3
Woolwich Building Society 81, 99

Yorkshire Bank 190
Yorkshire Penny Bank 23